The Best Breweries and Brewpubs of Illinois

The Best Breweries and Brewpubs of Illinois

Searching for the Perfect Pint

Robin Shepard

The University of Wisconsin Press

The University of Wisconsin Press
1930 Monroe Street
Madison, Wisconsin 53711

www.wisc.edu/wisconsinpress/

3 Henrietta Street
London WC2E 8LU, England

Library of Congress Cataloging-in-Publication Data
Shepard, Robin.
    The best breweries and brewpubs of Illinois:
    searching for the perfect pint / Robin Shepard.
        p. cm.
    ISBN 0-299-18894-9 (pbk. : alk. paper)
    1. Bars (Drinking establishments—Illinois—Guidebooks.
I. Title.
TX950.53.S53   2004
647.95773—dc21   2003006267

All information in this book is accurate to the best of the author's and publisher's knowledge at the time of printing, but some information is subject to change. The University of Wisconsin Press and the author assume no liability for inaccuracies or subjective opinions represented in this book. This book contains references to many businesses, people, places, and organizations. Any omission of factual information is unintentional. In writing this book every effort was made to ensure accuracy and completeness. All breweries were personally visited at least twice prior to publication, and each received a follow-up telephone call to confirm information herein. However, not all brewmasters, owners, or managers chose to participate in an interview. Opinions stated herein are not guaranteed or warranted to produce any particular results, and the advice and strategies contained herein may not be suitable for every individual. Neither the University of Wisconsin Press nor the author shall be liable for any loss of profit or any other commercial damages, including but not limited to special, incidental, consequential, or other damages. The author and publisher encourage readers to visit the breweries and sample their beer, and in doing so remind those who consume alcoholic beverages that they are responsible for their own actions and it is recommended that they travel with a nondrinking driver.

Contents

Preface

Okay, so this wasn't the most difficult book to research—it was, however, somewhat difficult to stay focused on the writing with a pint in my hand. While this book is indeed about beer, I hope you'll appreciate the many other elements that I've included. Inside these pages you'll find many styles of beer; tastes of food; things not to miss when you're quaffing a pint or two; the history of the breweries, the people and interesting facts about the communities; and even things to see along the way. Beer is indeed the central character in the book. However, the perfect pint is about the trip, the travel there, and acquisition of a new flavor. If beer is the destination, then this book is about the journey—one I hope you'll find as fascinating as I did as I traveled Illinois.

I began writing this book as a hobby, but it became much more than that! Just as many of the brewers you'll read about (or meet along the way) began with homebrewing, but it "got out of control" and they found themselves standing next to larger and larger equipment, until one day they stood above a boiling mash tun brewing their first commercial batch of beer—that's what it's been like for me. I too was captivated by homebrewing. That led to conversations with friends about different beers. From there, my hobby evolved into exploring different breweries and brewpubs. What I found about myself has not been just a love for good beer but also a thorough enjoyment of meeting and learning about the owners and brewers and how they got where they are today. I'd like to say "Thank you" to so many who took me seriously enough to sit down and open up their lives with stories about themselves. Most important, many of those conversations occurred as we shared a beer or two—all part of finding the perfect pint.

There are other special people who supported this book, including my wife, Kristi, and a number of friends who have been convinced to take a (sometimes not-so-short) detour to find Illinois's best. For Kristi it's meant giving up weekends and evenings to ride along to some of those out-of-the-way places. For the friends who occasionally traveled with me, they learned to expect that there's never a straight route to or from anywhere with me; it's best if the passenger takes care of the GPS receiver, not the driver; and there is always a good beer at the end of the road.

You might wonder how someone who lives in Wisconsin can give Illinois beer a fair review. I spent over two years traveling the state, purposely searching out the best breweries and brewpubs of Illinois. Along the way, each of the three dozen Illinois beer makers was visited at least twice, and some many more times. This book is a travel guide that's designed to be used. I hope you will follow some of my suggestions and methods for tasting and ground your quest for truth in my experiences. Don't just take my opinions—score the beers yourself.

The breweries and brewpubs of Illinois all have their own unique local characters, charms, and identities. Some are located in grand historical locations, such as America's Brewing Company in Aurora's C. B. & Q. Railroad Roundhouse, which was constructed in the 1850s. Some are anchors along the main streets of Illinois's old downtowns, like Emmett's Tavern and Brewing Company in West Dundee and the Elmwood Brewing Company in west central Illinois. Others are found in modern buildings that were designed to showcase the combination of restaurant and brewery operations in brewpubs like Prairie Rock Brewing Company of Schaumburg and Flatlander's Restaurant and Brewery in Lincolnshire. Furthermore, Illinois has national brewpub models in the Rock Bottom Restaurants and Breweries in downtown Chicago and Warrenville and the Ram Restaurants and Big Horn Breweries in Schaumburg and Wheeling. But for me, I've enjoyed the small brewpubs with the local community feel best of all. You'll understand what this means when you read the descriptions and then visit brewpubs like Mickey Finn's Brewery in Libertyville and Lunar Brewing Company in Villa Park.

While the Chicagoland area supports a majority of Illinois' breweries and brewpubs, you'll really miss out if you only concentrate there. Traveling across the "Land of Lincoln" will take you along some beautiful country. For example, Carbondale seems far from just about anywhere in the state, but the trip is part of the allure of the Copper Dragon brewery. Likewise, traveling the rustic Mississippi River roads, winding along North America's largest river valley, can't help but foster an appreciation for Illinois's spectacular natural resources.

Although I tried to list all of the Illinois microbreweries in existence at the time of publication, the actual number of breweries and brewpubs does change frequently. Consider my book as a work in progress, and you have an opportunity to record your opinions, score the beers, and find new breweries as they open. Just remember, this book is about enjoying Illinois's best local beer. The pursuit of the perfect pint is about quality, not quantity. Most important, be responsible for your own actions, consider public transportation and designated drivers, and know your limits. Have fun, enjoy yourself and the friends around you, and especially the communities where these establishments are located.

Cheers!

Introduction

The Best Breweries and Brewpubs of Illinois describes thirty-five Illinois beer makers and more than four hundred Illinois beers. It also offers short descriptions of each brewpub or brewery, the beers it serves, its menu, and a few ideas for other things to do or see while in the area. While this book is indeed about Illinois beer, there are also a number of good brewpubs and breweries that are found just beyond the state's border, within thirty miles or so. For those who live near the state line, or for those who enjoy short excursions, you'll find a listing of sixteen additional beer makers from the states of Indiana, Iowa, Missouri, and Wisconsin. The "Just Over the Border" section isn't all-inclusive, rather it will offer insights into some worthwhile stops in nearby states as you search for the perfect pint.

The book was designed to be taken along as you search for your own perfect pint. If you are like me, you probably like to try local beers and brewpubs when you travel. I also search for different brands and styles of beer at a tavern or restaurant and include friends in my pursuit.

Likes and dislikes in beer are personal and subjective. This book is not about getting you to agree with my perfect pint or that of the person sitting next to you at the bar. Rather, it should help guide your exploration, experimentation, and comparisons of beers that you personally find enjoyable.

A good place to begin is with a general understanding of beer and an appreciation for differences in its characteristics and styles. Beer tasting is about learning what you enjoy by distinguishing among the beers you drink. From there you can set out on your own tasting adventure for Illinois's best beers.

The Best Breweries and Brewpubs of Illinois is about more than just putting the glass to your lips and swallowing. If you really want to find your own perfect pint, try some of the tips I offer for tasting. The method is easy to learn. Most important, it provides a consistent approach to evaluating and comparing beers. While there is always a risk that you might look a little conspicuous if you walk into a pub or tavern carrying this book, take some pride in joining that special group of beer connoisseurs who are serious in their pursuit of the perfect pint! Don't be shy. Use the book to create a strategy, take notes as you seek those out-of-the-way places and quality brews, even ask the brewmaster to autograph their section.

In my critiques, from beer rankings to pub descriptions, I've tried to offer my assessment of things as I experienced them. Keep in mind, however, that I'm generally enthusiastic about microbrewing in Illinois, so don't just take this book as the definitive text on Illinois beer. Next to every beer listed is a place for you to record your own score. I've also included the beer tasting chart I developed in my travels. As you work with the tasting method, decide how my notes and perceptions stack up against your own.

For readers with Geographic Positioning System (GPS) receivers, I have included GPS coordinates in the directory sections in the back of the book. Depending upon the sophistication of your GPS receiver, these coordinates will give you directions, distances, and even travel times. Some of the brewpubs are difficult to find, and I've saved myself a fair amount of frustration on return visits by using my GPS receiver in combination with an address and city map.

As you search Illinois for your perfect pint, it's important to call ahead before visiting the brewpub or brewery, whether it's your first visit or a return trip. Hours can change (and for that reason have not been included in this book), especially between summer and winter. Almost all brewpubs and breweries offer tours, but most ask that you call ahead to schedule or check for weekend tour times. The availability of beers can change too. Brewpubs frequently produce seasonal specialties, alter or change a recipe, or just introduce a new beer. Menus also change frequently, especially with the seasons; a new chef might offer a different approach to food. These are reasons to make repeat visits, for each one can offer a different experience or a unique surprise.

Before you indulge, remember that the search for the perfect pint is about quality, not quantity—it's what you drink that counts, not how much you drink. Tasting isn't guzzling; it's best done in small samples. In fact, many brewpubs and breweries have beer samplers, where you can try a few ounces of several styles. Comparing beer is also about a consistent approach, which is the only fair way to compare one beer with another.

Some elements of consistency in beer tasting follow.

STYLE

Begin by observing the general classification or style—ale or lager—and then make comments that are appropriate for the style you are testing. In other words, evaluate ales against ales and lagers against lagers. Quality brewpubs clearly distinguish their ales from their lagers. You can't depend on catchy names to reveal this basic distinction.

As your tasting skills improve, try breaking down ales and lagers into types, such as Pilsners, bocks, Oktoberfests, nut browns, porters, and stouts. Then try to evaluate them within their specific style category; that is, evaluate porters against porters, not porters against pale ales or wheats. Over the years I've found that my own preferences for porters, nut browns, and Oktoberfests cause me to be more discriminating with these beers. If you are creating a beer list or data base, you'll find that your preference for certain styles will be recorded automatically, because you'll be drinking more of one style than another. If you need some help with beer styles, see the Beer Styles section in the back of the book for more specific descriptions of styles.

GLASSWARE

Different styles of glassware accent the qualities of certain beers. Most brew-pubs and taverns don't offer much of a glassware choice, but those that do are committed to being true to style.

As you might expect, Pilsner glasses are for Pilsners. They are designed to direct the floral hop aroma to the nose. Shaker and Nonick pint glasses are the most common pub glassware and are excellent for beers with abundant aromas and bouquets. Similarly, mugs have a wide opening for aroma but are sometimes better for displaying beers with heavy, thick heads. Weizen glasses are tall with a bowed or flared lip to help retain the beer's head and focus aromas. Finally, chalices, snifters, and thistles help concentrate more subtle aromas and allow the beer to develop a head without giving you a face of foam.

There are several stories about how the term growler came to be. The most common accounts say that it originated in the nineteenth century, when factory workers (some say the porters of London) regularly drank beer on break or with a meal. The local taverns would sell beer in open metal pails, and the custom was that local children would fetch the growler for a few pence. The most common story is that the growler gained its name in reference to the growling stomachs of the waiting factory workers. Another common tale is that when the metal pails were filled, the bartender would slide them down the bar to waiting customers. In doing so the pail sliding across the bar produced a growling sound—this allegedly coined another phrase, "rushing the growler," which could also be attributed to the children rushing back to the factory with a full growler. You decide which story you like best!

POURING THE BEER

Despite what you may have learned in college about a frothy head meaning less beer in the glass, beer with a head is what you want. As you pour the beer, start in the center of the glass—the beer needs an opportunity to explode into a rich, heavy foam. Look for a thick, creamy, and long-lasting head from kräusening, a secondary fermentation process that creates natural carbonation.

AROMA OR NOSE

It is a good idea to make your observation about aroma before you actually taste the beer. The aroma is usually greatest at the time of pouring the beer, so it makes sense to gather your impressions as the beer initially breathes and the head begins to dissipate. Determining aroma, or the beer's nose, takes practice. It is one of the most subjective judgments you'll make.

Immediately after you pour, raise the glass to your nose. Many complex flavor notes were created by malts, hops, and yeast during the brewing, fermenting, and aging processes. It may help to swirl the beer gently in the glass to release some of the carbonation and heighten the aroma. A sweet, caramel, chocolate, or coffeelike aroma comes from the malt varieties. A floral, tealike, citrus aroma comes from hops. Fruity aromas, such as apples, bananas, or

Pilsner Glasses

Designed to direct the floral hop aroma to the nose. The clear glass will highlight the clear golden color and effervescence of the beer. The Pilsner glass is designed for the Pilsner.

Shaker Pint (left)
and Nonick Pint (right)

The most common pub glassware. Suited as general, all-purpose beer glassware. The bulged side of the Nonick makes for better handling. Both have wide openings to allow the aroma to explode.

Mugs

The wide open mouth allows total exposure to the beer aroma, often recommended for strong, malty beers. The obvious emphasis of the mug is on its handling ease! Mugs are often used for full-bodied beers.

Chalice, Thistle, and Snifter (l. to r.)

The wide mouth allows for the aromas to explode, while providing greater space for a thick head. The shape and the stem allows the drinker to control the warming of the beer. Chalices are often used with Belgian ales, while thistles are associated with fine Scottish ales, and snifters are often used with barley wines.

Weizen

The clear, tall, and slightly bowed sides allow the aroma to concentrate and then escape while supporting a delicate head. This glass is well suited for the light fruit esters of the Weizenbier.

Growler

A growler is a container for beer bought by the measure. Usually half-gallon in size, many brewpubs will sell beer-to-go poured directly from the tap into the growler.

pears, are the esters, which are produced through the interaction of organic acids with alcohol in the fermentation process. It's fun to be creative when describing the beer's nose.

While the more common terms for aroma are malty, hoppy, sour, or fruity, the more specifically you can identify the smells, the more distinctive the description. If the nose is fruity, is it banana or citrus?

Some common aroma descriptors:

acetaldehyde	green apple
diacetyl	butter, butterscotch, or toffee
estery	various fruits
hoppy	odor associated with hop flowers, floral
malty	sweetness, can be caramel and/or chocolate
musty	stale, earthy, moldy
phenolic	medicinal, plastic
solvent	acetone or lacquer thinners
sulfur	rotten eggs
vegetal	cooked, canned, or rotten vegetables

APPEARANCE

The appearance of beer has two distinct elements: body and head. The color of the body is determined by the amount and type of malted barley used in brewing. Colors range from gold to amber to copper to brown to black, and these colors may come in light to dark shades. Some styles, such as porter and stout, even have a reddish hue. Cloudiness or clarity is also an important characteristic. Unfiltered wheat beers are often cloudy yellow or golden, while Pilsners take a clear or even bubbly appearance. The head of a beer can be as distinctive as the body. Notice its color and especially the texture of the head. Is it thick and creamy like a Guinness stout, or is it thin and bubbly like a Pilsner?

Filtering beer is a common part of the beer-making process in most breweries. It removes yeast and any suspended particles, leaving the beer bright and clear. This helps accentuate the qualities of some styles, as is the case with Pilsners. Some beer styles are traditionally nonfiltered, however. A true German Hefe-Weizen, for example, is a cloudy golden beer. This cloudy appearance is distinctive due to the special yeast that is used, which remains in suspension.

TEXTURE OR MOUTH FEEL

Let the beer roll around in your mouth. Does the texture feel thick and creamy or thin and watery? These adjectives can be helpful: crisp, silky, round, coarse. Texture can also refer to dryness or even a warming sensation.

TASTE

Appreciate the beer's varied flavor notes and its balance. Different parts of your tongue are stimulated in different ways. On the tip you should detect the sweetness of malt; toward the back on either side you sense bitterness from the hops. Is the taste balanced between the malt and the hops, or does one dominate, such as the hoppiness of an India Pale Ale? You may even want to comment on the intensity of the taste.

Serious tasters, such as professional tasters who judge beer competitions, say there are more than a hundred separately identifiable flavor elements. About forty of these are common and present in most beers.

Some common taste descriptors:

bitter	a bitterness derived from hops
dry	astringent, grainy, worty, sulfitic
fruity	apples, oranges, citrus
grainy	cereal-like
hoppy	flowery and aromatic hop qualities
malty	a sweetness, can be caramel and/or chocolate
medicinal	chemical or phenolic, solvent
musty	earthy, moldy
sour	a sharpness or fruity tone, vinegarlike, acidic
sulfur	skunky, burnt matches, rotten eggs, onion
sweet	associated with sugar
tart	acidic
yeasty	yeast, bouillon

FINISH

A good beer with character offers several different taste impressions, from the initial taste to the midtaste to the aftertaste, or finish. A common finish for a pale ale tends to feature a smokiness or even a dry bitterness. Beers with higher alcohol contents, such as Doppelbocks, can leave a warming sensation in the mouth. Crisp, clean-tasting beers, such as some Pilsners, may not have a detectable finish.

NOTE TAKING

If you are a serious note taker, jot down your observations of beers that have uniqueness. Focus on the most impressive or memorable part of the beer. This is also an opportunity for you to note its balance between the bitterness (hops) and the sweetness (malt). Or, certain styles accentuate bitterness or sweetness where one dominates the other. Some beers have distinctive taste segments that stand out and are worth noting. One might have a bitter or hoppy start but end with lingering caramel sweetness. Sometimes tastes can evoke images. I once had a Pilsner that actually had qualities of chicken soup! The more descriptive the better.

OVERALL SCORING

There are different methods of scoring beer. Some, such as those used by the Beverage Testing Institute (BTI) or at sanctioned competitions of the American Homebrewers Association (AHA), are numerical and can be quite detailed because they are used in competitions. For most of us at our favorite brewpub or brewery, a straightforward, simple method is quite sufficient. The tasting chart shown here, for example, uses a four-point (or mug) scale. After you've gone through a beer's taste qualities, rank your overall impression from good to bad. Don't be indecisive. Make a judgment of how much you enjoy this beer. An even number of choices, such as four, requires you to take a stand. There is no middle category of undecided.

🍺🍺🍺🍺	A great beer; distinctive; you'll have this beer over others.
🍺🍺🍺	A beer you enjoy, reliable, close to its described style.
🍺🍺	Problematic, lacks distinction, but probably worth trying again.
🍺	Not true to its style; you wouldn't recommend it to a friend.

SIGNING OFF ON YOUR VISIT

In my travels and in suggestions from readers of the previous companion book, *Wisconsin's Best Breweries and Brewpubs*, I've included an autograph block at the top of each brewpub/brewery description. As you hopscotch across Illinois visiting the state's beer makers, take this book along and have the brewery's brewmaster, owner, or waitperson sign his or her name and date your visit. Don't be shy as you travel the state to find Illinois's Best Breweries and Brewpubs and your own perfect pint. Asking for an autograph is a great way to strike up a conversation, and you might just be surprised where the discussion will lead about the brewery you're visiting. The persons responsible for making beer should be treated as celebrities, because it's their beer that's worth celebrating. So a signature at the top of their brewery's description is a way to say "Thanks for doing what you do so well!"

Taster Chart

BEER RATING SHEET:

Date: _____

Beer Name: _____

Brewery: _____

☐ Microbrewery   (or)   ☐ Brew Pub

City: _____

State/Province: _____

Country: _____

GPS Coordinates
N ____ ____ ____
W ____ ____ ____

Style (lager/ale/stout/etc.) _____

Nose/Aroma: _____

Appearance: _____

Mouth Feel/Body: _____

Taste: _____

Finish: _____

Comments: _____
_____
_____
_____
_____
_____

Beer Diagram:

Hoppy   *Malty*

Dark

A
L
E
S

3

1

5

2

General
Character Beers

Light
— *Color*
Light

L
A
G
E
R
S

4

6

Dark

Hoppy   *Malty*

Reference Beers
1. Anchor Porter
2. Berghoff Red Ale
3. Guinness Stout
4. Miller, Budweiser
5. Red Hook ESB
6. Spaten Oktoberfest

Overall Score For This Beer:

☐   4- 🍺🍺🍺🍺   = A great beer; distinctive; you'll have this beer over others.

☐   3- 🍺🍺🍺   = A beer you enjoy; reliable; close to its described style.

☐   2- 🍺🍺   = Problematic; lacks distinction; but probably worth trying again.

☐   1- 🍺   = A beer that isn't true to its style; you wouldn't recommend it to a friend.

Who Drank: _____

The Brewing Process

Brewing begins with four basic ingredients: water, barley, hops, and yeast. The amounts of these ingredients; the way they are mixed, heated, and cooled; and the storage of the beer all contribute to creating different styles of beer. Traditionally, many small brewers take pride in stating that they follow the *Reinheitsgebot*, the German Purity Law of 1516, which mandated that only those four ingredients (water, barley, hops, and yeast) be used in producing beer.

The equipment brewers use can differ from brewery to brewery. Illinois breweries are generally small by national standards. Brewery production is measured in barrels per year; most Illinois breweries average between three hundred and one thousand. Also, most have restaurant businesses that make them brewpubs. Breweries such as Goose Island (Chicago), Two Brothers (Warrenville), and Three Floyds (Munster, Indiana) are exceptions because they have capacities of several thousand barrels per year and are primarily breweries, although Goose Island does have two brewpub/restaurant locations and Three Floyds is expected to expand its brewery to include a restaurant bar. Big or small, Illinois brewhauses all have some basic elements in common, and the general concepts are summarized in the accompanying diagram.

A tour of a few brewpubs or breweries will offer further insights into the brewing process. Most brewmasters and owners enjoy offering tours. Breweries often have regularly scheduled tours, usually on weekends. Brewpubs are more likely to offer tours whenever they have time and interest from patrons. Just remember, it's always a good idea to call ahead if you would like a tour.

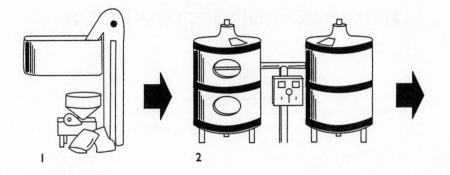

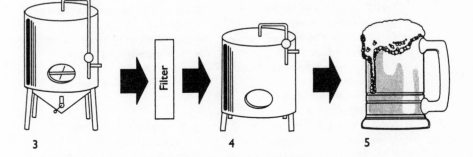

1. Milling
Malted barley is weighed, milled, and transported in a grain augering system or grain elevator.

2. Mash and Boil
The cracked malt is mixed with hot water and cooked in the "mash tun," converting starches to fermentable sugars. The malt is then rinsed, or "sparged," with hot water, creating the "wort." The wort is boiled, and hops are added.

3. Fermentation and Lagering
The boiled wort is cooled down, yeast is added to the fermenter, and fermentation begins. Ales take at least ten days to age and are kept at temperatures of 60–70°F. Lagers take at least thirty days and ferment at temperatures of 35–50°F.

4. Storage
Beer may be filtered to remove traces of yeast as it is transferred to the cold storage vessels.

5. Tapping
Brewpubs can draw beer directly from the cold storage vessels, which are usually near the bar. For breweries, beers go into kegs, bottles, or cans.

Breweries and Brewpubs Map

1. America's Brewing Company and Walter Payton's Roundhouse (Aurora)
2. Bent River Brewing Company (Moline)
3. Blue Cat Brew Pub (Rock Island)
4. Brass Restaurant and Brewery (South Barrington)
5. Carlyle Brewing Company (Rockford)
6. Copper Dragon Brewing Company and Pinch Penny Pub (Carbondale)
7. Elmwood Brewing Company and Parkview Restaurant (Elmwood)
8. Emmett's Tavern and Brewing Company (West Dundee)
9. FireHouse Restaurant and Brewing Company (Morris)
10. Flatlander's Restaurant and Brewery (Lincolnshire)
11. Flossmoor Station Restaurant and Brewery (Flossmoor)
12. Founders Hill Restaurant and Brewery (Downer's Grove)
13. Glen Ellyn Sports Brew (Glen Ellyn)
14. Goose Island Beer Company–Clybourn Avenue (Chicago)
15. Goose Island Beer Company–Wrigleyville (Chicago)
16. Govnor's Public House Restaurant and Brewery (Lake in the Hills)
17. Harrison's Restaurant and Brewery (Orland Park)
18. Illinois Brewing Company (Bloomington)
19. J. W. Platek's Restaurant and Brewery (Richmond)
20. Lunar Brewing Company (Villa Park)
21. Mickey Finn's Brewery (Libertyville)
22. Millrose Restaurant and Brewing Company (South Barrington)
23. O'Griff's Irish Pub and Brew House (Quincy)
24. Onion Pub and Brewery (Lake Barrington)
25. Piece (Chicago)
26. Prairie Rock Brewing Company (Elgin)
27. Prairie Rock Brewing Company (Schaumburg)
28. Ram Restaurant and Big Horn Brewery (Schaumburg)
29. Ram Restaurant and Big Horn Brewery (Wheeling)
30. Rhodell Brewery and Bar (Peoria)
31. Rock Bottom Restaurant and Brewery (Chicago)
32. Rock Bottom Restaurant and Brewery (Warrenville)
33. Taylor Brewing Company (Lombard)
34. Three Floyds Brewing Company (Munster, Indiana)
35. Two Brothers Brewing Company (Warrenville)

a. Aberdeen Brewing Company (Valparaiso, Indiana)
b. Anheuser-Busch (St. Louis, Missouri)
c. Back Road Brewery (LaPorte, Indiana)
d. Brewery Creek Restaurant and Microbrewery (Mineral Point, Wisconsin)
e. Brewmasters Pub–Friarswood (Kenosha, Wisconsin)
f. Bricktown Brewery & Blackwater Grill (Dubuque, Iowa)
g. Front Street Brewery and Beer Garden (Davenport, Iowa)
h. Gray's Brewing Company (Janesville, Wisconsin)
i. Joseph Huber Brewing Company (Monroe, Wisconsin)
j. Lafayette Brewing Company (Lafayette, Indiana)
k. Morgan Street Brewery (St. Louis, Missouri)
l. New Glarus Brewing Company (New Glarus, Wisconsin)
m. Route 66 Brewery & Restaurant (St. Louis, Missouri)
n. Schlafly Tap Room (St. Louis, Missouri)
o. Trailhead Brewing Company (St. Charles, Missouri)
p. Upper Mississippi Brewing Company (Clinton, Iowa)

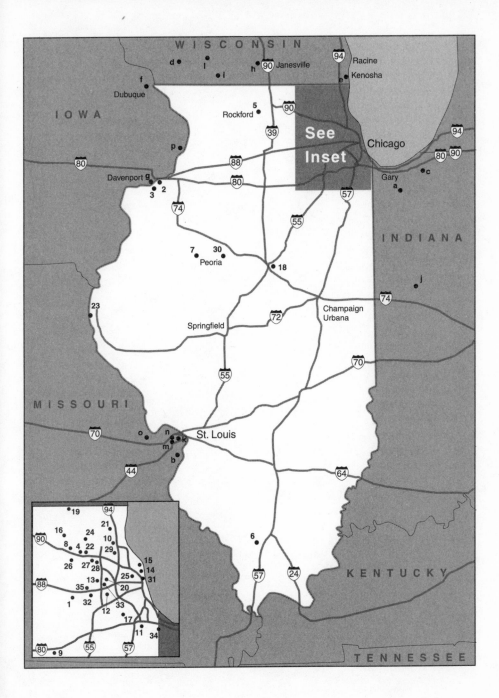

Illinois Breweries and Brewpubs

When searching for Illinois's best beer, always call ahead for brewpub and brewery hours and tour times and to double check directions. While those in larger cities have the most regular hours, some smaller businesses are more limited as to when they are open, especially between winter and summer schedules. Here are ten tips to finding Illinois's best beer:

Search the Internet. Good places to start are www.allaboutbeer.com, www.beerme.com, and even www.creamcitysuds.com.

Check with the hotel concierge; scan the local phone book for brewpubs, breweries, and beer.

Call a local homebrew supply store and ask advice for finding great local beer.

When arriving at a brewery or brewpub, pick up a copy of a beer newspaper to check area listings and brewmaster's special beers.

Look around at breweries and brewpubs for special postings of events and beer festivals.

Ask for taster samples or share a sample tray with friends as good way to introduce yourself to several beers and styles.

Talk with wait staff and the bartender about other area breweries.

Plan ahead to understand local transportation and get the phone number of a local cab company.

Take a brewery tour. Most breweries are open on weekends, whereas brewpubs offer tours at scheduled times or when there are enough interested patrons for a critical mass.

And always call ahead for hours, tour times, the need for reservations, directions, and the list of beers on tap.

America's Brewing Company and Walter Payton's Roundhouse

Aurora

Visit Date	Signed

ABOUT THE BREWERY

The complex comprising America's Brewing Company and Walter Payton's Roundhouse deserves more than just a casual visit. It is truly a destination. The building itself is worth seeing from its historical and architectural perspective alone. But, given that you can find excellent beer and food and many things to do in the city of Aurora, you'll want to allow plenty of time for a visit.

The brewpub is located in the former Chicago Burlington & Quincy Roundhouse along the east banks of the Fox River in Aurora. The structure is the only full-standing limestone roundhouse in the United States and is listed on the National Register of Historic Places. The roundhouse was renovated in 1996, but its original construction dates back to 1856–1865. It's a special experience just to walk through the building and envision how active the roundhouse would have been in the late 1800s. The circular structure has more than 72,000 square feet of space, including a landscaped courtyard where the locomotive turntable once spun great steam engines up to 360 degrees either into stalls so that they could be repaired or onto their original track to reverse their direction of travel.

Today the roundhouse not only has America's Brewing Company but also the Cognac Fondue Bar, the entertainment venue and night spot "America's Club," banquet facilities, and the Walter Payton Museum. During the warm weather months, the Roundhouse also hosts live entertainment from the gazebo in the courtyard.

America's Brewing Company regularly has a half-dozen of its beers on tap, with an assortment of bottles and an impressive wine list. You might also want to try the Roundhouse Root Beer. Of the house brews, the Czech-style Payton Pilsner is one of the most popular beers, but don't overlook the Sweetness Stout. Brewmaster Mike Rybinski is well known among Chicago beer enthusiasts for both of those beers. The Pilsner won a gold medal in the 2000 World Beer Cup competition, and the stout received a gold medal at the 2001 Great American Beer Festival. In 2002 the Bohemian Light was given a gold medal at the World Beer Cup. Rybinski has been around the Illinois beer scene for a few years. He began his career at the former Box Office Brewpub in DeKalb before coming to America's Brewing Company.

HISTORY

The majority of the Chicago Burlington and Quincy (C. B. & Q.) Railroad roundhouse was originally built over a ten-year period that began in 1856. The roundhouse was built in phases. The initial portions of the structure consisted of twenty-two stalls. Eight more were added in 1859, and the final ten completed the circular frame by 1865.

With additional buildings and related network of tracks, the roundhouse in its active day covered almost ten square blocks. Throughout the late nineteenth century C. B. & Q. prospered and expanded from Illinois into Missouri, Iowa, and Nebraska. During the early twentieth century it became part of the Northern Pacific Railroad Lines. In the mid-twentieth century rail service, locally as well as nationally, began declining, and by 1974 the roundhouse was abandoned.

The structure sat mostly vacant through the 1980s until the city of Aurora began looking for better uses when neighborhood revitalization took hold. Before long the surrounding blocks saw new hotels and the Hollywood Casino. Nearby, the Paramount Arts Center grew from what had been a 1931 movie theater. The roundhouse had actually been condemned and was in the process of being razed when the city of Aurora stepped in to stop it from being torn down. Ultimately the railroad gave the building to the city. When the developers of the brewpub, restaurant, and banquet facilities began their renovations on the roundhouse, it was in very sad condition and lacked public utilities. But despite those challenges the present roundhouse arose from its state of ruin in less than a year to open in March 1996.

Famous Chicago Bears football player Walter Payton was a major investor, but the husband and wife team of Scott and Pam Ascher are majority owners, president and vice-president respectively, and remain in active management roles associated with marketing and restaurant operations.

The brewpub was built on a three-way partnership of Payton, the Aschers, and Mark Alberts. The Aschers have been involved as developers in several projects in the Chicago area, including Goose Island Brewing Company in Chicago and Millrose Brewing in Barrington. They met Payton while working for him on a project in St. Louis. Alberts is well known in the Aurora area, and his background is as a certified public accountant. The brewery, restaurant, and banquet facility, with the help of revenue bonds for much of the project's financing, was developed for about $11 million. The renovation of the roundhouse has been recognized by the National Trust for Historic Preservation with its 1999 National Preservation Honor Award.

Walter Payton passed away in 1999, but his influence and presence are still felt in the Roundhouse. The Payton family is still an investor in the business, and many of the staff and management have fond memories to share about his visits. Walter was a big fan of the Roundhouse Root Beer, and his taste preference is still reflected in the recipe that he helped develop.

DON'T MISS THIS

The building itself is the obvious thing not to miss—but then again, it's hard not to appreciate the massive building and its historical character. It's fun just to walk around and explore the roundhouse. During the height of its usage, there were some forty different stalls where trains, engines, and railroad cars would be repaired. Some of those stalls now take on unique identities, such as the game room that's called "Bay 26." In another bay, football fans will want to allow time to visit the Walter Payton Museum. The ever-changing displays include Payton's Hall of Fame bust, game balls, Lombardi Trophy, and many awards won by the famous Bears running back.

In the main dining room, on the wall above the kitchen, make sure you notice the portrait of "The Bear Dance." The replica of the famous 1872 portrait was commissioned by Roundhouse owners Pam and Scott Ascher from three Champaign, Illinois, artists after the Aschers saw the portrait at the Metropolitan Museum of Art in New York. The reproduction was done on one piece of canvas and it took over six hundred hours to make.

In the Cognac Cigar Bar the historic-looking bar dates back to the 1890s. It's believed to have been made for the Columbian Exposition in Chicago in 1893. At that time it was very unique because of its rare use of electric light bulbs. The bar was constructed by Charles Passo, who upon arriving at the World's Fair with his bar, was inspired by the introduction of electricity throughout the fair. As a result, Passo drilled out the eyes and mouth of the lion's head in the center of the back bar. Then he added three light bulbs and created the world's first electric back bar.

In the wintertime you may want to sip a Reindeer Red Ale while you look out over the circular courtyard and watch for resident reindeer that roam the grounds during the holiday season.

AMERICA'S BREWING COMPANY BREWS

Aurora Amber Ale 🍺🍺🍺   *Your Ranking* _____
A light malty nose. Clear copper color with a thin, soft, off-white head. Full bodied. A light malty start to the taste with a balanced hoppy background. A smooth, light bitterness in the finish. Made with four different malts. A lighter version of an American pale ale.

Classic Dark
(a.k.a. Bubba's Brown Porter) 🍺🍺🍺🍺   *Your Ranking* _____
Very light malty nose. Deep bronze color with a thin, tan, soft head. Medium bodied and soft texture. A nice caramel sweetness with some hints of darker, chocolate malt in a toasted finish. This beer was described as a porter and listed as a brewmaster's special, so it may not be found very often at the Roundhouse.

Dancing Bear Honey Wheat Ale 🍺🍺   *Your Ranking* _____

No nose. Dark straw colored and slightly hazy. A thin, soft, white head. Medium bodied. Some sweet qualities, likely derived from the added local pure clover honey. A light smoky finish. Made with 20 percent wheat malt. Overall, one of the Roundhouse's best-selling beers. Best enjoyed while counting the dancing bears on the dining room wall—one patron actually counted 137 in the portrait.

Doppelbock 🍺🍺🍺   *Your Ranking* _____

A malty caramel nose with hints of sweet fruitiness. Cloudy, dark brown color and a thick, soft, brown head. Medium bodied and soft texture. Strong, sweet malty flavors. A light burnt sugar finish. This beer offers a heavy malt flavor that is very assertive.

Irish Red Ale 🍺🍺🍺🍺   *Your Ranking* _____

A clean, nicely balanced red ale. Begins with a light, crisp malty nose. Copper color with a light cloudiness. Medium bodied and soft texture. Smooth caramel flavor. A light smokiness in the finish, but overall this is a clean tasting beer.

Monk's Brown Ale 🍺🍺   *Your Ranking* _____

A light malty nose. Clear, light copper color with golden tints. A thin, bubbly, off-white head. Medium bodied. A light, thin caramel flavor. A sweet, cola-like finish. This beer gets high marks from many people, but it seems just too light of flavor for my tastes. A silver medal winner in the 2002 World Beer Cup competition.

Oktoberfest
(a.k.a. Hunt for The Red Oktoberfest) 🍺   *Your Ranking* _____

No nose. A very clean, somewhat thin beer. A deep gold to light copper color. Thin, bubbly, white head. A light malty flavor with hints but a weak hoppy finish. Brewed in the fall.

Payton Pilsner 🍺🍺🍺🍺   *Your Ranking* _____

A solid light lager with great flavor and assertive flavor character. A light hoppy nose begins this beer. Clear golden color with a thin, soft, white head. Medium bodied and soft texture. A light burst of hops slowly tapers but leaves a dominant mild bitter flavor with subtle maltiness. Winner of a gold medal in the 2000 World Beer Cup competition in the Bohemian Pilsner category. Named after Roundhouse co-owner and Chicago Bear Walter Payton.

Pumpkin Ale 🍺🍺   *Your Ranking* _____

Strong scent of ginger. Golden to copper color with a thin, bubbly, white head. Medium bodied and soft texture. Strong spicy qualities really provide a pumpkin flavor. A very sweet pumpkin ale.

Summer Blonde Kolsch 🍺🍺🍺   *Your Ranking* _____

This German-style wheat beer has some light fruity notes. Hints of banana in the nose. Golden color with a thick, bubbly, white head. Light and crisp body. A mild sweetness to the main body of taste. Just a mild, fruity, sour finish.

Sweetness Stout 34
(has been called Sweeney Stout) 🍺 🍺 🍺 🍺 *Your Ranking* _____

Strong sweet roasted aroma. Dark bronze body with a thick, soft, brown head. Full bodied and silky. Great sweet qualities; this beer really fits into a solid milk stout style. Some gentle, lightly roasted malt flavors finish this beer. Winner of a gold medal at the 2001 Great American Beer Festival.

Tripple 777 IPA 🍺 🍺 🍺 *Your Ranking* _____

A strong floral nose. Clear copper color and a bubbly, off-white head. Medium bodied and a soft texture. Firm hoppiness but somewhat passive bitterness. A dry finish.

OTHER AMERICA'S BREWING COMPANY BREWS YOU MAY WANT TO TRY

Berliner Weiss with Raspberry   *Your Ranking* _____

A German-style wheat beer. Made with raspberries for sweetness rather than tartness.

Cream Ale   *Your Ranking* _____

Similar to the Summer Blonde. Made with a percentage of corn. A fall seasonal.

Das En Hefe Weiss   *Your Ranking* _____

A cloudy, light German wheat. Overtones of banana and clove.

Golden Light   *Your Ranking* _____

Golden color with a thick white head. A light maltiness, with hints of honey.

Hemp Ale   *Your Ranking* _____

Brewed with sterilized hemp seeds. A nutty, malty flavor. Smooth texture.

India Pale Ale   *Your Ranking* _____

Made with Columbus, Cascade, and Centennial hops. Dry hopped in the end. Expect a strong bitterness from its sixty-three IBUs (International Bitterness Units). A winter seasonal.

Maizey Day   *Your Ranking* _____

Brewed with a percentage of corn. A light lager. Made as a spring seasonal.

Mild Ale   *Your Ranking* _____

A brown ale with mild malty flavor. A spring seasonal.

Payton's Pilsner Light (a.k.a. Bohemian Light) *Your Ranking* _____

A Bohemian-style Pilsner. Light in body and color and low in alcohol. A gold medal winner in the 2002 World Beer Cup competition.

Reindeer Red Ale   *Your Ranking* _____

Full bodied red ale. A caramel maltiness with a slightly dry finish. Made with Yakima Valley hops. Marks the return of reindeer to the courtyard for the holiday season.

Schwarzbier   *Your Ranking* _____

A German-style black beer with roasted tones. Smooth and mellow character. A summer seasonal.

Summer Blonde   *Your Ranking* _____

A light pale ale. Made for the summer season.

Wee Willie Wee Heavy Scottish Ale   *Your Ranking* _____

A winter warmer that'll take the chill off. Made with nine different malts.

Weiss Is Nice   *Your Ranking* _____

A traditional wheat. Straw color and mild spicy tones. Made as a summer seasonal.

BREWERY RATING

	Your Rating	Shepard's Rating (1 to 4 Mugs)	General Description
Location		ᕷᕷᕷ	Central city/community Entertainment district
Ease of Finding Location		ᕷᕷᕷᕷ	Close to major roads and intersections
Brewery Atmosphere		ᕷᕷᕷᕷ	Historic
Dining Experience		ᕷᕷᕷ	Family style/variety and fine dining
The Pint		ᕷᕷᕷ	A good experience

MENU

You should expect a changing menu and variety of options from Walter Payton's Roundhouse. Many of the choices are more upscale than what you would expect from a brewpub, but that shouldn't be surprising given the focus on special events and banquets at the Roundhouse. For example, among the entrees you'll find roasted salmon roulade with twisted potatoes on mango ginger beurre blanc. There is a five-spice pork tenderloin on sweet potatoes and chutney glaze; roasted prime rib is served with horseradish beer mustard; and there is a complement of seafood specials and a variety of pasta dishes. The Roundhouse also serves wood-grilled pizzas, about a half-dozen salads, and standard appetizers such as buffalo wings and brew-battered onion strings. If you are with a group, you might want to try the Taste of America sample platter, which offers portions of nearly all of the appetizers, including the deep-fried calamari and smoked barbeque ribs. For the really hungry person in the crowd, they'll want to ask about the twenty-ounce, double-cut prime rib! But if you're looking for something lighter, such as a sandwich or burger, the menu does offer a lunch section and separate pub category that describes about six to eight burger choices.

OTHER THINGS TO SEE OR DO IN THE AREA

Aurora is about forty miles west of Chicago in the Fox River valley. It was the first city in the world to have illuminated its streets with electricity and became known as "The City of Lights." It was also the first city to own its own electrical power plant. You can learn more about Aurora's past at the Aurora Art and History Center (20 E. Downer Place). The Center includes not just street lamps but maps, books, rotating exhibits, and even mastodon bones, which were actually found in local Mastodon Lake at Phillips Park in the 1930s.

The city of Aurora has excellent self-guided walking and driving tours. The Aurora Preservation Commission and the Aurora Convention and Visitors Bureau (1-800-477-4369, www.enjoyaurora.com) have developed a brochure that explains many of the historic sites and districts. It's one of the best guides for historical buildings in the state. The Roundhouse is indeed listed in the guide, but you'll also find descriptions and addresses for several other historical places like the homes and buildings on Stolp Island, the New York Street Memorial Bridge, the Paramount Arts Centre (23 E. Galena Boulevard), the Holbrook Mill (121 W. Benton Street), the Copley Mansion (434 W. Downer Place) of six-term U.S. Representative Col. Ira Copley, and the Coats Garage (53–54 S. LaSalle Street) in the Auto Row Historic District.

Also of historical note, but perhaps not quite the same historical significance, is the Hi-Lite Drive-In Theatre in Aurora (Montgomery Road and Hill Avenue). Built in 1947, it was Illinois's first drive-in movie theater. It still offers first-run movies. In the late 1800s and early 1900s Aurora was considered the corset center of the world. At least three corset factories thrived in Aurora. One of the largest was the Chicago Corset Company, which employed more than six hundred women and made more than two million corsets a year.

Since 1912 Aurora has hosted a farmers' market. On Saturdays from mid-June to mid-October you'll find fresh produce, plants, flowers, and various kinds of food at the Aurora Transportation Center (Route 25/233 North Broadway). Also in the summer, Music Under the Stars in Aurora is an evening concert series that moves weekly to a different park in Aurora. One park worth a walk through is Phillips Park (Smith Boulevard at Ray Moses Drive), with its more than three hundred acres and Mastodon Lake. There is a zoo with elk, otters, and pot-bellied pigs.

If you enjoy hiking and biking, the twelve-mile Virgil L. Gilman Trail connects Aurora with Montgomery. There is also access to the Illinois Prairie Path, the Fox River Trail, and the Great Western Trail.

The Hollywood Casino (1 New York Street) is directly southwest of the Roundhouse. Also close by is the Aurora Regional Fire Museum (New York Street and Broadway), which has displays of vintage firefighting equipment and photographs and memorabilia of the 1871 Chicago Fire.

The Kane County Flea Market is held the first Sunday of every month and the preceding Saturday afternoon at the Kane County Fairgrounds (Route 64 and Randall Road in St. Charles) and is considered among the largest in the Midwest. In July the Kendall County Historical Society (south of Aurora in Yorkville) sponsors a tractor and truck pull. In June the Mid-American Canoe Race stretches fifteen miles from St. Charles to Aurora along the Fox River. Island Park in North Aurora is a great place to view the race, where there is also an annual Arts and Crafts Fair.

Northeast of Aurora, the Kane County Cougars, a Class A professional baseball team, plays at Elfstrom Stadium in Geneva. Blackberry Farm's Pioneer Village (Galena and Barnes Road) is a living history park that contains a carriage museum, one-room schoolhouse and pioneer cabin, blacksmith shop, spinning and weaving demonstrations, and more than a dozen other old-fashioned stops.

On Aurora's lighter side, it became somewhat of a cultural icon when the movie *Wayne's World* was released. The movie was based on a *Saturday Night Live* spoof of an Aurora cable television access show. Some taping of the movie did take place in Aurora.

DIRECTIONS

Aurora is about forty minutes west of Chicago. Interstate 88 leads directly into the city from Chicago. Routes 25 and 31 are great roads to travel north and south of Aurora because they line the east and west banks of the Fox River.

America's Brewing Company and Walter Payton's Roundhouse is located in the heart of Aurora on Route 25, on the eastern banks of the Fox River. The Roundhouse is nearly directly east of Stolp Island. The I-88 and Route 25 interchange is approximately two miles north of the Roundhouse.

The Metra's Chicago-to-Aurora line will bring your directly to the Roundhouse, letting you off on the east steps of the brewpub.

Bent River Brewing Company

Moline

Visit Date	Signed

ABOUT THE BREWERY

Bent River is mainly a bar and brewery. Nestled in a series of brick buildings along the north side of Fifth Avenue, the green awnings offer a visual reference point for finding Bent River. The windows of the second floor have large arches of concrete and brick, which offer evidence of the building's construction during the early 1900s. This sense of history is further emphasized with old brewing memorabilia that are displayed in the building's large storefront windows.

Bent River is located in the historic Olde Town riverfront area of Moline. It's a place with atmosphere that a serious beer drinker really appreciates. As you walk into Bent River, you really get the impression that you are standing in the heart of a brewery. All that separates you from shiny copper brew kettles and stainless steel fermenters is a long, beautiful wooden bar with a copper top that measures nearly forty feet in length. Bent River is not short of character. Wooden floors, a pressed tin ceiling, and an almost exclusive focus on beer make for a memorable stop. Bent River is really two storefronts; the western side is the main bar, and the eastern half is composed somewhat like a German beer hall with lots of church pew seating.

Behind the building, accessible through a rear door to the bar, is a small outside area with a few tables and chairs that serves as a beer garden in the summer. While it might be a little shy on food and other elements for those looking for a restaurant, it more than makes up with its beer list. Look around—the more than two hundred mugs from the locals provide a strong endorsement of this brewery's product!

Bent River offers about a dozen beers throughout the year. You'll commonly find six to eight house beers on tap. The Mississippi Blonde is an excellent light beer, but the Bohemian Pilsner has more character as a light-to medium-bodied lager. One of Bent River's best sellers is the Pale Ale, and because it's so well liked, you might not always see it on tap. When you do, it's always worth filling the growler.

HISTORY

As a brewery, Bent River was established in 1997, but troubles over zoning with the city of Moline prevented actual brewing until 1999. Those who have followed Bent River may have seen, or even purchased, beer in the bottle, but bottling has not been a recent part of the brewery operations.

Bent River is actually supported by a partnership of about twenty major investors. Tim Koster is a major stockholder and brewer. Koster once worked at the local Rock Island Arsenal. After attending a mini course on brewing at Siebel Institute of Technology, he expanded from homebrew supply to actual brewing. You'll likely find Tim in the brewery most Saturdays. In fact, on Saturdays, when brewing starts, you'll even see a few friends there to help out.

Bent River takes its name from the bends in the Mississippi. Local legend explains that when the "Father of Waters" passed by the area, he was so tantalized by the beauty of the surrounding land that he turned his head to admire the view, and the result was that the Mississippi runs both east and west through the Quad Cities.

The building housing Bent River was built in the 1920s as a hardware store. Over the years it has contained a bakery and even a beauty school. The green pressed tin ceiling dates back to the building's original construction. In 1980 Tim Koster opened a homebrew supply store in the building, which helped him get his early thirst for brewing good beer. The homebrew store closed in 1999, when the brewery and bar expanded into the two rooms that make up Bent River today.

DON'T MISS THIS

There are more than two hundred mugs hanging on the center wall that divides the bar from an open seating area. The local Quad Cities homebrew club often hangs out here. M.U.G.Z. (Mississippi Unquenchable Grail Zymurgists) hold their regular meetings at Bent River. You might also look for Tim Koster's coaster collection hanging on the east wall of the dining room. But the inviting feature of Bent River is the broom that hangs over a backdoor on the beer hall side of the building. It once was tradition in England to hang a broom above the door to let the neighborhood know there was ale for sale inside!

BENT RIVER BREWS

American Style Wheat 🍺🍺🍺   *Your Ranking* _____
An unfiltered American wheat. No nose. Golden color with a creamy, soft, white head. Light bodied with a softness that offers hints of more body than it really has. Flavor dominated by a light, bitter hoppiness. No finish. A very clean, crisp wheat.

Bohemian Pilsner 🍺🍺🍺🍺 *Your Ranking* _____

A great, medium bodied Pilsner with some character from the Saaz hops. A light flowery nose. Golden body with a thin, soft, white head and a crispness to the texture. A nice hoppy start that is constant and steady and doesn't really let up, maintaining a crisp medium bitterness throughout. The finish has a hint of bitterness but is generally clean without an aftertaste.

Brown 🍺🍺🍺 *Your Ranking* _____

A light malty nose. Deep bronze color and slightly hazy. A thin, soft, brown head. Medium bodied and very carbonated. The taste is malty with a sharpness. Finishes clean and warm.

Citrus Ale 🍺🍺🍺🍺 *Your Ranking* _____

This is a fun beer. A fruity citrus aroma. Clear light copper color and a thick, soft, tan head. Light to medium bodied. A sharp fruity sour flavor that is actually well balanced with a smoky malty background. Finishes with a light fruitiness. This is as described by the brewery, "citrus and fruity," so it gets high marks for being what it is supposed to be and for Tim Koster's honesty.

Mississippi Blonde 🍺🍺🍺 *Your Ranking* _____

A light American-style lager. Clean, no nose or finish. Clear, light golden color. A bubbly, white head. Light bodied with a smooth texture. Malty from the beginning with a light, faint hoppy background.

Oatmeal Stout 🍺🍺🍺 *Your Ranking* _____

The tones of coffee, chocolate, and roasted barley will leave you wanting another one of these. A roasted, malty nose starts this beer off with a great indication of what will come. Very dark color with tints of brown. The head is thick, bubbly, and tan. Full bodied and highly carbonated. Strong caramel and chocolate malt qualities. The finish is mostly malty with a slight sharpness to the ending.

Pale Ale 🍺🍺🍺🍺 *Your Ranking* _____

Overall, my favorite of the Bent River brews. A great example of an American pale ale. A hoppy nose really starts this beer off with assertive character. Copper color with a slight haze. Thin, off-white head. Medium to full bodied, bubbly, and crisp. The hoppy bitterness is constant and firm throughout the finish. The bitterness might be a little mild for pale ale fans, but the firmness and consistency of the hoppiness makes this a great beer.

Raspberry Wheat 🍺🍺🍺 *Your Ranking* _____

An American-style wheat with raspberry flavor that really comes out in the nose and the finish. An unfiltered wheat, copper and slightly hazy. Thick, bubbly, white head. Medium bodied and soft. The raspberry flavors dominate the main elements of taste, including its finish. The raspberry flavor is strong but not overpowering.

Strawberry Blonde 🍺🍺 *Your Ranking* _____

A blonde lager with light strawberry flavor. Lighter than the raspberry wheat, a very strong fruity sweetness in both the nose and finish. Clear golden color with a thick, soft, white head. Sweet fruity strawberry flavors dominate most of the malt and hop characteristics.

Uncommon Stout   🍺🍺🍺   *Your Ranking* _____

A very, very malty nose. Dark color with bronze hues. A thick, soft, brown head. Full bodied. Strong malty qualities. The sweetness is complemented with a light coffee background that sets up a strong roasted finish. You'll really taste the coffee tones in this stout.

OTHER BENT RIVER BREWS YOU MAY WANT TO TRY

Jalapeño Pepper Beer   *Your Ranking* _____

A specialty lager. A version of the Bohemian Pilsner with jalapeño pepper taste.

Pepper Stout   *Your Ranking* _____

Pepper flavor added to the Oatmeal Stout.

BREWERY RATING

	Your Rating	Shepard's Rating (1 to 4 Mugs)	General Description
Location		🍺🍺🍺🍺	Central city/community
Ease of Finding Location		🍺🍺🍺	Difficult; traffic or roads are problematic
Brewery Atmosphere		🍺🍺🍺	Rustic
Dining Experience		n/a	No food
The Pint		🍺🍺🍺	A good experience

MENU

Aside from a few over-the-bar munchies, Bent River does not have food service.

OTHER THINGS TO SEE OR DO IN THE AREA

Moline is part of the Quad Cities: Davenport and Bettendorf in Iowa, and Moline/East Moline and Rock Island in Illinois. The Quad Cities are within a day's drive of Chicago, Des Moines, Minneapolis, or St. Louis, with connections to Interstates 80, 88, and 74.

The name Moline is from the French word *moulin*, meaning mill. The city was platted by a mill company in 1843. Some of the oldest areas of the city, between 7th and 18th Avenues, reflect the Belgian heritage. The Center for Belgian Culture (712 Nineteenth Avenue) offers historical information and demonstrations of how Belgian lace is made.

Moline is also home to John Deere and Company. Just two blocks from Bent River, the John Deere Pavilion and Collectors Center (1400 River Drive) houses vintage and modern John Deere equipment. You can even sit in the cab of a combine. The John Deere Commons is part of a revitalized riverfront in downtown Moline. The Deere-Wiman House and Butterworth Center (817 11th Street and 1105 8th Street) are beautiful mansions with elaborate gardens that offer a glimpse into the life of the Deere family. There are actually quite a number of old historic homes in this neighborhood that makes for an interesting drive.

The Great River Trail brings walkers, hikers, and bicyclists from Rock Island along the Mississippi through Moline and on to Cordova, Illinois. The trail is over sixty miles long and eventually stretches to Savanna, Illinois. Catching the trail in downtown Moline, near the John Deere Commons, you'll experience the Ben Butterworth Parkway out of Moline to East Moline. The Butterworth Parkway offers playgrounds, a marina, restaurants, and boat launches. Throughout Moline there are more than three dozen city parks.

If you want to see more of the Mississippi, consider the *Celebration Belle,* a nongaming riverboat that offers lunch, dinner, and sightseeing cruises. The *Channel Cat Water Taxi* offers a great view of the Quad Cities from the Mississippi River. Channel Cat service is available seven days a week from Memorial Day to Labor Day and on weekends through October as the weather holds. Docks are located at John Deere Commons and Ben Butterworth Parkway in Moline, Leach Park Landing in Bettendorf, and the Village of East Davenport Landing in Davenport.

The MARK of the Quad Cities is a twelve-thousand-seat arena that hosts performances, conventions, and sporting events. The MARK is home to the Quad City Mallards hockey team and the arena football team, the Steamwheelers.

The Rock Island Arsenal is on Arsenal Island in the Mississippi River. The island, while considered part of the city of Rock Island, actually spans the riverfront of Moline and Rock Island. Constructed in 1862, it was once considered the government's largest manufacturing arsenal. The island includes a museum, Confederate cemetery, and the Corps of Engineers' Clock Tower Building.

The area hosts a number of festivals and special events. Quad Cities Bald Eagle Days (Rock Island) is held in mid-January. The Rock Island Summer Fest is in mid-July. The Moline Riverfest offers live music, fireworks, and lighted boat parades in June (Mississippi and Ben Butterworth Parkways). And the Quad Cities Marathon in September encompasses a route through five cities in two states, crossing three bridges over the Mississippi.

Other stops in Moline might include the Fryxell Geology Museum (639 38th Street) on the Augustana College campus. The museum houses a collection of fossils, including sauropod dinosaur eggs. If you have a sweet tooth, try Lagomarcino's Confectionery (1422 5th Avenue), which is well known for its golden sponge candy.

Along the way to the Quad Cities, if you are traveling Interstate 88, you'll pass by Dixon, Illinois. Dixon was originally a trading post on the Rock River. Dixon is also known as the "Petunia Capital of the World" and celebrates annually with a Petunia Festival over the Fourth of July. Not far north of Dixon on Highway 2 is Grand Detour, the home of blacksmith John Deere.

DIRECTIONS

Take Interstate 74 into downtown Moline. Exit onto 7th Street and drive west. Within two-to-three blocks, turn north on 15th or 16th Street, and then within another two blocks you will come to 5th Avenue, where you should turn left (west). Bent River is located on the north side of the street. Look for the green awnings.

Blue Cat Brew Pub
Rock Island

Visit Date	Signed

ABOUT THE BREWERY

The Blue Cat Brew Pub (cat as in catfish, a popular fish found in the Mississippi River) is found in the heart of downtown Rock Island. The two-story brick building was once the local Veterans of Foreign Wars Hall. It has since been renovated into the Blue Cat, with two bars, a dining room, and pool hall. In the future the parking lot to the east of the building is expected to become a beer garden.

One of the most distinguishing features of the brewery (after the beer, of course) is the two-story interior atrium, which showcases a behind-glass brewhaus. The beer tower, as it is called, is clearly the focal point of the Blue Cat Brew Pub. The first-floor bar and dining room face the glass room, which contains the brew kettle and fermentation vessels. From upstairs on the second floor you can actually look over an iron railing and watch patrons as they drink the Blue Cat brews at the main bar.

The Blue Cat regularly has three or four of its own beers on tap, but it's always worth a stop to see what is brewing because you can expect to find more than twenty different styles throughout the year. Off the Rail Pale Ale and Wigged Pig Wheat are the standing favorites, but brewmaster and owner Dan Cleveland takes a lot of extra care in the brewing of his stouts, and you'll find several different varieties of that dark ale throughout the year.

HISTORY

The brother-and-sister team of Martha and Dan Cleveland established the Blue Cat Brew Pub in March 1994. The pair actually grew up in Rock Island.

Martha handles the restaurant side of the business, while Dan looks over the brewing. Dan was once a chemist at the University of Iowa Hospitals in Iowa City, where he provided support to the hospital's pathology department. But Dan developed a desire for brewing that led him to do a great deal of reading on the subject. Eventually he found himself in an apprenticeship at Denver's Wynkoop Brewpub. Dan said that when he brewed his first batch of beer at Blue Cat, he kept pulling samples for skeptical friends, just to make sure he was going to get beer. Today, with Dan's brewing skill, he's never short of friends for sampling.

The building occupied by Blue Cat is over one hundred years old. At one time it had a third floor, which was destroyed by fire in the 1960s. Local residents say that during the early 1960s that part of the building was a very popular spot for male burlesque. More recently, the building was better known as Rock Island's VFW hall.

Close by the Blue Cat is the Rock Island Brewing Company, which offers a couple of house brews that are brewed by Dan Cleveland at the Blue Cat. However, it's mainly just a popular bar. The original Rock Island Brewery dates back to the 1890s, reopened after prohibition, but closed in 1939.

The Blue Cat was almost known as Crooked River Brewing. But just before opening in 1994, Dan and Martha Cleveland received a registered letter from a brewpub in Ohio that had already claimed the Crooked River name, and they weren't so excited about sharing the moniker. The Clevelands had already had a sign made, but they eventually sent it back for changes.

DON'T MISS THIS

The building that houses the Blue Cat is full of history. When you ascend the steps to the upper bar, take a close look at the brick wall that lines the stairs. You can detect an old Bull Durham sign painted on the bricks, probably when it was the exposed exterior wall of the neighboring building.

While it sounds obvious, try not to miss the first-floor restaurant. Brewmaster Dan Cleveland says that the second-floor bar is so popular with his beer friends that some say they missed the first-floor dining room altogether.

BLUE CAT BREWS

Arkham Stout 🍺🍺🍺🍺   *Your Ranking* _____
A light roasted nose. Very dark with bronze tints and a thick, creamy, brown head. The flavor is dominated by a semisweet maltiness with a bitter hop balance. A roasted smokiness, medium hoppiness, and smooth texture. A silver medal winner in the 1996 World Beer Cup competition.

Big Bad Dog 🍺🍺🍺🍺   *Your Ranking* _____
An Old English Ale. Malty nose and flavor are aggressive. A mahogany to deep bronze color. A soft, tan head. Full bodied and soft texture. Sweet caramel flavors dominate and linger into the finish. Named by Martha's children, who enjoy watching the Rugrats on television and adopted the saying "Big Bad Dog" when needing to sound tough and assertive. This beer lives up to its

name. Winner of a silver medal in the 1996 World Beer Cup competition. A signature beer for Blue Cat.

Blue Cat Anniversary Ale VIII   *Your Ranking* _____
A special beer brewed for the Blue Cat's anniversary. No nose. Clear, dark copper color. A thick, soft, white head. Medium bodied and soft texture. Malty sweetness from beginning to end.

Finnigan's Irish Stout   *Your Ranking* _____
A lightly roasted nose. Very dark color and a thick, soft, brown head. Full bodied and dry texture. A malty start that has strong hop qualities that balance the chocolate flavor and leave you with a clean, crisp impression. The menu describes this as a drier stout than the Arkham.

Fuzzy Buzz Peach Ale   *Your Ranking* _____
A springtime seasonal. This beer is very sweet; there is no mistaking the peach aroma and flavor. This beer has its place with its distinctive sweet, fruity tones and is best enjoyed in the springtime so that its nose can compete with the aroma of fresh spring flowers. A light, bubbly texture with the peach flavor suggests that wine cooler drinkers might want to cross over to this special brew.

Guatemalan Coffee Stout   *Your Ranking* _____
A full-bodied, creamy stout with strong coffee aroma and flavor. Very dark color and a very thick, long lasting, bubbly, brown head. Those who like roasted coffee stouts will enjoy this beer.

Off the Rail Pale Ale   *Your Ranking* _____
A malty nose. Clear copper color and a thin, bubbly, white head. Medium bodied and smooth. There is a malty beginning followed by a burst of bitterness. The finish is bitter and crisp. Off the Rail is a longstanding flagship of the Blue Cat and was the first beer made by brewer Dan Cleveland.

Quad Cities Blonde   *Your Ranking* _____
A light malty nose. Vivid, clear golden color and a thick, soft, white head. Light to medium bodied with some creaminess. A malty start with a firm hoppy background. Fruity finish.

River Back Jack IPA   *Your Ranking* _____
A British-style India Pale Ale. Aged with oak chips. Strong hoppy, even resin-like aromas. Cloudy orange color with a soft, off-white head. Medium bodied and very crisp texture. The taste has strong bitterness. The finish is assertive yet crisp and clean. The bitterness leaves no doubt you are drinking an IPA. A bronze medal winner in the 1995 World Beer Cup competition.

Wigged Pig Wheat   *Your Ranking* _____
A light golden wheat. A light, fruity nose. Clear golden color with a head that is thin, bubbly, and white. Light bodied. Crisp, light hoppy flavors stand out above a mild, malty background that has faint hints of sweet banana. The clear golden color and hoppy qualities leave you with a very crisp impression.

BLUE CAT BREWS BREWED FOR THE ROCK ISLAND BREWING COMPANY

Baby Doc　🍺🍺🍺　　　　　　*Your Ranking* _____

An amber ale. The nose has a light malty quality. Cloudy amber color with a thin, soft, off-white head. Medium bodied and soft texture. A nice malty start with some dry bitterness that is way in the background and builds in the finish. Overall, smooth with just the right amount of hops to complement the caramel flavors. One of the owners of Rock Island Brewing is the son of a doctor and a doctor himself, so he got the name Baby Doc and gave it to this beer.

Cross Country Cream Ale　🍺🍺　　　*Your Ranking* _____

No nose. Light golden color. A thin, bubbly, white head. Light bodied and somewhat soft texture. Not much flavor, just some mild hoppy qualities that are latent within a light roasted malty body. This is one of Blue Cat's lightest beers.

OTHER BLUE CAT BREWS YOU MAY WANT TO TRY

Blue Cat Porter　　　　　　　　　*Your Ranking* _____

A smooth porter with a distinctive smoky taste. Deep copper color, medium body, and thick, rich head.

Bow Fish Imperial Stout　　　　　*Your Ranking* _____

A thicker body and higher use of hops in the tradition of Imperial stouts.

Classic Cranberry Ale　　　　　　*Your Ranking* _____

Brewed in time for Christmas.

Coriander & Orange　　　　　　　*Your Ranking* _____

A light specialty American wheat beer with spicy coriander tones and a subtle orange and ginger finish. A bronze medal winner at the 1997 World Beer Championships.

Crescent Moon ESB　　　　　　　*Your Ranking* _____

A dark, rich, full-bodied ale. Sweet and malty.

Ichabod's Pumpkin Ale　　　　　*Your Ranking* _____

A specialty beer brewed in October.

Rambling Raspberry　　　　　　　*Your Ranking* _____

Eighty pounds of raspberries are used to make this summertime beer. Tart flavor and distinctive fruity finish. A bronze medal winner in the 1995 World Beer Cup competition.

Red Toad　　　　　　　　　　　*Your Ranking* _____

An amber pale ale. A slightly hoppier beer than Off the Rail Pale Ale.

Scotch Terrier Rauch Bier　　　　*Your Ranking* _____

Smoky. A silver medal winner in the 1999 World Beer Cup competition.

Wee Bit Scotch Ale   *Your Ranking* _____

A light Scotch ale. Low hoppiness combined with a soft, malty flavor. A dash of Peated Malt provides a subtle, crisp, smoky finish. A bronze medal winner in the 1995 World Beer Cup competition.

BREWERY RATING

	Your Rating	Shepard's Rating (1 to 4 Mugs)	General Description
Location		🍺🍺🍺🍺	Central city/community Entertainment district
Ease of Finding Location		🍺🍺🍺	Easy, but requires some planning
Brewery Atmosphere		🍺🍺🍺	Family restaurant with sports bar accents
Dining Experience		🍺🍺🍺	Family style/variety
The Pint		🍺🍺🍺	A good experience

MENU

The Blue Cat menu is very ambitious. There are over a dozen appetizers, ranging from standard pub fare in poppers and hot wings to more eclectic offerings such as steamed mussels and Catfish Sate, which features curry-marinated catfish baked and finished with peanut sauce. Blue Cat makes a number of salads. You can expect a soup of the day that is homemade and served with fresh wheat bread. The heart of the menu features regional favorites, pastas, seafood, grilled specialties, and about a dozen burgers. If you are looking for something light, you might try the pan-seared halibut, which is finished with a white wine and jalapeño butter. But the regional favorites section of the menu is sure to gain the attention of the hungry traveler with choices like the brewmaster's meatloaf, the pot roast ploughman's platter, and the southern Dixieland special, which puts barbecued pork on fresh-baked corn muffins.

You may also want to ask about the Blue Cat's beer dinners, which often feature a five-course meal in which each course is paired with a special brew. Those who take part often receive a tour of the Blue Cat and share in some great conversation about matching their favorite beer with food.

OTHER THINGS TO SEE OR DO IN THE AREA

The Downtown Rock Island Arts and Entertainment District offers over thirty restaurants and pubs in an eight-block area. The District also features Jumer's Casino Rock Island (almost directly across the street from the Blue Cat).

Circa '21 Dinner Playhouse (1828 3rd Avenue) is a professional theater housed in the restored Fort Theater Building in downtown Rock Island. For summertime drama, check out Genesius Guild, an open-air theater in Rock Island Lincoln Park (near Augustana College on 38th Street).

Not far from the downtown to the south, the Painted Ladies of the Broadway Historic District provide a glimpse into the grand homes of Rock Island. More than five hundred homes in a thirty-block area feature Queen Anne, Italianate, and Colonial Revival architecture. The district contains twenty-one Rock Island landmarks and is nationally known for founding the "Great Unveiling" program, where a home's siding is removed to unveil the original historical parts of the structure. Above the Broadway Historic District, looking down from the hill is the Highland Park area that was home to the city's wealthiest residents at the turn of the twentieth century.

The Great River Trail is a scenic trail along the Mississippi River that stretches sixty-two miles from Rock Island to Savanna, Illinois. It's part of the 475-mile Grand Illinois Trail, which, when completed, will run from the Mississippi to Lake Michigan.

The Rock Island Arsenal is on Arsenal Island in the Mississippi River. The island, while considered part of the city of Rock Island, actually spans the riverfront of Moline and Rock Island. Constructed in 1862, in its earlier days it was consider the government's largest manufacturing arsenal. The island includes a museum, Confederate cemetery, and the Corps of Engineers Clock Tower Building. The Mississippi River Visitors Center is located on the west end of Arsenal Island. The island also has about four miles of bike trails.

The John Hauberg Indian Museum (1510 46th Avenue) explains the history of the Fox and Sauk Tribes. The museum and Watch Tower Lodge is located at the Black Hawk State Historic Site. Not only can you see Sauk and Fox Indian artifacts, there is also a network of walking paths along the scenic Rock River.

In January Rock Island holds the annual Bald Eagle Days Environmental Fair and Wildlife Art Show (see the Quad Cities Expo Center at 2621 4th Avenue). May features the Quad Cities Criterium, a European-style street bike race sponsored by the Downtown Rock Island Arts and Entertainment District. Summer evenings offer the baseball of the Quad City River Bandits, a farm team of the Minnesota Twins. Games are held in John O'Donnell Stadium in Davenport (directly across the river from downtown Rock Island). In August, the Great River Tug Fest is held in Port Byron, Illinois, and LeClaire, Iowa (about fifteen miles upriver from the Quad Cities). It's the annual Illinois-versus-Iowa tug-of-war across the Mississippi River. If you're headed this way in late summer, you might also want to check out the Amazing Maize Maze—a four-acre cornfield maze near Princeton, Iowa. The Rock Island Grand Prix features go-kart racing and is held in downtown Rock Island in September. Friday nights in October offer laser light shows and a haunted house in the Downtown Rock Island Arts and Entertainment District.

Another pastime is watching barges make their way through Lock & Dam 15 at the Rock Island District U.S. Army Corps of Engineers Mississippi River Visitors Center (just beyond the downriver edge of Rock Island itself). The first railroad bridge across the river remains, in part. In 1856 the first railroad bridge to span the Mississippi was built between Davenport and Rock Island, and the original log trestle still stands in the historic village of East Davenport.

DIRECTIONS

Blue Cat Brew Pub is located only about four blocks east of the Rock Island Centennial Bridge (Highway 67). When approaching from the south on Interstate 280, the easiest way to get to the Blue Cat is to follow the Centennial Expressway (Highway 92) east into downtown Rock Island. As you arrive on Route 92, go beyond the Centennial Bridge and look for Jumer's Casino, which is at approximately 18th Street. At this point look south, down 18th Street, for the white and blue awnings hanging over the Blue Cat's front windows.

When approaching from the north (Davenport, Iowa) and I-80, take exit 295 (Brady Street) and head south on Highway 61 into Davenport and continue to follow the signs to Rock Island and Centennial Bridge, which is about six miles from I-80. Once driving over the Centennial Bridge, exit onto Route 92 and head east to Jumer's Casino and look south, down 18th Street, for the Blue Cat's blue and white awnings.

Brass Restaurant and Brewery

South Barrington

Visit Date	*Signed*

ABOUT THE BREWERY

One of Illinois's newest brewpubs, the Brass Restaurant and Brewery is located in Chicago's northwest suburb of South Barrington. Given this brewpub's location near Interstate 90 and its proximity to a bustling entertainment and commercial neighborhood that includes a huge thirty-screen movie complex, it has great potential for attracting a strong following. Brass Restaurant and Brewery is a one-and-a-half-story building with a reddish masonry and glass exterior, built to the specifications of a modern brewpub and restaurant. You enter through a revolving door into a large lobby where the hostess greets you. On your left is the main dining room and on your right is the bar. Straight ahead is the restaurant's show kitchen. With all the glass, wood, brick, metal accents, receiving area, and revolving door there is a clear emphasis on making an impressive statement through a "grand entrance" to the Brass Restaurant and Brewery. But one of the best seats is in the beer garden that overlooks a small pond and restored wetland.

You can see into the brewhaus from inside the dining room, while at the bar, and even from outside in the beer garden. Many views offer a glimpse of the brewery's five fermenters and six serving vessels. One of the more unusual traits of this brewery is the two gunmetal-blue fermenters—a color you don't often find in a brewhaus. From the bar area, you might be overwhelmed by the 110-inch plasma television. During the warmer months, you may want to forgo the bustling interior for a light and smooth Weiss Guy Hefe-Weizen in the brewery's beer garden.

The Brass Restaurant and Brewery offers four standard beers and a couple of brewmaster's specials. Among the standard offerings, the Anticipation Amber is a nicely balanced red ale, and the Anytime Pale Ale is just like its name says—it's good anytime.

HISTORY

The Brass Restaurant and Brewery opened in 2003. Brewmaster Greg Browne is originally from Sydney, Australia. He first became acquainted with American beer while attending the Great Lakes Naval Training Center while in the Australian Navy in the late 1980s. After finishing his military service he returned to Illinois. After getting married, Greg decided to attend Siebel Institute of Technology in 1993 for a brewing short course. He brewed professionally at Chicago's Weinkeller brewpubs and Golden Prairie Brewing, which are both now closed. After enrolling in Siebel's Diploma Course, Greg went to work at Goose Island Brewing. Then in 1999 he tried his hand at owning and running a brewpub called Weeghman Park, but after nine months he decided to go back to work for Goose Island. Goose Island eventually purchased Weeghman Park Brewing and transformed the brewpub into what is now Goose Island–Wrigleyville. From 1999 to 2003 Greg was the brewmaster at Flatlander's in Lincolnshire, before taking over brewing operations at the Brass Restaurant and Brewery in 2003. Like many, Greg first learned brewing as a hobby. That's when, as Greg describes it, "I learned of the brotherhood of brewers, and it just seemed right for me!"

DON'T MISS THIS

As you walk through the revolving glass doors immediately on your left, there is a three-foot-tall golden parrot with ears that look like they belong to a mouse. In the dining room, along the north wall, you'll find a fifteen-foot-tall totem pole with five bird-like faces. The pole was made by a local artisan especially for Brass. Totem poles typically are carved to tell a story for the purpose of preserving local culture and heritage for future generations. Try as I might, I couldn't find any images of beer on this one.

BRASS BREWS

Anticipation Pale Ale   🍺🍺🍺🍺   *Your Ranking* _____
A smooth, very inviting floral nose. Rich copper color with a light haziness. Medium bodied and very bubbly texture. Firm, smooth hoppy flavor. Lingering bitter finish. This beer has the perfect name: I'm always anticipating my next visit for a pint of this pale ale.

Anytime Amber Ale   🍺🍺🍺🍺   *Your Ranking* _____
An English-style amber ale. A light malty aroma. Deep, hazy bronze color with a thick, bubbly, tan head. Medium bodied with some dry texture. Smooth malty beginning with emphasis on a caramel maltiness. Finishes with a balanced bitterness.

Pal's Porter   🍺🍺🍺🍺   *Your Ranking* _____
An assertive malty nose with chocolate tones. Deep dark color with bronze highlights in the bottom of the glass. Full bodied and round texture. A strong malty flavor in which the caramel notes come out first, followed by a smooth

chocolate malt background. Mild bitterness and dry texture in the finish. If it's a cool day in the beer garden, try this porter to take care of any chills.

Weiss Guy 🍺🍺🍺 *Your Ranking* _____

This is a perfect pint for the brewpub's beer garden and patio. A citrus nose. Cloudy, hazy copper color with a thick, soft, tan head. Light to medium bodied. A crisp, spicy fruitiness with a subtle sweet background combines to make a great German-style weissbier. The color and spicy tones stand out to make this a memorable beer.

OTHER BRASS BREWS YOU MAY WANT TO TRY

Hunter's Honey Wheat *Your Ranking* _____

The lightest of the Brass brews. This American-style wheat is made with fresh clover honey. Light golden color and a crisp malty aroma and flavor. A subtle honey finish.

BREWERY RATING

	Your Rating	Shepard's Rating (1 to 4 Mugs)	General Description
Location		🍺🍺🍺	Commercial/industrial
Ease of Finding Location		🍺🍺🍺🍺	Close to major roads and intersections
Brewery Atmosphere		🍺🍺🍺🍺	Family restaurant
Dining Experience		🍺🍺🍺🍺	Family style/variety
The Pint		🍺🍺🍺	A good experience

MENU

The Brass Restaurant and Brewery serves a combination of steaks, chops, and seafood. The menu supports an upscale tavern and family dining experience. Appetizers include coconut shrimp, quesadillas, wings, nachos, and beer-battered onions rings. You'll find about a half dozen salads. The brewpub's signature soups feature a white cheddar ale, baked potato, and Napa Valley onion. About ten different sandwiches and three or four pizza choices are attractive menu options among the local moviegoers. The entrees are ambitious with selections such as baby back barbecue ribs, lamb chops, stuffed chicken breasts, whiskey-roasted chicken, kabobs, salmon, halibut, and sea bass. But the dessert choices make Brass very unique. My recommendation is to go straight to the Brass Candy—a large margarita glass with fresh strawberries, blueberries, and whipped cream topped with homemade cotton candy. It's so large you'll be tempted to share with a friend, but for those who enjoy sweets the best of friends will each want to have their own.

OTHER THINGS TO SEE OR DO IN THE AREA

The Brass Restaurant and Brewery is located about five miles west of the Interstate 90 and 290 interchange. One of the local landmarks is Goebbert's Pumpkin and Farm Market (40 West Higgins Road). While known for its seasonal plants, pumpkins, and haunted house, Geobbert's also offers Animal Land, where you can feed goats, chickens, pigs, llamas, and kangaroos.

Probably the most recognizable landmark is the AMC South Barrington Thirty Theatres (175 Studio Drive) and the South Barrington Club (3 Tennis Club Lane). You'll drive right by the Brass Restaurant and Brewery on your way to and from the movie. The South Barrington Club offers tennis courts, a fitness center, a gymnasium, and a preschool.

South Barrington and a number of area villages combine to offer many options for an evening or weekend trip to Chicago's western suburbs. Northeast of South Barrington, the village of Palatine holds its street festival in August. Palatine also hosts a farmers' market from July to October at the Palatine Train Station (137 West Wood Street). In nearby Arlington Heights you'll find the Arlington Heights Historical Museum (110 West Freemont Street), and the Arlington Park Racecourse (Euclid Avenue and Wilke Road) features thoroughbred racing.

South of the Brass Restaurant and Brewery, you might want to visit the Lynfred Winery (15 South Roselle Road). North of the Brass Restaurant and Brewery, the Barrington Ice House Mall (200 Applebee Street) was once an ice house that was built in 1904. Located in the heart of downtown, the ice house has been transformed into a mall that includes many specialty shops and restaurants that link its historic architecture to the modern structure.

You may also want to check the brewery descriptions of Millrose Brewery (nearly across the street), Prairie Rock–Schaumburg, and Ram–Schaumburg for other things to see and do in the area.

DIRECTIONS

If traveling west on Interstate 90, exit at Barrington Road and go north to the stoplight, then turn left (west) on Center Road and Studio Drive for one block, then turn left (south) onto Hollywood.

If traveling east into Chicago on I-90, exit at Sutton Road (Route 59), go north to the light on Higgins Road (Route 72), then turn right (east/southeast) on Higgins and travel two and a half miles to Barrington Road; turn left (north) on Barrington Road and cross over I-90 to the light and then turn left (west) at Center Road and Studio Drive, then left onto Hollywood.

Carlyle Brewing Company
Rockford

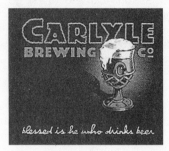

Visit Date	*Signed*

ABOUT THE BREWERY

Just over a block east of the Rock River, Carlyle Brewing is located in a century-old building that stands in the heart of Rockford's old downtown. The heavy double doors in the center of the façade of the two-story building offer an inviting atmosphere. Large windows, exterior masonry, and wooden accents really bring out a sense of history and charm for the structure.

Inside, dark wood tones and brick walls accentuate an old English pub feel. The building is divided in half. To the west (your right upon entering), you find the brewery. To the east is a seating area and bar. Owner and brewmaster Don Carlyle did much of the extensive remodeling of the building. After purchasing the building, Carlyle spent over a year completing renovation of the structure. Much of the first floor had to be reinforced to handle the tremendous amount of weight from the brewery. The brewing equipment was given another life when Carlyle purchased it from the Copper Tank Brewery of Dallas, Texas. The conditioning of the beer is completed in the basement of the building, where a twelve-hundred-square-foot walk-in cooler contains the brewery's serving tanks.

Carlyle Brewing is mainly a microbrewery and bar, but it does offer a light, pub-style appetizer menu. You can expect to find six to eight of its own beers on tap. Brewmaster Don Carlyle always has one or two import-style beers of his on tap and a variety of seasonal specials.

HISTORY

Making beer has been a lifelong goal for owner and brewmaster Don Carlyle, who got his start homebrewing. After spending fifteen years as an automotive technician, Carlyle attended Siebel Institute in 1997 and 1998, with a follow-up short course in 1999. After Siebel, he worked at the former McClintock Brewery and Grill of Beloit, Wisconsin, which closed in 2001.

Don had been looking for a building to house his brewery in the Rockford area for more than five years before finding the State Street location. The building in which Carlyle Brewing is located was originally constructed in 1901. It's rumored to have been a bordello in its early years. But locals may remember it and the attached buildings as part of a community theater called the Bijou. More recently it was home to the Estate Exchange Antique Store.

Don's love of beer has taken him to many places, including Europe, where he traveled with a backpack for nearly two months, sampling local beers and finding out what pub life was like. In 1997, his hiking took him to Germany, Belgium, Holland, Austria, and Luxembourg. In 1999, he toured Ireland and developed a taste for strong, dry stouts.

DON'T MISS THIS

As you walk through the main double doors of the building, the brewery is on your immediate right. Two ten-foot wrought iron gates, custom-made by a local craftsman, frame the entryway into the brewery.

CARLYLE BREWS

Belgian Special 🍺🍺🍺   *Your Ranking* _____
A light, fruity Belgian. A light, yeasty aroma. Clear body, deep golden to copper color with a thin, soft, white head. Medium bodied and soft texture. A light sweetness with some crisp wheat flavors. Finishes with hints of coriander.

British Pale Ale 🍺🍺🍺🍺   *Your Ranking* _____
This is a complex pale ale. No nose. A hazy copper color and a thick, soft, off-white head. Medium bodied and soft texture. Light malty start provides a light sweetness, but the hops found in the background transform the sweet, soft malty beginning into a firm, crisp, bitter beer. Finishes with a light dryness that doesn't linger long.

Raspberry Wheat 🍺🍺🍺   *Your Ranking* _____
A light raspberry aroma. Clear, golden body with a thin, soft, white head. Light bodied and soft texture. A light malty, somewhat earthy dominance. Finishes with sweet raspberry strength. Overall, the sweet fruitiness is memorable.

OTHER CARLYLE BREWS YOU MAY WANT TO TRY

Golden Ale   *Your Ranking* _____
This light ale has a clean aroma and taste. Subtle yet firm malty qualities.

BREWERY RATING

	Your Rating	Shepard's Rating (1 to 4 Mugs)	General Description
Location		🍺🍺🍺🍺	Central city/community
Ease of Finding Location		🍺🍺🍺	Easy, but requires some planning

	Your Rating	Shepard's Rating	General Description
Brewery Atmosphere		🍺🍺🍺🍺	Historic Rustic
Dining Experience		n/a	Limited (light snacks)
The Pint		🍺🍺🍺	A good experience

MENU

Carlyle is primarily a microbrewery, but it does offer a few light appetizers and snacks. You'll likely find a few sandwiches, sausages, brats, hot dogs, and soft pretzels on the bar menu.

OTHER THINGS TO SEE OR DO IN THE AREA

Rockford gets its name from the Rock River and the shallow ford used as a crossing point by the Galena-Chicago Stagecoach Line before the city was actually founded. You'll notice when traveling through Rockford that many of the streets are at odd angles to each other; that's because they were built to accommodate the river channel.

Rockford also has earned the nickname "The Forest City" because each block averages more than a hundred trees. There are great ways to enjoy the city, the river, and its trees: via boat, trolley, or walks through its numerous parks and gardens.

The *Forest City Queen* at Riverview Park (324 North Madison Street) is an excursion boat with a variety of cruises on the Rock River. Trolley Car 36, also at Riverview Park, is an open-air trolley that will take you on a forty-five-minute ride along the Rock River and into the Sinnissippi Gardens, Greenhouse, and Lagoon (1300 North Second Street). Sinnissippi Gardens offers an aviary, greenhouse, lagoon, and trails. Rockford's Klehm Arboretum and Botanic Garden (2701 Clifton Avenue) has more than 150 acres of trees and plants. In the summer months Rockford hosts "Music in the Park" (1401 North Second Street) with a variety of musical styles and events. A great time to visit Rockford is during the On the Waterfront Festival over the Labor Day weekend. Rockford's downtown is transformed into three days of food, music, and entertainment.

The Burpee Museum of Natural History (737 North Main Street) is housed in two Victorian-era mansions. Exhibits include *Tyrannosaurus rex* and woolly mammoth skeletons, rocks, birds, mammals, and collections of artifacts related to Native Americans.

Rockford Speedway (9572 Forest Hills Road) hosts NASCAR events. It also has become famous for the trailer races, amazing Double Decker race cars, and the "oval" enduro race. Also nearby, Blackhawk Farms Raceway (15538 Prairie Road, South Beloit) features sports car events and autocross, motorcycle, and go-kart races. Rockford is also home to the Frontier League's Rockford Riverhawks, who play at Marinelli Field (101 15th Avenue).

The Discovery Center Museum (711 North Main Street) in Riverfront Museum Park offers more than two hundred hands-on exhibits and makes a great stop for families. Also along the riverfront is the Rockford Art Museum (711 North Main Street). It's Illinois's largest art museum outside of Chicago and is well known for its permanent collection of nineteenth- and twentieth-century American art. Artspace, in the Clock Towner Resort (7801 East State Street, near Interstate 90), is a modern art gallery that showcases work by area artists.

Magic Water Waterpark (near Interstate 90 and Route 20) has water slides, a wave pool, tubes, and a water roller coaster. The Midway Village and Museum Center (6799 Guilford Road) is a late-nineteenth-century village with about two dozen historic buildings, including a one-room school, a jail, and a sheriff's office.

A great way to see the area around Rockford is by following the Boone County Historical Trail. The trail has four different routes, each about thirty miles long—approximately the distance one day's wagon ride would take you in Rockford's early years. Trail information is available from the Boone County Conservation District (815-547-7935).

About fifteen minutes south of Rockford, the city of Belvidere is known as Illinois's "City of Murals." Many are painted on the façades of buildings. Belvidere also offers downtown specialty shops, antiques, and galleries.

DIRECTIONS

From Interstate 90, take the State Street exit (Business Route 20). Travel west about seven miles into downtown Rockford. Stay on State Street; once Route 20 breaks off from State, Carlyle Brewery is about a half-mile ahead, just about a block east of the Rock River near the corner of State and Madison Streets.

Copper Dragon Brewing Company and Pinch Penny Pub

Carbondale

Visit Date	Signed

ABOUT THE BREWERY

The Copper Dragon Brewing Company is one of four business personalities: the Pinch Penny Pub, Pinch Penny Liquor, a live music establishment, and the brewery itself. The brewery part, called Copper Dragon, is in a former movie theater that has been renovated into a brewhaus and a concert hall for live entertainment. The brewery and former theater building is joined to the Pinch Penny Pub with a common, very large, beer garden.

Inside the old theater, where the Copper Dragon brewery is located, the area where the snack bar would have greeted movie patrons is now a bar. The brewhaus is to the left as you walk through the front doors. When the Copper Dragon first opened, it also served food and this area functioned as a restaurant dining room until 1998, when the restaurant business ended and Copper Dragon became focused on hosting live music and brewing beer.

Further inside, where the theater seating was once located has been transformed into a large dance floor that provides an indoor auditorium for bands. The walls of the former theater are painted to represent homes, doorways, and different landscapes. The scenes give you a sense that you are walking down a street similar to what one might expect to see in the French

Quarter of New Orleans, with wrought iron balconies and vines. However, some local college students have a different interpretation, saying the murals remind them of the television show *Sesame Street*.

In renovating the building, the sloped auditorium had to be dug out, mostly by hand. It was replaced with a basement and level floor. A U-shaped balcony wraps around the main floor. Where the projectors once ran, there is a small second-floor bar. If you're wondering what happened to all the old theater seats that once filled the auditorium, they were repurchased by the movie company that originally owned them.

The Copper Dragon Brewery is open only when live performances are scheduled, so it's best to call ahead for hours if you're interested in seeing the brewery or hearing live music. But the connected business, the Pinch Penny Pub, serves food and Copper Dragon beer, and the attached liquor store, Pinch Penny Liquors, also sells bottles of Copper Dragon beer. Overall, among the brewery, beer garden, pub, and liquor store, you'll find about seven of the Copper Dragon beers on any visit. The Blonde Ale, Weiss Bier, Pale Ale, and Porter are the most commonly available. The Oatmeal Stout is the best seller and the signature beer for Copper Dragon. Select styles are also available in twenty-two-ounce bottles at other Carbondale-area liquor stores.

HISTORY

The Copper Dragon Brewing Company was established in 1996 and is owned and managed with the Pinch Penny Pub, the companion tavern next door, and the attached Pinch Penny liquor store. The Pinch Penny Pub was opened in 1972 by the Karayiannis family and is one of the longest continuously held liquor licenses in Carbondale.

Opening the brewery involved a connected, yet unforeseen, set of circumstances for the Karayiannises. The building that contains Copper Dragon was the old Saluki movie theater, which entertained local residents until the early 1990s, when it closed and became vacant. At that time the Pinch Penny Pub needed two things: a sign and parking. Local ordinances would not allow the Pinch Penny to construct additional signage in the neighborhood, but the old theater had a sign that the Karayiannises could use. The parking was an added benefit.

Once the family had acquired the property with the parking lot and the valuable sign, then the question of what to do with the building became important. Jim Karayiannis and his mother and father, Ann and Fotios Karayiannis, decided that the interior of the theater would make an ideal venue for live entertainment, and, given the proximity to Southern Illinois University, live music was considered a major draw.

As renovations took shape, Jim, who enjoyed homebrewing and had attended Siebel Institute of Technology, was encouraged by his father to add a brewery to their plans. Jim says that Fotios had been harboring dreams of starting a winery in southern Illinois, so the idea of a brewery wasn't that far-fetched. Fotios's father had owned a winery in southern Greece.

At first both Jim and Fotios were very active as brewers, but as the management demands of the Pinch Penny Pub and Copper Dragon's live entertainment business grew, the beer making had to be handed to someone else, and a specific brewmaster's position was created for the company.

Deciding on the name "Copper Dragon" was a laborious ordeal for the Karayiannis family. After serious debate, they realized that the actual copper dragon in the courtyard between the Pinch Penny Pub and the theater building was well known to most area residents—so the name literally caught fire.

DON'T MISS THIS

The copper dragon for which the brewery is named is located in the courtyard and beer garden. The metal beast is attached to a propane tank, so every couple of minutes it will breathe flames into the courtyard! Family matriarch Ann Karayiannis is fond of dragons and collects them; she majored in medieval history in college. Mike Page, a local welder and artisan, made the fourteen-foot copper dragon, and Ann's father, who is an engineer, added the fire.

If you're fortunate enough to be in Carbondale when the theater and brewery building is open, inside there is a second copper dragon. It's even larger than the one in the courtyard, and it hangs from the ceiling above the dance floor, breathing smoke from a fog machine in its belly.

COPPER DRAGON BREWS

Best Bitter   *Your Ranking* _____
A malty nose. Clear bronze color and a thin, soft, brown head. Medium bodied and crisp texture. Strong, dry, hoppy flavor with a light acidic background. Light bitter finish.

Blonde Ale *Your Ranking* _____
Almost no aroma, just a light malty, earthy nose. A clear, light, golden color. The head is thin, soft, and white. Light bodied with a distinctive creamy texture. A very, very light citrus taste. Light, crisp ending. Brewed with two-row barley and wheat malts and finished with Saaz hops. This style was the very first beer served at Copper Dragon Brewery when it opened in 1996.

Dunkel Weizen *Your Ranking* _____
Light malty nose. A clear, bronze color and a thick, soft, white head. Medium bodied and soft texture. A slightly sweet caramel flavor. Lightly hopped. Finishes sweet with a light smokiness.

ESB (Extra Special Bitter) *Your Ranking* _____
Great flavor and color. A light, but sharp, floral aroma. Clear, vivid copper color and a thick, bubbly, tan head. Medium bodied and very carbonated. A hoppy start with a complex malty competition from a sweet background. The finish is mildly bitter and at first lightly dry; however, the bitterness lingers in the mouth and will actually build. While the Oatmeal Stout may be Copper Dragon's signature, this ESB is very well done and my pick of the brewery's beers.

IPA   *Your Ranking* _____
An India Pale Ale with a faint floral nose. Golden color with a slight haziness. A thick, soft, white head. Medium bodied and soft texture. Begins with a burst of maltiness, then becomes dry and mildly bitter. Finishes more dry than bitter.

There is some hoppiness here, but this IPA is very reserved in the hop characteristics.

Oatmeal Stout 🍺🍺🍺🍺   *Your Ranking* _____
Copper Dragon's best seller. A pointed, malty nose. Very dark color and a thick, bubbly, brown head. Full bodied and silky. The chocolate malt tones dominate, making this a strong, sweet-style stout. Finishes with a soft, smooth, maltiness. Made with organic oats and American two-row barley malt. Black malt and roasted barley give this stout its dark color and dry, roasted flavor. This is a great beer to be matched with the house special pizza from the Pinch Penny Pub.

Pale Ale 🍺🍺🍺🍺   *Your Ranking* _____
A very well done English-style pale ale. Light flowery nose. Clear copper body and a thick, soft, tan head. Medium bodied and round. Strong, aggressive bitter dominance that finishes dry. Brewed with Cascade hops for aroma and finish.

Porter 🍺   *Your Ranking* _____
Made with Fuggles and East Kent Goldings hops. Offers an inviting malty nose. Deep black color with a bronze hue. A thick, bubbly, brown head. Full bodied and round. Strong malty tones, but the overbearing sourness was relentless from the twenty-two-ounce bottle of Porter I purchased at Pinch Penny Liquors. My experience with this beer has only been one time, from a bottle that could have been old. I suggest giving it another try if you find it on tap at the brewery or Pinch Penny Pub.

Rye Wit 🍺🍺   *Your Ranking* _____
A sweet, lightly spiced nose. Cloudy orange color and a thick, bubbly, tan head. Medium bodied and crisp. Strong sweet fruity flavor with a caramel background. Finishes with a hint of orange and coriander.

Scotch Ale 🍺🍺🍺   *Your Ranking* _____
A malty nose. Deep, clear copper color. The head is thick, bubbly, and tan. Medium bodied and creamy texture. A rich, full, malty flavor with an initial bit of hops and a long-lasting sweet finish.

Weiss Bier 🍺🍺🍺   *Your Ranking* _____
An American-style wheat beer made with 50 percent two-row barley and 50 percent wheat malts. Slightly sweet with a subdued hop character. A floral nose. Hazy, golden color and a thick, bubbly, white head. Light bodied and round. A soft, smooth, malty flavor with a light earthy, even yeasty, finish. A mild, light weissbier.

OTHER COPPER DRAGON BREWS YOU MAY WANT TO TRY

Kolsch   *Your Ranking* _____
A summer seasonal at Copper Dragon. Similar to the Blonde Ale, only softer and with less hoppy finish.

Oktoberfest   *Your Ranking* _____
A seasonal beer for Copper Dragon, but not available every fall.

BREWERY RATING

	Your Rating	Shepard's Rating (1 to 4 Mugs)	General Description
Location		🍺🍺🍺	Entertainment district
Ease of Finding Location		🍺🍺🍺🍺	Easy, but requires some planning
Brewery Atmosphere		🍺🍺	Music venue (Copper Dragon) Sports (Pinch Penny Pub)
Dining Experience		🍺🍺	Pub fare (Pinch Penny Pub) No food (Copper Dragon)
The Pint		🍺🍺🍺	A good experience

MENU

The Copper Dragon Brewery does not serve food, but the nearby Pinch Penny Pub does. The Pinch Penny offers basic tavern food with sandwiches and pizza. The starters from Pinch Penny include common pub appetizers such as potato skins, onion rings, jalapeño poppers, and deep-fried mushrooms. There are also some unique choices, such as toasted ravioli and fried vegetables. The sandwich and burger menu offers selections such as the grilled pub special, with ham, Swiss, and cheddar cheese, and the Horseshoe, which is a one-third-pound burger served open face with fries and smothered with in cheese sauce. Other sandwiches include a Reuben and a grilled chicken. Pinch Penny pizzas come in two sizes: ten-inch and fourteen-inch. You can build your own with toppings that include sausage, pepperoni, spicy beef, onions, green peppers, mushrooms, ham, green olives, black olives, and tomato slices. The pub special pizza is made with sausage, green peppers, and onions, and the house special pizza features sausage, pepperoni, beef, ham, onion, green peppers, mushrooms, and black olives.

OTHER THINGS TO SEE OR DO IN THE AREA

The Copper Dragon hosts a variety of music events, so for those who enjoy live performances a call ahead might help you match your musical tastes with the beer that's on tap. A fun wintertime event in the brewery's beer garden is the annual Polar Beer night. Usually held around the last weekend in January, when there's snow and cold temperatures, the beer garden is opened, and hearty "polar bear" patrons pretend it's summer with lighter bodied beers and beach music.

Around town there's rich tradition and history. Carbondale's town square has more than two dozen historic buildings. Daniel Harmon Brush, the city's founding father, originally platted the town and left about ten acres open in the center of the town that were deeded to the Illinois Central Railroad. Throughout the nineteenth and twentieth centuries the area became known as the "public square" and remains a central focus of the town and its businesses. A walking tour map is available from the Carbondale Convention and Tourism Bureau (111 South Illinois Avenue, the Old Passenger Depot on the Town Square). The Town Square Pavilion offers a ten-week summer concert series. In 1996 Carbondale opened its new Civic Center. Located in the downtown, it provides a venue for small conferences and events.

The Woodlawn Memorial Cemetery (405 East Main Street) was the location of the first organized Memorial Day service in Illinois on April 29, 1866. The iron gate leading into the cemetery was originally from Carbondale College, which was built in 1860. Carbondale's West Walnut Street has had status as a national Historic District since 1975. Fifty-four historically significant properties are located in this neighborhood.

Carbondale is also home to Southern Illinois University (SIU). There are a number of interesting things to see on campus. The university's museum in the north wing of Faner Hall has prehistoric, historic, and scientific collections. Altgeld Hall, originally the Science Building, is the oldest building on campus. Built in 1898, Altgeld Hall resembles an English castle with its octagonal four-story tower and crenellated turrets. Shryock Auditorium is a center for performing arts and lectures. Part of the "old campus," the building was dedicated to Henry William Shryock, the president of Southern Illinois University from 1913 to 1935. Former President William Howard Taft gave the first public address when the building was dedicated in 1918. Inside, a Reuter pipe organ is located in the north balcony. The nine-ton organ contains over 3,000 pipes in fifty-eight ranks.

One of the most scenic ways to travel to Carbondale is from the west with a drive along the Mississippi River and Route 3 (the Great River Road National Scenic Byway). Northwest of Carbondale, the town of Chester is home of the cartoon character Popeye and birthplace of his creator Elzie Segar. There is a small museum in Chester that pays tribute to Popeye and his friends, many of whom were based on Chester residents.

About thirty miles southwest of Carbondale is the Shawnee National Forest with nearly 270,000 acres of natural lands. The forest is part of an area known as the Ozark and Shawnee Hills. The area has nearly 130 miles of hiking trails as well as picnicking and wildlife viewing opportunities. Southern Illinois is also known for its vineyards. The Scenic Shawnee Hills Wine Trail (south of Carbondale) boasts four award-winning wineries. The route will take you through rural areas with great views as you travel Jackson and Union Counties to visit the Pomona, Von Jakob, Alto, and Owl Creek Vineyards.

West of Carbondale, an area known as the Little Grand Canyon is a deep ravine accessible by a three-mile trail that descends through forests to a bluff from which, on a clear day, you can see the Mississippi River. (Little Grand Canyon is located seven miles south of Murphysboro on Route 127; turn right on Etherton Road and take the third turnoff to the trail entrance.) Also in this area, the Pomona Natural Bridge is one of only a handful of natural stone bridges in the United States. Murphysboro is located north of the Little Grand Canyon and northwest of Carbondale. Murphysboro is well known for its antique and craft shops. Murphysboro is also home to the General John A. Logan Museum (1613 Edith Street), which details the history of the Civil War general. The town erected a statue of General Logan (2125 Spruce Street) in 1928.

The Giant City State Park (336 South Church Road, Makanda) is located about twelve miles south of Carbondale. It includes Little Grassy Lake, Devils Kitchen Lake, and a twenty-five-site horse campground. At the entrance of Giant

City State Park, the town of Makanda is a former farming and railroad town that is now home to a community of artisans and craftspeople who display their work along the Makanda Board Walk (South Highway 51, then east at the Smiley Face Tower). Also in Makanda, along the railroad tracks in the heart of town, is a five-foot-tall stone monument to the hound dog Boomer. The legend of Boomer involves the dog trying to get the attention of his master, who was a railroad crewman on a train that had caught fire. Boomer is said to have had only three legs. As Boomer ran barking after the speeding train, he failed to see a bridge abutment ahead and ran headlong into the bridge, fatally injuring himself.

Southern Illinois University's mascot is also a canine of legendary proportions. This part of the state is sometimes called "Little Egypt," which is why in 1951 the university adopted as its symbol the Saluki, an Egyptian hunting dog of incredible stamina that literally runs its prey to death. In 1954 the original SIU mascot, a Saluki named King Tut, was run over by a car. King Tut is entombed in the northeast corner of McAndrew Stadium, sealed beneath the artificial turf and marked by a small pyramid.

DIRECTIONS

Carbondale is located about six hours south of Chicago or two hours southeast of St. Louis. If you are approaching from the north or south, Carbondale is about fifteen miles directly west of Interstate 57 on Route 13. If you are traveling from an east-west direction on Interstate 64, Carbondale is about fifty miles south from I-64's interchange with Route 51.

Once you arrive in Carbondale, the Copper Dragon Brewery and Pinch Penny Pub is located on the southern edge of the city and the northern edge of the Southern Illinois University campus. From the main intersection in Carbondale, Routes 51 and 13, travel south on 51 about three-quarters of a mile to Grand Avenue and turn left (east). The Copper Dragon and Pinch Penny Pub is about a half-mile to the east from the intersection of Grand and Route 51, on the north side of Grand Avenue. You'll want to turn into the parking lot on the east side of the Pinch Penny. The old theater building containing the Copper Dragon Brewery is mostly hidden from view until you're in the parking lot.

Elmwood Brewing Company and Parkview Restaurant

Elmwood

Visit Date	*Signed*

ABOUT THE BREWERY

Elmwood Brewing is a great find when you're looking for the combination of excellent food and a place that seems out of the way. Located about halfway between Peoria and Galesburg, only about ten minutes south of Interstate 74, Elmwood fits the bill of one of those "best-kept secret" type places, because unless you live in Peoria or Galesburg, it could very well be a destination in itself.

Elmwood, about twenty-five miles west of Peoria, is a community that is deeply tied to its small-town Illinois image and agrarian lifestyle. When you arrive in this city of two thousand, you realize you are in Illinois's agricultural lands. As in many small Illinois towns, the thriving downtown square is not what it once was, but the Elmwood Brewing Company provides what developers refer to as the anchor store effect. Located in the former Gabriel and Graham Building, it is found on the south side of the town square that surrounds a beautiful park—thus the name of the brewery's companion restaurant, the Parkview. While many of Elmwood's former downtown businesses have long since left, the Elmwood Brewing Company found its niche in great beer, fine dining, and catering.

Elmwood Brewing occupies an 1896 building that was once the home of the Odd Fellows and Rebekahs Lodge. It was purchased in 1997 by Matthew and Lyn Potts, after Matt saw its potential for the community and his own dream of owning a brewery. Once inside, you are immediately struck that this is a special place; the building and its fixtures have been painstakingly restored to respect the period of its original construction. Much of that renovation was by the hands of local craftsmen. The first floor is the main dining room, with a small bar that looks into the brewhaus. Just above those main windows over the back bar is one of many historical references in the building, with the original hand-painted front window from the Odd Fellows No. 102 and Rebekahs No. 319 lodge.

The building was restored by Potts between 1998 and 2001. While many patrons will likely spend most of their time in the Parkview's first floor dining room or bar, the upstairs was once the main room for the lodge and is now used for wedding receptions, banquets, parties, reunions, and live entertainment. Downstairs, the Underground Room—named in reference to the town's ties to the Underground Railroad—is used for private parties and special dinners.

Elmwood offers five to six regular beers on tap, plus a brewmaster's special or two. In 2003 the brewery added a bottling line, which means Elmwood beer can be found in Galesburg, Peoria, and Bloomington. At the brewpub, the Amber is the best seller, but it's wise not to overlook the Nut Brown Ale.

HISTORY

Elmwood Brewing and the Parkview Restaurant began with a homebrewing kit. At the encouragement of his wife, Lyn, Matthew Potts started learning to home-brew in 1991. Matt credits his desire not to hold back as he jumped in, trying from the beginning to understand how to brew the best homebrew. He also studied the equipment that would help ensure that he got the most out of his hobby. In 1997 Matt's hobby changed dramatically. In his job as a real-estate attorney, Matt attended a public auction in Elmwood that included the sale of the community's lodge hall. At the mere waving of his hand he entered the brewing business and soon found himself deeply involved in an extensive renovation project that would involve constructing a restaurant and building a brewery.

Matt purchased much of his brewery equipment from a failed brewery in Portland, Oregon. When taking a tour, you might imagine Matt's eye for detail when you consider that, when he took the trip to Oregon to see the equipment, he had never worked in a brewery nor even taken a commercial brewing class. With his self-taught knowledge and the help of talented local plumbers and electricians, he was able to construct his brewhaus and restaurant. It was close; just observe how snugly the main brew kettle and lauter tun fit between the floor and ceiling. Snug isn't the adequate term, because there are just inches to spare.

Elmwood Brewing was established in December 2001.

DON'T MISS THIS

Elmwood Brewing has a deep commitment to the history of the building in which it's located. The behind-the-scenes stories make Elwood Brewing and its companion restaurant, the Parkview, a very special place. From the old restored front window of the Odd Fellows and Rebekahs to the Elmwood City Plat Map from 1896 in the dining room, there's a story nearly everywhere. If you have a chance to see the second-floor banquet hall, take special care to observe the draperies over the large windows and the chandeliers. The lighting fixtures are reproductions that were made especially for the building by H&H Industries of Elmwood.

ELMWOOD BREWS

Amber Ale *Your Ranking* _____

This Irish red is the flagship beer of Elmwood. Clean and crisp. No aroma. A clear, copper color with a thick, bubbly, tan head. Medium bodied and a crispness that is almost a sharp texture. The taste focuses on a smooth and solid caramel flavor. A light hint of hops in the finish.

American Pale Ale *Your Ranking* _____

A crisp American-style pale ale that begins with a light, hoppy nose. Light golden color with a thin, soft, white head. Medium hoppiness accents the crispness of the beer. A nice finish. Brewed with American barley, wheat malt, hops, and honey.

Hefeweizen *Your Ranking* _____

This unfiltered wheat has a very inviting banana aroma. Deep golden color that has a light hazy quality. The head is white, thin, and soft. Light textured and medium bodied. A smooth malty balance that includes banana and clove flavors from beginning to end.

Nut Brown Ale *Your Ranking* _____

A cross between an English-style nut brown and a brown porter. A great find. Begins with a light, mild, malty nose. Nice roasted, nutty qualities. Deep bronze color and a soft, tan head. Full bodied. Malty. The malty tones are most aggressive in the beginning and they stay firm throughout the taste with solid caramel tones. The roasted malts bring a great finish to this beer, with English malt and hops.

Stout *Your Ranking* _____

The strong chocolate aromas from this beer are easy to detect. Very dark, opaque color with a thick, soft, brown head. Full bodied and a silky texture. The malty tones really stand out in the taste, complemented by a coffee finish. Described by the brewery as an Irish stout, but there is considerable emphasis on malty sweetness.

Strawberry Ale *Your Ranking* _____

A special beer brewed for the Elmwood annual strawberry festival. There is a strong strawberry nose that lingers throughout, especially in the finish. Golden and slightly cloudy with a light body, this is a refreshing summer brew.

OTHER ELMWOOD BREWS YOU MAY WANT TO TRY

Apricot Ale *Your Ranking* _____

Light amber color with fruity apricot. Made in small special batches, and rotates among Elmwood's taps as a brewmaster's special.

Blonde Ale *Your Ranking* _____

This light ale has a clear, straw color and white bubbly head that has great retention. Crisp and lightly hopped. Clean finish.

Pumpkin Ale   *Your Ranking* _____

This seasonal ale has a rich amber color with lots of pumpkin flavor. Served in the fall. This special beer doesn't last long. Made with fresh pumpkin.

BREWERY RATING

	Your Rating	Shepard's Rating (1 to 4 Mugs)	General Description
Location		🍺🍺🍺	Central city/community
Ease of Finding Location		🍺🍺🍺	Close to major roads and intersections
Brewery Atmosphere		🍺🍺🍺🍺	Historic
Dining Experience		🍺🍺🍺🍺	Family style/variety Fine dining
The Pint		🍺🍺🍺🍺	A perfect experience

MENU

The Parkview is Elmwood Brewing Company's companion restaurant. It offers a number of choices with an aggressive menu. Elmwood native David Howard oversees the menu, which features hearty entrees such as New York strips, rib eyes, baby back ribs, grilled salmon, herb roasted chicken, and fried catfish. The pasta selections include spaghetti and fettuccine. The sandwich options feature an eight-ounce Angus burger, Reuben, patty melt, turkey club, portobello burger, and a grouper sandwich. The Parkview also has a range of salads and soups. On the lighter appetizer side, you might try the soft pretzels with cheese sauce. For desserts, the French chocolate cake matches well with an Elmwood Stout!

OTHER THINGS TO SEE OR DO IN THE AREA

Elmwood is about a half-hour west of Peoria. The square is the focal point of the community. In Elmwood's Central Park, across from Elmwood Brewing and Parkview Restaurant, is the statue *The Pioneers* by Lorado Taft (in 1926 Elmwood raised $15,000 for the sculpture). The Lorado Taft Museum (302 North Magnolia) is also located in Elmwood. Taft's works are also exhibited at the Art Institute of Chicago and several other Windy City parks.

Elmwood's seasonal events include the annual Strawberry Festival in June, which offers not only the best in berries but also craft booths, a car show, and three-on-three basketball. In the winter, the Annual Christmas Walk offers caroling and horse-drawn carriage rides.

South of Elmwood the scenic Spoon River Drive connects Fulton, Knox, and Stark Counties. The annual Spoon River Festival is held the first two weekends in October in Ellisville.

Jubilee College State Park (nineteen miles east of Elmwood) offers out-door recreational opportunities. Jubilee College was one of the first colleges in

Illinois, founded in 1839 by Bishop Philander Chase (who is buried in the churchyard). Chase was a western missionary of the Episcopal Church.

Galesburg is about a half-hour west of Elmwood. The Carl Sandburg State Historic Site (331 East Third Street) marks the birthplace of Sandburg. A visitor center and museum is devoted to the life of the Pulitzer Prize-winning poet and Lincoln biographer. The Galesburg Railroad Museum (423 Mulberry Street) offers a restored 1921 Pullman parlor car and railroad memorabilia. Railroad Days are held in late June. The national Stearman Fly-In, held every year in September, celebrates the Stearman biplane, used to train early twentieth-century military pilots.

Fifteen miles west beyond Galesburg is Monmouth, the birthplace of Wyatt Earp, and the community celebrates Earp's birthday each year in mid-June.

DIRECTIONS

From Interstate 74, take the Canton/Kewanee exit about twenty-five miles west of Peoria. Elmwood is located on Highway 78, about eight miles south of I-74. As you drive into the town, Elmwood Brewing is located on the southern part of the town square.

Emmett's Tavern and Brewing Company
West Dundee

Visit Date	Signed

ABOUT THE BREWERY

You'll get a strong sense of history and tradition as you settle in with a pint at the bar of Emmett's Tavern and Brewing Company. The three-story cream-colored brick building was constructed in the nineteenth century. Inside, old photos, wooden accents, and a hearty upscale menu all combine for a warm atmosphere, fine beer, and feeling of what dining in days gone by must have been like.

The main bar takes full advantage of the large front windows, which were once part of the original occupant's mercantile façade when the building served as a dry goods store. Today the display windows offer wide views of West Dundee's Main Street. The bar is somewhat small, but a counter against the Main Street window offers an excellent vantage point for people watching.

The main floor of Emmett's has two distinct dining areas. The more open and active dining area is to the south, sharing a large room with the main bar. To the north, or left of the entryway, the main dining room has wooden floors, area rugs, paintings, and table candles that all combine for a quieter and more intimate feeling. Emmett's also has a large banquet hall on the second floor and a private party room, called the Board Room, on the third floor.

The renovations to get the building into its current condition were extensive, and most of the original fixtures had long been removed before Emmett's made changes. That makes the commitment to period restoration even more impressive, considering that remodeling had to be done just right to keep the building on the National Registry of Historic Places and in tune with the Dundee Historical District.

To the right of the main doorway, behind glass, is the heart of Emmett's brewery. The shining copper brewhaus is an incredible visual display. It seems to match perfectly with the wooden interior and the dim, yet sharp, lighting that sparkles on the mash tun.

Emmett's keeps at least six of its beers on tap. The Harvest Gold is the most popular, but the Old Dundee Scottish Ale is one of Emmett's most recognized beers, especially after being named "Best Beer in Chicago" in the 2001 Brewpub Shootout. It's also a good idea to watch for special events at Emmett's. You might catch Irish/Celtic music on Friday nights, which will go well with an Oatmeal Stout. Brewmaster Ryan Clooney hosts a brewmaster's dinner several times a year. Each September, Emmett's celebrates its own birthday with special events. At the end of September the annual Oktoberfest Celebration blocks off Second Street for music, food, and beer.

HISTORY

Emmett's Tavern and Brewing Company was established in 1999. At the intersection of Second and Main Streets, Emmett's occupies the "Hunts Block" building, which was constructed in 1871 and to this day is a cornerstone of West Dundee's downtown Historical District. At the time of its construction it was referred to as "Hunt's Folly" because it was one of the first multi-story brick buildings in the downtown. It loomed over a shantytown of small one-story wooden shacks that had been built along the Fox River. The original owner, Henry Hunt, built it for a cost of $12,000 to house his dry goods store. Over the years the building was also used as a hardware store and as the First Bank of Dundee (which is where the safe in the restaurant's foyer came from). More recently, the history of the building and that of downtown West Dundee was showcased in a scene from the 2002 movie *Road to Perdition,* starring Tom Hanks and Paul Newman. In the making of the movie, vintage automobiles and fake snow were brought in to accent the strong historical features found along Dundee's Main Street.

Emmett's is a family-run business. Andrew Burns and his father, Timothy, are the owners. Their ending up in West Dundee was somewhat by chance, or perhaps fate, as Andy has described it. He and his father were returning to their Long Grove homes late one night after an investors' meeting when they decided to take a detour and drive through West Dundee. Andy had not been through the town in several years and isn't sure why they took that turn that night, other than that his father is the type of person who is always looking for a new route home. As chance would have it, at about 1:00 A.M., he noticed the Hunts Block building was for sale. The next morning Andy drove back to West Dundee to take a closer look, and that's when the present collided with the past to create a sense of history for Emmett's Tavern and Brewing Company.

Emmett's brewmaster, Ryan Clooney, got his job by skill, luck, and chance—or, some say, it was just fate. In 1995 he read an article in the *Chicago Tribune* about homebrewing and was interested enough that he clipped the article. But he ended up misplacing the clipping, only to discover that his wife had tucked it away. When Christmas came around, she had taken the clipping to the local homebrew supply store and purchased the best gift a beer lover could want—a homebrew kit. At the time, Ryan had been working as a union carpenter in the area. But his hobby had led him to a lot of reading, then a short course at Siebel Institute, and eventually an internship at Mickey Finn's Brewery in Libertyville. In 1999 he saw an advertisement for the brewmaster position at Emmett's and decided to apply for the job. After Burns had looked at more than sixty applications and done a great deal of sampling, Ryan Clooney was chosen to become the brewmaster. While the brewery was in the process of being built, Ryan went back to Siebel for its Diploma Course and was ready for professional brewing when Emmett's opened for business in September 1999. Just as with the business's sense of history, there is an interesting tie in Ryan Clooney's past with that of owner Andy Burns. When Ryan was interviewing for the job, he and Andy discovered that both had attended the same high school in Mundelein and graduated within a year of each other!

DON'T MISS THIS

Emmett's has many references to history throughout the Hunts Block building. As you walk through the front door you'll be facing the original safe from the First Bank of Dundee. Keeping with a respect for the building's historical charm, many of the black-and-white photos you see on the walls were collected with help from the Dundee Township Historical Society. You'll find some fun references to beer in the photos such as Frank Cahill's Downer & Bemis Ale & Lager Beer, along with O'Neills Whiskeys and several images of the Dundee area from the nineteenth and twentieth centuries.

Just inside the entryway is a framed portrait of Emmett Burns, the family patriarch whose name was taken for business. Emmett was Andy Burns's grandfather and Timothy Burns's father. Emmett was a man the community knew well, but unlike a brewmaster, he wasn't someone that you wanted to apply his craft. Emmett spent most of his life as an undertaker in Buffalo, New York.

In a different vein, near the bar you'll come face to face with an antique, six-foot-tall cigar store Indian. It stands to the right of the ornate wooden back bar—deadpanning over Emmett's beer list of daily specials!

EMMETT'S TAVERN AND BREWING COMPANY BREWS

Amber Ale 🍺🍺🍺   *Your Ranking* _____
A light hoppy nose. Clear copper color with a thin, soft, off-white head. Medium bodied and soft texture. A malty start with a hoppy background. The use of Pacific Northwest hops provides a great floral finish.

Dunkle Weizen 🍺🍺🍺🍺   *Your Ranking* _____
Lots of fruity banana esters in the nose and main body of taste. Cloudy copper color and a thick, soft, white head. Medium bodied. Great sweet, fruity qualities showcase a banana flavor. A yeasty finish. A very well done Dunkle Weizen. This is one of my overall Emmett's favorites.

Harvest Gold (a.k.a. Golden Ale) 🍺🍺🍺🍺   *Your Ranking* _____
A light hoppy nose. Clear, golden straw color with a thick, bubbly, white head. Light bodied and crisp. Some nice assertive flavors, especially with a sharp hoppiness continuing through the finish. The most popular beer from Emmett's. Brewed with American malt and Saaz hops.

Oatmeal Stout 🍺🍺🍺🍺   *Your Ranking* _____
Begins with a mildly roasted nose. Very dark black color with a thick, soft, brown head. Medium to full bodied and slick texture. A strong malty sweetness dominates. A roasted coffee finish that is firm but not overpowering. Each batch is brewed with forty pounds of oatmeal combined with English and Belgian dark malt. Served on a nitrogen tap.

Oktoberfest 🍺🍺🍺🍺   *Your Ranking* _____
A great fall seasonal. A malty nose. Clear copper color and a thick, soft, tan head. Medium bodied. A malty start with a mild hoppy background. A light, crisp, bitter finish. There are some great flavors and a complexity to this beer that make it worth more than one pint.

Old Dundee (a.k.a. Scottish Ale) 🍺🍺🍺   *Your Ranking* _____
A firm, malty nose. Reddish copper color. A thick, soft, tan head. Full bodied. Strong malty, caramel, sweet flavor with a mild roasted background. It finishes with the roasted tones building through the sweetness; there is a light warmth in the finish. Made with eight different malts and a touch of peat malt at the end, this beer is a favorite of the locals.

Porter 🍺🍺🍺🍺   *Your Ranking* _____
Lots of chocolate malt in the nose. Very dark and even looks thick. A creamy, tan head. Full bodied and silky. The dry, chocolate flavors dominate. A light fruity finish. Watch for this beer also on cask.

Special Bitter 🍺🍺🍺   *Your Ranking* _____
Made with 100 percent English malt, hops, and yeast, then dry hopped. A faint malty nose. Clear deep copper color with a thick, soft, white head. Medium to light bodied. Some light hoppy flavors with a complex malty sweetness and touch of caramel tones. It finishes with a lingering hoppiness.

Strong Ale 🍺🍺🍺🍺   *Your Ranking* _____
This winter warmer has a strong caramel malt nose. Deep, dark brown color and a thick, bubbly, brown head. Full bodied and round texture. Caramel malty flavor dominates with a smoothness that really makes this beer inviting. Finishes with a mild hoppy bitterness.

Victory Pale (a.k.a. American Pale Ale) 🍺🍺🍺   *Your Ranking* _____
A hoppy to spicy nose. A hazy golden color and a thin, bubbly, off-white head. Medium bodied and lightly dry. A sharp bitter flavor dominates despite a smooth malty start and hints of a fruity background. The finish is mildly bitter. A silver medal winner at the 2001 Great American Beer Festival.

OTHER EMMETT'S TAVERN AND BREWING COMPANY BREWS YOU MAY WANT TO TRY

Belgian White   *Your Ranking* _____
A special seasonal beer from Emmett's. Some light bitterness with a background accented by coriander and orange.

Brown   *Your Ranking* _____
Made with Maris-Otter English malt and all English hops. Known for a rich malty flavor, especially in its caramel sweetness.

Dopple Bock   *Your Ranking* _____
A silver medal winner in the 2002 World Beer Cup competition.

1871 Pre-prohibition Lager   *Your Ranking* _____
A clear copper color. Medium bodied and a complex malt-to-hops balance, with a light lingering hoppiness that leaves you with a clean impression.

English Style Mild   *Your Ranking* _____
A smooth, well balanced brown ale.

German Pilsner   *Your Ranking* _____
A clean, light Pilsner with a slight emphasis on a crisp hoppiness.

Hefeweizen   *Your Ranking* _____
A traditional German-style Hefe-Weizen, brewed for summer.

India Pale Ale (IPA)   *Your Ranking* _____
Intense bitter tones. Another favorite of the local, neighborhood crowd, especially when it's available as a cask-conditioned brewmaster's special.

Maibock   *Your Ranking* _____
A late winter through spring seasonal.

Robust Porter   *Your Ranking* _____
A rich mahogany color with a dense tan head. Medium to full bodied with a soft bitterness and caramel sweetness.

BREWERY RATING

	Your Rating	Shepard's Rating (1 to 4 Mugs)	General Description
Location		🍺🍺🍺	Central city/community
Ease of Finding Location		🍺🍺🍺	Easy, but requires some planning
Brewery Atmosphere		🍺🍺🍺🍺	Historic
Dining Experience		🍺🍺🍺🍺	Family style/variety, and fine dining
The Pint		🍺🍺🍺🍺	A perfect experience

MENU

Emmett's Tavern and Brewing Company offers an upscale American-style menu. There is a full range of options, from sandwiches to beef, pork, lamb, seafood, and pasta. The appetizer choices include baked artichoke and spinach dip, toasted ravioli, teriyaki duck tenders, pastrami smoked salmon, Emmett's onion loaf, and fresh baked pretzels. You might also consider the Tavern Cheese Fondue for Two. There are at least five different soups, such as the sweet corn chowder, the black bean chili, and the portobella mushroom. The lighter sandwich selections include the brewpub boursin burger, which is served with garlic herb boursin cheese and sliced portabella mushrooms. The All-American burger is the basic hamburger. But the ostrich wrap is a favorite, with grilled ostrich meat and sautéed onions and peppers wrapped in a tortilla and served with Emmett's own house-made potato chips. The main entrees on Emmett's menu are well beyond basic pub fare! You'll find Chambord Moullard duck, turkey marsala, cedar planked whitefish, potato crusted tilapia, pretzel crusted lamb, and peppercorn sirloin. There are also some straightforward main dishes that you'd expect in any family restaurant with a T-bone and the petite filet of beef. Pasta selections range from the mildly spicy chicken and andouille farfalle to the grilled vegetable lasagna. The only shortcoming to Emmett's menu is a limited choice of vegetarian options. To finish your meal, ask about the apple strudel.

OTHER THINGS TO SEE OR DO IN THE AREA

The Dundee Township Visitor's Center (319 North River Street), also known as the Depot, is a good place to find tourism information on local history, area attractions, and events.

A great way to enjoy East and West Dundee is by taking a walking tour of some of Dundee's historic and architecturally significant downtown buildings. The Dundee Historical District is located along Main Street, on both sides of the Fox River through East and West Dundee. The Dundee Township Historical Society Museum (426 Highland Avenue) has items and exhibits that feature life in Dundee since its settlement in 1835. In the summer, the Dundee Main Street and Dundee Township Historical Society offer a variety of guided tours that will take you to see historic buildings and homes and even on cemetery walks. Both East and West Dundee have an extensive number of old homes that bear white plaques displaying their date of construction.

One of West Dundee's most famous residents was Allan Pinkerton, who founded the famous detective agency in Chicago in 1850. Prior to that he was a cooper (cask and barrel maker) and had a shop in West Dundee just down the street from Emmett's Tavern and Brewing Company. A historical marker (3rd and Main) indicates the home where Pinkerton lived from 1844 to 1850 and sheltered slaves escaping to freedom. Pinkerton later became sheriff of Kane County and was head of the Union Army's spy service during the Civil War. Pinkerton became famous across the country when he put an end to a plot to assassinate President Abraham Lincoln.

The Heritage Festival in Dundee is in mid-September. The three-day event offers music, food, a car show, an antique fair in Graffelmann Park, and over a hundred crafters will line Lincoln Avenue's river walk (north and behind Emmett's). East Dundee Day is held in July, so you'll see not only fireworks but also an annual 5K race and many other activities. Also each July, the East Dundee Firefighters Association hosts a festival. Throughout the winter holiday season, the Dundee Jaycees sponsor "Dickens in Dundee" with gingerbread-house decorating, a community sing-along, and a tree lighting ceremony.

The Fox River Bike Trail offers thirty-six miles of paved bike trails with lines to Crystal Lake to the north and Aurora to the south.

Santa's Village is a twenty-five-acre amusement park that includes Old McDonald's Farm, Coney Island, and more than forty rides. It's located two miles north of Interstate 90 on Route 25 (intersection of Routes 25 and 72). Dolphin's Cove Family Aquatic Center (Routes 25 and 68, Carpentersville) has water slides, a zero-depth pool, and picnic areas.

If you're looking to shop, try the Spring Hill Mall (Routes 31 and 72, West Dundee/Carpentersville). Haeger Potteries (Maiden Lane and Van Buren Street, East Dundee) is an active pottery and ceramic factory. At the factory there is a museum, a video presentation, and one of the world's largest hand-thrown vases—at 650 pounds and more than eight feet tall, it's been listed in the *Guinness Book of World Records.*

DIRECTIONS

Emmett's Tavern and Brewing Company is located in West Dundee, just two blocks west of the Fox River at the corner of Main Street (Route 72) and Second Street.

When approaching on Interstate 90, exit on Route 31 (exit mile 24) and drive north approximately two miles to the intersection of Route 31 and Route 72. Then turn right (east) and travel past two stoplights, to the corner of Second and Main. Emmett's is located on the northeast corner of the intersection. Parking is available behind the building.

FireHouse Restaurant and Brewing Company

Morris

Visit Date	Signed

ABOUT THE BREWERY

From the outside, if you took away the large grain bin and the brewpub's logo from above the door, you would swear that the FireHouse Restaurant and Brewing Company is a firehouse. The large steel and glass garage doors and a circular drive help you imagine that you could actually see a fire truck with its lights on pulling out of the bays of the two-story brick building.

The FireHouse is easy to find, on the edge of downtown Morris. If you were to throw a rock from the FireHouse parking lot across Illinois Street, you could almost hit the waters that flow between the banks of the historic Illinois and Michigan Canal.

Inside the brick and cinder block building the openness is filled with a dining room, two private party rooms, the brewhaus, and a second-floor mezzanine that looks down on the main dining room. There is even a second-floor private party room with a great view of the entire brewpub. The bar—a square island, surrounded by about fifteen bar stools, in the middle of this large warehouse building, with four fermentation vessels perched directly over it in a towering, glass-enclosed loft—greets you as you walk through the front doors. The only thing that is missing is a fire pole.

But the best seats in the FireHouse are actually outside. On one of Illinois's warm summer evenings you may find the large glass garage doors opened for an inside, yet outside, merging of dining room and beer garden. Just envision a ladder truck leaving on a call—the doors rise, the red lights go on—and here you sit in the location where the engine would roll out of the firehouse.

The FireHouse keeps five to seven house beers, plus at least one brew-master's special, on tap for most visits. The FireHouse Light, Prairie Fire Wheat, Fire Engine Red, Night Watch Dark, and Spotted Dog Pale Ale are the standard beers. If you are looking for a great light lager, try the brewmaster's special, Potawatomie Pilsner. Other brewmaster's specials that should prompt a special visit include the FireHouse Bock and the Nut Brown.

HISTORY

The FireHouse Restaurant and Brewing Company was opened in May 2000 by local residents Wayne McFarland, John Keegan, and John Peacock. The trio wanted to add another restaurant option to their town, while also offering something unique in food and drink.

FireHouse brewmaster Matt Van Wyk walked into brewing out of high school—in a manner of speaking. Matt was a high school science teacher for five years before his hobby became so serious that he decided to pursue it professionally. A teacher often has summers off. So when the school year ended and Matt had a vacation from his Glen Ellyn High School biology classes, he became friends with Glen Ellyn Sports Brew (formerly Glen Ellyn Brewing Company) brewmaster Mike Engelke. One summer break Matt even volunteered to help Engelke in exchange for a few pints and lunch. Matt went on to attend a short course at Siebel Institute and then took a part-time job as assistant brewer at Glen Ellyn Brewing Company. Then one day in the spring of 2002, Matt happened to be in the FireHouse for a pint and a meal when he struck up a conversation with the former FireHouse brewmaster and found that he was leaving. At that point, there was a "fire within" Matt Van Wyk, and he applied for the job as the FireHouse brewmaster and became a full-time brewer in May 2002. It sounds like the stories you hear about the kid who always hung around the firehouse only to grow up to be a firefighter!

DON'T MISS THIS

Everything, from the way the building has been designed to the interior decor and names of signature dishes, works to support the firefighting theme. If you look closely on a ledge above the bar, you'll find a collection of firefighter hats from Illinois towns such as Gardner, Lockport, Long Grove, and Kinsman. There are also helmets from Cincinnati, Kansas City, and Washington, D.C.

FIREHOUSE BREWS

Fire Engine Red    *Your Ranking* _____
A robust and full-bodied amber ale. A light malty nose. Clear, deep reddish-copper color and a thick, soft, off-white head. Great malty start with some hints of roasted nuttiness. There is a firm hoppy background and light, dry finish.

FireHouse Bock   *Your Ranking* _____
This German lager has a strong malty nose. Clear, deep copper color with a thin, bubbly, white head. Medium to full bodied and smooth. Great caramel flavor in the main body of taste. Smooth and warm finish. This beer has great

smooth, warm flavor and individualistic character; too bad it's a brewmaster's special and is not always available.

FireHouse Honey Brown   🍺🍺🍺   *Your Ranking* _____

A malty nose. Clear bronze color with a thick, soft, tan head. Medium bodied and soft texture. A strong malty flavor and sweet finish. Overall a soft, smooth, malty beer. The honey accents are found in the background of the taste and very subtly in the sweet finish.

FireHouse Light   🍺🍺   *Your Ranking* _____

This ale is one of FireHouse's most popular beers. A very light hoppy nose. Clear, light golden to straw color and a thick, creamy, white head. Light bodied and bubbly. A mild malty, somewhat earthy flavor, finishing with a fruity sourness. This beer is very effervescent and is indeed a light beer. It's the FireHouse's version of mainstream big-brewery light beer.

Night Watch Dark   🍺🍺🍺🍺   *Your Ranking* _____

This porter has hints of coffee and caramel. A light coffee nose. Very dark with bronze tints. A thick, soft, tan head. Full bodied and soft texture. Firm bodied, caramel malty flavor with a mild hoppy background. The finish includes both bitter and light roasted coffee flavors that complement the hoppy tones.

Nut Brown   🍺🍺🍺   *Your Ranking* _____

An English brown ale. Malty nose. Deep, clear bronze color and a thin, soft, tan head. Medium bodied and smooth texture. The dominant flavor is malty and smooth with a nutty background. It finishes with some sweetness and a slight roastedness.

Potawatomie Pilsner   🍺🍺🍺🍺   *Your Ranking* _____

A very well done light lager. No nose. Clear, dark golden color and a thick, bubbly, white head. Light bodied and bubbly. A smooth malty beginning with a crisp hoppy background and light bitter finish. Given a choice of light-bodied beers, I preferred the Potawatomie Pilsner to the FireHouse Light.

Prairie Fire Wheat   🍺🍺🍺   *Your Ranking* _____

No nose. A hazy, golden color and a thin, bubbly, white head. Medium bodied and a soft texture. Smooth malty flavor that finishes with a light citrus fruitiness. Brewed with generous portions of Midwest-grown white wheat malt for added body and flavor.

Spotted Dog Pale Ale   🍺   *Your Ranking* _____

A light floral nose. Clear, golden color and a thick, bubbly, white head. Medium bodied. Dominated by a mild dry hoppiness that continues to build during the entire pint. Finishes with a light bitterness and subtle dryness. Made with Cascade and Columbus hops for aroma and finish. I had great hopes for the Spotted Dog, but on two occasions it never came when called—perhaps it's worth another try on a future visit.

OTHER FIREHOUSE BREWS YOU MAY WANT TO TRY

Cream Ale   *Your Ranking* _____
A light colored and light bodied ale. Served on a nitrogen tap for creamy smoothness.

Oktoberfest   *Your Ranking* _____
Copper to orange color with a sweet malty aroma. Balanced with Noble hops.

Raspberry Wheat   *Your Ranking* _____
A smooth and flavorful unfiltered American wheat.

Spiced Winter Lager   *Your Ranking* _____
Spiced with a blend of cinnamon, nutmeg, cloves, honey, cranberries, and real vanilla. The beer menu describes this as, "a fruitcake in every glass."

Strawberry Blonde   *Your Ranking* _____
A light crisp ale with a subtle infusion of strawberries.

BREWERY RATING

	Your Rating	Shepard's Rating (1 to 4 Mugs)	General Description
Location		🍺🍺🍺	Central city/community
Ease of Finding Location		🍺🍺🍺	Easy, but requires some planning
Brewery Atmosphere		🍺🍺🍺	Family restaurant
Dining Experience		🍺🍺🍺	Family style/variety
The Pint		🍺🍺🍺	A good experience

MENU

The FireHouse menu is composed of American cuisine, with most of the offerings being grilled or barbequed and named with a fire or firefighting description. For example, the appetizer part of the menu is referred to as FireStarters and includes the Tinder Box chicken strips, BonFire nachos, FireWings, and loaded fries. A fun appetizer to share is the FireStix, which are shredded chicken and a special blend of cheeses wrapped in a white flour tortilla and then deep-fried. To begin a meal you'll also get a choice of Road-House chili, a FireHouse Caesar salad, or the soup of the day. For a lighter lunch or meal, the FireHouse offers baked potatoes plain or topped, including one with chili and cheese; a stuffed potato with grilled chicken and sliced red onions; and The Pig with pulled pork, onions, and cheddar and jack cheese. The FireHouse also makes several sandwiches, burgers, quesadillas, and pizzas. The entrees all come with a salad, fresh-baked Milano dinner rolls, and cinnamon honey butter. Among the signature dishes you'll find the

Firefighters strip steak and roasted garlic smashed potatoes. The Backdraft barbeque ribs are smoked pork ribs covered with the FireHouse special Backdraft barbeque sauce. Among other favorites, the Mile-High meatloaf is served over garlic mashed potatoes, covered with chive gravy, and topped with fried Backdraft onions. The blackened catfish consists of two fillets seasoned with Cajun spices. But the FireHouse mint salmon is a special treat; it is prepared in wrapped paper to seal in natural flavor and moisture, and it just flakes off the fork with a mild minty aroma and taste. There are only a few vegetarian options at the FireHouse. Among those are a portabella mushroom dinner and the FireBreak fettuccini with roasted vegetables. The ending to the perfect meal at FireHouse includes a chocolate volcano made from triple chocolate cake smothered with hot molten chocolate sauce.

OTHER THINGS TO SEE OR DO IN THE AREA

Located about sixty miles southwest of Chicago, Morris makes a great weekend destination. But if you travel there, a number of other nearby small towns may keep you occupied more than just a few days.

Morris is perhaps best known for its location on the Illinois and Michigan Canal. The canal is visible from the FireHouse Restaurant and Brewery by looking directly south. The I&M Canal was built to connect Lake Michigan to the Mississippi River and eventually to the Gulf of Mexico. Its construction began in 1836, but it wasn't officially opened until 1848. At the height of its usage, the I&M Canal was ninety-six miles long and had an average depth of six feet. The canal helped Chicago and a number of cities like Morris to grow and prosper. But as railroad transportation began to dominate in the mid-nineteenth century, use of the canal decreased. The canal continued to be used until 1933, when the Illinois Waterway opened. The city of Morris was incorporated in 1842 and named after Isaac Newton Morris, a commissioner with the Illinois and Michigan Canal.

A great way to enjoy the history and natural beauty of the area is by tracing the Illinois and Michigan Canal Corridor. The seventy-five-mile driving tour will take you on back roads and into canal towns and expose you to scenic parks and historic sites. The route extends from Lemont on the east to LaSalle/Peru on the west, with Morris about halfway between. Blue and yellow signs labeled "I&M Canal" mark the route. The signs with a boy and mule pay tribute to the young men who worked long hours tending the mules that pulled the boats and barges through the canal. One noteworthy stop along the Illinois and Michigan Canal Corridor is Lockport (about thirty miles north and east of Morris). Lockport was founded in 1836, when construction began on the canal, and it remains one of the best-preserved canal towns in the country. There is a walking tour of Lockport's Pioneer Settlement and the Illinois and Michigan Canal Museum (803 State Street). Lockport also hosts Old Canal Days (in the downtown) each June with a carnival, flea market, arts and crafts, and family entertainment.

In Morris, along Illinois Street at the south end of Liberty Street, the Riverfront Commission constructed Canaport Plaza. It provides access to the Illinois & Michigan Canal; you may also want to note the steel silhouettes of the Armstrong family, the pioneers who helped to found Morris and build the canal. Elsie Armstrong and her three sons arrived in Morris in 1831, leaving Ohio and Elsie's drunken husband behind. Armstrong and her sons were very active in building the I&M Canal, and a street on the northern edge of the downtown bears their name.

The Grundy County Courthouse Square is in the heart of Morris. The courthouse was constructed in 1912–1913 and stands on the same site where the first two-story wooden courthouse was built in 1842. There are a number of war memorials on the courthouse grounds, but pay particular attention to the twenty-foot cedar pole. According to legend, the pole is a tribute to Chief Nucquette. It was originally placed to mark a burial mound from about 1700, located near where the FireHouse Restaurant and Brewing Company is today. The pole was moved to the courthouse lawn in the 1920s. Numerous Native American burial mounds dating from 900 to 1500 A.D. were destroyed during construction of the I&M Canal.

The second Saturday of each month from May through September is Cruise Night with classic and antique vehicles driving along Liberty Street. Also on select nights in June through August, the City of Morris sponsors Concerts on the Courthouse Lawn. In June the National Skydiving League 4-Way Competition takes off at the Morris Airport. Also in June, Morris hosts the Fireman's Carnival (an appropriate event to attend when visiting the FireHouse Restaurant and Brewing Company). Morris's annual Corn Festival is held in September. The downtown event includes a huge craft and flea market, a farm fair, carnival, fireworks, and parade. In October the Morris Lions Club holds a Classic Car Show (Route 6, approximately six miles east of Morris). The annual Home for the Holidays celebration in late November features carriage rides, caroling, and lighting of the courthouse christmas tree.

If you enjoy the performing arts, the Morris Theatre Guild (507 Liberty Street) presents full-length comedies and dramas, musicals, and murder mystery dinner theater. The guild is an adult comedy troupe with many local people and familiar faces on stage.

The Heritage Tractor Adventure is held in June. This event features vintage tractors that roll along the I&M Canal from Joliet to Streator, Illinois. In nearby Wilmington (about twenty miles east of Morris) during July there's an annual antique tractor and thresher reunion.

The FireHouse Restaurant and Brewing Company represents a modern brewpub, but there are also historical brewing roots in Morris. You may want to walk or drive by the old Gebhard Brewery (west of the Fire-House at the end of Washington Street). The brewhaus and bottling plant portions of the brewery still survive. The Gebhard Brewery was founded in 1866 by German immigrant Louis Gebhard. The I&M Canal was important to the brewery because boats would deliver barley and hops. During the 1870s the brewery used almost a third of all corn produced in Grundy County. The Gebhard Brewery closed with Prohibition in 1919. Gebhard Woods State Park is located west of the FireHouse and the old Gebhard Brewery grounds. The park was purchased from Mrs. William Gebhard by the Grundy County Rod and Gun Club in 1934. The Rod and Gun Club later donated the property to the State of Illinois to be developed and maintained as a state park. The thirty acres of parkland are bordered on the south by the I&M Canal and on the north by Nettle Creek. In July Gebhard Woods is host to the Dulcimer Festival, with concerts and workshops that highlight a range of folk instruments.

DIRECTIONS

Morris is about an hour southwest of downtown Chicago, about a half-hour east of La Salle/Peru, and seventy-five miles northeast of Bloomington. The main interstate connection to Morris is Interstate 80. The FireHouse is located on the southern edge of downtown Morris, on the north bank of the I&M Canal. It's about one and a half miles south of the Route 47 (exit 112) interchange with I-80. As you approach Morris from the north on Route 47 (known locally as Division Street), just before you cross the I&M Canal Bridge, turn right (west) onto Illinois Street. The FireHouse is located within three blocks at the intersection of Illinois and Wauponsee Streets.

Flatlander's Restaurant and Brewery
Lincolnshire

Visit Date	Signed

ABOUT THE BREWERY

Flatlander's boasts an impressive modern brewpub and restaurant design. It stresses its restaurant business with a separate and distinctive dining room called the Harvest Room, while the brewery and main bar are located in the Tap Room. Flatlander's will appeal to both beer enthusiasts and those looking for upscale dining matched with good beer.

The focal point of the Harvest Room is a large see-through fireplace along the north wall. Tables are in the center, while booths line the edges of this large rectangular room. There are also banquet facilities at Flatlander's, and a smaller party room is available.

The Tap Room features not only the main bar but lots of seating with large booths and high tables. There is a stage for live entertainment, but if you are curious, look behind the stage curtain and you'll find the brewhaus. Actually, one of the most impressive views is from the outside along Old Half Day Road. The brewhaus is visible through large windows, and the building is designed to showcase the brewery in its own isolated chamber.

Also from the outside, approaching the main doors on the building's eastern side, you'll see a large fountain and small garden that creates a traffic circle for the Village Green. To the south of Flatlander's entry way is the beer garden. With vines and an overlook of the fountain, it's perhaps one of the most comfortable outside patios you will find in the Chicago area.

Flatlander's keeps about eight of its own beers on tap, plus you'll find a nice selection of bottled beers and wines. The Flatlander's Light, Lincolnshire Lager, Harvest Amber Ale, Abe's Honest Ale, and Locomotive Stout are the standard beers you can count on being available. The Light is a strong seller for Flatlanders, but Abe's is an assertive pale ale that is a very memorable beer. If you're looking for something with a little more body and distinctive character, you might try the 80 Shilling Ale when it's available. Flatlander's does bottle a few of its beers. On every label the company offers its motto, which will make any Illinois-Flatlander proud: "Drink Good Beer, Be Kind, Tell The Truth."

HISTORY

Flatlander's was established in 1996. The building was constructed for Flatlander's, and it was the first occupant of Lincolnshire's Village Green business park and shopping area.

Flatlander's brewmaster Anthony Carolla developed a taste for homebrewing and fine ales in the mid-1990s. Anthony is a local kid who grew up in Vernon Hills and went to high school in Libertyville. Anthony's brewing orientation was accelerated by the influence of the local homebrew club Brewers on the Bluff (BOB) and an occasional visit to Mickey Finn's, which taught him the finer nuances of what ales can be. Anthony was one of the first Flatlander's employees and has been with the company since it opened in 1996. He worked as an assistant brewer with Flatlander's first brewmaster, Kris Huber, from 1997 until 1999. Huber moved on to work for a malting company in Germany. From 1999 until 2003 Greg Browne was the brewmaster at Flatlander's. Browne is well known in the Chicago beer industry for his involvement with Goose Island, the former Weeghman Park Brewing (which became Goose Island–Wrigleyville), Flatlander's, and more recently the Brass Restaurant and Brewery in South Barrington.

Behind the scenes, Flatlander's is helped along by longtime brewery insider Henry Knuer, a former vice president at the Froedtert Malting Company in Milwaukee. Froedtert is a major supplier of malt to big breweries such as Anheuser-Busch, Miller, and Coors. Knuer is now retired and lives in the Lincolnshire area, but his advice and recommendations shine through a number of Flatlander's brews, especially the Marzen-style amber lager.

DON'T MISS THIS

The main bar area, or Tap Room as it is known, is more than two stories high. The back bar makes use of the high ceiling with plenty of room for stacking liquors and spirits. But high above the bar shelving, continue looking upward. Through the glass windows you'll see the 466-gallon serving tanks for the main taps! The Tap Room is large and somewhat hollow with its tall ceiling height and concrete floor. It goes with the rural image of the name Flatlander's, almost leaving you with a feeling that this room could have been a farm machine shop building. But we like it much better as a brewery and Tap Room! If you're taking a Flatlander's tour, you'll see coasters on the walls with the name Knuer. Those coasters are actually from breweries that Henry Knuer, Flatlander's helper and local beer idol, once owned in Germany. Look even more closely and you might see Henry helping out in the brewhaus.

FLATLANDER'S BREWS

Abe's Honest Ale 🍺🍺🍺🍺 *Your Ranking* _____

An American pale ale. A firm hoppy nose. Clear, copper color with a thick, soft, white head. Medium bodied and bubbly. Nice hoppy start, remaining bitter through the finish. Some very firm, not overly bitter, just great hoppy flavor. Made with Cascade hops from the Pacific Northwest. Dry hopped for bitter flavor and aroma. This beer has remained virtually unchanged since it was originally brewed for Flatlander's Grand Opening in 1999.

**Abe's Honest Ale
(cask conditioned)** 🍺🍺🍺🍺 *Your Ranking* _____

Similar in appearance to Abe's (described above) on a cold tap line. There is a little less head, and it's softer. The hoppiness is really accented. If given the choice, and you enjoy a smooth hoppy beer, try this one!

Czech Pilsner 🍺🍺🍺 *Your Ranking* _____

A faint sweetness to the nose. Clear golden color. A thick, very soft, white head. Medium to light bodied and crisp texture. A light hint of maltiness, but overall firm hoppy crispness. Some excellent hoppiness with a round to soft feel. The hoppiness will build over the finish and continue to linger with a light dryness.

80 Shilling Ale 🍺🍺🍺🍺 *Your Ranking* _____

A Scottish-style ale. Strong spicy nose. Dark brown color with a thick, soft, tan head. Full bodied and soft. A rich malty flavor with hints of smoke, finishing sweet and warm. While it was described as malty sweet with roastedness and hops, the maltiness and roasted tones overshadow any hoppy flavors. This ale is brewed with a small amount of peat malt to give it that smoky tone.

Executioner 🍺🍺🍺🍺 *Your Ranking* _____

A malty nose. Dark color with bronze highlights. A thick, bubbly, brown head. Full bodied and somewhat slick texture. Firm malty flavors with a coffee background. Finishes warm and bitter. There is great flavor and assertive character in this beer.

Flatlander's Light 🍺🍺🍺🍺 *Your Ranking* _____

The lightest of Flatlander's beers. A lager with a light malty nose. A clear straw color and a thin, bubbly, white head. Light bodied and very effervescent. Despite a faint maltiness to the nose, this beer is very clean and crisp with a firm, hoppy flavor. This is a light beer with some great flavor!

Harvest Amber Ale 🍺🍺🍺 *Your Ranking* _____

A British-style pale ale. A light hoppy nose. A light copper color and a little hazy. A thick, soft, tan head. Medium bodied and round. Begins with a light maltiness but is well balanced with a firm malt flavor up front with firm hoppy background and a strong, clean, bitter balanced finish. Watch for this on a cask-conditioned tap.

Honey Brown 🍺🍺🍺   *Your Ranking* _____

Lots of sweet, caramel malty flavor in this beer. A malty nose, dark color, and a thick, bubbly, tan head. Medium bodied and creamy. Caramel malty body with a sweet honey finish.

Lincolnshire Lager 🍺🍺   *Your Ranking* _____

A Munich-style lager. The nose seemed a little vegetal. Great clear golden color with a thin, bubbly, white head. Light bodied. Mild maltiness with a sour background. A light roasted finish.

Locomotive Stout 🍺🍺🍺   *Your Ranking* _____

A dry Irish-style stout. Strong malty aroma, especially the roasted notes. Black color with a bronze tint. The head is thick, soft, and creamy thanks to being served on a nitrogen tap. This creaminess carries into the texture, which is medium and soft. Assertive chocolate malt flavors really build and remain in a long-lasting finish. The roasted nose and finish also have hints of coffee.

Old Orchard Ale 🍺🍺🍺   *Your Ranking* _____

A light bodied wheat ale made with red cherries. No nose. A cloudy amber color with a thick, soft, white head. Full bodied and creamy. Very sweet malty tones, has some cherry accent, but the sweetness is more earthy and malty. Finishes with a lingering sweetness.

Prairie Wheat 🍺🍺   *Your Ranking* _____

A light fruity nose. Clear, light golden color and thin, soft, white head. Light bodied and soft. Malty flavors dominate with a crisp hoppy finish. All of the flavors are a little quiet for this wheat beer. Could be much more assertive, but if you're looking for a light-bodied, clean beer, this is a good choice. It is brewed with Czech hops for bitterness and aroma.

Snow Melt 🍺🍺🍺🍺   *Your Ranking* _____

This Duvel-like Belgian beer has an assertive sweet fruity flavor and warm finish that makes a near perfect winter warmer. Heck, it'll warm your taste buds anytime, and if it's on the beer list it'll be what I'm having on that visit. A light, earthy, sweet nose. Hazy golden color with a thin, bubbly, white head. Medium to full bodied. Strong sweet fruity flavors dominate with a sweet, warm finish. This beer is near perfection. Just be careful, with its warmth and high alcohol qualities, not to overdo it.

OTHER FLATLANDER'S BREWS YOU MAY WANT TO TRY

Belgian White   *Your Ranking* _____

A seasonal offering. Light and smooth with hints of coriander and orange.

English Mild Ale   *Your Ranking* _____

Similar to a brown ale but lighter in body.

Hefeweizen   *Your Ranking* _____

A summertime seasonal at Flatlander's.

Kolsch   *Your Ranking* _____

Light golden and light bodied. Some light fruitiness. A summer seasonal.

Oktoberfest   *Your Ranking* _____

A hearty, burnt-orange colored German lager. Full bodied and a rich malt flavor with just enough hops to provide balance. A fall seasonal.

BREWERY RATING

	Your Rating	Shepard's Rating (1 to 4 Mugs)	General Description
Location		🍺🍺🍺	Neighborhood/residential
Ease of Finding Location		🍺🍺🍺	Easy, but requires some planning
Brewery Atmosphere		🍺🍺🍺	Family restaurant Music venue Sports
Dining Experience		🍺🍺🍺	Family style/variety
The Pint		🍺🍺🍺	A good experience

MENU

In keeping with the rural strength found in the name Flatlander's, you can expect plentiful and flavorful Midwestern food that matches well with a house beer. It's hard to surpass the one-pound meatloaf dinner paired with an Abe's Honest Ale, or the full rack of barbecued ribs that are made with a blend of Harvest Amber Ale barbecue sauce. Another favorite is the Kansas City strip, which is a peppercorn encrusted bone-in strip steak served with button mushrooms and Locomotive Stout sauce and onion rings. The Amish chicken breast is topped with Harvest Amber barbecue sauce, smoked hickory ham, smoked Monterey Jack cheese, diced tomatoes, and chives. For seafood, the fresh Lake Superior whitefish is herb crusted, baked, and served over a bed of spinach. About a dozen sandwiches and half-dozen burgers are also found on Flatlander's menu. The burgers come in choices of ground beef, buffalo, and turkey. Sandwiches include a blackened prime rib, a Lincolnshire club sandwich, a chicken parmesan, and a grilled vegetable, which is a portabella mushroom with roasted bell peppers and mixed squash. Pasta selections feature a vegetable lasagna, linguini primavera, stuffed ravioli, and a sausage and pepper marinara. Deciding on a dessert isn't easy with choices like the chocolate chip cookie pie, fresh baked carrot cake, and the apple cinnamon pretzel sprinkled with cinnamon sugar and served with French vanilla ice cream.

OTHER THINGS TO SEE OR DO IN THE AREA

Lincolnshire hosts its annual Art Festival in early July at the Village Green Center (Old Half Day Road and Route 21), which is nearly in Flatlander's parking lot! Also close by to Flatlander's is Marriott's Lincolnshire Resort and Theatre (Milwaukee Avenue and Half Day Road). The Marriott supports an award-winning theater that presents Broadway-level programs.

If you're looking for shopping, Hawthorn Center (Milwaukee Avenue/Route 21 and Route 60) is a two-level regional shopping center. Also north of Flatlander's in Vernon Hills, the Cuneo Museum and Garden (1350 North Milwaukee) includes seventy-five acres of grounds, a conservatory, lakes, and a Venetian-style mansion with a forty-foot-high great hall, stained glass windows, and a grand piano.

About eight miles northwest of Flatlander's, Mundelein holds its Community Days celebration in Krauck Lauer Park (Seymour Street and Courtland Street) in early July. Quig's Orchard (300 South Route 83, Mundelein) is another area stop to consider. Here you'll find apple cider, apple pie, homemade fudge, a garden gift shop, and a greenhouse. In nearby Prairie View, Didier Farms (16678 West Aptakisic Road) holds an annual Pumpkin Festival in October, complete with hayrides and pick-your-own pumpkins.

About five miles to the southwest, Long Grove hosts several festivals in its downtown, including the Chocolate Festival in May, the Strawberry Festival in June, and the Art Festival in August. Long Grove is also home to a historic village, with ninety-plus specialty shops. It is also well known for the Long Grove Confectionery Company (220 Robert Parker Coffin Road), which makes over three hundred different gourmet chocolates.

If you enjoy hiking and biking, the Des Plaines River Trail runs through Lake County. The southern section of the trail connects to Wright Wood Forest Preserve and Half Day Forest Preserve, both in Vernon Hills. Plans call for this trail to stretch over thirty miles through Lake County. In northern stretches the valley is wide and the river meanders through open prairies and savannas. In southern stretches the river is straighter and the valley is narrower, with woodlands and forests. The Tamarak Picnic Grounds (across from the Marriott Lincolnshire) is a densely wooded ten-acre park with playgrounds, tennis and basketball courts, swimming pool, pavilion, and picnic tables. The Discovery Picnic Ground (Route 22 and Milwaukee Avenue) is a ten-acre facility with an Olympic-sized swimming pool, soccer field, and picnic tables.

Set on thirty-six acres of woodlands and green space, the Ravinia Festival (400 Iris Lane, Highland Park) runs from June through early September, featuring the Chicago Symphony Orchestra, jazz, pop, and many other musical performers. Highland Park also offers an annual Evening of Smelt (Park Beach, 31 Park Avenue) every April. Highland Park is located about eight miles east of Lincolnshire.

You may also want to check the brewery descriptions for Ram (Wheeling) and Mickey Finn's (Libertyville) for other things to see and do in the area. Both of these brewpubs are within ten minutes of Flatlander's.

DIRECTIONS

Flatlander's is located at the corner of Route 45 (Old Half Day Road) and Route 21 (Milwaukee Avenue). This intersection is north of Route 22 (Half Day Road).

From Chicago take Interstate 90 west either to Interstate 94 North (Edens Expressway) toward Milwaukee or to Interstate 294 (Tri-State Tollway), which will join I-94 and continue north toward Milwaukee. Exit on Route 22/Half Day Road and turn west on Route 22. Proceed two miles to Old Half Day Road and turn right, continuing on about a quarter of a mile, and Flatlander's will be on your right-hand side (north) just before you reach Route 21 (Milwaukee Avenue).

From the south take Illinois 88, East/West Tollway, toward Chicago. Take I-294 toward Milwaukee. Exit on Route 22/Half Day Road and turn west on Route 22. Proceed two miles to Old Half Day Road and turn right, continuing on about a quarter of a mile, and Flatlander's will be on your right-hand side (north) just before you reach Route 21 (Milwaukee Avenue).

Flatlander's is also near two other brewpubs. Ram–Wheeling is located about four miles south on Milwaukee Avenue. Mickey Finn's is located about six miles north on Milwaukee Avenue in Libertyville.

Flossmoor Station
Restaurant and Brewery
Flossmoor

Visit Date	Signed

ABOUT THE BREWERY

Flossmoor Station has all of the qualities of a great brewpub. The 1906 railroad station offers historical character and neighborhood charm. It provides a fun destination for anyone from Chicago or Greater Illinois. The menu has variety at reasonable prices, and you'll find an excellent list of standard house beers along with an ambitious and ever-changing array of specialty beers. For a brewpub of its size, Flossmoor Station achieves solid and consistent beer offerings in styles such as a Belgian Wit, Belgian Tripel, Imperial stout, and cask-conditioned barley wines.

The former Illinois Central Railroad depot really offers an ideal venue for the brewpub. You walk up several steps into the building, just like many passengers once did as they caught trains into Chicago during the early 1900s. The interior has been restored to keep the feel of an open railroad station. The main bar is located in the entry room, and the open archways that once led to the train platform are now large windows. The dining room is basically one large room with lots of natural lighting and open space that helps to create a busy, bustling atmosphere.

Flossmoor Station has received a number of awards for its food, beer, and overall business. It was named "Best Brewery" of 2002 by *Chicago Magazine* in its annual "Best of" issue. In 1998, its owners, Dean and Carolyn Armstrong, were voted "Small Business Persons of the Year" by the Chicago

Southland Chamber of Commerce. Visiting Flossmoor Station, you quickly learn why it has received so much recognition. Staff is attentive and knowledgeable; the old depot makes great use of its space, and it has great views throughout the building. Furthermore, the restoration of the old depot has preserved a major community landmark.

Flossmoor Station regularly offers ten of its own beers on tap. The standard ones include Zephyr Golden Ale, Gandy Dancer Honey Ale, Station Master Wheat Ale, Panama Red Ale, Iron Horse Oatmeal Stout, and the brewpub's flagship beer—Pullman Nut Brown Ale. Brewmaster Todd Ashman likes to travel and research his beer recipes, so it's worthwhile to watch for his interpretations of Belgian styles, German bocks, or the strong Scotch ale called the Kilt Kicker Wee Heavy. You'll likely find something new on every visit, because Ashman brews over two-dozen beer styles throughout the year.

HISTORY

Flossmoor Station Restaurant and Brewery is located in an Illinois Central Railroad station building that was constructed in 1906. At the time it was built there were only six homes in the community of Flossmoor. The area was a weekend retreat for many wealthy Chicago families, aided by train service. But as rail passenger service declined, the station building eventually fell from use in the 1970s. A Metra platform was constructed behind the station, so the building's life as a train station was over. The building sat vacant until the 1990s, when it was remodeled to house a number of specialty shops. When that venture failed, local residents Dean and Carolyn Armstrong saw potential in restoring the station into a restaurant and brewpub. After the Armstrongs purchased the station building and invested more than $1.5 million, Flossmoor Station was opened in July 1996.

The Armstrongs were met with a number of hurdles as they rebuilt the old station. Perhaps the most challenging was that local community residents expressed fear and concern over how a brewery in the middle of the downtown might affect their quality of life. But the Armstrongs persevered through opposition and cost overruns, acting as their own general contractor, and even oversaw much of the remodeling, down to the miniature tiles that spell "The Brewhouse" on the floor of the brewery and "Flossmoor Station" on the steps leading into the main dining room.

Flossmoor Station's brewmaster, Todd Ashman, found quality microbeer as many of us did, while in college. Todd describes his "awaking" as the first day of classes while at Santa Rosa Junior College in Texas. After that first afternoon he found himself in a local pub enjoying a Sierra Nevada Pale Ale. That, he says, started the ball rolling in his quest of looking for beers with strong flavor and character. From that experience he ventured into homebrewing, and after returning home to his native California he joined the "Sonoma County Beerocrats" homebrew club. By 1995 he had enrolled in the University of California Davis Extension program for brewing. That led him to brewing jobs at Bison Brewing in Berkeley, California, and later at Kegs Brewery in Alamogordo, New Mexico. By June 1996, Flossmoor Station was looking for a fulltime brewmaster, and Todd was hired just two weeks after the brewpub's grand opening. Todd is very serious about researching beer styles and learning what history has to offer in the way of recipes and inter-esting approaches to making beer. You'll find an acute commitment to such styles as Belgian ales, Imperial stouts, and cask-conditioned barley wines.

DON'T MISS THIS

The obvious aspect you really can't miss is the arrival of Metra trains on the plat-form next to the building. You can feel the trains go by the station. Large windows in the bar allow for some great train and people watching. There are also a num-ber of old historic photos hanging throughout Flossmoor Station. In the bar, along the northern wall, there is a fascinating photo of an "iron horse" making its way over flooded tracks. If you have ever wondered what the inside of a Pullman car looks like, one of the photos in the main dining room will give you an idea. But my favorite is in the corner of the bar area, near the entry into the main dining room: a photo of two elderly men enjoying a beer, one drinking from a tin cup.

FLOSSMOOR STATION BREWS

Abbaye Dubbel 🍺🍺🍺🍺   Your Ranking _____
Sweet aroma. Clear, mahogany color and a thick, bubbly, tan head. Full bod-ied and very soft. Strong malty flavors and a yeasty finish. Made with black-strap molasses for color and flavor. A gold medal winner at the 2002 Great American Beer Festival.

Framboise de Flossmoor 🍺🍺🍺   Your Ranking _____
A Belgian Wit ale made with raspberry puree, grape concentrate, and a cham-pagne yeast. Very distinctive reddish purple color with a thick, bubbly, white head. A light cherry nose. Medium bodied and very bubbly. Strong cherry fla-vor, but not sour. Actually very smooth. There is a fruity dryness to the finish.

Gandy Dancer Honey Ale 🍺🍺🍺   Your Ranking _____
A light, sweet, honeylike nose. Dark copper color and a thick, tan, bubbly head. Medium bodied and soft. Malty flavors stand out with a roasted finish. Made with four types of malt and flaked rye. Hopped with Centennial and Crystal hops. Orange blossom honey is added to the recipe. Winner of a sil-ver medal at the 1999 Great American Beer Festival.

Iron Horse Oatmeal Stout 🍺🍺   Your Ranking _____
A light malty, roasted nose. Very dark, opaque and a thick, soft, brown head. Medium to full bodied. Flavor is rich in caramel, toffee, and espresso tones. Fin-ishes with a strong flavor of coffee. Brewed with baked oats for a roasted accent.

Le Chien Blanc Witbier 🍺🍺🍺🍺   Your Ranking _____
This Belgian-style Wit is spiced with orange, lemon, grapefruit, coriander, and chamomile. You find many of these in the initial aroma. A lightly cloudy, golden color with a thin, bubbly, white head. Medium to light bodied and soft. A spicy start, then some yeasty flavor. Sweet, fruity finish. A very special treat when found on tap at Flossmoor. A summertime specialty beer.

Panama Red Ale 🍺🍺🍺🍺   *Your Ranking* _____

An American-style amber ale brewed with pale ale malt and Belgian caramel malts. Hopped with Centennial and Amarillo. A light, malty nose. Clear copper color and a thin, bubbly, white head. Medium bodied and round. A mild malty taste with hints of hoppiness that actually come out strong after building in the finish. Dry hopped in the keg!

Pullman Nut Brown Ale 🍺🍺🍺🍺   *Your Ranking* _____

This American-style brown ale is Flossmoor's signature beer. A malty nose. Dark bronze color with a thick, tan, bubbly head. Full bodied and smooth. Strong malty tones with a roasted background that lingers throughout the finish. Made with molasses and hand-toasted oats. Four-time gold medal winner (1997 to 2000) at the Great American Beer Festival and bronze in 2002, as well as silver in the 2000 World Beer Cup competitions. An exceptional beer.

Roundhouse Raspberry Wheat Ale 🍺🍺🍺🍺   *Your Ranking* _____

The raspberry flavors are most evident in the aroma and finish, and the berry sweetness couples well with the beer's soft texture, making for a very smooth fruity beer. A hazy, light golden color and a thin, bubbly, white head. Light bodied, bubbly, and very soft. Mild wheat start with the berry flavor in the finish.

Station Master Wheat Ale 🍺🍺🍺   *Your Ranking* _____

A spicy nose. Clear golden color. A thin, bubbly, white head. Medium bodied and soft texture. A light, hoppy start with a mild, malty flavor. A clean finish. Made with 33 percent wheat malt.

Todd and Bill's Excellent IPA 🍺🍺🍺🍺   *Your Ranking* _____

An English-style India Pale Ale. A strong, assertive hoppy nose. Hazy golden color and a thin, bubbly, white head. Full bodied. A sharp bitterness. Very bitter and long-lasting hoppiness for the finish. Brewed with Marris Otter malt and Centennial and Amarillo hops. An exceptional beer.

Todd's Tupelo Tripel 🍺🍺🍺   *Your Ranking* _____

A sweet nose. Clear, deep golden color with a thick, bubbly, off-white head. Full bodied and soft. A light warm beginning and ending. Smooth sweetness with a mild bitter background. Great yeasty flavor. Instead of traditional Belgian candy sugar, this Tripel is made with Tupelo Honey from Florida.

Zephyr Golden Ale 🍺🍺🍺   *Your Ranking* _____

The lightest of the Flossmoor beers. A flowery nose. Clear, light golden color. A thick, white head. Light bodied and soft. Smooth, grainy body and smoky finish. Brewed with three varieties of hops and a touch of rice.

OTHER FLOSSMOOR STATION BREWS YOU MAY WANT TO TRY

Chessle Cherry Wheat Ale   *Your Ranking* _____

A light-bodied fruit beer with a blend of red cherries and wheat ale. Slightly sweet, yet tart.

Dark Star Imperial Stout   *Your Ranking* _____

A stout aged in a Jack Daniel's whiskey barrel. Dark, rich, and aromatic. Brewed once every three years. Served in a brandy snifter.

Dunkleweizen   *Your Ranking* _____

A German-style Dunkel Weizen.

El Diablo Belgian Strong Ale   *Your Ranking* _____

Strong aggressive maltiness. Deep bronze color.

Imperial Eclipse Stout   *Your Ranking* _____

A gold medal winner at the 1998 Great American Beer Festival.

Kilt Kicker Wee Heavy   *Your Ranking* _____

A strong Scotch ale with smoky flavors.

Munich Helles   *Your Ranking* _____

A spring seasonal.

Old Conundrum Barley Wine   *Your Ranking* _____

A very special barley wine brewed with palm sugar from India. Ask the bartender; you may get a choice between an Old Conundrum aged in a Jack Daniel's barrel with whiskey flavor or one aged in a traditional oak barrel. A sweet, malty nose. Clear copper color and a thin, bubbly head. Full bodied and warm from beginning to end. Winner of a bronze medal in 2002 and a silver medal in 1999 at the Great American Beer Festivals, as well as a silver medal in the 2000 World Beer Cup competition.

Terminal Bourbon Stout   *Your Ranking* _____

Lots of malt with a warm bourbon aroma and finish. A gold medal winner at the 2002 Great American Beer Festival.

A Train Wreck of Flavor   *Your Ranking* _____

A blend of Flossmoor's Pullman Brown Ale and Old Conundrum Barley Wine, further aged in a Jack Daniel's barrel. A myriad of flavors. Watch for this beer at an area beer tasting event.

BREWERY RATING

	Your Rating	Shepard's Rating (1 to 4 Mugs)	General Description
Location		🍺🍺🍺🍺	Central city/community
Ease of Finding Location		🍺🍺🍺	Difficult, out of the way, need a map
Brewery Atmosphere		🍺🍺🍺🍺	Historic Family restaurant
Dining Experience		🍺🍺🍺🍺	Family style/variety
The Pint		🍺🍺🍺🍺	A perfect experience

MENU

The Flossmoor Station menu is a combination of family dining and upscale pub offerings. Appetizers include the heaping portion of Macho Nachos, Brew-Schetta with garden fresh northern Italian tomato-basil relish, hot and spicy buffalo wings, Hophead's Big Cheese Dipper of sharp cheddar and green chili beer dip, and the brewery platter of ribs, onion rings, buffalo wings, and celery. There are a variety of salads and soups, including beer cheese and Brew Kettle chili. There are about a dozen sandwiches on Flossmoor's menu. The brewery burger is a half-pound steak burger. The Pullman Pork Beer-B-Que is in a special Flossmoor Station sauce. The Kegger dog is a quarter-pound, all-beef kosher hot dog, blanched in Station Master Wheat Ale. The entree selections provide a range of steak, chicken, fish, and pasta. The Roundhouse Beer-B-Que ribs feature baby back pork ribs, slow-smoked and finished on the grill with Station Master Beer-B-Que sauce. The Zephyr Lake perch platter is a choice of sautéed or fried Canadian lake perch served with a cilantro-Zephyr Golden Ale tartar sauce. A great way to finish a visit to Floss-moor Station is by stopping at the Old Caboose Ice Cream Shoppe on the brewpub's south lawn. Beyond ice cream, you'll find soft pretzels in several flavors, such as cream cheese, cinnamon apple, pizza, jalapeño, or plain. Churros are another special treat made like a stick-shaped pastry that is lightly flavored with cinnamon. You might also ask for a Goober Brau root beer made in Flossmoor Station's brewery—it's named after the pub's mascot dog.

OTHER THINGS TO SEE OR DO IN THE AREA

Flossmoor is located south of Chicago, just minutes off Interstate 94, the Tri-State Tollway (I-80/94), Interstate 57, and U.S. Route 30. The Metra will let you off at Flossmoor Station Restaurant and Brewery, and you'll also be in the heart of downtown Flossmoor. Across the street from the brewpub, the Tudor-style Civic Center building, built in 1929, features a unique mix of retail stores, restaurants, offices, and apartments. Flossmoor Commons (3301 West Vollmer Road) also offers many options for shopping, with exclusive stores and neighborhood boutiques.

The Homewood-Flossmoor Park District maintains over two hundred acres of open space and thirty-three parks and recreational facilities. Over the Fourth of July, the Homewood-Flossmoor Park District hosts Family Fun Fest with a parade. The Homewood Chamber of Commerce and Park District sponsor an annual Art Fair each spring. The Park District also supports the Starry Nights concert series during the summertime with performances by the Symphonic Pops Orchestra of Chicago and other popular artists.

About eight miles south of Flossmoor the internationally recognized Nathan Manilow Sculpture Park is located at Governors State University (Governors Highway and University Parkway, University Park). It's home to twenty-two sculptures by world-renowned artists. Also on the campus of Governors State University is the Center for Performing Arts with its twelve-hundred-seat theater. Nearby is Thorn Creek Nature Center (247 Monee Road, Park Forest), with its wildlife displays and exhibits. The Iron Oaks Environmental Learning Center (2553 Vollmer Road, Olympia Fields) is a thirty-three-acre nature preserve with a cross-country ski center, an adventure center, and numerous exhibits. The thirty-nine-mile Burnham Greenway to Joliet segment of the Grand Illinois Trail roughly parallels U.S. Route 30 and can be picked up about five miles south of Flossmoor in Richton Park.

North of Flossmoor, you can see the Cook County Cheetahs baseball team of the professional independent Frontier League. The Cheetahs play at Hawkins Ford Field (4545 Midlothian Turnpike, Crestwood). Crestwood is also home to Hollywood Park (5051 Cal Sag Road), an amusement park with two miniature golf courses, over a hundred games, bumper cars, and an indoor children's playland.

North and east of Flossmoor, in the town of South Holland, the Midwest Carver's Museum (16236 Vincennes Avenue) boasts a thousand woodcarvings created by local and internationally known artists. Also north and east of Flossmoor, near Thornton, the local historical society hosts an annual (June) Thornton Quarry Tour of the largest limestone quarry in the world. The quarry is atop a four-hundred-foot deposit of limestone that is over four hundred million years old. The Thornton Quarry was first developed in the 1830s, and today it annually produces more than seven million tons of rock worth about $40 million. Interstate 80 is actually built over the quarry!

Thornton is also the home of the former Biefeldt Brewery (400 Margaret Street). John S. Biefeldt founded his brewery there in 1857. Today there are a few buildings that remain on the site. One of the old brewery buildings is home to the restaurant called Widow McCleary's. The Biefeldt Brewery changed hands and operated under several different names but finally closed in 1957, when the owner at the time, Joe Sadauskas, shut the doors after claiming that Chicago gangsters had demanded "protection" money to keep the brewery open. After he declined to pay, about 140,000 gallons of beer ended up being dumped mysteriously in the nearby Thorn Creek. The old brewery complex is believed to be haunted. During renovations in 1951, skeletal remains were discovered in a sealed room. The victims were thought to have been entombed alive, allegedly on the orders of Al Capone, as an example of what could happen when debts were not paid. There is an exhibit on the Biefeldt Brewery at the Village of Thornton Historical Society Museum (114 North Hunter Street).

DIRECTIONS

Flossmoor is located south of Chicago. The brewpub is across the street from the Flossmoor Post Office and Public Library and set on the east side of a small traffic circle. Perhaps the easiest way to get there from downtown Chicago is on the Metra, because it lets you off at the brewpub!

You can reach Flossmoor from Interstate 57 by taking the Vollmer Road exit, turning east, then take Route 50 north to Flossmoor Road and again turn to the east. That'll take you directly into the village of Flossmoor.

Approaching from the east and west is a little more difficult on Interstate 80. Look for the Route 1 exit (Halsted South) and turn south. Take 183rd Street right (west) into Homewood. Just beyond the railroad tracks, turn south on Western, which eventually becomes Sterling and takes you directly into the Village of Flossmoor and to Flossmoor Station Restaurant and Brewery.

Founders Hill Restaurant and Brewery

Downers Grove

Visit Date	Signed

ABOUT THE BREWERY

Founders Hill Restaurant and Brewery is located in downtown Downers Grove. Its name pays tribute to that city's founders, who lie in peace across the street in the local cemetery. Both the brewery and cemetery are uphill from the central city of Downers Grove.

The brewpub is located in a building that was originally constructed in the late nineteenth century. The building once served as the Cresay Auditorium, but most locals will remember the two-story brick building as housing various car dealerships, including Baughman Motors and later Stillwell Buick. Prior to its renovation into a brewpub, the building had a car elevator that would lift vehicles to the second and third floors; however, a fire in the late 1930s destroyed the third story of the building. From the outside the building shows off some of its historical character and charm. Between the first- and second-floor windows there are painted scenes of olden times that offer a visual tie to this business's sense of times past.

As you walk into Founders Hill, you can gain an appreciation for the building's massive frame. Huge wooden timbers, large beams in the ceiling, iron accents, and a second-floor loft that is now an additional dining room all provide visual cues of the building's prior uses. Tables along the front windows offer a great view of street activity. The high ceiling has large fans, exposed ventilation ducts, and wooden beams.

The bar area is located in the southern half of the first floor. The long, cherry-colored bar is eye-catching, but the focal point of the main barroom is the brewery itself. The two-story brewhaus reaches upward in its own glass-enclosed room, which requires an atrium-type arrangement for the tall forty-five-barrel fermenters. Special lighting makes it really stand out, both from inside when you are in the bar and even when you're outside passing by on the street; the large front windows expose the stainless steel vessels. In the summer Founders Hill has a beer garden along the front of the building on Main Street. On some weekends the brewpub will host live music.

Founders Hill commonly offers six beers on tap, with an additional brewmaster's special or two. While the Founder's Light Lager and Heritage Wheat are among the best sellers, brewer Karl Fitzloff always has something special that's worth a stop. Around Thanksgiving time, watch for his Christmas ale called Santa's Little Helper; just in time for spring, the Main Street Maibock finds its way from the brewhaus.

HISTORY

Founders Hill Brewing Company was established in 1996. Head brewer Karl Fitzloff has been with Founders since it began operations, and he actually helped build the brewhaus. Originally a Chicago native, Fitzloff began his brewing career in 1994, when he took a job at the former Weinkeller Brewery in Westmont. After attending the Siebel Institute in 1994, he brewed for a short time at the Main Street Brewery in Cincinnati, Ohio. In 1995 he joined Founders Hill in time to help pick out the brewing equipment and brew the very first batch.

Fitzloff's taste for beer began early. Before he was twenty-one, he figured out that he could brew beer even though he couldn't legally buy it. But what influenced him dramatically was a trip to Germany on his twenty-first birthday. Because of his age, Karl had never gotten accustomed to America's mainstream beers, so his first taste of commercial beer came while in Germany. As Karl says, he never had a chance to get used to anything but the best! So when he became a professional brewer, it just seemed normal to him to offer a variety of beers with character to his customers.

DON'T MISS THIS

As you approach the front door from outside, you might notice brewer Karl Fitzloff's personal hops plant. Inside, there's a fun look around at some of the antiquelike fixtures as well as a Jack Nicklaus trophy from a golf tournament on December 12, 1961, and the old horseshoe that contractors found during the building's renovations and inspired Founders' Blacksmith Stout.

FOUNDERS HILL BREWS

Bernardine's Honey Brown   🍺🍺🍺   *Your Ranking* _____
An American brown ale. Three pounds of apple blossom honey are used in every keg. Brewer Karl Fitzloff's mother, Bernardine, actually raises the honey used in this beer. A strong malty nose. Deep bronze color with a thin, bubbly, tan head. Medium bodied and soft texture. A sweet malty flavor. The honey comes in lightly in the finish. Available in summer. Considered Karl's favorite fishing trip beer.

Blacksmith Stout 🍺🍺🍺   *Your Ranking* _____

Robust and creamy is a good way to describe this beer, which begins with a strong roasted malt nose. It has a very dark bronze body with a slight cloudiness and a thick, soft, tan head. This stout is full bodied with a creamy texture. There is ample sweet chocolate malty flavor, which is complemented by a subtle roasted background. The roasted tones help accent a mild dryness to the finish. Overall, it is more sweet than dry or hoppy. Made with six types of malted barley and accented with oats for smoothness. Downers Grove once supported two local blacksmiths, who set up their business not far north on Main Street. During renovations for Founders Hill, contractors found an old horseshoe in the building, and that inspired this brew. You might look around and try to find the shoe hanging on the wall.

Chill on the Hill 🍺🍺🍺   *Your Ranking* _____

A clear malt beverage. An alternative for those looking for something with less color but lots of character. In the brewing process this beer is filtered so many times that brewer Karl Fitzloff loses about 30 percent of the batch before it even reaches the serving tanks. The nose offers a strong citrus aroma. The body has a cloudy white color. There is virtually no head, just a few white bubbles. This beer is light bodied and round. The taste is somewhat cola-sweet, similar to a saccharine flavor. Citrus and sweet continue through the long-lasting finish. It is as described: a unique "malternative" beverage.

Founders Light Lager 🍺🍺   *Your Ranking* _____

This American light lager is light yellow to clear straw in color, with no nose. The head is thin, bubbly, and white. The light, crisp body provides delicate character; it has a very smooth, mild malty body. The ending is a little grainy with just a hint of fruitiness, which seems somewhat out of place.

Herb's Smoked Porter 🍺🍺🍺   *Your Ranking* _____

A light malty nose. Very dark color and a thick, bubbly, brown head. Full bodied and round. Strong sour qualities overwhelm the malt. Some faint roasted qualities in the finish, but the aggressive cherry puree really dominates. A nice porter, but the fruity, sour side distracts from the beer flavor, unless you enjoy an aggressive cherry-like accent.

Heritage Wheat 🍺🍺🍺   *Your Ranking* _____

Brewed with 40 percent wheat. A very light, fruity nose. A slightly cloudy, yellow color and a thin, soft, white head. Light body and very crisp. There is a meaty-wheatiness to this beer that is very distinctive. The finish has a light whiff of roasted malt that competes with a very light hoppiness. It is made with Hallertau and Willamette hops.

Hidden River Red Ale 🍺🍺🍺🍺   *Your Ranking* _____

An aggressive malty nose that is very alluring. Clear copper color and a thick, soft, white head. Medium bodied and round texture. A clean, crisp caramel start with hints of fruitiness in the background. Finishes with a lingering light crisp bitterness. Made with caramel malt for color and Willamette and Hallertau hops for bitterness. Named after the local St. Joseph Creek, which mysteriously disappears into the ground near Founders Hill.

Main Street Maibock   🍺🍺🍺   *Your Ranking* _____

A traditional German-style lager. An almost hidden hoppiness for nose. Light, clear copper color and a thick, bubbly, white head. Medium bodied and very carbonated. Great sweet flavors and a pleasant hoppy balance that comes in late in the taste and lingers through the finish. An early spring to summer seasonal.

Pierce's Pale Ale   🍺🍺🍺   *Your Ranking* _____

This is a very clean pale ale. No nose. A golden to light copper color with a thick, soft, off-white head. Medium body and smooth. There is a mild, soft, malty start, and the bitterness builds in the finish and continues to stay with you. It might be a little subtle for some pale ale fans, but give it a chance for its smooth, clean, mildly hopped tones. It gets its distinctive aroma and bitterness from East Kent Goldings hops. It is named after town founder Pierce Downer, whose grave you won't find in the Founders' Cemetery across the street, because Pierce was buried on the family farm near his Downers Grove home.

Santa's Little Helper   🍺🍺🍺🍺   *Your Ranking* _____

A full-bodied holiday ale. Aged for a year. Smooth and well balanced. Made with cinnamon, orange, and cloves. A strong malty nose. Dark, translucent deep bronze. A thin, soft, tan head. Full bodied and creamy. Dominated by a caramel malty sweetness. The cinnamon is light and well in the background. The ale finishes with a malty sweetness. You'll find Santa's Little Helper available in the fall beginning around Thanksgiving until just after the holidays. You'd better be good, because this beer should be on your list to Santa!

Scarlett's Raspberry Wheat   🍺🍺   *Your Ranking* _____

A strong raspberry nose. Light yellow and hazy body. A thin, soft, white head. A thin, yet round texture. The sweet fruitiness of raspberries is very dominant from the beginning through the finish. There is a light hint of bitterness in the initial taste, but the raspberry flavor doesn't let much else come through. Fruit beer drinkers will really enjoy the crisp sweetness of this beer.

OTHER FOUNDERS HILL BREWS YOU MAY WANT TO TRY

Blackburn Dopplebock   *Your Ranking* _____

A German-style doppelbock. Strong malty character. A rich copper color and caramel flavor.

Brown Ale   *Your Ranking* _____

An American brown with a thick chocolate flavor. Accented by East Kent Goldings hops.

German Hefe Weizen   *Your Ranking* _____

A traditional German Hefe. Made with a 50-50 mixture of wheat and two-row barley. Very yeasty. Originally brewed to commemorate Founders' fifth anniversary.

Grunder Hugel Oktoberfest *Your Ranking* _____

A Vienna-style lager brewed in the fall. Medium bodied and brilliant orange color.

BREWERY RATING

	Your Rating	Shepard's Rating (1 to 4 Mugs)	General Description
Location		🍺🍺🍺🍺	Central city/community
Ease of Finding Location		🍺🍺🍺🍺	Easy, but requires some planning
Brewery Atmosphere		🍺🍺🍺	Historic, and a family restaurant
Dining Experience		🍺🍺🍺	Family style/variety
The Pint		🍺🍺🍺	A good experience

MENU

Founders Hill has an ambitious menu, not only appealing to a hungry late-night bar crowd but also pleasing those looking for upscale dining. The menu is not extensive, but it does offer a variety of very tempting core dishes. Of the pub style of fare, you'll find that the Founders' Favorites will have a combination of burgers, chicken, grilled vegetables, and the always-favorite "Not Your Mother's Meatloaf" with whipped potatoes, chopped tomato, and Mary Rose sauce. For those looking for a more complete dining experience, Founders offers Lake Superior whitefish, pan-seared swordfish, and North Atlantic salmon. A Meat Lover's section provides a range from Kansas City ribs, smoked pork chops, pot roast, and barbecue chicken breasts. The appetizer menu provides some great options for sharing among friends, with choices such as the Three Way bruschetta, coconut shrimp, crispy calamari, and a combo platter of ribs, onion rings, chicken wings, and beer-battered vegetables with blue cheese and barbecue sauces.

OTHER THINGS TO SEE OR DO IN THE AREA

Downers Grove was settled in 1832 by Vermonter Pierce Downer (after whom Pierce's Pale Ale is named). The Pierce Downer home (4437 Seeley Avenue) is a private residence. Downer was buried on what was part of the family farm (4525 Linscott), but the area is now maintained by the local Park District.

During the pre-Civil War days the community of Downers Grove was a transfer point for the Underground Railroad. More local history is uncovered at the Downers Grove Museum (831 Maple Avenue), which is located in an eleven-room Victorian house that once belonged to the Blodgett family. If you enjoy walking tours and looking at historic homes, the village of Downers Grove has some 150 Sears Catalog Homes that were built between 1908 and World War II. The Downers Grove Visitors Bureau (1-800-934-0615) has a brochure that features photos, floor plans, and addresses, making a very interesting walking tour.

One of the most distinguished buildings of Downers Grove is the Tivoli Theater (5021 Highland Avenue). The Tivoli opened in 1928 as the second theater in the United States to feature sound movies. Despite extensive remodeling, the theater still has its original grand style, and it continues to offer movies and live performances.

Throughout the summer Downers Grove hosts a farmers' market, Friday Night Car Spectacular, and Concerts in the Park. On the last weekend of June the Heritage Festival Street Fair is held. In August the Sports Grand Prix championship races bring some of the world's best cyclists and in-line skaters to town. For a midwinter break, the Ice Sculpture Festival is held for two days at the end of January. Ice carvers from throughout the Midwest compete for prizes in a variety of categories.

Downers Grove has made a commitment to some outstanding public recreational areas. The Belmont Prairie (Haddow Avenue and Cross Street) is a twenty-five-acre site that offers a glimpse of what the Illinois prairies were like. Lyman Woods (33rd Street east of Highland Avenue) offers one and a half miles of marked trail through a 135-acre natural area of oak savanna, prairie, and marshland. If you enjoy golf, the Downers Grove Golf Course (2420 Haddow Avenue) was established in 1892 and is considered the oldest nine-hole course in the nation.

Near Downers Grove you can see an operating waterwheel gristmill at the Graue Mill and Museum (York and Spring Roads, Oak Brook). The Graue Mill also has a museum and authentic Underground Railroad station. Just west of Downers Grove is the nineteenth-century village of Naper Settlement (523 Webster Street, Naperville), where exhibits and docents provide an interpretative look at life from the 1830s to the early 1900s. In nearby Lisle, Station Park (918 Burlington Avenue) is home to a Chicago, Burlington, and Quincy Railroad depot. The station was originally built in 1874; it also has a wooden caboose and an 1830s tavern.

DIRECTIONS

Downers Grove is located about twenty miles west of downtown Chicago. The major intersection of Interstates 88 and 355 is a good landmark to give perspective for where this village is with respect to Greater Chicago. From I-88 take the Highland exit and travel south on Highland, which becomes Main Street in Downers Grove. From I-355, take the Route 34 exit and travel east into Downers Grove, then turn south on Main Street. Founders Hill Restaurant and Brewery is about a mile south of the intersection of Route 34 and Main Street. If approaching from the south, the Lemont Road exit from Interstate 55 will take you north. Watch for Main Street to split off to the east from Lemont (just north of 75th and Lemont). Stay on Main Street to Founders Hill. There is parking on the street and in the parking lot behind the building.

You can save yourself some driving stress by taking the train. A Metra stop is two blocks north of Founders Hill on Main Street. You might consider a two-brewpub pub crawl, because this line also runs to Aurora and lets you off at America's Brewing Company and Walter Payton's Roundhouse.

Glen Ellyn Sports Brew

Glen Ellyn

Visit Date	Signed

ABOUT THE BREWERY

The Glen Ellyn Sports Brew makes exploring Chicago's suburban communities a worthwhile adventure. Formerly known as the Glen Ellyn Brewing Company, the brewpub remodeled to a sports theme in 2003, adding televisions and eliminating the linen tablecloths it was known for as a fine dining restaurant. There is always something new from brewmaster Mike Engelke, who makes more than two dozen beer styles in a year. Engelke likes to brew small batches, so he's known for rotating a lot of beers on his taps.

Despite the interior fourteen-foot ceilings, the bar area is small and intimate. About a dozen barstools line a short bar that has a gorgeous, very large, ornate oak back bar. There are thick brick interior walls and wood accents with large windows that offer views of the street and plenty of ambient light. The main dining room occupies the northern half of the building's ground floor and consists of a large room with a glass-enclosed brewhaus.

Strict visual sign ordinances in Glen Ellyn mean that many of the town storefronts are rather uniform. Glen Ellyn Sports Brew has great exposure at the corner of Main and Duane, but there is limited identification on the building. The brick building's green awnings do stand out above the front door, but you need to look closely to identify the brewpub. The most striking visual evidence of a working brewery is that some of the brewhaus equipment can be seen through the building's corner windows. There is actually a great deal of natural light that filters into the main dining room because of the windows and the reflecting sunlight that bounces off of the stainless steel fermenters and brew kettle.

Glen Ellyn Sports Brew has six or more house beers during most visits. There is usually at least one lager on tap at any time. Root beer, cream soda, and specialty sodas are available. The Glen Ellyn (G. E.) Lite and the Honey Apricot are almost always available and are perhaps the most popular brews. However, the Hefeweizen and Rooftop Smoked Porter are special treats when they are in season. But for a truly great beer, attend a brewmaster's dinner at Glen Ellyn, because it's about the only way you'll get to sample brewmaster Mike Engelke's Devil's Kriek.

HISTORY

Glen Ellyn Sports Brew was established in 1996 as the Glen Ellyn Brewing Company. Like many professional brewers, brewmaster Mike Engelke got his start homebrewing. Mike was part of the "Class of 1996" who completed a Siebel Institute brewing short course, along with Jonathan Cutler (Piece) and Tim Koster (Bent River).

The brewpub has captured some impressive recognition in the Chicago area, voted "Best Brewpub in the Western Suburbs" in 1998 by the DuPage County magazine *Word of Mouth.* In 1999 it won several honors, including recognition from fellow brewpubs in the Chicago Brewpub Shootout, a four-star rating from the *Naperville Sun,* and the designation "Best Brewpub" by *Chicago Magazine.*

Brewpubs often have to overcome many challenges before they are successful, but one that couldn't be planned for was a fire within days of its grand opening. Glen Ellyn opened on June 26, 1996, but four days later, workers making repairs on the roof of the building accidentally caused a rooftop fire that forced the brewery to close its doors. After a month of smoke and water damage repairs, it reopened. This inspired Mike Engelke to make his special Rooftop Smoked Porter that is released every summer to mark the anniversary of the fire and double grand opening.

DON'T MISS THIS

With the sports theme you'll find a number of team logos and banners in Glen Ellyn Sports Brew. Look behind the bar and you'll see several autographed footballs, including ones signed by Barry Sanders and Tony Dungy. Perhaps the most striking visual aspect of Glen Ellyn Sports Brew is the way the brewhaus has been enclosed in its own glass room. There are glass windows exposing views from outside, and glass walls that separate the equipment from the main dining room. There's always a good chance that while you're dining you'll see brewmaster Mike Engelke working on his next batch.

GLEN ELLYN BREWS

Chatterin' Jon's IPA 🍺🍺🍺   *Your Ranking* _____

Strong hoppy nose. Clear, deep golden color and a thin, soft, white head. Medium bodied with a round texture. Strong hoppy bitterness from beginning to end. There are also light hints of fruity bitterness in the finish.

Devil's Kriek 🍺🍺🍺🍺   *Your Ranking* _____

This Kriek-style lambic has a light, crisp fruit filled taste with a firm, not over-powering, tangy cherry nose and finish. A hazy bronze color with a thin, bubbly, reddish-tan head. Medium bodied and very crisp. Some cherry flavor but nicely complemented with a hoppiness. This beer is rarely available over the bar. A special treat of brewer Mike Engelke at his brewmaster's dinners. Mike keeps most of this for special occasions and himself, stating, "If I talked about this beer, I'd have to sell it and there would be less for me!" An exceptional beer.

Diablus Belgian Strong Ale 🍺🍺🍺   *Your Ranking* _____

This is a full-bodied Belgian strong ale. Some assertive fruity tones, especially in the nose and finish. A cloudy, copper to brown color and a thick, soft, brown head. Strong malty flavors are nearly as strong as fruity qualities. You might detect some sweet flavors of banana. A warm finish. The beer menu described this as "Devil's Brew" for its 666 pounds of malt per batch.

Dirty Bird British Bitter 🍺🍺   *Your Ranking* _____

An unfiltered special bitter. Starts with a light floral nose. Copper color and a thick, bubbly, tan head. Medium bodied and highly carbonated. A light sweetness in the beginning with a strong aggressive dryness that builds and builds in the finish. There are some complex flavors in this beer that are interesting; however, it may not be as bitter as some ESB fans would like.

80 Shilling Scottish Ale 🍺🍺🍺   *Your Ranking* _____

An assertive malty nose. Dark copper color with brown highlights. A thick, bubbly, brown head. Medium bodied and round. The mild malty flavors are smooth and semi-sweet with a crisp fruity background. Finishes with a smoky peat earthiness. A smooth Scottish ale with all the right flavors, just a little quiet for fans of this style.

Flander's Belgian Brown 🍺🍺🍺🍺   *Your Ranking* _____

The sweet fruity aromas are strong. Clear, rich copper color and a thin, bubbly, off-white head. Medium bodied and soft texture. Sweet fruity flavors, especially hints of banana, amid the yeasty tones you would expect in a Belgian. A light sour finish.

Glen Ellyn (G. E.) Lite 🍺🍺🍺   *Your Ranking* _____

Lightest of the Glen Ellyn brews. A light smoky nose. Clear light golden color. A thick, soft, white head. Light bodied and crisp. It begins with a light, sharp malty flavor with a mild hop complement in the background that lingers through the finish.

Glen Ellyn Red   *Your Ranking* _____

This Irish-style red ale is one of the flagship beers for the brewpub. Clean, no aroma, and great balance. A deep bronze to amber color with a thick, bubbly, off-white head. Medium bodied and round. A crisp finish that is almost equal in malt and hops qualities.

Golden Apricot   *Your Ranking* _____

One of Glen Ellyn's most popular beers, just not one of my favorites because I'm not that fond of apricots. A strong scent of apricot in the nose. Clear, deep golden color and a thick, soft, white head. Light bodied and soft. Strong sweet apricot flavor that overwhelms most of the beer qualities. If you like sweet fruity beers, this beer is worth a try. If you don't like apricot flavor, better pass.

Hefeweizen   *Your Ranking* _____

An unfiltered German-style wheat beer. Hints of clove in the nose. Cloudy, golden color. A thin, soft, white head. Medium bodied and soft. Strong yeast qualities and banana flavors. Finishes crisp and clean.

Honey Apricot   *Your Ranking* _____

The nose is aggressive with its apricot tones. Clear, deep golden color and a thick, soft, white head. Light bodied and soft. Strong, sweet apricot flavors. Finishes with a slight dryness and smokiness. Not much evidence of honey, except in the roasted finish. A summer seasonal at Glen Ellyn.

IPA   *Your Ranking* _____

Brewmaster Mike Engelke really makes a solid, firm, well-hopped IPA. This beer has great flavor, and there's more than just hops. A strong resiny nose. Clear, deep golden to copper color, but it looks somewhat thick and translucent. A thin, soft, white head. Full bodied. Strong hoppy flavor from beginning to end. A firm malty burst in the middle offers an accent to its aggressive bitterness. It's not over-the-top in hops, just a strong bitter flavor and long-lasting dryness you'll appreciate. This is a great beer for those looking to try an IPA without getting something that the hops totally dominate so that you lose the rest of the beer flavors.

Kolsch   *Your Ranking* _____

Light malty nose. Very clear golden color and a thin, soft, white head. Light bodied and soft texture. Sweet, lightly roasted qualities with a mild hoppiness. Finishes with a lingering sweetness. There are some syrup qualities that are a little confusing to this beer's overall style. It's definitely worth another try when you see it.

Lady Red Ale   *Your Ranking* _____

Considered the flagship of Glen Ellyn Sports Brew. A light malty nose. Amber color with a slight cloudiness. A thick, soft, tan head. Medium bodied and silky. A smooth caramel malty flavor with a firm hoppy accent. Finishes with a slight warmth. Made with seven kinds of malt and three varieties of hops.

Maibock   *Your Ranking* _____

A strong malty nose. Clear copper color. A thick, soft, off-white head. Medium bodied and creamy texture. This German lager has a hearty malty sweetness with caramel tones and a firm hoppy background. There is also some warm bitterness to the ending.

Milky Way Stout 🍺🍺   *Your Ranking* _____
An English-style cream stout. Very strong roasted nose. Dark color with a bronze hue. Thick, soft, tan head. Medium bodied. Rich malty flavors of chocolate malt. A gentle balance with hops, but a fruity sour finish that is overpowering.

Oktoberfest/Vienna 🍺🍺🍺   *Your Ranking* _____
A very crisp clean beer. No nose. Clear copper color with a thin, bubbly, off-white head. Medium to full bodied. Deep rich malt flavors and a subtle hop finish that leaves a very crisp, clean impression.

Pumpkin Ale 🍺🍺   *Your Ranking* _____
A soft, sweet aroma of pumpkin and ginger. Light copper color with a thick, soft, white head. Medium bodied and soft. Strong spicy flavor, especially ginger. Hints of pumpkin and cloves in the finish. This beer was offered in fall 2000, but future appearances are uncertain—just like Linus's Great Pumpkin.

Rooftop Smoked Porter 🍺🍺🍺🍺   *Your Ranking* _____
A strong roasted beginning in the nose. A clear dark ale with bronze tints. A thick, soft, tan head. Full bodied. Strong roasted qualities with a touch of hoppiness. The chocolate and smoky notes of the aroma complement a gentle sweetness of caramel malt. The finish is delicately accented by alder wood smoke flavor. Created to commemorate the fire that damaged the building during its renovation to a brewpub. Released annually around June 26.

Trapp's Belgian Strong 🍺🍺🍺🍺   *Your Ranking* _____
This Trappist-style Belgian ale has a nutty, warm nose. Dark bronze, almost black color and a thick, soft, brown head. Medium to full bodied and very bubbly. Strong sweet caramel flavor. A warm malty finish. Lots of carbonation and yeasty qualities.

Vienna Uber Alles 🍺🍺🍺   *Your Ranking* _____
No nose. Clear, light copper color and a thick, bubbly, tan head. Medium bodied and soft. A smooth malty flavor. This Vienna-style lager is a very clean tasting beer with nice balance.

OTHER GLEN ELLYN BREWS YOU MAY WANT TO TRY

Belgian Wit   *Your Ranking* _____
A Belgian white ale. Light bodied and unfiltered. Spicy tones of coriander and bitter orange peel.

Black Forest Dunkleweizen   *Your Ranking* _____
An unfiltered dark wheat beer with citrus taste, hints of clove and banana. A touch of roastedness.

Czech Pilsner   *Your Ranking* _____
A golden Bohemian Pilsner with noticeable floral aroma. Medium bodied.

Equinox ESB   *Your Ranking* _____
Golden color, unfiltered. The hint of fruity esters complements the well-balanced, imported English hops. Available to celebrate the autumnal equinox.

Flander's Belgian Bronze   *Your Ranking* _____
Unfiltered, medium bodied and spicy.

Kona Stout   *Your Ranking* _____
A rich roasted black stout with smooth creamy texture. Made with Hawaiian Kona coffee.

Little Angel German Alt   *Your Ranking* _____
A deep copper colored German ale. Medium bodied. A complex blend of imported malts and hops with a crisp finish.

Paddy's Irish Stout   *Your Ranking* _____
A dry Irish stout with chocolate tones and some roasted qualities. A gentle, hoppy, bitter finish.

Prospect Park Pale Ale   *Your Ranking* _____
A West Coast-style pale ale. Medium bodied. Made with Cascade hops.

Serenity Now Saison   *Your Ranking* _____
An unfiltered Belgian ale. Golden straw color. Sweetened with honey, lightly hopped, and spiced with coriander.

St. Hubbin's English Ale   *Your Ranking* _____
A medium bodied English bitter. Slightly fruity, moderately hopped, and unfiltered. To be true to style, it is served a little warm.

Winter Warmer Spiced Christmas Ale   *Your Ranking* _____
Made with cranberry, ginger, anise, and chocolate. Full bodied. Often served in an eight-ounce snifter.

BREWERY RATING

	Your Rating	Shepard's Rating (1 to 4 Mugs)	General Description
Location		🍺🍺🍺🍺	Central city/community
Ease of Finding Location		🍺🍺🍺	Difficult; traffic or roads are problematic
Brewery Atmosphere		🍺🍺🍺🍺	Family restaurant
Dining Experience		🍺🍺🍺🍺	Mix of tavern food and fine dining
The Pint		🍺🍺🍺	A good experience

MENU

Glen Ellyn Sports Brew has an impressive menu that is more extensive than that of most sports bars. The roasted garlic and beer nut goat cheese is served on Italian bread for a wonderful starter. Other appetizer choices include crab cakes, calamari, and Brewery bruschetta. On the lighter side, there are several choices of salads, such as a wilted spinach, warm brie and raspberries, sweet apple salad, or just a straightforward house salad. The soup selections offer cheddar and ale or a chef's soup of the day. You can get a burger, but the choice isn't easy among about eight sandwiches, including the Brewhouse Stilton, the Roasted "Porter" Abello mushroom, or the brewery barbecue turkey. Entrees feature steak, pork, fish, poultry, and pastas. The filet mignon is grilled and topped with melted brie over wild mushroom ragout and sautéed spinach. The four-cheese ziti, shrimp fettuccini, chicken and penne pasta, and mixed vegetables complete the pasta menu. There are also nightly specials that have ranged from Tuesday lobster boil to a Friday fish fry. But the perfect finish for the evening is the Brewmaster's Summer Sundae for Two, composed of vanilla and chocolate ice cream, pecans, banana, strawberries, raspberries, chocolate, whipped cream, and a special stout caramel sauce!

OTHER THINGS TO SEE OR DO IN THE AREA

The Glen Ellyn Park District maintains twenty-six parks that cover about three hundred acres of land. The twenty-five-acre Lake Ellyn Park and Lake Ellyn offer fishing, clay tennis courts, walking and jogging paths, and the park hosts special events. Lake Ellyn is eight to ten blocks northeast of Glen Ellyn Sports Brew. In June, Lake Ellyn hosts the Great Cardboard Boat Regatta.

Bicyclists can catch the Illinois Prairie Path, which runs through town on the south side of the Union Pacific tracks. Sunset Park (483 Fairview Avenue) contains ball fields, a playground, and a water park. The Willowbrook Wildlife Center (525 South Park Boulevard at 22nd Street) is a wildlife rehabilitation facility with over ninety species of injured native wild animals on exhibit.

The Hidden Lake Forest Preserve (east side of Route 53, and south of Butterfield Road, Route 56) takes its name from the south lake, which is mostly hidden from view. With nearly four hundred acres it has preserved old oaks, wetlands, and nature trails. The Morton Arboretum (Route 53, north of East/West Tollways, Lisle) is a 1,700-acre outdoor museum that offers examples of plants from around the world.

One of the most visible landmarks is the cupola-topped village hall (Civic Center, 535 Duane Street), and it's just a short walk from Glen Ellyn Sports Brew. The structure originally served as Glen Ellyn's junior high school and then as the fifth- and sixth-grade Duane Street School during the late 1950s.

Stacy's Tavern (557 Geneva Road) is a restored 1840s tavern located at Five Corners. Built in 1846, it originally served as a way station for travelers heading east to Chicago and west to the Fox River. It is now home to the Glen Ellyn Historical Society.

There are as many ongoing as special events in Glen Ellyn. Farmers' markets are held on Fridays from May through October. The local Jaycees help coordinate a village fair in May. Also in May, the annual Taste of Glen Ellyn is held. In July, Glen

Ellyn Brewing's Annual Golf Tournament tees off. The annual Snowflake Ball is held in February, and Pet Parade is held in March.

Glen Ellyn is actually part of a western Chicago "Triangle" of great brewpubs. Within about fifteen minutes of each other, Taylor Brewing, Lunar, and Glen Ellyn Sports Brew all provide unique choices for good food and beer. You might also check those brewpub listings for Other Things to See or Do in the Area.

DIRECTIONS

The most common way to get to Glen Ellyn for out-of-towners is to take Interstate 355 and exit at Roosevelt Road (Route 38) and turn west. About a mile on Route 38, watch for the stoplights and intersection with Main Street, then turn north. It can be a little challenging navigating Glen Ellyn because of the one-way streets.

Glen Ellyn Sports Brew is located in an early 1900s building along the town's main street. The town of Glen Ellyn's Civic Center is a good landmark. The brewery is also just a block off the Metra train stop. There is parking across the street, and if you're lucky enough to find a street meter, you can still park in Glen Ellyn for five cents.

Goose Island Beer Company–Clybourn Avenue
Chicago

Visit Date	Signed

ABOUT THE BREWERY

The company motto, "We celebrate beer, rather than just serving it," really sums up a visit to Goose Island. When one thinks of a Chicago brewery and brewpub, Goose Island is one of the most recognized beer makers in Greater Chicago—and out of state too, for that matter. For those who appreciate good beer, when you inquire around town where to find the perfect pint, and an equally impressive meal, you hardly get the question asked before Goose Island is suggested.

Located in a three-story brick building in Chicago's Clybourn Corridor, a section of the Lincoln Park and DePaul neighborhoods, Goose Island should be given tremendous credit for restoring Chicago's microbrewery industry. Its beginnings in the late 1980s paved the way to show others that brewpubs not only could make it in Chicago—they could thrive. It's therefore fitting that the structure has ties to the city's past brewing industry. The building was once in the heart of a cluster of Chicago's pre-Prohibition breweries. In the early 1900s it was home to a brewery supply company.

You experience a great deal of character and warmth as you enter Goose Island. Interior brick walls have been maintained and carefully accented with wood and soft lighting. Where some building renovation projects would have been tempted to gut the interior, Goose Island has protected the compartmentalization of the structure. You'll find several distinct party rooms, a two-level main dining room, a second-floor mezzanine that doubles as a game room, and a glass-enclosed, greenhouse-style patio and beer garden. The main bar is very large and square. It is set in the middle of a large room, nearly filling the space. From the main bar you can look through glass into the heart of the brewpub's brewery.

Goose Island always has something new and inviting on its beer list. On any one visit you'll find over ten Goose Brews. Among the standards that Goose Island has become known for are the brewery's hoppy flagship beer, Honker's Ale. Other well-known Goose Island beers are the Goose Pils, the Hex Nut Brown Ale, IPA, and Kilgubbin Red Ale. The brewmaster's specials to watch for include the medium-bodied, crisp Oktoberfest and a very special Trappist-style Belgian beer referred to only as Blue! On my discovery of Blue I requested a small taste before ordering. When the bartender sat the sample in front of me he looked right at me and said, "You won't be disappointed, this is a special gift from Mother Goose." Kind of funny, all I could think of was, this must have been how the nursery rhyme "Old King Cole" was inspired, because after a glass of Blue I was indeed a merry old soul. If you remember other Mother Goose rhymes, there are also a few lines in "Old Mother Hubbard" that seem to apply:

> She went to the alehouse
> To get him some beer,
> But when she came back
> The dog sat in a chair.
> She went to the tavern
> For white wine and red,
> But when she came back
> The dog stood on his head.

One recommendation: if you find yourself reciting nursery rhymes, or if you see a dog standing on its head in Goose Island—it's time to go home!

HISTORY

John Hall founded the Goose Island Beer Company in 1988. The original location was here at the Clybourn Avenue brewpub.

Goose Island gets its name from the mile-long Goose Island in the Chicago River, and the neighborhood surrounding it. Over a twenty-year period in the mid-nineteenth century, the artificial island was created from dredging that formed the North Branch Canal. The area around Goose Island became its own neighborhood, known for its Irish immigrant heritage. The Goose Island brewpub is actually part of what is referred to as the Lincoln Park/DePaul neighborhood, which is more or less bounded by Diversey Parkway to the north, Ashland Avenue and the Chicago River to the west, and Lincoln Park itself to the east; its south-southeast border fronts the neighborhood of Old Town Triangle along a diagonal from Armitage Avenue to North Avenue.

John Hall started Goose Island after twenty-one years with Container Corporation of America. John's transition into brewing was literally like a "stroke of lightning." In 1986 John was on a trip when his flight was delayed due to a thunderstorm. As he waited, he picked up an in-flight magazine and became intrigued by an article on boutique beers. As he read, he became even more interested. Two years later he walked away from his executive position and into the brewing business.

His son, Greg, joined the brewery in 1988 as an assistant brewer. Greg says his father didn't play favorites; as assistant brewer Greg earned only minimum wage, and "the people answering the phones made more an hour than I did." While working in the brewery, Greg earned degrees from the U.S. Brewers Academy and Siebel Institute of Technology. He also took time to travel throughout Europe researching brewing techniques. In 1991 Greg became Goose Island's main brewmaster.

Goose Island opened its second brewpub in the Wrigleyville/Lakeview neighborhood (3535 North Clark) in April 1999. Located just a block south of Chicago's historic Wrigley Field, it takes on a sports bar atmosphere. Prior to becoming Goose Island, the building was home to Weeghman Park Restaurant and Brewery.

Each of Goose Island's brewpubs has its own brewing facilities, but the company's main brewing and bottling is done at 1800 West Fulton Street. This facility was opened in November 1995, and within a year the expanded brewery operations pushed Goose Island into the regional microbrewery market with an annual production of over 24,000 thousand barrels. In the fall of 1997 Goose Island began producing the classic Bohemian-style Pilsner, Baderbrau. In 1998 Baderbrau Vienna Style Lager was added to the brewery's portfolio. By 2003 total production at Goose Island topped 100,000 barrels per year. Also, in 1997 Goose Island began making craft-brewed soda with Goose Island Root Beer and Orange Cream Soda.

DON'T MISS THIS

Goose Island–Clybourn Avenue has several different rooms in which you can enjoy a meal or party. In the main dining room, look around on the walls at the old photos. On the south wall there is a photo of the construction of Soldier Field. Another is that of an Atlas Prager horse-drawn beer wagon on the streets of Chicago. On the west wall there is a touch of Chicago brewing history, with a Fox Deluxe Beer sign showing the beers of the day, which included Fox Deluxe, Atlas Prager, Edelweiss, and Monarch. Interestingly, the sign also lists a few out-of-town beers, which included Wisconsin's old giant breweries such as Blatz, Pabst, Schlitz, and Fox Head 400 (the latter, a Waukesha brewery, is believed to have once had ties to Chicago's organized crime bosses).

GOOSE ISLAND–CLYBOURN BREWS

Blonde Ale   🍺🍺   *Your Ranking* _____
The lightest of the Goose Island beers. A light malty nose. Clear golden color and a thick, soft, white head. Medium bodied and a soft texture. Mild hoppy flavor with hints of sweetness in the background. A light, mild, dry finish. Brewed with pale and wheat malts. A pleasant floral nose due to liberal use of Mt. Hood hops. A gold medal winner at the 1999 Great American Beer Festival.

Blue   🍺🍺🍺🍺   *Your Ranking* _____
This Belgian Trappist-style ale has lots of flavor and unique character. A musty nose. Very dark bronze color and a thin, soft, tan head. Full-bodied, silky tex-

ture with a warmth from the initial sip. Strong, pronounced malty flavor. Very warm and earthy finish. This is Goose Island's interpretation of a Chimay Grand Resérve, served in a goblet. When one is pressed to pick an overall favorite Illinois beer, Blue makes the list of exceptional beers.

Demolition 1800 Ale 🍺🍺🍺🍺 Your Ranking _____

A golden strong ale. A light, subtle, hoppy nose. Deep golden color and highly carbonated. A thin, bubbly, white head. Creamy texture. Bitter strength throughout. A smooth, warm finish. Brewed with Saaz and Styrian Goldings hops at thirty pounds per ten-barrel batch. Served in a goblet.

Dorset Bitter 🍺🍺🍺 Your Ranking _____

An English-style best bitter. No nose. Rich copper color. A thick, soft, tan head. Medium and very soft. A firm, constant bitter flavor with some caramel malt balance. A light fruity finish. This beer was served as a cask-conditioned ale and made an excellent companion to a mushroom and Swiss burger.

Dublin Stout 🍺🍺 Your Ranking _____

A light roasted nose. Very dark black color with a thin, soft, creamy tan head. Medium to full bodied and soft. A light roasted flavor with a bitter background and finish. Some strong flavors with a slight dominance of roastedness.

Dunkel Munich Lager 🍺🍺🍺🍺 Your Ranking _____

A dark lager beer in the Munchener style. A light roasted coffee aroma in the beginning. Dark color and a thin, bubbly, brown head. Medium to full bodied and soft texture. A smoky, chocolate body. Roasted finish. This beer's long aging period helps provide smooth body and balance. This is a great beer to enjoy at the bar while waiting for friends to join you before having a meal at Goose Island. It has great flavor; just don't let it seduce you into too many—you might not have room for dinner!

Goose Pils 🍺🍺🍺🍺 Your Ranking _____

No nose. A clear, light golden color and thick, soft, white head. Medium bodied and soft texture. A soft, constantly building hoppiness. Finishes with dryness. Made with Czech Slovenian hops. A silver medal winner at the 2002 Great American Beer Festival. Available in bottles.

Hex Nut Brown Ale 🍺🍺🍺🍺 Your Ranking _____

A full-bodied English brown ale. A malty nose with a light coffee background. Dark brown color and a thick, bubbly head. Medium bodied and sharp. A strong malty body with a hoppy balance. Finishes with a sweet nuttiness. Overall, slightly more sweet than bitter. A great beer, and even better when you have the choice of a cask-conditioned version. Available in bottles.

Honker's Ale 🍺🍺🍺🍺 Your Ranking _____

Goose Island's flagship beer. Almost no nose, just a light floral aroma that requires concentration to find. A reddish golden color and a thick, creamy, off-white head. Medium bodied and soft. A firm bitterness dominates over a smooth caramel background. Made with pale, wheat, and caramel malts with a touch of barley. Honker's unique flavor comes from Styrian Goldings hops. A gold medal winner in the 1994 and 1995 World Beer Championships and the 1997 Great American Beer Festival. Available in bottles.

Hopscotch Ale　🍺🍺🍺　　　　　　　*Your Ranking* _____

A light hoppy nose. Clear copper color and a thin, soft, white head. Medium bodied and very bubbly texture. Strong hoppy firmness. A dry and smoky finish. One of Goose Island's most popular seasonal beers, usually found in mid- to late winter.

India Pale Ale　🍺🍺🍺　　　　　　　*Your Ranking* _____

Strong hoppy nose. A clear, deep golden color. Thick, soft, white head. Full bodied. Strong bitter flavor. Dry and smooth from the beginning through the finish. Made with Centennial, Fuggles, and Cascade hops. Watch for this beer on draft—especially at Goose Island on Clybourn Avenue. It is also available in bottles.

Kilgubbin Red Ale　🍺🍺🍺　　　　　　*Your Ranking* _____

No nose. A cloudy amber color and a thin, soft, tan head. Medium bodied and round. A burst of hoppiness in the beginning, giving in to malty dominance. No finish. A clean, crisp beer. Most often found around St. Patrick's Day. Available in bottles. Kilgubbin is the Gaelic name for the Goose Island neighborhood.

Lincoln Park Lager　🍺🍺🍺　　　　　　*Your Ranking* _____

A light hoppy nose. Clear, reddish amber color and a thin, very soft, off-white head. Medium bodied and soft texture. A malty start with a light hoppy background and floral finish. This Vienna-style lager is offered in February to mark Abe Lincoln's birthday.

Nelson Algren Alt Beer　🍺🍺🍺　　　　　*Your Ranking* _____

No nose. A cloudy copper color and a creamy, white head. Light to medium bodied. A mildly hoppy beer. A crisp bitter finish. Brewed with Northern Brewer, Mt. Hood, Saaz, and Tettnang hops. Named for famed Chicago author of *Walk on the Wild Side, Somebody in Boots,* and *Never Come Morning.*

Oktoberfest　🍺🍺🍺　　　　　　　　*Your Ranking* _____

A lager with a vivid reddish copper color and a thick, bubbly, tan head. Medium bodied and round texture. Smooth caramel start with a crisp hoppy background. A mildly bitter finish. A crisp, clean Oktoberfest brewed for the fall. Available in bottles.

Robert Burns Scottish Ale　🍺🍺🍺　　　*Your Ranking* _____

The nose is sweet, malty, and even earthy. Dark reddish copper color and a thin, bubbly, off-white head. Full bodied and round texture. Malty tones really stand out and emphasize the smooth qualities of this beer. The finish is a mild dryness, but not really that hoppy because the strong malty qualities continue to linger. Brewed with pale, caramel, and peat smoked malt for earthy aroma and finish. Made to celebrate the poet's birthday of January 25, 1759.

Summertime Kolsch Bier 🍺🍺   *Your Ranking* _____

A slightly fruity nose with hints of sourness. A cloudy light yellow to straw color and a thin, soft, white head. Light bodied and creamy. Some fruity tones in the beginning before the hops eventually win the flavor contest. Finishes with a mild, earthy bitterness. Goose Island says the secret to this beer is the temperamental yeast strain, which makes life difficult for the brewers but makes the results a refreshing beer for you. This beer won a gold medal at the 2002 Great American Beer Festival.

XXX Porter 🍺🍺🍺   *Your Ranking* _____

This porter has loads of flavor and a strong bitterness. A light floral nose. Deep dark and bronze hues. A thin, soft, tan head. Full bodied and round texture. A strong malty start, but the hops come in loud and strong. Finishes bitter and dry. This beer offers assertive flavor, texture, and finish.

OTHER GOOSE ISLAND–CLYBOURN BREWS YOU MAY WANT TO TRY

Christmas Ale   *Your Ranking* _____

This beer began as a different ale each year to celebrate the winter holidays. But the recipe has become refined to a Belgian with deep garnet color and rich malty flavor. It has also picked up a couple gold medals from the World Beer Championships.

Dunkel Weizenbock   *Your Ranking* _____

A Bavarian-style wheat beer with strong clove and banana flavors. A rich malty middle and finish. Brewed with pale, wheat, caramel, and chocolate malts and Saaz hops. Served in a goblet.

Extra Special Bitter (ESB)   *Your Ranking* _____

Brewed with nineteen pounds of hops per batch. Bittered with Northern Brewer and finished with Fuggle and Goldings for a full hops aroma and a long hoppy finish. Matched with a blend of four malts to create a rich, sweet, full-bodied beer.

Fest Ale   *Your Ranking* _____

A deep golden beer with strong malt character. Made for Goosefest and the music that brings the Goose to flight! Pale and Munich malts are used for flavor and body.

Hefeweizen   *Your Ranking* _____

This unfiltered, Bavarian-style wheat beer is brewed with 50 percent wheat malt and German yeast.

Oatmeal Stout   *Your Ranking* _____

A black, ruby color and a creamy tan head. Smooth, creamy middle with a long, oily finish. Made with roasted and black barley. Available in bottles.

Old Aberration Barley Wine   *Your Ranking* _____

Also known as Old Abe. Goose Island's original barley wine, available as a winter seasonal.

Pagan Porter   *Your Ranking* _____

Contains Centennial hops and Maris Otter English-style malts. A subtle licorice taste and rich dark color.

Pilgrim Pale Ale   *Your Ranking* _____

Golden color. A medium bodied pale ale. Brewed with Willamette hops.

Red Felt Ale   *Your Ranking* _____

Bitter flavor and finish stand out. Brewed with Amarillo, Cascade, and Columbus American hops. The name refers to the red felt pool tables at Goose Island–Clybourn Avenue.

Rotweizen   *Your Ranking* _____

A red wheat beer. Made with caramel malt to be a bit sweeter and fermented with German weizen yeast. Brewed for summer.

Schwarz Lager   *Your Ranking* _____

A dark German lager. Made with German roasted barley for a smooth character and color.

Smoked Porter   *Your Ranking* _____

Goose Island smokes its pale malt over cherry wood in its own kitchen to create this beer with a smoky finish. Watch for this beer when served cask conditioned. This beer also goes by the name Q.

Sticke Ale   *Your Ranking* _____

This is a special, rare, Alt-style beer. Described by some as an Alt-Bock style. It's brewed as an occasional treat. For the purist, this style is unique to the area around Düsseldorf, Germany, and served there in the traditional manner from wooden casks and a gravity feed. *Sticke* roughly translates to "secret." The local pubs around Düsseldorf don't advertise its availability; rather, they merely hang a sign outside the pub that says "Tomorrow Sticke." Wait for the sign to go up at Goose Island–Clybourn Avenue; you won't be disappointed.

BREWERY RATING

	Your Rating	Shepard's Rating (1 to 4 Mugs)	General Description
Location		🍺🍺🍺🍺	Entertainment district
Ease of Finding Location		🍺🍺🍺	Easy, but requires some planning
Brewery Atmosphere		🍺🍺🍺🍺	Family tavern Sports
Dining Experience		🍺🍺🍺🍺	Family style/variety
The Pint		🍺🍺🍺🍺	A perfect experience

MENU

Goose Island's menu features a number of hearty entrees, burgers, sandwiches, and salads. The appetizer choices offer the basic Goose Fries, onion strings, potato skins, quesadillas, Maryland crab cake, and fresh baked pretzels that are matched with Düsseldorf mustard and garlic cheddar cheese spread. Goose Island offers a half-dozen salads that include versions of the house Goose Island salad, a farmers' market, Caesar, Cobb, Asian chicken, and crispy chicken. There are about a dozen burgers to choose from. The most basic is the pub burger served on an onion roll. The Clybourn melt is topped with cheddar cheese, beer onions, and thousand-island dressing and served on marble rye bread. The Legendary Stilton burger is a half-pound of black pepper-crusted ground beef grilled and topped with roasted garlic cloves, English Stilton cheese, and Düsseldorf mustard. Among the main dishes, from which it is difficult to pick a favorite, is the home-style meatloaf, which is served with mashed potatoes, mushroom gravy, and the chef's vegetables. On one visit the chef's vegetables were steamed broccoli and asparagus, which matched perfectly with meatloaf and a XXX Porter. Other entrees include shepherd's pie, shrimp and penne pasta, and jambalaya. On Friday's the special is fish and chips, which feature Honker's Ale-battered walleye and Goose Fries. There is also a late night menu, an abbreviated list of burgers and appetizers. Finishing the meal is another tough choice between the Oatmeal Stout cheesecake and Minnie's black velvet cake.

OTHER THINGS TO SEE OR DO IN THE AREA

You might consider theater when in the Goose Island area. The Apollo Theater Center (2540 North Lincoln Avenue) is one of the oldest commercial theaters in Chicago. The 350-seat auditorium brings in big-budget productions of off-Broadway shows. If you're looking for that costume you saw in the play, or that perfect Halloween getup, the Chicago Costume Company (1120 West Fullerton Avenue) sells everything from monsters to tutus. By the way, nearby the Chicago Historical Society (1601 North Clark Street) houses one of the nation's largest nineteenth-century women's costume collections, along with architectural records and artifacts from the Great Chicago Fire.

The Steppenwolf Theatre (1650 North Halsted Street) is a regional theater that has produced such acting talent as John Malkovich, Laurie Metcalf, and Gary Sinise. Second City (1616 North Wells) was a nightclub founded in the late 1950s by a small group of theater lovers. Second City gained its name from a 1950s profile of Chicago published in *The New Yorker*. It helped a number of struggling actors become big names today, including Alan Arkin, Ed Asner, Robert Klein, Shelley Long, Jerry Stiller, Robin Williams, and *Saturday Night Live* alums Dan Aykroyd, Bill Murray, and John Belushi.

The Red Lion (2446 North Lincoln Avenue) is a favorite English pub in the neighborhood. It claims to be haunted by a man and a woman whose voices are occasionally heard near the bar. The name Red Lion isn't exactly original; it is a very popular public house name in Britain dating back to the fourteenth and fifteenth centuries, when the rulers in power demanded the red lion of Scotland be displayed in public places throughout England. The Biograph Theater (2433 North Lincoln Avenue) is where gangster John Dillinger was shot by the FBI after seeing the movie *Manhattan Melodrama* on the evening of July 22, 1934.

DePaul University (Fullerton Avenue, between Halsted and Clifton) was established in 1898. Today this Catholic university covers about twenty-five acres in the area and also has a downtown Chicago campus.

One of my favorite places for a walk is Oz Park (intersection of Larrabee, Geneva, and Lincoln). A brief stroll will bring you face-to-face with the Tin Man and the Cowardly Lion. Oz Park was named in honor of Frank Baum, author of *The Wizard of Oz,* who once lived in Chicago.

For local festivals and events, in late July, north of Goose Island–Clybourn Avenue, the Taste of Lincoln Avenue (Lincoln Avenue between Fullerton Parkway and Wrightwood Avenue) is an annual street festival. If you're around in August, the annual Goose Island Fest occurs just west of the brewpub (1800 North Kingsbury from Willow to Wisconsin).

Lincoln Park, on the shores of Lake Michigan (directly east of Goose Island), is the largest park in Chicago, with almost six miles of lakefront. One of the park's highlights is the Lincoln Park Zoo (2200 North Cannon Drive). The Farm-in-the-Zoo is a replica of a working prairie farm and features hands-on exhibits for kids, the South Pond offers some great paddle boating, the Lester Fisher Great Ape House contains more than forty gorillas, the Kovler Lion House is home to endangered and threatened species, the Robert McCormick Bear and Wolf Habitat features a 250,000-gallon polar bear pool, and the Rookery is an urban refuge for migrating birds. The Peggy Notebaert Nature Museum of the Chicago Academy of Sciences (2430 North Cannon Drive) offers a variety of permanent exhibitions that show the relationship between the environment and people.

Numerous statues in Lincoln Park might make a fun game of "can you find them," including the Standing Lincoln, Storks at Play, William Shakespeare, and Hans Christian Andersen. If you think you see a mausoleum in the park, you probably have. A wrought-iron fence surrounds the Couch family tomb. The Ira Couch family took their case all the way to the state Supreme Court to stop the mausoleum from being removed. Lincoln Park was once a cemetery. Only the Couch tomb and another grave, that of David Kennison, who took part in the Boston Tea Party, remain on the grounds today.

The area around Goose Island and the Clybourn Corridor has been home to several breweries, many of which died with Prohibition. A driving tour of the area will offer a few relics of this once thriving industry. In his book *The History of Beer and Brewing in Chicago 1833–1978,* Bob Skilnik identifies the Independent Brewing Association as operating a brewery in the 821–825 blocks of West Blackhawk. The brewery ran from 1915 to 1920, then during Prohibition it became known as the Primalt Products Company. In the 1930s Primalt merged with Bismark Brewing Company, which operated until 1941. The West Side Brewery Company operated between 1890 and 1919 in the 900 block of North Paulina; the Pfeifer's Berlin Weiss Beer Company was in business from 1892 to 1909 at 718–742 North Leavitt Street; and the City Brewery Company operated under several names, including Francis J. Dewes, from 1882 to 1906 at 764 West Chicago Avenue. Brand Brewing Company was in existence from 1899 to 1935 at 2530 Elston Avenue. The Brand Brewing building was also home to another short-lived brewery, the Golden Prairie Brewery, which operated in the 1990s. Just north of the Brand Brewery was the Home Brewery at 1654 West Elston Avenue, which began in 1910 and closed in 1920.

DIRECTIONS

Exit Interstates 90/94 (Kennedy Expressway) at North Avenue (Route 64) and turn east. After about one mile, turn left on Sheffield. Two blocks north, Sheffield intersects with Willow, where you will turn left. Goose Island will be directly in front of you at the intersection of Willow and North Marcey Street. Goose Island is also near the CTA Red Line (North/Clybourn stop).

Goose Island Beer Company–Wrigleyville
Chicago

Visit Date	Signed

ABOUT THE BREWERY

Although I like sports, ordinarily I'm just not a big fan of sports bars. But Goose Island–Wrigleyville is a compliment to sports bars, offering a vibrant atmosphere without being loud and full of cheap beers and televisions. As you would expect, being less than a city block from Wrigley Field, you'll get a strong dose of baseball. There are painted murals and photos of baseball superstars throughout the two-story brick warehouse-type building. There are even a number of televisions, a couple of large-screen ones, and a stage area for live entertainment. But the mahogany bar, the high ceiling with its open beams, the behind-glass brewery, and the large windows that expose Clark Street all seem to really make Goose Island dispel the noisy, crowded sports bar image.

There are actually two bars on the main floor of Goose Island. During most afternoons you'll find that the focus of the brewpub is up front, near the entryway, where the dining room is on two levels and a number of tables look through those picture windows to the intersection of Clark and Eddy Streets. There are large, green leather booths, hanging lights, and a wooden parquet floor that complement the copper light from the brewhaus. Deeper into the brewpub, there is a second dining area, with a large-screen television and a huge painted mural of baseball greats.

There is a second floor to Goose Island–Wrigleyville. Upstairs you'll find more quiet party rooms and additional fermentation tanks and beer storage. Outside, to the north of the building, there is an area between the buildings that serves as a beer garden, and you can only imagine how busy it is on Cub game day!

Goose Island often has over ten Goose Brews for any visit. The sampler trays are big-sized beers, served in wine glasses. Among the common offerings that Goose Island has become known for include the brewery's hoppy flagship beer, Honker's Ale. Other well-known Goose Island beers are the Goose Pils, the Hex Nut Brown Ale, IPA, and Kilgubbin Red Ale. The brewmaster's specials to watch for include the medium bodied, crisp Oktoberfest and the Wrigleyville Wheat. But to borrow a baseball metaphor, the strong Belgian ale called Trippel Play is "out of the park" compared to other beers.

HISTORY

Goose Island–Wrigleyville was the second brewpub in the Goose Island family. It opened in April 1999. Located just a block south of Chicago's historic Wrigley Field, it takes on a sports bar atmosphere, and inside, some of those baseball greats are featured in photos and murals. Prior to becoming Goose Island, the building was home to Weeghman Park Restaurant and Brewery, which was rather short lived, closing in 1999 and turning over most of its equipment to Goose Island. Wrigley Field was once called Weeghman Park.

John Hall started the Goose Island Beer Company in 1988, after twenty-one years with Container Corporation of America. The Goose Island Brewpub on Clybourn Avenue in Lincoln Park was the company's original location. Goose Island's Fulton Street brewery operations were added in 1995.

John's transition into brewing was literally like a "stroke of lightning." In 1986 John was on a trip when his flight was delayed due to a thunderstorm. As he waited, he picked up an in-flight magazine and became intrigued by an article on boutique beers. As he read, he became even more interested. Two years later he walked away from his executive position and into the brewing business.

His son, Greg, joined the brewery in 1988 as an assistant brewer. Greg says his father didn't play favorites; as assistant brewer Greg earned only minimum wage, and "the people answering the phones made more an hour than I did." While working in the brewery, Greg earned degrees from the U.S. Brewers Academy and Siebel Institute of Technology. He also took time to travel throughout Europe researching brewing techniques. In 1991 Greg became Goose Island's main brewmaster.

Each of Goose Island's brewpubs has its own brewing facilities, but the company's main brewing and bottling is done at 1800 West Fulton Street. This facility opened in November 1995, and within a year the expanded brewery operations pushed Goose Island into the regional microbrewery market with an annual production of over 24,000 barrels. In the fall of 1997 Goose Island began producing the classic Bohemian-style Pilsner, Baderbrau. In 1998 Baderbrau Vienna Style Lager was added to the brewery's portfolio. By 2003 total production at Goose Island topped 100,000 barrels per year. Also, in 1997 Goose Island began making craft-brewed soda with Goose Island Root Beer and Orange Cream Soda.

Goose Island gets its name from the mile-long Goose Island in the Chicago River between North Avenue, Halsted Street, and Elston Avenue.

Over a twenty-year period in the mid-nineteenth century, the artificial island was created from dredging that formed the North Branch Canal. The area around Goose Island became its own neighborhood, known for its Irish immigrant heritage (the Irish called it Kilgubbin).

DON'T MISS THIS

With Goose Island–Wrigleyville's proximity to Wrigley Field there are some obvious ties to baseball in the pub's decor. As you walk around, be sure to notice the black-and-white photos of former Chicago Cubs players as well as other baseball legends. You'll find the likenesses of Bob Feller, Lefty Grove, Dizzy Dean, Paul Dean, Mel Ott, Riggs Stephenson, Gabby Hartnett, Bill Herman and his son, Lou Boudreau, and Mickey Mantle. Near the main door there is a large mural of "Mr. Cub," Ernie Banks. Cub fans remember Banks as the ballplayer who said, "What a great day for baseball. Let's play two!" That would make a good beer motto for Goose Island–Wrigleyville.

GOOSE ISLAND–WRIGLEYVILLE BREWS

Blonde Ale   *Your Ranking* _____
The lightest of the Goose Island beers. A light malty nose. Clear golden color and a thick, soft, white head. Medium bodied and a soft texture. Mild hoppy flavor with hints of sweetness in the background. A light mild dry finish. Brewed with pale and wheat malts. A pleasant floral nose due to liberal use of Mt. Hood hops. A gold medal winner at the 1999 Great American Beer Festival.

Dopplebock   *Your Ranking* _____
A strong, assertive malty nose. Dark brown and hazy color. A thick, bubbly, brown head. Full bodied. Strong caramel sweetness and a smooth, sweet background. Finishes with warmth and a mild bitterness. There seems to be a smoky accent that builds after several sips of this beer. It's best described as flavorful, smooth, and warm.

Dortmunder Pils   *Your Ranking* _____
Not much nose, just a light maltiness. A deep golden color and subtle bitterness from the use of Saaz hops. Full bodied with a bittersweet finish.

Dunkel Munich Lager   *Your Ranking* _____
A dark lager beer in the Munchener style. A light roasted coffee aroma in the beginning. Dark color and a thin, bubbly, brown head. Medium to full bodied and soft texture. A smoky, chocolate body. Roasted finish. This beer's long aging period helps provide smooth body and balance.

Goose Pils   *Your Ranking* _____
No nose. A clear, light golden color and thick, soft, white head. Medium bodied and soft texture. A soft, constantly building hoppiness. Finishes with dryness. Made with Czech Slovenian hops. A silver medal winner at the 2002 Great American Beer Festival. Available in bottles.

Hex Nut Brown Ale   🍺🍺🍺🍺   *Your Ranking* _____

A full-bodied English brown ale. A malty nose with a light coffee background. Dark brown color and a thick, bubbly head. Medium bodied and sharp. A strong malty body with a hoppy balance. Finishes with a sweet nuttiness. Overall, slightly more sweet than bitter. A great beer, and even better when you have the choice of a cask-conditioned version. Available in bottles.

Honker's Ale   🍺🍺🍺🍺   *Your Ranking* _____

Goose Island's flagship beer. Almost no nose, just a light floral aroma that requires concentration to find. A reddish golden color and a thick, creamy, off-white head. Medium bodied and soft. A firm bitterness dominates over a smooth caramel background. Made with pale, wheat, and caramel malts with a touch of barley. Honker's unique flavor comes from Styrian Goldings hops. A gold medal winner in the 1994 and 1995 World Beer Championships and the 1997 Great American Beer Festival. Available in bottles.

India Pale Ale   🍺🍺🍺   *Your Ranking* _____

Strong hoppy nose. A clear, deep golden color. Thick, soft, white head. Full bodied. Strong bitter flavor. Dry and smooth from the beginning through the finish. Made with Centennial, Fuggles, and Cascade hops. Watch for this beer on draft—especially at Goose Island on Clybourn Avenue. It is also available in bottles.

Kilgubbin Red Ale   🍺🍺🍺   *Your Ranking* _____

No nose. A cloudy amber color and a thin, soft, tan head. Medium bodied and round. A burst of hoppiness in the beginning then it gives in to malty dominance. No finish. A clean, crisp beer. Most often found around St. Patrick's Day. Available in bottles. Kilgubbin is the Gaelic name for the Goose Island neighborhood a few blocks south of Goose Island–Wrigleyville.

Maduro   🍺🍺🍺   *Your Ranking* _____

A strong, full-bodied brown ale. Roasted nose. Dark, reddish color and a thick, soft, white head. Malty and clean taste and dry bitter finish. Brewed with seven different malts. Complex and lightly hopped for balance.

Oktoberfest   🍺🍺🍺   *Your Ranking* _____

A lager with a vivid reddish copper color and a thick, bubbly, tan head. Medium bodied and round texture. Smooth caramel start with a crisp hoppy background. A mildly bitter finish. A crisp, clean Oktoberfest brewed for the fall. Available in bottles.

Summertime Kolsch Bier   🍺🍺   *Your Ranking* _____

A slightly fruity nose with hints of sourness. A cloudy light yellow to straw color and a thin, soft, white head. Light bodied and creamy. Some fruity tones in the beginning before the hops eventually win the flavor contest. Finishes with a mild, earthy bitterness. Goose Island says the secret to this beer is the temperamental yeast strain, which makes life difficult for the brewers but makes the results a refreshing beer for you. This beer won a gold medal at the 2002 Great American Beer Festival.

Trippel Play 🍺🍺🍺🍺   *Your Ranking* _____

A light, sweet, fruity nose. Copper color and hazy. A thick, soft, off-white head. Full bodied and very soft. Sweet, malty flavor with a gentle, spicy background. Warm and malty finish. This is similar in malty flavors to a smooth, lighter version of a Scotch ale. Great candy sweetness. A unique, flavorful beer that is served in a tulip glass. This strong Belgian ale is made at Goose Island–Wrigleyville.

Wrigleyville Wheat 🍺🍺   *Your Ranking* _____

This American-style wheat has a light malty nose. Light golden to deep yellow color. A thick, soft, white head. Light bodied and soft texture. Dominated by a grainy, malty flavor. Finishes with a light hoppiness. Smooth texture and mild malty tones stand out, but the strength of the sweetness is a little distracting.

XXX Porter 🍺🍺🍺🍺   *Your Ranking* _____

This porter has loads of flavor and a strong bitterness. A light floral nose. Deep dark and bronze hues. A thin, soft, tan head. Full bodied and round texture. A strong malty start, but the hops come in loud and strong. Finishes bitter and dry. This beer offers assertive flavor, texture, and finish.

OTHER GOOSE ISLAND–WRIGLEYVILLE BREWS YOU MAY WANT TO TRY

Christmas Ale   *Your Ranking* _____

This beer began as a different ale each year to celebrate the winter holidays. But the recipe has become refined to a Belgian with deep garnet color and rich malty flavor. It has also picked up a couple gold medals from the World Beer Championships.

Dunkel Weizenbock   *Your Ranking* _____

A Bavarian-style wheat beer with strong clove and banana flavors. A rich malty middle and finish. Brewed with pale, wheat, caramel, and chocolate malts and Saaz hops. Served in a goblet.

Extra Special Bitter (ESB)   *Your Ranking* _____

Brewed with nineteen pounds of hops per batch. Bittered with Northern Brewer and finished with Fuggle and Goldings for a full hops aroma and a long hoppy finish. Matched with a blend of four malts to create a rich, sweet, full-bodied beer.

Fest Ale   *Your Ranking* _____

A deep golden beer with strong malt character. Made for Goosefest and the music that brings the Goose to flight! Pale and Munich malts are used for flavor and body.

Hefeweizen   *Your Ranking* _____

This unfiltered, Bavarian-style wheat beer is brewed with 50 percent wheat malt and German yeast.

Oatmeal Stout   *Your Ranking* _____

A black, ruby color and a creamy tan head. Smooth, creamy middle with a long-lasting, oily finish. Made with roasted and black barley. Available in bottles.

Pilgrim Pale Ale   *Your Ranking* _____

Golden color. A medium bodied pale ale. Brewed with Willamette hops.

Rotweizen   *Your Ranking* _____

A red wheat beer. Made with caramel malt to be a bit sweeter and fermented with German weizen yeast. Brewed for summer.

Schwarz Lager   *Your Ranking* _____

A dark German lager. Made with German roasted barley for a smooth character and color.

Smoked Porter   *Your Ranking* _____

Goose Island smokes its pale malt over cherry wood in its own kitchen to create this beer with its smoky finish. Watch for this beer when served cask conditioned. This beer also goes by the name Q.

Sticke Ale   *Your Ranking* _____

This is a special, rare, Alt-style beer. Described by some as an Alt-Bock style. It's brewed as an occasional treat. For the purist, this style is unique to the area around Düsseldorf, Germany, and served there in the traditional manner from wooden casks and a gravity feed. Sticke roughly translates to "secret." The local pubs around Düsseldorf don't advertise its availability; rather, they merely hang a sign outside the pub that says "Tomorrow Sticke."

BREWERY RATING

	Your Rating	Shepard's Rating (1 to 4 Mugs)	General Description
Location		🍺🍺🍺🍺	Entertainment district
Ease of Finding Location		🍺🍺🍺	Easy, but requires some planning
Brewery Atmosphere		🍺🍺🍺	Sports
Dining Experience		🍺🍺🍺	Family style/variety
The Pint		🍺🍺🍺	A good experience

MENU

Goose Island's menu features a number of hearty entrees, burgers, sandwiches. and salads. The Wrigleyville brewpub seems to place a little more emphasis on daily burger and sandwich specials than its sister location on Clybourn Avenue. The appetizer choices offer the basic Goose Fries, onion strings, potato skins, quesadillas, Maryland crab cake, and fresh baked pretzels that are matched with Düsseldorf mustard and garlic cheddar cheese spread. You can actually select cheddar jalapeño, parmesan, or classic Bavarian pretzel styles. On one quiet afternoon a friend and I ordered a basket of all three, and they were nearly a meal for both of us. I suggest taking a group if you order the sample basket! Goose Island offers a half-dozen salads that include versions of the house Goose Island salad, a farmers' market, Caesar, Cobb, Asian chicken, and crispy chicken. There are about a dozen burgers to choose from. The most basic is the pub burger served on an onion roll. Reggie's Home Run burger is a half-pound burger mixed with serrano chilis and cilantro and topped with pepperjack cheese. The Legendary Stilton burger is a half-pound of black pepper-crusted ground beef grilled and topped with roasted garlic cloves, English Stilton cheese, and Düsseldorf mustard. Among the main dishes is the home-style meatloaf, which is served with mashed potatoes, mushroom gravy, and the chef's vegetables. Other entrees include shepherd's pie, shrimp and penne pasta, and jambalaya. Finishing the meal is another tough choice between the Oatmeal Stout cheesecake and Minnie's black velvet cake.

OTHER THINGS TO SEE OR DO IN THE AREA

Wrigleyville, as you would expect, refers to the area surrounding Wrigley Field, the home of the Chicago Cubs. It's part of a larger neighborhood called Lakeview and the area supports many other restaurants, bars, and shops.

The Lakeview/Wrigleyville neighborhood is roughly bordered by Irving Park Road on the north, Diversey Parkway on the south, Ashland Avenue on the west, and North Lake Shore Drive to the east. Lakeview began as a settlement where farmers grew vegetables and flowers through much of the mid-nineteenth century. While wealthy Chicagoans built their homes along the lake, working-class families built more affordable homes in this area. By the 1880s the German saloons and beer gardens and even Schlitz Brewing Company taverns emerged in this area. By the early twentieth century there were more than fifty Schlitz-tied houses in Chicago, and many were in what is now Lakeview. Schubas Tavern (3159 North Southport Avenue) is one of those early Schlitz saloons. Built in 1900, the two-story brick building has one of the most evident examples of brewery-related history, with a Schlitz globe high above on its front windows.

Wrigley Field (1060 West Addison Street) was built in 1914 and was originally called Weeghman Park, after Charles Henry Weeghman, the owner of the Federal League's Chicago Whales. When the team folded, Weeghman purchased the Cubs and moved them to his ball field. Chewing gum magnate William Wrigley bought the team in 1926, and the park's name was changed. Afternoon games are truly special at Wrigley Field.

Wrigley's home (2446 North Lakeview Avenue) remains a private residence but is well worth a drive by, especially for Wrigleyville and Wrigley Field fans. The German neoclassical mansion was constructed in 1896 and is one of the few remaining mansions on Lakeview Avenue.

Some of the most famous Chicagoans call Graceland Cemetery home (Clark Street and Irving Park Road). Headstones bear the names of Bertha and Potter Palmer, Marshall Field, Philip Armour, detective Allan Pinkerton, and George Pullman, inventor of the Pullman sleeping car.

The Lakeview neighborhood hosts a number of community events. Mayfest and Rock around the Block are two very popular summertime street festivals. It's also a good plan to watch for announcements for the Father's Day Ribfest held along Lincoln Avenue from Irving Park Road to Warner Avenue. The Lakeview Clark Street Fair (Clark and Addison Streets) is held in August. Also in August, the North Halsted Market Days (North Halsted Street, between Addison Street and Belmont Avenue) regularly draw more than 250,000 people for a two-day festival that features craft vendors, music, and food. Later in the fall, North Halsted Street hosts an annual Halloween parade. In late July, south of Goose Island–Wrigleyville, the Taste of Lincoln Avenue (Lincoln Avenue between Fullerton Parkway and Wrightwood Avenue) is another annual street festival.

A fun stop that many locals enjoy is the Vic/Brew & View (3145 North Sheffield Avenue). It's actually two theaters in one. As the Vic, it is a popular concert spot for live entertainment. When no concerts are scheduled, it becomes a second-run movie theater, called the Brew & View because it sells beer during the shows.

DIRECTIONS

When approaching from Interstates 90/94 (Kennedy Expressway), exit at Addison Street (exit 45) and turn east. About three and a half miles from the Kennedy, Addison will intersect with Clark. On the left you'll see Wrigley Field. Turn south (right) onto Clark, and Goose Island–Wrigleyville is almost immediately on your left at the corner of Clark and Eddy Streets. You can also take the CTA Red Line train to the Addison stop. The CTA's no. 22 Clark Street bus runs right in front of the brewpub.

Govnor's Public House Restaurant and Brewery

Lake in the Hills

LAKE IN THE HILLS, ILLINOIS

Visit Date	Signed

ABOUT THE BREWERY

To its credit, Govnor's Public House lives up to its company motto, "Céad Míle Fáilte (One Hundred Thousand Welcomes) in the house of our friends—old and new—may we all feel as one in the Pub." Govnor's Public House in Lake in the Hills is an example of a large, modern brewpub in a bustling suburban atmosphere of shopping and entertainment opportunities. Built new for Govnor's, the two-story building has a striking exterior that has been designed with brick, wood, and prominent cottage-style windows that give it the impression of a local Irish pub—only larger than the small neighborhood gathering places you might find in the Celtic countryside. Govnor's is visually impressive with its landscaping that includes a pond, a fountain, and great views from the wraparound beer garden and outside deck.

Inside the brewpub, the stone accents and Irish images are abundant. You walk through a large stone arch as you enter the front doors. In the foyer you see an ornate, antique cabinet that blends in nicely with the dark wooden accents throughout. The main dining room has a see-through fireplace to the outside. Several smaller, more intimate rooms offer a cozier experience. Square French-style doors and windows allow for a great deal of ambient light, but the bar's wooden floor and high ceiling seem to soak up the sunlight and keep it dim as you'd find in a Irish pub.

The brewery is mostly out of sight in the basement of the building. In the main bar you'll see four serving tanks and two fermentation vessels behind large glass windows. The brewhaus, consisting of more than ten other vessels, a mash tun, and a brew kettle, is actually below the bar.

Govnor's hosts live entertainment and a number of beer events throughout the year. In July it holds an annual Brew Daze and opens its parking lot to other local brewers. St. Patrick's Day, as one might expect, is very special at Govnor's.

The brewpub regularly has ten of its own beers on tap. Brewmaster and part owner Ron Buck keeps about half of those taps dedicated to rotating brewmaster's specials. The standard offerings include the Celtic Cream Ale, Leprechaun Light, Public House Pale Ale, O'Kelly's Hefeweizen, and Shamrock Stout. There is always a bitter beer on tap to appeal to hops lovers, and both the Public House Pale Ale and Veronica's American Pale Ale are great examples. However, whenever I'm at Govnor's, I ask for one of Ron Buck's Belgian-style ales, especially the Anvers Cent Tripel.

HISTORY

Govnor's Public House Restaurant and Brewery has ties in ownership and theme to Govnor's Pub of Chicago (207 North State Street). The Lake in the Hills brewpub is run by a four-person partnership of Jim Dziubla, Steve Carlson, Don Klein, and Ron Buck. Jim and Steve have been involved in a number of local restaurant businesses, including the founding of Govnor's Pub in Chicago back in 1986. Govnor's Pub of Chicago does not brew on the premises, but it does serve the beers from Govnor's Public House. Don also helped with the Chicago bar business, and Ron is Govnor's brewmaster.

Ron Buck found himself brewing at Govnor's Public House after being the long-time accountant of Jim Dziubla. Ron brewed at home during the 1980s and handled the books for Govnor's Pub. After attending Siebel Institute from 1999 to 2000, Ron expanded his role from that of accountant to partner and brewmaster when Governor's Public House opened in April 2001. With the Irish theme for both restaurants you might expect strong Celtic ancestry from the partnership, but actually Ron is the only Irishman of the group.

DON'T MISS THIS

Govnor's Public House is full of Irish accents, from the stonework and fireplaces to photos of Irish faces and places. A couple of oddities to look for that seem somewhat out of place include a large metal lion above the main bar. The five-foot, welded sheet metal artwork was made by a local ironworker. During the warm summer months, in the pond that Govnor's outer deck overlooks, you might find a floating alligator head that seems to be scanning the fountain for a meal. Given that Ireland has neither native alligators nor lions, the significance of these is not clear, but nevertheless they'll bring a smile when you're looking about.

GOVNOR'S PUBLIC HOUSE BREWS

Able-bodied Barley Wine   🍺 🍺 🍺 🍺   *Your Ranking* _____
A nice example of a more Americanized barley wine style with a firm hoppiness. Begins with a light spicy nose. Cloudy, light copper color and a thin, soft, tan head. Full bodied and sharp. A smooth caramel malt beginning with a very sharp hoppy background and lingering bitterness that builds in the finish. Served in a tulip glass, this makes for an excellent following to one of Govnor's hearty entrees.

Anvers Cent Tripel   🍺 🍺 🍺   *Your Ranking* _____
A strong sweet nose. Rich golden color and clear. The head is thick, soft, and white. Full bodied and very soft. Strong sweet fruity tones dominate with a

light hint of clove and spiciness. A warm, sweet finish. Initially brewed as Govnor's hundredth batch of beer and served on the brewpub's first anniversary.

Celtic Cream Ale 🍺🍺🍺 *Your Ranking* _____
No nose. A clear light golden color. A thin, soft, white head. Light bodied and soft. This beer offers a light, malty sweetness that is smooth. A clean finish with just a hint of bitterness. This golden ale is commonly served on a nitrogen tap by Govnor's.

Donegal IPA 🍺🍺🍺🍺 *Your Ranking* _____
A light hoppy nose, a little mild in aroma, but a taste that fills with strong firm bitterness. Dark golden to a light copper color. A thick, soft, white head. Full bodied and creamy. Strong, firm bitterness that lingers throughout the finish. A very smooth IPA. This beer is made with two pounds of whole Fuggles hops in the serving tank to ensure a big hops flavor.

Emerald Isle Blonde Ale 🍺🍺🍺 *Your Ranking* _____
No nose. A very clear, bright, golden color. Thin, soft, white head. The body has a soft texture. Smooth maltiness with a light roasted finish. Some balance and smooth malty qualities.

Fomharfest (a.k.a. Oktoberfest) *Your Ranking* _____
A light malty nose. Clear copper color and a thick, bubbly, tan head. Medium to full bodied and soft texture. Strong malty character that continues through the finish. A sweet, caramel Oktoberfest. A fall seasonal beer for Govnor's. *Fómhar*, pronounced "foh-ur," is Gaelic for autumn or harvest.

Govnor's Gaelic Golden 🍺🍺🍺🍺 *Your Ranking* _____
A Belgian strong golden ale. Sweet, yeasty nose. Cloudy golden color and a thick, soft, white head. Medium bodied and soft texture. Fruity qualities stand out, especially the flavor of banana. A crisp, fruity finish. It reminded me of a very strong Hefe-Weizen.

GPH Abbey Ale 🍺🍺🍺 *Your Ranking* _____
A traditional Belgian singel. No nose. A cloudy, golden to copper color and a thick, soft, white head. Medium bodied. A mild malty character that is blended with the spicy qualities for a crisp, fresh taste. Mild hop flavor and bitterness overall, but it offers a dry, floral finish. A brewmaster's special for Govnor's.

Heaven Hill Stout 🍺🍺 *Your Ranking* _____
A strong bourbon flavor overtakes the beer qualities. An earthy nose. Very dark color and a thin, bubbly, brown head. Full bodied and leathery. Strong warmth from the initial sip. Smooth malty flavors, but they remain hidden behind the bourbon aroma and taste.

Kilkenny Kolsch 🍺 *Your Ranking* _____
Light grainy or earthy nose. Clean golden color and a thin, soft, white head. Light bodied and round. Malty, earthy flavors. A sweet, vegetal finish. Just a little too grainy for my taste.

Leprechaun Light 🍺🍺🍺   *Your Ranking* _____

This Pilsner-style lager is crisp and complex. A light malty nose. Clear straw color and a thin, bubbly, white head. Light bodied and crisp texture. A mild malty body with a light hoppiness in the background and finish. Brewed with domestic grains and imported European hops.

O'Kelly's Hefeweizen 🍺🍺🍺🍺   *Your Ranking* _____

A Bavarian-style wheat beer. Strong banana esters in the nose. A cloudy, deep golden color with a thick, soft, white head. Light bodied and soft. Sweet fruity qualities with a light hoppy background. Sweet finish.

Public House Pale Ale 🍺🍺🍺🍺   *Your Ranking* _____

A traditional English pale ale. A mild hoppy nose. Clear copper color and a thin, bubbly, tan head. Full bodied and soft. A mild maltiness begins this beer, but some assertive hoppy qualities develop late. The finish is mild and fruity. Four additions of hops in the brewing process help support the great hoppy qualities.

Shamrock Stout 🍺🍺🍺   *Your Ranking* _____

Described as an Irish stout with tones of coffee and cacao from generous amounts of roasted barley. The roasted qualities come out in the nose and finish. Dark copper hues within a very dark body. The head is thick, soft, and tan. This stout is medium bodied with a slick texture. Malty flavors dominate with a roasted finish. Overall, my pint emphasized the malty sweetness more than Irish stout fans might expect, but this is still a great beer; it's served on a nitrogen tap line.

Solstice Wit 🍺🍺🍺🍺   *Your Ranking* _____

A light Belgian-style Wit. The nose is spicy with a light aroma of coriander. A slightly hazy golden color and a thin, bubbly, white head. Light bodied and very bubbly. Sweet fruity flavors stand out in the main body of taste. A light dry finish. Spiced with coriander and orange peel, resulting in an elegant and complex wheat-based ale. A brewmaster's special for Govnor's.

Veronica's APA 🍺🍺🍺🍺   *Your Ranking* _____

An American adaptation of an English pale ale. A firm hoppy nose. Golden color with a light haziness. A thick, soft, off-white head. Medium bodied and soft texture. Great smooth bitter flavor and a long-lasting hoppy finish. Some light citrus qualities tend to build over the quaffing of a pint of Veronica's. Brewed with two pounds of whole Cascade hops in the serving tank for strong hop flavor and aroma.

Weefolk Cherry Weiss 🍺🍺   *Your Ranking* _____

The menu offers some insight into this very fruity brew by calling it a "light bodied fruity Malternative." There certainly is a lot of cherry flavor, so much that you may find it difficult to find the malty qualities. Even though it has a very memorable nose, one of the most striking qualities of this beer is its vivid red color and soft white head. It is light bodied with a very sweet cherry flavor and finish. Most of the flavor of this brew is from the wheat malt and sweet cherries. Other versions of this beer have featured apricot.

OTHER GOVNOR'S BREWS YOU MAY WANT TO TRY

Brown Eye Brown Ale _Your Ranking_ _____

Malty, with a hint of caramel. A southern English version of a brown ale with a gentle moderate sweetness. A brewmaster's special for Govnor's.

Dingle Dubbel _Your Ranking_ _____

Rich malt character with a hint of clove spice. Served in a twelve-ounce glass. A brewmaster's special for Govnor's.

Dublin Dunkelweizen Bock _Your Ranking_ _____

A very complex combination of beer styles. Many flavors are found in this beer, including caramel and chocolate malts, banana aromas, and hints of clove and raisin. It is a fall seasonal at Govnor's Public House.

BREWERY RATING

	Your Rating	Shepard's Rating (1 to 4 Mugs)	General Description
Location		🍺🍺🍺	Entertainment district
Ease of Finding Location		🍺🍺🍺🍺	Close to major roads and intersections
Brewery Atmosphere		🍺🍺🍺	Family restaurant
Dining Experience		🍺🍺🍺🍺	Family style/variety
The Pint		🍺🍺🍺	A good experience

MENU

Govnor's menu features some great Irish flavor as well as American favorites. Overall, it is a combination of upper-level pub food and family-oriented offerings. The appetizers include selections of mushrooms, chicken fingers, buffalo wings, nachos, and blackened chicken egg rolls. There are a variety of soups and salads. One favorite is the Caveman chili in a sourdough bread bowl. Salads range from the basic classic Caesar to Mrs. Gallagher's beef tip salad with its sautéed peppers and beef tips. House specialties feature chicken, steak, pork, pasta, and fish. The tuna steak Francisco is pan seared and served over a bed of calico rice and topped with sautéed vegetables. McFarland's chicken is charbroiled, topped with shaved smoked ham and melted Swiss cheese, and served over rice with a creamy white wine sauce. A great treat is the Cajun meatloaf and shallot mashed potatoes covered in a spicy Creole sauce. As in many Irish pubs you'll also find corned beef and cabbage, fish and chips, and even a steak and stout soup. On the lighter side of the menu, Govnor's will make about a half-dozen burgers and an equal number of chicken sandwiches. Pizzas and pastas are also on the menu. To finish a meal you might consider the bread pudding with whiskey sauce, the crème brûlée, or the praline pecan fudge ball.

OTHER THINGS TO SEE OR DO IN THE AREA

The community of Lake in the Hills emerged in the 1920s when Judge Walter J. LaBuy bought about five hundred acres in the area, built a home, and dammed Woods Creek to create a small lake, for which the community was named. Today, it continues to be a community known mostly for its quiet residential streets and modest population growth.

In June Lake in the Hills hosts an annual Air Show (corner of Rakow Road and Pyott Road). The event features static displays and plane and helicopter rides. Also, each November the community celebrates its birthday with a variety of activities. The Lake in the Hills Fen is a 160-acre preserve for endangered species of plants and wildlife. It joins the twenty-six-acre Barbara Key Park, and together they provide great opportunities for nature walks and outdoor enjoyment. For indoor activities such as shopping, try the River Point Shopping Center (Algonquin and Randall Roads) and the Centre at Lake in the Hills (across Randall Road from Govnor's).

When traveling to Govnor's Public House and Restaurant on Interstate 90, be sure to notice the three-story round barn located at the Randall Road exit. It is the future site of the Ag Tech and Agricultural Education Center. While traveling from Interstate 90 north toward Lake in the Hills, you'll drive through Sleepy Hollow, a community founded in 1958 by Floyd Falese. Nestled in the rolling hills just south of Lake in the Hills, the town brings to life familiar names from *The Legend of Sleepy Hollow*, offering such streets and locations as Crane Drive and Lake Ichabod.

Algonquin, located east of Lake in the Hills, was originally a boarding place for wagons carrying settlers from the east and a staging point for farm products from the west heading into Chicago. By the early twentieth century it became a popular summer vacation area for Chicago businessmen and their families. It may have been best known for the Algonquin Hill Climbs of the early twentieth century, in which automobiles would race up Algonquin Hill (also known as Jayne's Hill), Philip's Hill, or Perry Hill to earn the coveted Algonquin Cup. Another type of ride involves the *Algonquin Princess* (20 West Algonquin Road, 1-847-658-5300), a beautiful turn-of-the-century paddleboat.

In nearby Gilberts, Gilberts Days in June are celebrated downtown with a street dance, a parade, bands, fireworks, and even a horseshoe contest. West of Lake in the Hills and Govnor's in the town of Union (north of Interstate 90 just east of Route 20) is the Railway Museum (7000 Olson Road). The museum also has several other special events including free admission for dads on Father's Day, the annual Showcase Weekend in September, which pays tribute to its members and volunteers, and its annual Harvest Festival Weekend in October. Also in Union, the McHenry County Historical Society Museum (6422 Main Street) hosts an annual Cider Festival in October. Just a little further west in McHenry County, downtown Marengo holds a three-day Settlers' Days festival in October.

Moraine Hills State Park is located north of Lake in the Hills near McHenry. In the park, Lake Defiance (about three miles southeast of McHenry off of South River Road) contains a 120-acre floating sphagnum moss and leatherleaf bog, surrounded by a moat of open water. Also north of Lake in the Hills, the community of Crystal Lake hosts an annual Lakeside Festival and Gala Week each June that features a Taste of Crystal Lake, the America's Cardboard Cup Regatta, a parade, fireworks, and other lakefront activities. Crystal Lake is the largest city in McHenry County and is home to a renovated historic downtown with over a hundred specialty shops and services and the restored Raue Center for the Arts (26 North Williams Street). The Raue Center opened in 1929 as El Tovar to showcase talking movies, while today it is home to live theater performances. The Crystal Lake Historical Society periodically hosts a cemetery walk through Lake Avenue Cemetery with costumed interpreters presenting first-person stories about the life and times of Crystal Lake's earliest settlers. Also in Crystal Lake, every Thursday evening in the summer is Classic Car Cruise Night—over five hundred classic cars have been known to show up for some events.

DIRECTIONS

When traveling either from or toward the greater Chicago area on Interstate 90, take the Randall Road exit (near mile marker 27), and travel north approximately seven miles. Govnor's is located just north of the Randall Road intersection with Algonquin Road. If traveling on Route 14, turn south on McHenry Road (which becomes Randall Road) and continue about four miles south. The Metra Union Pacific Northwest Line to Harvard stops in nearby Crystal Lake (Woodstock Avenue and Great Street).

Harrison's Restaurant and Brewery
Orland Park

Visit Date	Signed

ABOUT THE BREWERY

Harrison's Restaurant and Brewery is a family-oriented, upscale casual restaurant located in the southwestern Chicago suburb of Orland Park. The brewpub is situated along busy LaGrange Road (Route 45), but its size and location at a stoplight make it difficult to miss. It's a large red brick building with accents of white concrete stonework, green awnings, and lots of windows, and in the summer the flowers and shrubbery help make it stand out among a number of storefronts and businesses.

As you walk inside Harrison's, you're greeted by a large stone and copper fireplace. To the left is the main bar area, while to the right is the spacious dining room. The main dining area is in the center of the building and forms a square, with other building features basically wrapping about it. The ceiling of the main dining area is vaulted, with unique lighting that shines on sculptured fruits, vegetables, breads, and grains, giving them the appearance of an intricate carving. Surrounding this main dining area on the west is a semiprivate area for parties.

The bar is long, with room for about two dozen patrons. In the bar area there is lots of wood, from the bar itself to the back bar, high tables, windows, and floor. There's also a private cigar room with a Pac Man video game. Throughout the bar area are photos of movie stars and famous people such as John Travolta, Michael Douglas, Raquel Welch, Frank Sinatra, Dean Martin, and President John Kennedy. The brewery is located at the south end of the bar, and it sparkles from the sunlight that shines through windows into the brewhaus. On a bright day it offers warm, glistening backlighting for the brew kettle and fermenters. As you approach the building from the parking lot, or if you are outside in the beer garden, you can actually see inside the brewhaus.

Harrison's brewmaster, Joachim Mekoum, came to Orland Park in September 1998 from the Monte Carlo Brewery, Resort, and Casino in Las Vegas. Joe offers about ten of Harrison's beers on tap for most visits. You can't go wrong with a pint of the brewpub's flagship brew, Harrison's Red. Other standard beers include Millennium Pale Ale, LaGrange Golden Light, Black Diamond Stout, Raspberry Wheat, and Harrison's Wheat. If you enjoy fruit beer, Harrison's offers one of the most aggressive approaches to flavored wheats. You might catch the Kiwi-Mango or the Apricot or the Peach.

HISTORY

Harrison's Restaurant and Brewery is very much a family business. It's owned by four partners related through marriage. Husband and wife Chris and Marie Mastorakos, along with Marie's brother Harry and his wife, Catherine Nakos, founded Harrison's in 1997. The first beer was brewed in April 1998, and the brewpub's doors opened on May 4 of that year. The four-person family team has been owners in several other Chicago area restaurant businesses, including the Copper Palace Restaurant in Oak Forest and Harry's in Midlothian.

The idea for a brewpub came to Chris Mastorakos as he traveled through Tennessee in 1992. Since Mastorakos was involved in several restaurants he decided to pay a visit to the Blackstone Brewpub in downtown Nashville. The brewpub business intrigued him because his father was a wine maker in Europe, and at the time he and his brother were learning to homebrew. After a few years passed, Mastorakos sold a business and decided to reinvest in a brewpub for his Orland Park restaurant.

The building containing Harrison's was only two years old when the Mastorakoses and Nakoses decided to purchase it and remodel it into a brewpub. Its previous use was as a Piccadilly Cafeteria.

In case you're wondering about the name Harrison's—no, despite the mural with Harrison Ford, the actor does not own it. Rather, the brewpub's owners just selected a name that sounded good to them.

DON'T MISS THIS

If you look around the main dining room you'll see a large painted mural on the south wall. The playful painting includes the likenesses of Harrison Ford wearing a chef's jacket, Antonio Banderas as a brewer, and Jack Nicholson and Sharon Stone smoking cigars and having a beer. To the far right are the special likenesses of family patriarchs Harry and Bessie Nakos (Marie and Harry's father and mother).

HARRISON'S BREWS

Black Diamond Stout 🍺🍺🍺   *Your Ranking* _____
A smooth, dry version of an Irish stout. An oatmeal stout with a very dark color and light bronze highlights in the bottom of the glass. A thick, soft, brown head. Full bodied and silky. A sweet malty stout with a slightly sour finish. This stout has some strong sweetness and a silky, smooth texture.

Cherry Ale Your Ranking _____

A strong cherry nose that lasts through the taste and finish. Clear golden color and a thick, soft, white head. Medium bodied and thin texture. A strong cherry flavor dominates the body and finish. It is actually served with a cherry. Those that like strong, sweet cherry flavor will enjoy this beer.

Harrison's Red Your Ranking _____

No nose. A clear, dark copper color. A thin, soft, white head. Medium bodied and round. A caramel malty dominance with a light roasted or toffee flavor. A firm, crisp, hoppy finish. This is a complex, yet well balanced beer with great flavor and a dry hoppy ending. It is made with Munich malt and three types of hops.

Harrison's Wheat Your Ranking _____

An American-style wheat with a prominent fruity nose. Cloudy golden color and a thin, soft, creamy, white head. Medium to light bodied and crisp. A light fruity and malty start with a light hoppy background. Finishes with a grainy texture. There is some nice bitterness in this wheat.

Honey Blonde Your Ranking _____

A malty nose. Clear golden color and no head. Medium bodied. A sweet, honey flavor dominates. The honey is crisp in the finish.

IPA (cask conditioned) Your Ranking _____

Wow, this is a great India Pale Ale. This beer is one of those you'll need to ask for, because it is not always mentioned by the restaurant waitstaff. It has an abundant floral aroma, cloudy golden color, and a thin, soft, white head. It is full bodied with strong, firm, smooth bitterness from beginning to end. The intensity of flavor really lives up to the introduction offered by this beer's nose.

Kiwi Your Ranking _____

One of those seasonal specials from brewmaster Joachim Mekoum. A light yeasty nose. Clear golden color and a light, bubbly, white head. Light bodied and soft. A yeast-like beginning with a maltiness that eventually is dominated by a sour citrus flavor. A fun beer, and definitely different, but the serious beer crowd might not appreciate it—so just don't make a big deal about it if you are surrounded by beer geeks.

Lager Light Your Ranking _____

No nose. Clear straw color and a very thin, soft, white head. Light bodied with a mild sharpness and low bitterness. Overall, grainy and earthy flavors win out.

LaGrange Golden Light Your Ranking _____

No nose. A clear, light golden color. Thin, soft, off-white head. A light body with a bubbly texture. A light dry start to the taste with a sweet malty back-ground. Some assertive crispness that gives it unique character. This light beer is a delicate ale with smooth flavors and a crisp, clean, dry finish.

Millennium Pale Ale 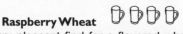   *Your Ranking* _____

A light hoppy nose. Vivid copper color and a thin, soft, tan head. Medium bodied and bubbly texture. A strong bitterness with some quiet caramel malt flavors in the background. Finishes with a subtle graininess. Strong flavors and bubbly texture are memorable.

Oktoberfest   *Your Ranking* _____

This traditional German lager has a faint malty nose. A cloudy bronze color with a thick, soft, tan head. Medium bodied and soft texture. The malty flavor is rather quiet and thin, but there is a smooth sweetness that builds. Finishes with a light hoppy bitterness. Many great Oktoberfest qualities, but just a little withheld. A fall seasonal at Harrison's.

Raspberry Wheat   *Your Ranking* _____

A very pleasant find for a flavored wheat beer. A light raspberry nose. Light golden to orange color with a hazy, light cloudiness. A thick, soft, white head. Medium to light bodied. A mild malty flavor with a light, crisp raspberry taste, aroma, and finish. Raspberry nose and finish make a nice complement to the wheat maltiness; they are not overdone or too sweet. The raspberry flavors do build, but it takes a while for the fruitiness to dominate.

OTHER HARRISON'S BREWS YOU MAY WANT TO TRY

Brewmaster's Special Fruit Beers   *Your Ranking* _____

Several variations on the flavored wheat beer are found at Harrison's, including apricot, blackberry, blueberry, peach, kiwi, and kiwi-mango,

Honey Wheat   *Your Ranking* _____

A brewmaster's special. Light bodied with a firm sweetness.

Maibock   *Your Ranking* _____

A seasonal special to watch for each May. Copper color and smooth malty flavors.

BREWERY RATING

	Your Rating	Shepard's Rating (1 to 4 Mugs)	General Description
Location		🍺🍺	Commercial/industrial Entertainment district
Ease of Finding Location		🍺🍺🍺	Close to major roads and intersections
Brewery Atmosphere		🍺🍺🍺	Family restaurant
Dining Experience		🍺🍺🍺🍺	Family style/variety
The Pint		🍺🍺🍺	A good experience

MENU

Harrison's menu has a lot of diversity in choices—referred to by owner Chris Mastorakos as "American Eclectic." The signature dishes include touches of Creole found in the jambalaya to an American flair with a range of steaks. For starters, the appetizer selections offer wings, nachos, quesadillas, and Cajun popcorn shrimp. There are also Bayou crab cakes, stuffed mushrooms, and beer-battered onion rings. Harrison's offers about six different salad selections, such as a classic Caesar and a Fuji salad with chicken, Napa cabbage, bean sprouts, and fresh apple slices. The entrees, which make a dinner choice difficult, include ale-battered fish and chips, grilled Atlantic salmon, fajitas, pecan-crusted catfish, and roasted vegetable pasta. Many of the entrees are served with rice or vegetables. Harrison's steaks are well known, especially for those who enjoy large cuts. The restaurant's specialty is the thirty-two-ounce porterhouse. The filet mignon is a sixteen-ounce broiled portion served with sautéed mushrooms and vegetables. The barbecued baby back ribs are hickory smoked and basted with Harrison's chipotle barbecue sauce with a touch of Black Diamond Stout. Several of Harrison's other dishes also include beer. The Brewhouse Reuben is made with Harrison's Wheat, the beer brat is simmered in Millennium Pale Ale, and the cheddar and potato soup features Harrison's Red Ale. For dessert, a great way to finish the evening is with Louisiana sweet potato pecan pie or the fruity burrito, which features fresh fruit and white chocolate wrapped in a chocolate tortilla and fried.

OTHER THINGS TO SEE OR DO IN THE AREA

Harrison's is located on the busy LaGrange Road (Route 45). Nearby are numerous opportunities for retail shopping, bookstores, and small strip malls. There is a large Target store to the brewpub's east and Orland Park Place (153rd and LaGrange Road) is across LaGrange Road to the west. Other shopping centers include Orland Square (151st Street and LaGrange Road), which is a two-level shopping center with more than 150 stores. Also, if you enjoy antique hunting, the antique shops of Beacon and Union Avenues offer a row of dealers all along one block.

Franklin E. Loebe Recreation Center (14650 South Ravinia Avenue) includes classrooms, an indoor playground, a walking track, and dance rooms. Franklin Loebe was a former Orland Park village treasurer. The village operates more than five hundred acres of park land, including Centennial Pool (15520 West Avenue) and Orland Park Ice Arena (10700 West 159th Street). Along with Centennial Pool, the Humphrey Sport Complex encompasses twenty acres of softball, baseball, and soccer fields. It was named for Orland Park's first mayor, John Humphrey. Orland Park's Lake Sedgewick in Centennial Park (15600 West Avenue) hosts an annual Fishing Derby during July and August. The village's Recreation and Parks Department also oversees the Orland Park Sportsplex (159th Street, west of Wolf Road), a ninety-thousand-square-foot sports and fitness complex.

About ten miles west of Orland Park and Harrison's on the Illinois and Michigan Canal is Lockport. Lockport was founded in 1836 when construction began on the canal, and it remains one of the best preserved canal towns in the country. There is a walking tour of the Pioneer Settlement (803 South State Street). The Illinois and Michigan Canal Museum (also 803 State Street) offers insight into nineteenth-century life along the canal, and there is a walking tour of the early settlement features. Lockport hosts Old Canal Days (in the downtown) each June with a carnival, a flea market, arts and crafts, and family entertainment. A little further west is the charming town of Plainfield, with its historic nineteenth-century architecture and more than thirty unique downtown shops and restaurants along the Lockport Street corridor.

West and north of Orland Park, the Island Rendezvous is held at Romeoville's Isle a la Cache Museum (501 135th Street). You can relive the fur trade era with reenactors portraying the voyageurs and Native Americans of the nineteenth century.

North of Orland Park, Palos Park is home to Swallow Cliff Sports Area (Routes 83 and 45). The Forest Preserve District of Cook County operates a six-lane toboggan slide during the winter, with toboggans available for rent. In Palos Heights, Lake Katherine Nature Preserve (7402 West Lake Katherine Drive) consists of 158 acres, three miles of trails, and the twenty-acre Lake Katherine. In Worth, Gale Moore Park (109th and Depot Streets) features Civil War Weekend in June, with battle reenactments and demonstrations. The Fine and Performing Arts Center is located on the south side of the Moraine Valley Community College campus (about a half-mile east of LaGrange Road between 107th and 111th Streets).

Nearby Joliet is known for gambling and speed! Joliet is home to two casinos; the Empress Casino (Route 6 and Empress Drive) and Harrah's (151 North Joliet Street). The Chicagoland Speedway (3200 South Chicago Street) offers NASCAR Busch and Winston Cup Series Races, demolition derbies, car shows, and concerts. Joliet is also home to the Rialto Square Theater (102 North Chicago Street), which opened in 1926 and today offers venues for big-name entertainers, dinner theater, conventions and annual events. The Rialto was built as a Vaudeville movie palace during the Golden Age of movies. There are over one hundred Czechoslovakian crystal chandeliers and light fixtures throughout

the theater. The chandelier in Rialto's rotunda is called "The Duchess"; at twenty-two-feet and weighing over two tons it is one of the largest crystal chandeliers in the United States. Tours of the Rialto are available.

If you enjoy independent baseball, consider Hawkinson Ford Field (4545 Midlothian Turnpike) east of Orland Park in Crestwood, the home of the Cook County Cheetahs of the Frontier League.

DIRECTIONS

Harrison's is located on LaGrange Road (also Route 45) just north of the intersection with Route 6 (159th Street). The brewpub is approximately ten miles south of Route 45 and Interstate 294, or about three and a half miles north of where Route 45 connects to Interstate 80.

Illinois Brewing Company
Bloomington

Visit Date	Signed

ABOUT THE BREWERY

The Illinois Brewing Company is in downtown Bloomington, just to the southwest of the town square and McLean County Courthouse. The brewery is located in a former Montgomery Ward department store building that was originally constructed between 1918 and 1920. The brewery is in the southwest part of the four-story red brick building, which adjoins a six-story building that houses the well-known Bloomington Antique Mall.

Illinois Brewing has a memorable look from the outside. As you approach the corner of southbound Route 51 and West Front Street, you immediately notice the building's glass corner. As you look through the large windows, you can see down into the brewhaus or up into the bar. Patrons in the bar actually sit above sidewalk level, on what appears to be a floating floor. When you're inside, getting a seat by the windows will offer an interesting perspective, because you look down to see pedestrians on the outside sidewalk, while they have a great view of your feet!

Illinois Brewing has multiple personalities. It's a tavern, a sports bar, and a dance hall. All you have to do is walk through the building to get a sense of the transformation this bar is capable of—all depending upon what type of crowd shows up. For example, to the south, where the windows look on West Front Street and southbound Route 51, there are tables and a dining area. A long, multi-angled bar stretches from north to south in the middle of the main floor. The north third of the bar is an open area that doubles as a stage and dance floor. There are also multiple levels in this part of the building that feature a second-floor stage that looks down onto the dance floor. While it offers a quiet place for a lunch, the after work and evening crowd can transform the bar into a thriving nightclub atmosphere.

Illinois Brewing regularly has up to ten of its own beers on tap, including a brewmaster's special or two. You'll also find a variety of other microbrews on tap and in the bottle. Throughout the year, brewer Tim Hilton and owner Jeff Skinner offer about fifteen different styles of their beers. The Newmarket Pale Ale and the Uptown Amber Ale are the most popular, but the Porter from Hell is Skinner's pride and joy.

HISTORY

The Illinois Brewing Company was established in 1995, but because of extensive renovations and licensing requirements it wasn't until June 1999 that the bar opened. It took even longer for the brewing to begin. Beer didn't flow at Illinois Brewing until December 2000.

Owner Jeff Skinner is well known among local homebrewers. Skinner started homebrewing about 1980. In 1988 he opened a homebrew supply store in his house, called Brewmaster Beer and Wine Making Supplies. Today, Skinner continues to supply homebrewers with whatever they need, operating the homebrew supply business out of Illinois Brewing. With a laugh, Jeff will tell you his homebrew supply business went from his living room to under the bandstand. He is certainly serious about beer, and that's why Illinois Brewing is a full-service business, from homebrewing supplies to a working brewery to a multifaceted bar business.

A historic piece of Bloomington's brewing past still stands near the Highland Golf Course on South Main Street. Although only a few buildings are left, the Meyer and Wochner Brewery (also known as the Meyer Brewing Company and originally as the Gambrinus Brewery) spanned over one hundred acres of land and had caves for lagering, stables, barns, well-kept grounds, and the owners' homes. That brewery operated from 1861 to 1920.

DON'T MISS THIS

About midway down the bar, on the west wall, there is a fire bell, or what firefighters call a "water gong." This unusual-looking red metal device is actually an alarm. In the event of fire, the water flowing through the contraption will make the sound of a ringing bell.

ILLINOIS BREWING COMPANY BREWS

Big Beaver Brown Ale 🍺 🍺 🍺 🍺   *Your Ranking* _____
A brown that begins with a strong, malty nose. Very dark color with a thick, soft, white head. Full bodied. Great roasted qualities that complement the maltiness without seeming burnt. A light bitterness is barely detectable in the finish.

Clover Hill Honey Ale 🍺 🍺 🍺   *Your Ranking* _____
A light malty nose. Golden color with a slight haze. The head is thin, soft, and white. Medium bodied and soft textured. A mild sweetness dominates. There is a smooth, roasted honey finish.

High Beam Barleywine   🍺 🍺   *Your Ranking* _____

A very malty nose. Cloudy bronze color. The head is very thin, bubbly, and white. Full bodied and slick textured. Strong sweet caramel flavors. Syrupy sweet. A sugary finish. This barley wine is aged in Jim Beam oak barrels.

Kurt's Kolsch   🍺 🍺 🍺   *Your Ranking* _____

No nose. A cloudy golden color and a thin, bubbly, white head. Medium bodied and round. A dry hoppy beginning with a light sour malty background. The light dry, hoppy flavors build in the finish, but this really isn't a bitter beer. Overall it strives for balance despite a sour background.

Newmarket Pale Ale   🍺 🍺 🍺   *Your Ranking* _____

Light hoppy aroma. A slight cloudiness to the golden color. A thin, bubbly, white head. Medium bodied and smooth. The bitterness has some dryness that builds into the finish. This ale is made with all Cascade hops.

O'Turly's Lyte Ale   🍺 🍺   *Your Ranking* _____

An American-style light beer with the crispness of a lager. No nose. Cloudy, light yellow color and a thin, soft, white head. The flavors are very light, just hints of sweet maltiness with a citrus background. The finish has some fruitiness that allows this beer to end on a crisp, clean note.

Porter from Hell   🍺 🍺 🍺 🍺   *Your Ranking* _____

The signature beer for owner Jeff Skinner. According to the beer menu this porter is heavy and robust, but that's an understatement. A strong, aggressive malty nose. The color is very dark with a thick, soft, brown head. Full bodied and silky. The chocolate malt flavors dominate this beer from the nose through the finish. Made with brown sugar molasses. Skinner gets extra credit for his creativity in this recipe by using a secret ingredient: the caramel used by a friend who is a local candy maker—oops, it's not so secret any more!

Raspberry Wheat   🍺 🍺   *Your Ranking* _____

A strong fruity nose that is sweet and clearly lets you know you'll be drinking a raspberry-flavored beer. Golden color with a thin, soft, white head. Thin to medium bodied and soft. A light malty sweetness at the beginning, but the fruity sweet raspberry flavor takes over. The finish actually offers more raspberry than the beginning. For those who enjoy raspberry beers, you'll get your fill of raspberries in this brew.

Stumblin' Stout   🍺 🍺 🍺   *Your Ranking* _____

A full-bodied, creamy, sweet, Midwestern stout with a dry finish. Begins with a malty nose. Very dark color with bronze highlights and a thin, bubbly, brown head. A thick, even slick, texture helps accentuate the malty flavors. There is a slight sour background that competes with the chocolate malt finish.

Uptown Amber Ale   🍺   *Your Ranking* _____

No nose. The color is a brownish copper with a slight haziness. The head is thin, bubbly, and off-white. Medium bodied and round texture. A malt-dominated taste, with a slight fruity background that lingers into the finish. This beer comes off just a bit too sour for my preference of what an amber can be.

Wee Willy's Wheat Ale 🍺🍺🍺   *Your Ranking* _____

An American-style wheat ale. No nose. A light yellow color. A thick, bubbly, white head. Light bodied with a subtle softness. There are some very nice wheat qualities with a mild graininess and hints of fruitiness to the flavor. Finishes with a light sourness.

White Chocolate 🍺🍺   *Your Ranking* _____

This is interesting, albeit somewhat of a novelty beer. The white chocolate really comes through in the aroma and accents the finish; beyond that this beer has some of the Wee Willy's characteristics: a hazy, light gold to yellow straw color and a thick, bubbly, white head. Light bodied and soft, this beer is worth a try, but the serious beer fan might find it just a bit too whimsical.

OTHER ILLINOIS BREWING COMPANY BREWS YOU MAY WANT TO TRY

IPA   *Your Ranking* _____

A traditional English India Pale Ale.

Old Dublin's Barley Wine   *Your Ranking* _____

Full bodied, dark, and heavy maltiness.

BREWERY RATING

	Your Rating	Shepard's Rating (1 to 4 Mugs)	General Description
Location		🍺🍺🍺	Central city/community
Ease of Finding Location		🍺🍺🍺	Close to major roads and intersections
Brewery Atmosphere		🍺🍺🍺	Family tavern Music venue Sports
Dining Experience		🍺	Pub fare
The Pint		🍺🍺	Okay, but wasn't perfect

MENU

The Illinois Brewing Company has a basic tavern menu with choices of bar munchies, soups, salads, pizza, and sandwiches. Appetizers include hot wings, nachos, and brew pub pretzels. Pizzas come in four sizes with basic toppings of cheese, sausage, pepperoni, a supreme, and white garlic. Sandwiches are straightforward and inexpensive, including a standard hamburger, grilled chicken, pork ribeye, Italian beef, Polish sausage, bratwurst, and a BLT.

OTHER THINGS TO SEE OR DO IN THE AREA

Bloomington was named in 1822 for its flowers! Every year in early September the city celebrates its Harvest Bloom Festival. The next attraction after the flowers of Bloomington, and the focal point of the city skyline, is the Old McLean County Courthouse on the square in the heart of the city. The American Renaissance-style structure was built from 1901 to 1904. The rotunda is over one hundred feet high in the center and is finished at the top with an allegorical painting called "Peace and Prosperity."

The McLean County Historical Society (200 North Main) has four galleries that depict the history of the county and life on the prairie. The David Davis Mansion, also known as "Clover Lawn" (1000 East Monroe Drive), was built in 1872 for U.S. Supreme Court Judge David Davis and his wife. Davis was a friend and mentor of Abraham Lincoln and is credited with helping him win the nomination for the presidency. Major's Hall (Front and East Streets) marks where Abraham Lincoln gave his famous "Lost Speech" about the abolition of slavery in 1856. The speech got this name because, allegedly, reporters became so enthralled with the speech that none of them took notes.

The Adlai Stevenson family called Bloomington home. Adlai Stevenson I was vice president for Grover Cleveland. Adlai Stevenson II was governor of Illinois and twice Democratic candidate for the presidency. Both now rest in the Evergreen Cemetery (302 East Miller Street). Also buried at Evergreen is the wife of Adlai I, Letitia Green Stevenson, who was the second National President General of the Daughters of the American Revolution. The Stevenson homes are located in the Franklin Park Historic District (bound by Walnut, McLean, Chestnut, and Prairie Streets), along with many more nineteenth-century Victorian homes.

The Ewing Manor Cultural Center, also known as Ewing Castle (Emerson Street and Towanda Avenue) was the home of Hazel Buck Ewing and was built in 1929. Ewing's father was associated with William Wrigley Jr. of the Wrigley Company and Wrigley Field in Chicago. In July and early August, the Illinois Shakespeare Festival is held on the Ewing Manor grounds.

In nearby Normal, the Normal Theatre (209 North Street) opened in 1937 as the city's first theater for sound films. It has been restored to its original condition. The Funk Prairie Home, about fifteen miles south in Shirley, is the restored 1864 residence of Lafayette Funk, Illinois state senator and cofounder of Chicago's Union Stockyards. Highway buffs might want to take note that Old Route 66 runs southwest through Bloomington toward St. Louis.

If you are into heights, the Upper Limits (1304 West Washington Street) claims to be the tallest indoor climbing facility in the world. The Watterson Towers dormitory (corner of Beaufort Street and Fell Avenue in Normal) on the Illinois State University campus takes credit for being the world's largest college residence hall at twenty-eight stories. And the Prairie Aviation Museum (Route 9, near Central Illinois Regional Airport) offers a theater and aircraft models including a 1942 DC-3, an A-7A Corsair, and a UH-1 "Huey" Helicopter.

Bloomington is also home to one of the ultimate complements to beer—Beer Nuts Incorporated (103 North Robinson Street). Beer Nuts were originally called "Redskins" because of their red skins and glaze. The company has a retail store and tours are available.

DIRECTIONS

When approaching Bloomington, you have a couple of options for routes. Old Highway 51 will take you through Bloomington in a north and south direction. On the south side of the square, after 51 splits into one-way roads, Illinois Brewing is located southwest of the courthouse, at the corner of East Front and southbound Highway 51.

Another option is to take Interstate 55. On Bloomington's west side, watch for exit 160 and turn east (Highway 150/Market Street) toward the downtown. Market Street will intersect with Highway 51, where you should turn south and watch for Front Street. Illinois Brewing is located on the northeast corner of the intersection of Front and Highway 51.

J. W. Platek's Restaurant and Brewery

Richmond

J.W. PLATEK'S
Restaurant • Brewery

Visit Date	Signed

ABOUT THE BREWERY

J. W. Platek's Restaurant and Brewery is located in northern Illinois, only about two miles from the Wisconsin border. The brewery and restaurant are in a two-story building that is trimmed with cream-colored siding, a brown roof, and blue awning over the main door. Its residence-like appearance reminds one of a bustling roadhouse from the early twentieth century. In fact, the building was originally constructed in the 1920s as a restaurant.

Richmond is a quaint northern Illinois town of about 1,100 citizens. When you visit Platek's, the crowd is dominated by many return visitors not only from Richmond, but also from Chicago's northern suburbs. The waitstaff are very friendly, and you quickly get the impression that you would become a local after just a visit or two.

Inside you can easily envision that this building could be someone's house. Actually, part of the building is a home. The upper story is an apartment, and owners Jim and Bonnie Platek lived upstairs at one time. The brewery is located in the basement. Platek's is probably the smallest Illinois brewery, making only about eighty barrels per year from a barrel-and-a-half system. Jim Platek describes it as a Frankenstein system that takes advantage of fifty-five-gallon stainless steel drums, small electric pumps, and a carbon-dioxide-driven transfer process.

Seating in Platek's is somewhat limited, so reservations are always recommended. To the right of the front door the square bar is large enough for only about ten stools. The main dining room is also somewhat cozy with about a dozen tables. Large wooden booths and a few small tables make up the smoking area of the restaurant. Dark wooden accents, dim lighting, table candles, and lots of mirrors that reflect light all help accent the upscale menu and offer an inviting supper club feeling.

Platek's keeps four or five beers on tap, plus domestic bottles and a very extensive wine list. For house beers, the American Wheat and Belgian White are among the most popular. But the American Pale Ale has great hoppy character and will be appreciated by those looking for a distinctive beer. Brewer and owner Jim Platek also makes a memorable Brown Ale that is well worth a pint or two.

HISTORY

J. W. Platek's Restaurant was established in 1989. The brewery was added in 1997. The husband and wife team of Jim and Bonnie Platek owns the brewery. The pair met while working at the Big Cedar Restaurant in West Bend, Wisconsin. Jim takes care of the brewing, and Bonnie manages the restaurant. Like many brewers, Jim got his start homebrewing. As the hobby grew, it eventually became part of his restaurant.

The building housing Platek's was built in the 1920s. Originally the Red Star Inn, it offered dining and dancing. When the building changed to its current form, the Plateks found old newspapers in the walls—one dated back to the 1960s Cuban missile crisis—as well as a 1950s Boy Scout booklet. During the renovations to its present condition, Jim Platek says several local residents came in to share their memories and photos of how the restaurant has been a constant fixture for the community, everything from a well-known eatery to allegedly hosting gaming machines in the 1940s.

DON'T MISS THIS

Outside the front exposure of Platek's is a four-foot-high wooden fence that blocks the windows and patrons from view. From the outside you might expect it to be hiding a beer garden. But from the inside of the dining room as you look outside, you find that it provides a small area for seasonal displays. On one visit it contained a small wooden windmill. The wooden fence does help block the constant traffic lights and highway noise—throughout Platek's you quickly get an impression that the interior of the restaurant was completely thought out and planned to accent the supper club feel.

J.W. PLATEK'S BREWS

American Pale Ale　　　　　　　　　　　　　　*Your Ranking* _____
Described by the brewery as an American version of a British classic pale ale. Some great hoppy qualities. A light floral nose, clear deep copper color, and a thick, bubbly, white head. Medium bodied. Strong dry bitter flavor will build throughout the aftertaste.

American Wheat　　　　　　　　　　　　　　　*Your Ranking* _____
A malty nose and body. Clear bronze to copper color with a thick, bubbly, white head. Light bodied and soft. A strong syrupy sweetness is difficult to get beyond. The wheat qualities just never materialize. Don't rule this beer out, just ask for a sample first.

Belgian White　　　　　　　　　　　　　　　*Your Ranking* _____
Somewhat light in color and body for the style, but this beer will grow on you. A light fruity nose has just a hint of orange. The color is a hazy, light golden. The head is thick, bubbly, and white. Overall it is light bodied with a crispness. The light malty flavor builds, and the orange and coriander stand out in the finish.

Brown Ale　　　　　　　　　　　　　　　　*Your Ranking* _____
A malty nose. Dark color with reddish to bronze highlights. A thick, bubbly, tan head. Medium bodied and soft texture. Strong caramel malt flavor dominates

the taste, and with the soft texture this beer comes off very smooth. The finish is clean and almost nonexistent.

Stout 🍺🍺🍺🍺   *Your Ranking* _____

A beer that comes off as it is described: dark and rich with coffee flavors, one that fans of sweet, roasted stouts will enjoy. A strong roasted nose gives you a great impression that you have found some roasted chocolate malt to enjoy. Very dark color with a thick, soft, tan head. Full bodied and silky. The body of flavor is malty with very assertive roasted tones that build into coffee-like flavors in the finish.

OTHER J. W. PLATEK'S BREWS YOU MAY WANT TO TRY

Belgian Strong Ale   *Your Ranking* _____
Copper colored and malty. A fall seasonal.

Bock   *Your Ranking* _____
Full bodied, copper, and well balanced. A late winter into spring seasonal beer.

Dunkel Weizen   *Your Ranking* _____
Fruity and dark. A fall to winter seasonal.

Honey Chocolate Porter   *Your Ranking* _____
A Christmas time treat. Full bodied, lots of malt, and very dark.

Weizen   *Your Ranking* _____
Medium bodied and crisp. A summertime seasonal beer.

BREWERY RATING

	Your Rating	Shepard's Rating (1 to 4 Mugs)	General Description
Location		🍺🍺🍺	Commercial/industrial
Ease of Finding Location		🍺🍺🍺	Easy, but requires some planning
Brewery Atmosphere		🍺🍺	Out of sight
Dining Experience		🍺🍺🍺🍺	Supper club, family dining
The Pint		🍺🍺🍺	A good experience

MENU

J. W. Platek's has limited hours and seating, so it's always a good idea to call ahead for reservations. Platek's menu is focused on hearty dishes of steaks, ribs, and seafood. The entrees are the type found in many upscale supper clubs and fine restaurants. Some of the choices include beef Wellington, shrimp

DeJonghe, blackened fillet of catfish with spicy Dijon mustard sauce, barbecued baby back pork ribs, and a sixteen-ounce New York strip with mushroom garnish. There are a number of specials to watch for, such as the Tournedos Farci, which features twin petite filet mignons stuffed with French Brie, or a similar version called the Grilled Tournedos, with two filets topped with a green peppercorn cream sauce and fresh vegetables. The special Wellington is a filet mignon topped with chicken liver mousse, baked in a puff pastry, and served on Bordelaise sauce. Platek's menu also features a number of daily specials that are dependent upon the availability of special ingredients, such as buffalo, venison, wild boar, rabbit, and even alligator. There is a lighter sandwich side to the menu that includes a tenderloin sandwich, chicken breast sandwich, half slab of ribs, or the half order of deep-fried shrimp. Your meal will likely begin with a vegetable plate that may also include cheese, dressings, beets and onions, or chicken liver mousse. If you have the choice, the house soups are excellent, especially the Hungarian goulash. Desserts include the Chocolate Indulgence, a flourless chocolate cake served with warm raspberry sauce, and the Italian dessert, tiramisu, consisting of Italian cream cheese (mascarpone), ricotta, brandy, and lady fingers. The one limited side to Platek's menu is the lack of vegetarian options; otherwise the food experience was incredible.

OTHER THINGS TO SEE OR DO IN THE AREA

Richmond is about sixty miles northwest of downtown Chicago, just a few miles from the Illinois-Wisconsin border. The town is a great destination for its antique dealers, custom furniture makers, pottery, and gift stores. There is also a homemade chocolate shop, an ice cream parlor, and a number of bed and breakfasts.

If you have a sweet tooth to conquer, Anderson's Homemade Candies (10301 Main Street) is known for hand-dipped English toffees, fudge, and old-fashioned candy bars. The well-known Illinois confectioners began in 1919 on Armitage Avenue in Chicago, but when rent for the store doubled in 1926 from ten to twenty dollars per month, Anderson moved his store to Richmond. Richmond is also home to one of the few remaining Dog 'n' Suds drive-up restaurants (11015 U.S. Highway 12).

If you visit in the summer you might try to plan your trip around Richmond Round-Up Days, which features a parade, live music, a community-wide garage sale, and an arts and craft show. Later in the fall, Christmas of Yesteryear on Thanksgiving weekend offers holiday lighting, shopping, and even caroling.

About seven miles west of Richmond is the town of Hebron (on Route 173), with its basketball water tower that pays tribute to the 1952 state championship team. About fifteen miles southwest of Richmond, in Woodstock, is the Woodstock Opera House (121 Van Buren). Built in 1890, the opera house is listed on the National Register of Historic Places. A number of famous notables have performed there including Paul Newman, Tom Bosley, and Orson Welles. But the opera house is thought to be haunted by the ghost of a woman who is believed to have jumped from the bell tower. The ghost, named Elvira, occupies the balcony in seat DD-113. Reports of sightings include banging noises and booing and hissing during rehearsals. Woodstock was the filming location for the 1992 movie *Groundhog Day*, and the town celebrates Groundhog Day with self-guided walking tours of many of the sites that were part of the movie. Other famous Woodstock residents include Chester Gould, the creator of the Dick Tracy comic strip. Every June the town celebrates Dick Tracy Days with a parade and drum corps competition. The McHenry County Courthouse in Woodstock has been home to a number of other famous mugs, including activist and political candidate Eugene Debs.

The nearby Chain O'Lakes State Park (near Spring Grove to the east of Richmond) contains Illinois's largest concentration of natural lakes. Chain O'Lakes State Park (8916 Wilmont Road, Spring Grove) offers opportunities for boating, fishing, and skiing. The park borders three natural lakes—Grass, Marie, and Nippersink—and the Fox River, which connects the other seven lakes: Bluff, Fox, Pistakee, Channel, Petite, Catherine, and Redhead. Altogether the Chain O'Lakes contains nearly 6,500 acres of water and 488 miles of shoreline. The Illinois State Fish Hatchery and Spring Grove Fisheries Resource Center (2314 Hatchery Road) on the Chain O'Lakes offers tours by appointment.

About fifteen miles south of Richmond (on Route 31) is Moraine Hills State Park (914 South River Road, McHenry). Lake Defiance in the park features a 120-acre floating sphagnum moss and leatherleaf bog. Pike Marsh (in the southeast corner of Moraine Hills) contains the largest known colony of pitcher plants in Illinois. Pitcher plants attract, trap, and digest insects. The Pike Marsh Nature Trail features a floating boardwalk.

DIRECTIONS

Richmond isn't difficult to find, but it does take some planning. Because it is located about sixty miles from downtown Chicago, and only a mile from the Illinois-Wisconsin border, it's good to check a map before venturing out. Platek's is located on the west side of Highway 12, just a few feet north of the intersection of Highway 12 and 31—about a mile south of Richmond's town center. There's really no main route to get to Platek's. The best advice is to allow some time for two-lane highways, and enjoy the roads that take you through the northern suburbs of Chicago.

Lunar Brewing Company
Villa Park

Visit Date	Signed

ABOUT THE BREWERY

Of all the Illinois brewpubs and breweries, Lunar Brewing Company is among the most distinctive in local neighborhood character and identity. Lunar is bordered by busy St. Charles Road on the south and a residential area to the north. Once you step through the door you really get a feeling that you're in a true neighborhood beer bar. Adding to this sense of community is the stonework stating "Villa Park Hall" above the building's central door (leading into the main part of the structure from St. Charles Road), evidence that the building was once the Villa Park Hall.

As you would expect with a name like Lunar, there are a great many opportunities to tie a celestial theme into the interior decoration and beer names. Mobile-like moons and stars hang from the ceiling everywhere, and you almost expect to hear Van Morrison singing "Moondance." But Lunar is a little more rustic than that. It has all of the markings of an old saloon. With its long, narrow interior, dark wood, and low lighting, it will indeed turn day into night; and the nightlife and fine beer found at Lunar can be out of this world (pardon my slip into the nonterrestrial world of Lunar's name and marketing).

Lunar is special because it's not large and it's not marketed as a mainstream brewpub, just a neighborhood tavern that makes its own beer. Most important, it's the type of place you walk into and do a doubletake, because there's a handful of faces at the bar, and everyone seems to know everyone. Lunar can indeed be packed on weekend nights, especially because there is a small stage in the back for live entertainment. But Lunar caters to repeat visitors and especially those who live nearby. It's the type of tavern you bring a good friend to, because, from the people who work behind the bar to the building itself, it all feels like a good friend. You quickly understand what this means, because the great old wooden bar and its accompanying back bar draw you to the barstools—while the high table seating and the other tables and chairs in the far part of the pub just seem to take care of the overflow. The moment you walk into Lunar, you want to belly up to the bar and have a few Lunar brews! Owner and brewmaster Jules Roels says, "Even for those on their first visit, the bar, its back bar, and old antique-looking fixtures will make you feel at home."

The beer lists for Lunar are kept on chalkboards above and at the end of the bar. As for the beer selection, it has something for everyone. Lunar has about ten of its own beers on tap, but the coolers contain an extensive selection of beers, including many hard-to-find imports. Lunar has an ambitious group of in-house brewed beers, from lighter bodied Pilsner-types to heavy, full-flavored stouts and porters. It seems that Roels is always cooking up something in his very small, three-barrel system. The brewery is actually the envy of anyone who has brewed at home in the kitchen. That's because the brewhaus is actually in the room behind the bar, in what was a former kitchen when the business served food. Lunar is full of unique beers, and there are always several to choose from. But despite the expansive list of house beers, at only 125 to 130 barrels per year, it's one of the smallest brewery/brewpubs in Illinois.

For the beer enthusiasts, Lunar always has an interesting and intriguing variety of house beers on tap. Mickey's Pils is a traditional light German lager, while the Moondance IPA and Polaris Porter offer assertive flavor and memorable character. The only true regular beers for Lunar are the Raspberry Cream Ale and the Kosmic Kolsch. But a hands-down, game-over favorite beer is Lunar's Belgian-style strong ale called Neil Armstrong Ale. After a few of these, you just might think the person sitting on the barstool next to you is Neil Armstrong!

HISTORY

The building that is home to Lunar was constructed in 1933. It served as a community gathering place and dance hall up until the 1950s, when political changes in the community instituted so-called "footloose laws" to reduce the dancing and the decadence that was believed to ensue in such establishments. Villa Park also constructed a new village hall about that time, so the building changed to a tavern and restaurant. In 1963 the structure survived a devastating fire that gutted the building and left only the exterior walls standing. After rebuilding it was occupied by a number of owners and businesses. The most recent tenant, before it became Lunar, was a bar called Adam's Place. Jules and Michele Roels purchased the building in 1996 and opened Lunar Brewing in May of that year.

Jules Roels, like many beer enthusiasts, became involved in the brewery ownership through an interest in homebrewing, but for Jules it's a much deeper infatuation than a mere hobby. Jules says he's genetically predispositioned to brewing, being part Belgian and having a grandfather who operated a small brewery there.

In the 1980s Jules was a corporate vice president in the electrical division of the Dover Company. One day co-workers were talking about homebrewing, and the conversation captivated his interests. Later, while purchasing home-brew supplies as a Christmas gift for one of those friends, Jules says he was just too tempted and soon found himself surrounded by his own homebrewing equipment.

Jules continued to read anything he could find about brewing. He soon became involved in the Brewers of South Suburbia (B.O.S.S.) and won a homebrew competition with his Mickey's Pils. By the 1990s Jules and his wife, Michele, were looking for a brewpub opportunity. They actually looked for about four years before finding what they considered a building with an "intrinsic feel" and character all its own. Once you've visited Lunar, you quickly understand how buildings can have their own personalities. And Jules has matched "intrinsic feel" with unique and distinctive beers.

After the Roelses found the location, selecting a name was done some-what by fate. In 1995 Jules and Michele were enjoying Christmas with friends. As Christmas Eve turned into Christmas morning, gifts were exchanged, and a friend gave Michele a pendant showing a crescent moon and elves shoveling pearls into the mouth of the moon. Suddenly it dawned on the Roelses: The name of their brewpub would be Lunar.

DON'T MISS THIS

The inside decor of Lunar is a vast collection of beer mirrors, hanging half-moons and stars, and a touch of history. The bottled beers are kept cool in an old icebox-style cooler behind the main bar. The iceboxes date back several owners. There's a small collection of beer steins high above the back bar. The back bar itself is a local product, constructed in the 1950s by a local Chicago craftsman. But if you're interested in beer advertising, look closely above the doorway to the restrooms for a two-dial clock from Lowenbrau—one set on local time, the other on Munich time.

LUNAR BREWS

Bella Luna Best Bitter 🍺🍺🍺🍺   *Your Ranking* _____

A firm hoppy nose. A light cloudiness to the copper color and a soft, tan head. Medium bodied and smooth texture brings out a light malty flavor, then the hops provide a strong bitter accent that competes with the caramel sweetness but really offers a nice balance. The hoppiness continues on into the finish for a firm, solid bitter beer. This traditional English bitter is made with Goldings and Fuggle hops for flavor and aroma.

Black Star Stout 🍺🍺🍺🍺   *Your Ranking* _____

A malty, somewhat grainy nose. Beautiful, deep, dark opaque color. The head is very, very thick, light brown, and soft. My pint supported almost an inch of that soft head above the glass! This stout is medium to full bodied and silky. The chocolate tones dominate, but the dry hoppy background is strong enough to be almost perfectly balanced. This is an excellent rendition of the dry Irish-style Guinness you get in Ireland—so much in balance you might think you're drinking a perfect porter.

Chateau de Lune 🍺🍺🍺   *Your Ranking* _____

This is a French-farmhouse style ale. A light musty nose. Cloudy, light golden to straw color and a thick, soft, white head. Medium bodied. Mild malty flavor with a crisp hoppy background. Finishes with a dry bitterness. Similar to the Mickey's Pils in flavor, but a little smoother and more balanced.

Lunar Pumpkin Ale 🍺🍺   *Your Ranking* _____

A pumpkin beer with lots of pumpkin flavor that will stand out for its assertive spiciness. A cinnamon and clove nose. A cloudy orange to copper color. A thin, soft, white head. Medium bodied, thin, bubbly, and soft. A mild caramel flavor, but the pumpkin really dominates. The sweet pumpkin, with a light dry hint of clove and even a little hops, comes out in the end.

Mickey's Pils 🍺🍺🍺   *Your Ranking* _____

Brewed as a traditional Pilsner lager. A fruity nose. Cloudy yellow to golden with a thick, soft, white head. Medium bodied and very bubbly. A light malty flavor with a sour background. The finish is crisp and bitter, even a little tart. There is a complex variety of flavors from fruity sour, to earthy, to bitter, and all seem to have some distinctive phases in the bulk of this beer's profile. This beer started it all for owner and brewmaster Jules Roels. Named after his wife, Michele, whose nickname is Mickey.

Moondance IPA 🍺🍺🍺🍺   *Your Ranking* _____

This is an aggressive, rough, strong India Pale Ale. If you like a well-made IPA, this beer is something to appreciate. Strong hoppy nose that does not disappoint you in the delivery of all the bitter and resin tones. Cloudy copper color and a thick, soft, tan head. Full bodied and rough, somewhat sharp textures because of the strong hoppy flavors. Dry from beginning to end. Made with Columbia hops. You get strong hop aroma and flavor as you dance to the moon.

Nebula Nut Brown 🍺🍺🍺   *Your Ranking* _____

This is a mild English-style brown. Begins with a light fruity nose. Cloudy bronze color and a thick, bubbly, brown head. Medium bodied. A soft, caramel malty flavor with a strong fruity background. The mild malty flavors transform into light roasted nutty tones in the finish.

Neil Armstrong Ale 🍺🍺🍺🍺   *Your Ranking* _____

An exceptional beer, a Belgian-style strong ale. Hints of coriander and sweetness in the nose. Clear, deep gold color with a delicate, soft, white head. Medium bodied with a soft texture. Sweet malty flavors are refined and smooth. There is a candylike sweetness in the background and finish. The ending has just a light hint of hoppiness that accents well, even lightens, its personality a touch. Made in celebration of Lunar's sixth anniversary, it is served in a snifter to enable you to appreciate its color and gentle aroma. One too many of these and you feel as if you're on the moon.

Oktoberfest 🍺🍺🍺   *Your Ranking* _____

A light, roasted, malty nose. Cloudy copper color with a thin, soft, tan head. Medium bodied and bubbly. Malty flavor with a crisp hoppy finish. Overall, the hoppiness is strong and memorable.

Polaris Porter 🍺🍺🍺🍺   *Your Ranking* _____

An excellent smooth, sweet porter. A light chocolate malty nose. Dark color with great bronze tints in the bottom of the pint. A thick, soft, tan head. Full bodied and silky. Malty flavors are very abundant, especially a smooth chocolate malty flavor with a roasted background that lingers into the finish for a great coffee-like accent. Made with eight malts and three hops. Served on a nitrogen tap line. A great full-bodied porter for a crisp, cool fall afternoon.

Third Stone from the Sun 🍺🍺🍺   *Your Ranking* _____

A German Stein (stone) lager. A roasted nose. Clear, light copper color and a thin, soft, white head. Medium bodied and round. A maltiness to the initial taste but well balanced with some bitterness, leaving you with a clean, crisp beer.

Total Eclipse 🍺🍺🍺🍺   *Your Ranking* _____

Smooth and solid malty flavors that combine for great balance. An export-style oatmeal stout served on a nitrogen tap line. The nose offers a strong aroma of chocolate malt. The color is deep and dark as a starless night. A thick, soft, brown head. Medium to full bodied and smooth. It actually looks much heavier than it feels. There is a great mixture of caramel and chocolate malt flavors at just the right strength to accent a smooth texture. This is a great stout.

OTHER LUNAR BREWS YOU MAY WANT TO TRY

Jumping Cow Cream Ale   *Your Ranking* _____

A pre-Prohibition ale. Smooth and soft. Hopped like a lager, but has some of the interesting fruity qualities of an ale.

Kosmic Kolsch   *Your Ranking* _____

Light and dry with some spicy aromas. Made with Noble hops. One of the standard beers you'll find on Lunar's taps.

Mc Red   *Your Ranking* _____

First served for St. Patrick's Day in 2003. A rich red ale with notes of toffee and a dry finish.

Moonbeam Steam   *Your Ranking* _____

An amber lager brewed as an ale. Made with Cascade hops.

Moonshine Stout   *Your Ranking* _____

A rich imperial stout. Secondary fermentation in Jack Daniel's whiskey barrels leaves this brew complex and enticing.

Orion Oatmeal Pale   *Your Ranking* _____

A silky oatmeal texture that's been well seasoned with Styrian hops.

Pale Moon   *Your Ranking* _____

An American pale ale with a big Cascade hop signature from start to finish.

Raspberry Cream Ale   *Your Ranking* _____

A lightly hopped cream ale with raspberry tones. A touch of vanilla rounds out the finish. A standard beer that is always available.

Summer Solstice Wit   *Your Ranking* _____

A summertime seasonal.

Yellow Moon Rice-in'   *Your Ranking* _____

An American Pilsner, brewed in a pre-Prohibition style.

BREWERY RATING

Rating	Your Rating	Shepard's Rating (1 to 4 Mugs)	General Description
Location		🍺🍺🍺	Neighborhood/residential
Ease of Finding Location		🍺🍺🍺	Difficult, out of the way, need a map
Brewery Atmosphere		🍺🍺🍺🍺	Rustic
Dining Experience		n/a	Limited; frozen pizza
The Pint		🍺🍺🍺🍺	A perfect experience

MENU

Lunar is more of a neighborhood tavern type brewpub with a very limited menu. There are frozen pizzas available, but the concentration is distinctively on its beer.

OTHER THINGS TO SEE OR DO IN THE AREA

A starting point for a visit to Villa Park is with a stop or call to the Villa Park Chamber of Commerce. The chamber is located in the Ardmore Avenue Train Station (10 West Park Avenue, 1-630-941-9133), which was constructed in 1910 and is listed on the National Register of Historic Places. Also on the National Register of Historic Places is the Villa Avenue Train Station, which served the Chicago, Aurora, and Elgin (C. A. & E.) Railroad. It is now home to the Villa Park Historical Society Museum (220 South Villa Avenue, at the Illinois Prairie Path). Built in 1929, it served passenger trains until 1957. The abandoned railroad right of way is now part of the sixty-one-mile-long Illinois Prairie Path recreational trail. The on-site museum contains artifacts from the railroad, village, and Ovaltine factory. The malt drink Ovaltine was once made in Villa Park at the Ovaltine Factory complex (1 Ovaltine Court) from 1917 to 1987. More recently the buildings have been part of a redevelopment area for Villa Park with lofts and apartments. Although the factory machines have long since been quiet, current residents claim the buildings are haunted by former workers, citing examples of strange noises and doors slamming for no reason. As for Ovaltine, which is now part of the Novatis Nutrition Corporation of Basel, Switzerland, it is thought of as a health drink in the

United States, in Britain it is considered a nighttime comforter, while in Thailand it can be bought on draft like beer!

DuPage County's largest sports and exposition facility is Odeum Sports and Expo Center (1033 North Villa Avenue). Odeum hosts concerts, sporting, and special events. It is also the site of "Scream Fest" haunted house during the Halloween season. The Enchanted Castle Indoor Entertainment Center (1103 South Main, Lombard) offers indoor fun with laser tag, rides, miniature golf, and other games. For outdoor enjoyment, try the Morton Arboretum (4100 Route 53, Lisle) with its seventeen-hundred-acres of trees and plants and twelve miles of hiking trails.

The Elmhurst Art Museum (150 Cottage Hill) is located in the steel and glass home of architect Ludwig Mies van der Rohe. It contains five galleries, with one permanently devoted to exhibiting works by members of the Elmhurst Artists' Guild. The Lizzadro Museum of Lapidary Art (220 Cottage Hill) is the result of more than fifty years of work by collector Joseph F. Lizzadro. It shares the beauty of hard stone carvings while promoting the study of earth science. The museum houses one of the largest collections of Chinese jade carvings in the country and features a unique gift shop. The York Theatre Building (152 North York Street, second floor) is home to the Theatre Historical Society of America. The society's American Movie Palace Museum includes artifacts, renderings, photos, ads, and other exhibits related to the great motion picture palaces built throughout the United States. The Elmhurst Historical Museum (120 East Park Avenue) is located in the 1892 Glos Mansion and provides galleries and national touring exhibits. The museum also sponsors a local cemetery tour with costumed interpreters who portray historic citizens of Elmhurst as they tell their life stories beside the tombstones.

The Mount Carmel Cemetery (1400 South Wolf Road/Harrison and Hillside Avenues, Hillside) is home to over four hundred private family mausoleums. Among the most visited is the Bishops' Mausoleum, which received over fifty thousand visitors in the two months after the death of Joseph Cardinal Bernardin in October 1996. But to many, Mount Carmel is just as famous for the graves of a number of Chicago gangsters—including Alphonse "Al" Capone, Earl "Hymie" Weiss, and Dion "Deany" O'Banion. Mount Carmel is also believed to be haunted by Julia Buccola Petta, also referred to as "The Italian Bride," who died in childbirth in 1921 at the age of twenty-nine. Her grave is depicted by a life-size statue of a woman in her wedding dress. There have been reports of an apparition of a woman in a white dress near her grave.

A little further east in Oak Park, the Ernest Hemingway Museum and Birthplace (339 North Oak Park Avenue) is located in the Victorian home where Hemingway was born. Oak Park is also home to the world's largest collection of Frank Lloyd Wright-designed buildings and houses, with twenty-five structures built between 1889 and 1913. Guided tours of the Home and Studio Complex (951 Chicago Avenue) take visitors through the complex and architectural laboratory used by Wright from 1889 to 1909.

For shopping, the Villa Park French Market (Ardmore Avenue and Prairie Path) is an open-air market setting for homegrown and commercial goods. The local farmers' market in Villa Park runs from June through October. Nearby, Elmhurst Crossing (St. Charles and Route 83) is about a mile east of Lunar, and the Elmhurst City Centre (209 North York Street) has a variety of opportunities with more than seventy-five shops, restaurants, and a restored movie theatre. Also in

Elmhurst is the well-known Elmhurst Public House (683 West St. Charles Road), with its monthly beer specials, a dozen-plus taps, and various bottled beers.

Lunar Brewing is actually part of a western Chicago "triangle" of great brewpubs. Within about fifteen minutes of each other, Lunar Brewing, Glen Ellyn Sports Brew, and Taylor Brewing all provide unique choices for good food and beer. You might also check those brewpub listings for other things to see or do in the area.

DIRECTIONS

Getting to Lunar will take a little planning for those who don't live in Villa Park or a surrounding suburb. It's highly recommended that you check a map, especially for exits and entrances to Interstates 290, 294, 355, and 88. The major roads bringing traffic east and west include South Addison Road (Route 64/North Avenue) and West Roosevelt Road (Route 38).

Lunar Brewing is located on busy St. Charles Road. The Villa Park water tower is about one block west of Lunar. For those approaching from the north or south on I-290, Lunar is about three and a half miles west of the I-290 interchange with St. Charles Road. If you see the Elmhurst water tower you're about a mile east of Lunar.

If you are approaching on Interstate 355 it's probably best to take the South Addison (Route 64) exit, travel east to North Ardmore Road, and turn south on Ardmore to St. Charles Road. Once at the corner of St. Charles and North Ardmore, turn back east, and Lunar is only about two blocks away.

Mickey Finn's Brewery
Libertyville

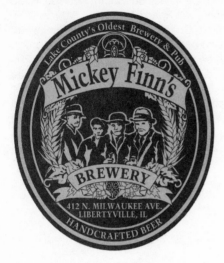

Visit Date	Signed

ABOUT THE BREWERY

When you're looking for a brewpub with strong ties to the community, the type you find with a local neighborhood tavern, you should try Mickey Finn's in Libertyville. Located on the town's square, across from Cook Memorial Park and Rose Garden on Milwaukee Avenue, you get a great feeling of community history in this old tavern. It's almost always busy, and it is able to maintain an intense personal feel when you walk through the door. Once you enter the main barroom you'll quickly see why it's been a long-time local gathering place. Brick walls, wooden accents, a pressed tin ceiling, old photos, and an incredible old back bar all give Mickey Finn's a "well worn" feel.

The service is also something that is distinctive and memorable. You're greeted with a smile from the time you walk through the door, and no matter how busy the place is, the wait never seems long because staff are so attentive. You'll also find all of the staff are very knowledgeable about the beer that's served in Mickey Finn's. This is due in part to the classroom-style orientation to beer that each staff member must go through before becoming a server. Staff actually take a Mickey Finn's exam before they're allowed to serve beer.

Mickey Finn's encompasses roughly fourteen thousand square feet of bar and restaurant space. The main bar is on the first floor, to the right of the front door. The dining room shares some space with the brewhaus. Upstairs there is a full-service bar and large seating area that is often used on weekends and for special parties or banquets. In the summertime Mickey Finn's has a very inviting beer garden nestled between the buildings with its own full-sized trees and overlook of Cook Park. When approaching Mickey Finn's from Milwaukee Avenue, you actually walk through the beer garden on your way to the front door.

Mickey Finn's regularly has eight or more of its own beers on tap, plus you'll find occasional cask-conditioned beers. Mickey Finn's Wheat Ale is always served; it's actually one of the brewpub's original beer styles from when it opened in 1994. A great deal of thought has also been put into the beer names, which reference Libertyville history or local places, such as Abana Amber Ale, Five Springs Oatmeal Stout, and Mr. C's Pale Ale (as in Ansel Cook, see description below). But Mickey Finn's doesn't just try to pass off cute names; the beers live up to expectations. Just try the Gudenteit Hefe Weizen. It's one of the most popular brewmaster's specials and is well worth a trip, especially if you have an opportunity to enjoy it in the outdoor beer garden.

HISTORY

Mickey Finn's was established as a brewery in 1994. However, the name Mickey Finn goes back a lot further—to Chicago's nineteenth century. In his 1940 history of Chicago's underworld, *Gem of the Prairie*, Herbert Asbury described the original Mickey Finn as a notorious Chicago tavern proprietor in Chicago's South Loop: "Finn was the lowliest and by far the toughest of the princes of Chicago's Whisky Row. This terrible little man—he was only five feet and five inches tall and weighed about a hundred and forty pounds—was the veritable Mickey Finn whose name became synonymous for a knockout drink. It tickled Mickey Finn's fancy to have a customer order by 'his' name the drink which would knock him out."

In 1896 Finn opened a bar called the Lone Star Saloon and Palm Garden at the southern end of Whisky Row near Harrison Street. In the Lone Star and Palm Garden Finn allegedly fenced stolen property, ran a school of instruction for young pickpockets, and, with his wife Kate Roses, oversaw "girls" of questionable character! Finn hooked up with a voodoo doctor named Hall to develop "knockout" drinks by means of which Lone Star patrons mysteriously passed out and were dragged into a back room, stripped of their valuables, and then dumped in an alley. Finn's trademark was that he always put on a derby hat and a clean white apron before he robbed his unconscious victim. By 1903 Mickey Finn was shut down by Chicago police, but a little cash in the right account supposedly helped him avoid prosecution. His legacy, however, is that "Mickey Finn" became the slang for any sort of knockout drink.

The Libertyville building containing the modern Mickey Finn's Brewery dates back to the 1920s. During Prohibition the tavern "posed" as a barbershop. The present Mickey Finn's brewpub got its start by chance. One evening in the early 1990s, Libertyville businessman Pat Elmquest was on his way home and stopped into the former Mickey Finn's tavern. Pat somewhat jokingly told his friends he was looking to try something different, when one of them remarked he should buy the place. And in a few months he did. In 1992 Elmquest entered into a partnership with Bill Sugars, who also was looking for a business opportunity. Sugars had looked around in different cities, but luckily for Libertyville, Sugars settled on Mickey Finn's. Sugars knew Elmquest, and with some extensive ideas for expanding the tavern into a brewpub, plus the right business plan and financing, they were able to create today's Mickey Finn's. Elmquest unfortunately passed away in 2002. Sugars remains very active in the business, and you'll likely see him almost anytime at the brewpub, greeting patrons and even pitching in when needed.

Brewmaster Luke Kazmierski also has an interesting story about how he ended up at Mickey Finn's. Like Elmquest, he also happened to be dining in Mickey Finn's one evening with his wife. As an avid homebrewer, Kazmierski, in a casual conversation with the waiter, made a passing remark about offering to help out around the brewpub. But as fate would have it, there turned out to be an opening for an assistant brewer. Luke says that at the time he didn't think much about his over-dinner offer to help out, but in a few days he got a call from former brewmaster Ryan Ashley. After coming in a couple of times, Luke made an impression and was offered the job. Despite being locally employed with Abbott Laboratories, Luke decided it was time for a change and became a professional brewer in January 2000. He took over for Ashley to become Mickey Finn's head brewer in 2002.

DON'T MISS THIS

The historical references throughout Mickey Finn's really accent the charm and character of the old tavern. The interior walls offer numerous old photos of Illinois bars and turn-of-the-century beer drinkers. Look closely at the large black-and-white photo behind the main first-floor bar and you'll notice that this 1935 photo is an heirloom of Mickey Finn's showing the actual back bar that is still in use today. This photo is used by Mickey Finn's in its logos and packaging.

MICKEY FINN'S BREWS

Abana Amber Ale 🍺🍺   *Your Ranking* _____
A light hoppy nose. Clear copper color and a thin, soft, white head. Medium bodied and very bubbly. Hoppy bitterness that is strong and dominant, not overwhelming. A mildly dry finish. This beer has great color and flavor. Its name comes from Abana Spring, which was a major source of water for Libertyville's Grabbe and Newberry bottled water company of the 1880s. Abana Spring on the Grabbe and Newberry property was supposedly named after a famous well in the Holy Land.

Alt Bier 🍺🍺🍺   *Your Ranking* _____
A fairly clean beer with a light fruity background. No nose. Clear, deep copper color and a thin, tan, bubbly head. Medium bodied and very bubbly. A mild malty flavor with a light, yet firm, fruity background. Finishes with a light bitterness and hints of dryness. The bubbly body and light fruity accents stand out.

Five Springs Oatmeal Stout 🍺🍺🍺🍺   *Your Ranking* _____
A strong malty nose with light hints of roasted coffee. Dark color with reddish to bronze highlights. A very thick, soft, brown head. Full bodied and soft. Strong sweet and smooth malty tones stand out. A firm sweet chocolate malt finish with a subtle dryness that builds. This beer won a silver medal and a bronze medal for Best of Show in the 2000 Real Ale Festival. In 1994 it won

Best of Show at the Chicago Beer Society's Fall Tasting. The name pays tribute to the local springs used by American Indians for medicinal purposes. The Indians valued several such springs near Rockland Road and the Des Plaines River. The Grabbe and Newberry company, which bottled water in Libertyville in the nineteenth century, sold some of this water as "Vital Water." Historical information from the Cook Memorial Public Library described it as being "put into brown glass bottles because the sun's rays shining through the clear glass activated the chemicals and generated gas which sometimes exploded the bottle"—sounds like beer!

Gudendark Dunkel Weizen   Your Ranking _____

A darker version of the Hefe Weizen. A little more malty aroma. Cloudy copper color with a thick, soft, tan head. Medium bodied and bubbly. A malty, even caramel-type sweetness that is slightly more prominent than the fruity banana and clove flavors. Winner of a gold medal in the 1998 Great American Beer Festival and a gold medal in the 1998 World Beer Cup competition.

Gudenkrisp Kolsch   Your Ranking _____

No nose. A light golden color and somewhat hazy. Thin, very soft, white head. Light bodied with a soft texture. Crisp, sweet, malty flavor that lingers into a light finish. A light-bodied beer with plenty of color.

Gudenteit Hefe Weizen   Your Ranking _____

Not always on tap, but one of the most sought-after Hefe-Weizens in Illinois when it is. Strong, assertive spicy aroma. Cloudy golden color with a thick, soft, white head. Light to medium bodied, bubbly and somewhat soft texture. Full of wheat malt flavor with a fruity finish. A gold medal winner in 2001 and 1998 and a bronze medal winner in the 1996 Great American Beer Festival. An exceptional beer.

Imperial Delusion   Your Ranking _____

A malty nose. Very dark, thick-looking body. A thick, bubbly, brown head. Full bodied and chewy. Strong chocolate flavor. Warm and earthy finish with a sticky sweetness. This imperial stout was first brewed at the end of 1999 for the Y2K craze. Fermented in Jack Daniel's whiskey barrels.

Little Fort Porter   Your Ranking _____

Dark and full bodied with smooth roasted qualities. Begins with a light roasted aroma. Dark black color with brown highlights. A thin, soft, off-white head. Full bodied and soft textured. Sweet caramel and chocolate maltiness. A sweet finish. The name pays tribute to the Great Lakes Naval Training Center, which is located about ten miles east of Libertyville.

Mickey Finn's Raz   Your Ranking _____

Mickey Finn's Wheat Ale with raspberry flavor, a summertime seasonal. Strong raspberry nose. Dark yellow to golden and cloudy. A thin, bubbly, white head. Light bodied and highly carbonated. The raspberry flavors stand out in the taste, but there is a subtle background of clove and spiciness. The beer finishes with the fruity raspberry flavors and aroma.

Mickey Finn's Wheat Ale   🍺🍺🍺   *Your Ranking* _____

Considered the mainstay of Mickey Finn's because this beer has been on tap since the brewery opened in 1994. A spicy nose. Hazy golden color and a thick, soft, white head. Medium bodied and soft texture. A sweet, malty flavor with a mild, fruity background that leaves you with a sweet finish. There is a light graininess in the end. Brewed with 50 percent wheat malt, this beer has a subtly sweet flavor balanced with a faint spicy aroma. Until 2002 this beer was available locally in a six-pack of bottles.

Mr. C's Pale Ale   🍺🍺🍺   *Your Ranking* _____

A complex nose that has some bitterness and hints of earthy maltiness. A dark yellow to golden color with a thick, bubbly, white head. Medium bodied. Smooth hoppiness dominates. A light dry finish. A nitrogen-charged version is called Mr. C's Nitro Pale Ale and is very similar except for the more pronounced, softer texture. This beer honors Libertyville patriarch, Ansel Cook. Mr. C. farmed near Libertyville and eventually became an Illinois state legislator. The Cook Mansion was the first permanent dwelling in Libertyville and is located directly across the street from Mickey Finn's in Cook Park.

R. K.'s IPA   🍺🍺🍺🍺   *Your Ranking* _____

A flowery nose. Clear copper color and a thin, soft, tan head. Medium bodied with a sharpness to the texture. Bitterness dominates and remains firm and long lasting. A dry finish. There seems to be a slight maltiness in the beginning, but the hoppiness takes over. The bitterness seems light at first but it will continue to build. This is a solid, well-done IPA that hopheads will truly enjoy.

Ridiculously Conspicuous IPA   🍺🍺🍺   *Your Ranking* _____

The hops do make this a conspicuous beer! A strong floral nose. Deep golden to copper color and a thick, tan head. Medium bodied and soft texture. Overall a strong, firm bitter IPA. The floral aroma is assertive and really adds to the ridiculous hoppy nature of this beer.

Scapegoat Doppelbock   🍺🍺🍺🍺   *Your Ranking* _____

Lots of caramel flavor and warmth in this bock. A light malty nose. Deep, dark bronze color. A thick, bubbly, brown head. Medium bodied and soft. Strong caramel malt flavor. A sweet, warm finish. A well-done, full-flavored doppelbock.

Wee Heavy   🍺🍺🍺🍺   *Your Ranking* _____

Lots of malt from the nose to the finish. Deep bronze color and a thick, rich, soft, tan head. Full bodied. Malty caramel flavors with a warm finish. A very smooth and soft Wee Heavy that accentuates the maltiness. A bronze medal winner in the 2002 World Beer Cup competition. A silver medal winner at the 1997 Great American Beer Festival.

Wit-Engeltje   🍺🍺🍺🍺   *Your Ranking* _____

A Belgian-style Wit beer. A tart nose. Light golden color with a thin, soft, white head. Light bodied and soft texture. The taste is tart, almost a sharp fruitiness. There are hints of orange and coriander in the background and finish. A refreshing beer. This Flemish titled beer means "White Angel," and it marks the July 2000 birth of former brewmaster Ryan Ashley's daughter.

OTHER MICKEY FINN'S BREWS YOU MAY WANT TO TRY

Butler Ballpark Dark   *Your Ranking* _____
This dark ale is named after the nearby baseball fields.

German Pilsner   *Your Ranking* _____
A crisp, floral aroma. Golden colored and light to medium bodied.

Mickey Finn's Classic Irish Stout   *Your Ranking* _____
Dark color with a thick, soft, tan head. Strong malty flavor. You expect a great stout from a bar called Mickey Finn's.

Mickey Finn's Oktoberfest   *Your Ranking* _____
Deep copper and well balanced.

Old Rondout Pale Ale   *Your Ranking* _____
Named after the town of Rondout, located about three miles east of Libertyville on Route 176.

Santa's Magic   *Your Ranking* _____
Released on the Friday after Thanksgiving. Belgian strong ale made with twenty-five pounds of honey and thirty-five pounds of dark Belgian candy sugar in each ten-barrel batch.

Scottish Ale   *Your Ranking* _____
Deep copper color and full of warm malty tones.

Vardin's Best   *Your Ranking* _____
An English bitter named after Englishman George Vardin, who was the first to build a log cabin in a grove of trees that would become Vardin's Grove, which grew into the town of Libertyville. When the Vardin family moved out of their cabin, the structure eventually became Libertyville's first post office.

Whiskey Barrel Imperial Stout   *Your Ranking* _____
Similar to the Imperial Delusion. This strong, full-bodied stout is stored in Jack Daniel's whiskey barrels for up to a year before serving.

BREWERY RATING

	Your Rating	Shepard's Rating (1 to 4 Mugs)	General Description
Location		🍺 🍺 🍺	Commercial/industrial
Ease of Finding Location		🍺 🍺 🍺	Easy, but requires some planning
Brewery Atmosphere		🍺 🍺 🍺	Family restaurant Family tavern

	Your Rating	Shepard's Rating	General Description
Dining Experience		🍺🍺🍺🍺	Family style/variety
The Pint		🍺🍺🍺🍺	A perfect experience

MENU

The food at Mickey Finn's ranges from banquet, family restaurant, or tavern to lighter bar and pub fare. On the munchies portion of the menu, you'll find a common assortment of bar appetizers such as seasoned fried chicken wings called Killer Wings, a cheesy artichoke dip, chicken taquitos, and Finn's skins (potato wedges filled with bacon, melted cheddar, and green onions). For groups of friends the beer cheese fondue is a fun dish. About a half-dozen salad choices, a soup of the day, and Mickey's beer bread are on the lighter side of the menu. Mickey Finn's offers a number of sandwich and burger choices, including the red-hot cayenne pepper Cajun chicken sandwich, the Alpine chicken with sautéed fresh mushrooms and melted Swiss cheese, a tuna melt, and a Reuben. The basic burger is known as the Mickey burger, and the "Pat E" Melt pays tribute to late owner Pat Elmquest. A special section of the menu features Mexican fare, with chicken and pork burritos, chicken quesadillas, green enchiladas, and the Pancho's special quesadilla, which offers a combination of steak, onions, peppers, tomatoes, and cilantro. Mickey Finn's also serves a few pitas, daily specials, and pizza. The heart of the pub specials include chicken pot pie, Irish pot pie made with ground beef and vegetables, whitefish filet, broasted chicken dinner, baked cheese tortellini, and linguini with marinara sauce. For dessert you might finish your meal with cheesecake.

OTHER THINGS TO SEE OR DO IN THE AREA

Libertyville is located in south central Lake County, approximately thirty-five miles north of the Chicago Loop and seven miles west of Lake Michigan. As you arrive in Libertyville, you'll likely travel on Milwaukee Avenue (Route 21). This road is a historic one, paralleling the Des Plaines River. For hundreds of years it served as a principal route between the Chicago Portage (between the Des Plaines River and the Chicago River) and then on to Green Bay—connecting the Mississippi to the St. Lawrence Seaway.

In Cook Park, directly across the street from Mickey Finn's, you can tour the home of Ansel B. Cook, contractor, builder, and state legislator, after whom the park is named. The home was built in 1878 and stands on the site of George Vardin's original homestead, which was the first cabin in what would become Libertyville. The property was later the place where Dr. Foster, the first doctor to practice in Libertyville, had his office. It also served as the first post office for Libertyville and the surrounding area. Today the Cook Mansion serves as headquarters of the Libertyville-Mundelein Historical Society.

Famous Chicago architect David Adler left his estate to the village of Libertyville. The Adler Cultural Center (1700 North Milwaukee Avenue) contains artwork and provides music classes. It also hosts an annual Festival of the

Arts each August. The David Adler home and its eleven acres are listed on the National Register of Historic Places. One of Adler's most ambitious projects in the Chicago area was an estate he designed just west of Lake Forest for the Lasker family, with its private swimming pool, theater, and golf course. In the 1920s, Adler was also a trustee of the Art Institute of Chicago.

On its historic Main Street, Libertyville has many distinctive shops, galleries, and award-winning restaurants. Libertyville's farmers' markets are on Thursdays. And Libertyville hosts a big sidewalk sale several times a year.

About ten miles north of Mickey Finn's the town of Gurnee (Interstate 94 and Route 132) is a mecca for shopping and outdoor amusements. The Gurnee Mills Mall (6112 West Grand Avenue) features over two hundred stores with discount, outlet, and specialty vendors. A little further north of Gurnee, near the Wisconsin border, the Tempel Lipizzans are majestic white stallions that prance and dance as they perform a centuries-old tradition of classical dressage at Tempel Farms (17000 Wadsworth Road, Wadsworth). Performances are held mid-June through August. Six Flags Great America (542 North Route 21) has over one hundred different rides, including the Déjà Vu—the worlds tallest and fastest suspended looping boomerang coaster—and numerous shows. One of Illinois's most unusual homes is located in this area between Gurnee and Wadsworth. The Gold Pyramid House (near Route 132 and Dilley's Road, for directions call 847-662-6666) is fifty-five feet tall and painted gold, with a statue of Pharaoh Ramses II standing guard.

Along the Lake Michigan shore, the Great Lakes Museum at the Great Lakes Naval Training Center provides insight into life at a "boot camp" training facility. A special section of the museum is dedicated to the expanding role of women in the United States Navy. The museum is located in the Camp Barry area of the training center.

South of Mickey Finn's and the Libertyville town square, the Cuneo Museum and Gardens in Vernon Hills (1350 North Milwaukee Avenue) has seventeenth-century tapestries, oriental rugs and paintings. The thirty-room estate was built in 1914 by Samuel Insull, a one-time secretary to Thomas Edison and later the first chairman of the Commonwealth Edison Company.

The Kolbe Shrine (1600 West Park Avenue, about two miles west of Libertyville along Route 176) honors the life of Franciscan priest and Polish saint Maximilian Kolbe. Mosaics depict his life as well as his death in a German concentration camp during World War II. Marytown also holds both an arts and crafts fair and a city festival every August.

Lambs Farm (Route 176 and Interstate 94) is a pet shop and interactive facility for developmentally disabled adults. In addition to the pet shop, the farm has Aunt Mary's Country Store and Bakery, an ice cream parlor, and a thrift shop. The Discovery Center at the farm gives visitors a chance to learn what wool or a goat's horn feels like. Rides include a miniature train, which travels along the shore of Lambs Lake, and the Old World Carousel. Lambs Farm also hosts a summer arts and crafts show. Mickey Finn's sponsors a 5K race each year, raising money for disabled youths and adults.

If you enjoy hiking and biking, there are some great trails in the Libertyville area. The Independence Grove Forest Preserve (River Road, north from Route 137) covers eleven hundred acres and offers hiking and bicycling trails. Independence Grove is one of the early names of Libertyville. Just west of town the Butler Lake Bike Path will allow you to explore Butler Lake Park, and east of Libertyville is the Des Plaines River Trail. Plans call for this trail to stretch over thirty miles through Lake County. In northern stretches the valley is wide and the river meanders through open prairies and savannas. In southern stretches the river is straighter and the valley is narrower with woodlands and forests.

About ten miles southwest of Libertyville, Wauconda is the site of the Lakewood Forest Preserve's Lake County Discovery Museum (27277 Forest Preserve Drive, near Route 176 and Fairfield Road). It's home to the Curt Teich Postcard Archives, which is the world's largest collection of picture postcards. You can also speed back twelve thousand years in the Vortex Roller Coaster Theatre, shop for ideas in the Mall of History, or enjoy the two thousand acres of forest preserve. Also west of Libertyville in Volo is the Illinois Auto Museum (27582 West Volo Village Road) with its 250 classic and Hollywood cars, three hundred antique dealers, 1950s-style food court, and memorabilia shop.

You may also want to check the brewery descriptions for Flatlander's (Lincolnshire) and Ram (Wheeling) for other things to see and do in the area.

DIRECTIONS

Mickey Finn's is located in downtown Libertyville near the corner of Church Street and Illinois Route 21 (Milwaukee Avenue). Milwaukee Avenue is the main north-south road. But if you choose to drive the tollway system, it can be a little tricky.

From Chicago take Interstate 90 west either to Interstate 94 North (Edens Expressway) toward Milwaukee or to Interstate 294 (Tri-State Tollway), which will join I-94 and continue north toward Milwaukee. Exit either Route 176 or Route 137. When you reach Milwaukee Avenue (Route 21) turn north if you're on Route 176, or turn south if you're on Route 137. Mickey Finn's is located on the east side of the town square. If you're traveling from Wisconsin, it's best to

exit at Route 137 because there is no southbound off-ramp at the Route 176 interchange.

Mickey Finn's is also near two other brewpubs. Flatlander's is located about six miles south on Milwaukee Avenue in Lincolnshire, and Ram–Wheeling just about four miles beyond Flatlander's.

The Metra North Central Service Line has stations in Libertyville (2401 West Harris Road) and Mundelein (205 North Archer Avenue). However, the locations of these stations would likely require a short connecting cab-ride between the brewery and the train depot.

Millrose Restaurant and Brewing Company

South Barrington

Visit Date	Signed

ABOUT THE BREWERY

Millrose Restaurant and Brewing Company has a very distinctive appearance; it is actually a building complex composed of six barns that were originally constructed in the mid-nineteenth century. All of the barns were either moved or taken apart and reassembled into what Millrose is today. As one of the Millrose brochures states, "Why close the barn after the cows are out?"

On the outside there is a barn look, but actually the silo catches your eye first. You really can't appreciate how many barns are involved or the overall interior floor plan until you are inside. Each barn makes a distinctive contribution to the restaurant, brewery, banquet facilities, and country store components of Millrose. For example, one barn was used for the country store, another became the pub room, another helped give rise to the gift shop, and still another makes up the Rosewood Tavern. All are connected in ways that open directly from one interior section to another. Inside, the individual barns also serve as additional private dining or banquet rooms.

The decor is as rural as you would expect in a barn-bar. Antique tools, chandeliers made with antlers, bent willow chairs, leather booths, and Southwestern-style rugs all help establish a rustic atmosphere. There are at least six stone fireplaces throughout the rooms, or rather barns. The main bar is square with about twenty-five stools. It is located in the center of a large A-frame, cathedral-like room. From here you can walk into the main dining room, into the country store, toward one of the two patios, or up a small staircase to a loft and private dining rooms. The Rosewood Tavern is to the right of the main entryway. It is actually from a local barn, built in the

1840s by the Busse family, that once stood near West Cuba and Quentin Roads. The Rosewood is decorated in a Western decor and has small tables, its own bar, and comfortable lounge seating. It leaves you with the feeling that you've stepped into the private study of a Western cattle baron's home.

The Millrose is well known for its banquet facilities, which meet the needs of wedding receptions, small conferences, and private parties. The menu is extensive, even expansive from a page-by-page perspective. The restaurant was founded by a meat-packing company, so they give extra attention to dishes featuring ribs, pork, and steak.

Millrose regularly offers four to six of its own beers, plus various national macrobrewery beers and a wine list. The Country Inn Ale and Prairie Pilsner are the best sellers, but give the Panther Ale a try if you're looking for an amber ale. Another favorite to watch for is the occasional appearance of the General's Ale.

HISTORY

Millrose Restaurant and Brewing Company grew from a long-time Chicago-area meat-packing company. Rose Packing Company began in 1924, near Midway Airport. In the 1950s, company owner William Rose decided to bring his family to the village of South Barrington, where he was also involved in helping to establish the village. In 1973 Rose relocated the meat-packing company headquarters to the present lot it shares with Millrose Restaurant and Brewing Company. The country store was the first addition to Rose's business, in what would become a restaurant, country store, gift shop, banquet facilities, and brewery.

The barns that make up Millrose date back to the 1840s through the 1870s. The first arrived on-site in 1975, when William Rose needed extra space for his country store. Rose had purchased farmland in the Barrington area and decided that moving the barns would support his country store theme and also make good use of the barns. By 1981 he had moved the second barn from the former Magnuson farm, located about a mile north on Barrington Road. But the most ambitious barn relocation occurred in 1984, when Rose moved a barn that had been built in 1870 from the farm of Chris Heinrich. The barn, the largest of the Millrose barns, had originally sat near Route 72 and Interstate 90. To move the barn meant bringing it across the Barrington Road overpass of I-90. What a sight it was, as the structure inched its way across the bridge while traffic flowed underneath the overpass.

Through the late 1980s the number of barns continued to grow on the site. It was Rose Packing Company vice-president Mike Sherian who spent a couple of years researching microbreweries and designing ideas for the restaurant and brewery. The brewery finally opened in October 1992.

DON'T MISS THIS

Every visit to Millrose seems to bring out something from its decor that you didn't see before. Just take some time to walk about. It's hard to miss the ten-foot-diameter antler chandelier that hangs in the main bar. Or, in the Rosewood Tavern room, you'll find a four-foot bear made from willow branches standing on a rooflike platform above the bar.

Country Inn Ale 🍺🍺🍺

Your Ranking _____

A mild hoppy nose. Clear, light golden color and a thin, soft, white head. Light bodied with a soft texture. Mild hoppy flavor, but overall only a light bitterness. A very faint sweet ending, but not much of a finish.

Dark Star Lager 🍺🍺🍺

Your Ranking _____

This has the most distinctive character of the Millrose brews. A light malty nose. Clear, dark bronze color and a thin, bubbly, off-white head. Medium bodied. A clean, crisp malty flavor with just a light bitter background. A mostly clean finish with just a light roasted caramel malt ending.

General's Ale 🍺🍺🍺

Your Ranking _____

An American-style pale ale brewed with pale and caramel malts. Begins with a faint flowery nose. Deep golden color with a light haziness. Thick, soft, tan head. Medium bodied with a soft slickness. Mild flowery, resiny bitterness dominates and lingers into the finish. This beer has a nice hoppy start, but it just seems a little timid. A brewmaster's special at Millrose, it pays tribute to one of the original business partners, who was a general in the United States Marine Corps.

Panther Ale 🍺🍺🍺

Your Ranking _____

This amber ale has a light malty nose. Clear copper color and a thin, soft, white head. Medium to light bodied. A sweet caramel malt flavor stands out from the very start. Finishes with a light, very mild bitterness. This is a solid amber ale.

Prairie Pilsner 🍺🍺

Your Ranking _____

A very light Czech-style Pilsner. No nose. A clear light straw body with a thin, bubbly, white head. Light bodied and soft. A dryness to texture and flavor but no attempt at malty qualities.

Raspberry Wheat 🍺🍺

Your Ranking _____

A light raspberry wheat, difficult to identify as a flavored beer by aroma and appearance. Virtually no nose, the aroma of raspberries was especially absent. Golden color with a light cloudiness. Very light bodied and soft texture. There is a mild, sweet raspberry fruitiness to the taste, but the flavor is actually very light. Most of the sweet raspberry flavor builds from the beer's finish, but only after several sips.

Rose's Red Ale 🍺

Your Ranking _____

A malty nose. Clear, dark, reddish bronze color. A thick, soft, tan head. Light body with a soft, slick texture. A malty beer with caramel tones that stand out. Finishes very sweet. This beer was just a little too reminiscent of sweet wort.

Rosewood Oatmeal Stout 🍺🍺🍺

Your Ranking _____

Strong roasted nose. A clear, very dark color with a thick, creamy, tan head. Begins with a slight bitterness that helps accent the roasted malt aroma and taste. Finishes with a light roasted chocolate malty flavor. There is some nice taste and flavor in this beer, especially the light dryness. Overall, this beer is best described as a light, dry stout; or it could pass for a roasted rye porter.

Wheat and Honey 🍺🍺   *Your Ranking* _____

No nose. Golden color with a light cloudiness. Very light bodied and soft texture. There is only a mild flavor of malt; the emphasis is on a sugary type sweetness to the main body and finish. It is described as Millrose's Blonde Ale with honey.

OTHER MILLROSE BREWS YOU MAY WANT TO TRY

Blonde Ale   *Your Ranking* _____

Light bodied, golden color, and crisp hoppy flavor.

Porter   *Your Ranking* _____

A brewmaster's special. Dark, full bodied, and roasted.

BREWERY RATING

	Your Rating	Shepard's Rating (1 to 4 Mugs)	General Description
Location		🍺🍺🍺	Commercial/industrial
Ease of Finding Location		🍺🍺🍺🍺	Close to major roads and intersections
Brewery Atmosphere		🍺🍺🍺	Family restaurant
			Rustic
Dining Experience		🍺🍺🍺	Family style/variety
The Pint		🍺🍺🍺	A good experience

MENU

Given the Millrose rural theme and the restaurant's decor, you can expect some hearty country cooking. The quantity and quality of what the menu offers is clearly a focus for Millrose. It is also a good idea to check your watch to see which menu (brunch, lunch, dinner, or banquet) you'll be ordering from, because each has its own specialties that make every visit new and interesting. The basic choices on the menu include appetizers, soups, salads, sandwiches, burgers, pasta, and vegetarian main entrees and Millrose specialties. Many of the choices are made with beer. The appetizers that you'll find include chicken wings, fried jalapeños, fried onion straws, potato skins, and a sampling of nearly all the appetizers with the Taste of Millrose, which is a meal in itself or a party for friends! The soups are hearty and thick, and choices include the Millrose chili, beef vegetable, and baked French onion. There are more than a half-dozen salads and at least that many sandwiches and burgers. Five pastas are on the menu, with a couple that are vegetarian options. Dinner entrees can be more expensive than you would expect to find in most brewpubs, but you'll get some generous portions and excellent pairings such as the aged ribeye served with southwestern roasted peppers or the baby back ribs glazed with Millrose sauce. Other dishes include lamb, poultry, and seafood.

OTHER THINGS TO SEE OR DO IN THE AREA

Millrose is located about five miles west of the Interstate 90 and 290 interchange. South Barrington and a number of area villages combine to offer many options for an evening or weekend trip to Chicago's western suburbs.

One of the local landmarks of South Barrington is Goebbert's Pumpkin and Farm Market (40 West Higgins Road, Barrington). Although known for its seasonal plants, pumpkins, and haunted house, Geobbert's also offers Animal Land, where you can feed goats, chickens, pigs, llamas, and kangaroos. Also, very close to Millrose is the AMC South Barrington 30 Theatres (175 Studio Drive, Barrington).

Northeast of South Barrington, the village of Palatine holds its Street Fest in August. Palatine also hosts a farmers' market from July through October at the Palatine Train Station (137 West Wood Street). In nearby Arlington Heights (about twelve miles east and north of Millrose Restaurant and Brewing Company) you'll find the Arlington Heights Historical Museum (110 West Freemont Street), and the Arlington Park Racecourse (Euclid Avenue and Wilke Road), which features thoroughbred racing. In the general vicinity area of Arlington Heights, the Rolling Meadows Park District headquarters (3000 Central Road) is home to William B. Fosser's Puppet Production "Opera in Focus." With fully staged scenes from well-known operas, the performances run about one hour. A demonstration of the operation of the puppets and a tour of the highly technical backstage area follows each performance.

South of Millrose, the Hoffman Estates Park District runs the Seascape Family Aquatic Center (1300 Moon Lake Boulevard). Continuing south on Roselle Road toward Roselle, you may want to consider a visit to the Lynfred Winery (15 South Roselle Road).

Directly north of Millrose, the Barrington Ice House Mall (200 Applebee Street, Barrington) was once an actual ice house built in 1904. Located in the heart of the downtown, the ice house has been transformed into a mall that includes many specialty shops and restaurants that link its historic architecture to the modern structure. Also in Barrington, you can walk inside a giant heart, fill a cavity on a colossal tooth, or take a video ride in an ambulance during a visit to Health World (1301 South Grove Avenue).

Barrington also is known for a legendary gun battle that took place on November 27, 1934, at the entrance to North Side Park. The shootout left two federal agents dead and mortally wounded outlaw "Baby Face" Nelson, who escaped but later bled to death from seventeen bullet wounds. The agents who died in the confrontation, Samuel Cowley and Herman F. Hollis, had only four months earlier been part of the ambush that killed John Dillinger outside the Biograph Theater on Chicago's near west side (see the brewery description for Goose Island–Clybourn Avenue).

You may also want to check the brewery descriptions for Prairie Rock–Schaumburg and Ram–Schaumburg for other things to see and do in the area.

DIRECTIONS

Millrose Restaurant and Brewing Company is located at the corner of Central Road, Studio Drive, and Barrington Road, just a stoplight north of the Barrington Road overpass of Interstate 90. It's easy to find when traveling westward from downtown, but a little more complicated when traveling eastward toward Chicago.

If traveling west on I-90, exit at Barrington Road-North, go north to the stoplight, then turn right (east) into Millrose.

If traveling east toward Chicago on I-90, exit at Sutton Road (Route 59), go north to the light on Higgins Road (Route 72), then turn right (east/southeast) on Higgins and travel two and a half miles to Barrington Road, turn left (north) on Barrington Road, cross over I-90 to the light, and then turn right (east) into Millrose.

O'Griff's Irish Pub and Brew House

Quincy

Visit Date	Signed

ABOUT THE BREWERY

Quincy may seem a little out of the way for some, but if the beer doesn't bring you here, the scenic drive and history of the area will provide a great weekend getaway. O'Griff's Irish Pub and Brew House is located in Quincy's downtown square, on the north side of Washington Park (also called John's Square), where in 1858 the famous Lincoln-Douglas debate took place.

O'Griff's Pub is on the north side of the town square, in between the Washington Theater and the former Ricker National Bank (now called the Griffin Center). The building housing O'Griff's Brew House was originally built in the 1870s and served as a trading post. Prior to renovations in the 1990s, the building's stone walls and dirt floor presented challenges to the brewery's owner, brewer and local developer Dan Griffin. But after extensive renovations and acquisition of some used brewing equipment, O'Griff's now provides great beer for thirsty local Quincy University college students, as well as travelers exploring the Mississippi River Valley.

The building's interior is long and narrow. The pub and restaurant occupy the western half of the structure. The brewhaus is visible from the outside through large windows; it actually sets in an adjoining room to the east and shares space with an open area that doubles as a dance floor and small banquet hall. Interior walls are painted green, with brick and wood accents, complementing an Irish theme. Along the western wall of the pub, you find a large mural, which is actually just an outdoor billboard from a popular macrobrewery. On my first visit, the mural featured life-sized Clydesdales and the Budweiser beer wagon. It was later rotated with a larger-than-life-sized image of Dale Earnhardt Jr. and his red Bud car. There are televisions, pool tables, a dart board, and a variety of electronic games.

You can expect to find about six to ten O'Griff's beers on tap for any visit, plus a selection of other bottled beers and taps that will top two hundred different beers. O'Griff's target brewing capacity is about a thousand barrels per year.

HISTORY

Owner Dan Griffin, a local contractor and property developer, opened O'Griff's in July 1994. As a local bar, O'Griff's developed a reputation for its extensive beer list. A few years later, Dan was having lunch with a fellow developer when the two struck up a deal over some used brewery equipment that was once part of Capital City Brewing in Springfield. Before lunch was over, Dan owned a brewery.

With some consulting help from Saaz Brewing and his own construction know-how, Dan was able to install the equipment in the eastern half of the building that houses O'Griff's. The first beer flowed at O'Griff's in September 2001.

DON'T MISS THIS

Near the front of the pub, in the southwest corner, you'll see an old St. Louis Blues hockey jersey. Dan Griffin is a hockey fan and once posted a Chicago Black Hawks jersey in the bar. In 1994 a bar patron was complaining about the Black Hawks with Dan over a beer, when Dan quipped back, "If we had a Blues jersey, we'd burn the Black Hawks one!" So that's what happened— the patron brought in a Blues jersey, there was a ceremonial bonfire and beers, and the Blues jersey was retired into the rafters of O'Griff's.

If an opportunity presents itself, a visit next door to the Griffin Center is very worthwhile. Renovated in the early 1990s and opening in 1993, the Griffin Center is in the former Ricker National Bank. Its high ceilings and open main room provide an expansive ballroom and banquet hall. The Ricker National Bank operated from 1875 until the 1930s and was known for printing its own money bills. The ornate back bar in the Griffin Center was rescued from a local farmer's barn and restored to provide a tremendous focal point for the banquet hall. It is believed to be nearly a hundred years old.

O'GRIFF'S IRISH PUB BREWS

Blueberry Ale　　　　　　　　　　　　　　*Your Ranking* _____
Ordinarily it's difficult for a fruit beer to get high marks from me, but this beer has a subtle blueberry accent that doesn't overpower the beer flavors. It begins with a faint berry nose, has a clear golden to light copper color, a thick, bubbly, white head, and is light bodied and soft. It has a malty start with a very light fruity background, and it finishes with a berry aroma but not much taste. Overall, it is smooth and malty with a pleasant blueberry accent.

Dark Honey Brown　　　　　　　　　　　　*Your Ranking* _____
A stronger version of the Light Honey Brown. The malty tones really stand out in the nose. Clear, deep bronze color with a thick, soft, brown head. Medium bodied and soft texture. Malty sweetness dominates. A firm roasted finish. Each batch is made with locally produced Wheelan Honey from Barry, Illinois. Overall, this is the one of the best O'Griff's brews.

Golden Canadian Ale　　　　　　　　　　　*Your Ranking* _____
No nose. A deep golden color with a thin, soft, white head. Light to medium bodied and round texture. A light malty start, then a firm but light hoppy back-

ground. Clean finish. The hoppy background stands out. It is as described: a light, golden ale.

India Pale Ale 🍺🍺🍺 *Your Ranking* _____

Begins with a very light hoppy nose. Clear, deep copper color. Thin, soft, tan head. Medium bodied and somewhat soft texture. A light sweet malty beginning, but the bitterness comes through in the finish. This beer has a pleasant, smooth bitterness that makes it a great companion to O'Griff's lasagna and garlic. However, it's just a little mild for hops lovers.

Irish Amber 🍺🍺🍺🍺 *Your Ranking* _____

A malty nose. Clear bronze to dark brown color. Thick, soft, tan head. Medium bodied and very bubbly. A strong caramel malty flavor with a crisp clean finish. After about a half-pint, the finish becomes somewhat dry.

Light Honey Brown 🍺🍺🍺 *Your Ranking* _____

Light sweetness with hints of earthiness to the nose. A clear, reddish color and a thin, soft, tan head. Medium bodied and soft. Malty flavors, especially the caramel malts, stand out, but the flavors are very withheld. A faint roastedness to the finish.

Oatmeal Stout 🍺🍺🍺 *Your Ranking* _____

A mild malty nose. Deep, dark bronze color. Thick, soft, brown head. Full bodied and very soft. Great caramel and chocolate malty flavors. There is a very light, faint bitter accent. While described as a dry stout, this beer is more like a sweeter milk stout. A great find.

Porter 🍺🍺 *Your Ranking* _____

A faint malty nose. Deep dark bronze color with a copper hue. A very soft, tan head. Medium bodied and thin. A malty start to the taste with a strong fruity background. A light fruitiness continues to linger into the finish. This beer is worth another try and will likely improve. On one occasion the server admitted that there was a problem with carbonation and the tap lines, which could have contributed to the thin texture.

Red Ale (a.k.a. O'Griff's Irish Amber) 🍺🍺🍺🍺 *Your Ranking* _____

No nose. A clear, reddish copper color with a thin, soft, tan head. Medium bodied and soft texture. A floury start with some aggressive malty tones. The caramel malt eventually wins out. A very light trace of hops in the finish.

OTHER O'GRIFF'S IRISH PUB BREWS YOU MAY WANT TO TRY

Strawberry Blonde *Your Ranking* _____

Probably one of the most popular O'Griff's brews. A mild, light beer. Clear golden color with a thick, bubbly, white head. Light bodied. Clean taste that has a soft, smoky malty flavor. Strawberry comes out in the aroma and finish. This beer was first brewed in June 2002.

BREWERY RATING

Rating	Your Rating	Shepard's Rating (1 to 4 Mugs)	General Description
Location		🍺🍺🍺🍺	Central city/community
Ease of Finding Location		🍺🍺🍺	Easy, but requires some planning
Brewery Atmosphere		🍺🍺🍺	Sports
Dining Experience		🍺🍺🍺	Pub fare
The Pint		🍺🍺🍺	A good experience

MENU

O'Griff's offers a variety of basic pub foods. There are about a dozen sandwiches to choose from, including a grilled chicken breast, Reuben, BLT, tuna melt, and gyros. There are also homemade pizzas, ranging from a mini to a large, with your choice of about ten different toppings. There are also daily specials such as tacos on Tuesdays, lasagna and garlic on Thursdays, and spare ribs on Fridays.

OTHER THINGS TO SEE OR DO IN THE AREA

Quincy is known for its many nineteenth-century river homes and estates, among them the Villa Katherine, Eells House, and the home of Governor John Wood. The Villa Katherine is home to Quincy's Tourist Information Center (532 Gardner Expressway). This Mediterranean villa is located on a bluff overlooking the Mississippi River. The home of Dr. Richard Eells (415 Jersey Street) was a station for the Underground Railroad during the 1840s. The mansion of John Wood, the founder of Quincy and former governor of Illinois (425 South 12th Street), was built in 1835.

Quincy has a beautiful town square called Washington Park with old oak trees and a bandstand. Washington Park was the site of the sixth senatorial debate between Lincoln and Douglas in 1858. A granite boulder was placed in the park to commemorate the famous event. For those who wish to learn more about Quincy's history, the Quincy Museum is housed in the 1891 Newcomb-Stillwell Mansion (1601 Main Street). And the Quincy Art Center (1515 Jersey Street) is located on the grounds of the former Lorenzo Bull mansion. Also on the square, and next door to O'Griff's Irish Pub and Brew House, is the Washington Theater. Designed in typical Mediterranean Revival style, it was constructed in 1928.

The Quincy Convention and Visitor's Bureau offers an excellent pamphlet with "Fifty Great Things to See and Do." For example, you may want to look for the double-decker tour bus and take a tour of Quincy. Information on bus tours is available from the Quincy Convention Bureau (800-978-4748). Another interesting piece of historical trivia is the Quincy Maid-Rite (507 North 12th Street), said to be the oldest restaurant in Illinois serving the Maid-Rite loose ground beef sandwich. It began in 1928 with just three tables and four chairs.

Quincy has a fascinating history with the Mississippi River. The Quincy Levee provided calm water for the summer steamboats to run between

Quincy and Hannibal. Riverview Park (Northeast Quincy) overlooks the Mississippi and was the site of a Black Hawk War skirmish. Quinsippi Island (Front and Cedar Streets) is reached by a one-lane wooden planked auto bridge. The island offers picnic areas, beaches, and replicas of log homes. There is also an Antique Auto Museum with sixty-five antique cars.

O'Griff's Irish Pub and Brew House

In nearby Pittsfield, Pig Days are held during the summer (1-217-285-2971). Pittsfield considers itself the pork capital of the world. In early September, Nauvoo holds its annual Grape Festival. Quincy's festivals include the Annual Dogwood Parade and Festival in May, and Quincy's farmers' market takes place in Washington Park from May to October.

Quincy once had a thriving brewery industry. The Dick Brothers Brewery (9th and York Streets) is no longer in operation, but some of the buildings remain. You can still see the words "Brew House" on the main building, near the top of the five-story brick structure. Caverns were built under the buildings in 1875 that were once used for storage and lagering.

The Harrison Brewery (9th and Harrison) brewed in the 1870s and 1880s. It was started by Michael Becker and later became the Yeck & Becker Brewery when brewery partner Charles E. Yeck bought out Becker. Eventually, it became Gem City Brewery.

The Eber and Hoerring Brewery was located at 6th and Chestnut Streets and operated in the 1860s by brothers Henry and Rudolph Eber and Leonard Hoerring. Hoerring eventually sold his interest in the brewery, and it became Eber Brothers Brewery. Eber Brothers sold the brewery in the 1880s to Gottlieb Schanz and Fritz Wahl, and the brewery became the Schanz Wahl Brewery. Disagreements between the two would eventually make it the Wahl Brewery when Schanz sold out. Sometime before 1910 the brewery closed. When Schanz left, he purchased the Harrison Brewery. He eventually sold it to a group of saloon keepers in the 1890s, and it became Gem City Brewery, which closed in 1895.

Other Quincy breweries at the turn of the twentieth century included the Washington Brewery (6th and State), the Jefferson Brewery (6th and Jefferson), the Fischer Brewery (11th and Washington), the Schultheiss Brewery (3rd and Jefferson), the Western Brewery (7th and York), and the M.X. 8 Brewery (near 5th and Oak).

DIRECTIONS

Take exit 14 (Broadway and Highway 104) west from Interstate 172. O'Griff's is about five miles west of the interstate. Turn left (south) at the last stoplight before the Mississippi River bridge. Within two-to-four blocks, again turn left (east) and travel two blocks looking for Washington Park Square (the town square). O'Griff's is located on the north side of the square. Look for O'Griff's green awnings near the Washington Theater marquee.

Onion Pub and Brewery
Lake Barrington

Visit Date	Signed

ABOUT THE BREWERY

Describing the Onion Pub and Brewery is a lot like peeling an onion; every time you uncover one layer to the story, there's another layer, another tale to tell. Whether it's the company's humble beginnings as a microbrewery, the transformation of an abandoned quarry, or the luck of hitting a lottery windfall, all are found in the layers of Onion's story.

The Onion Pub and Brewery is somewhat secluded, considering that it's a couple of blocks north of Northwest Highway (Route 14), bordered by an industrial park and twenty acres of land with the eight-acre Pepper Lake. The Onion Pub and Brewery was constructed on and around the site of a former rock quarry. Great effort was taken to build a brewery and be sensitive to its natural surroundings, even to improve upon what was left behind by the property's former owners. The Onion's extensive landscaping and prairie restoration make a contribution to the local environment, but they are also a statement that the brewery's owners are committed to an ecologically sensitive design. For example, the walls of the brewpub were constructed using a modern, state-of-the-art process that combines concrete and styrofoam for high energy efficiency. The temperature of the building is regulated with heating and cooling coils that extend into the waters of Pepper Lake.

The exterior of the brewpub has light earth-toned stucco walls and a brown cedar roof. Inside the brewpub, large Douglas fir timbers from Oregon and Washington actually frame the main part of the building's interior. Wood trim and stucco-looking walls all help accent the earthen qualities of the Onion Pub and Brewery. Look closely at the bar. It was made by a local artisan who constructed it from salvaged wooden panel doors. The primary dining room, the bar, a semi-private party room, and a patio all take advantage of some great views that really capitalize on the brewpub's landscaping, the native plants, and Pepper Lake.

The Onion Pub and Brewery is well known for its Paddy Pale Ale, an assertive American pale ale with a strong hoppy flavor. Paddy is a hearty beer for those who enjoy bitterness. You can also expect to find the Golden Lager and Jack Stout on tap for most visits. Brewmaster's specials to watch for include the Summer Wit, a traditional Belgian-style white beer.

HISTORY

The Onion Pub and Brewery is a second-generation brewery, originally called the Wild Onion Brewing Company. The name "Wild Onion" refers to the Potowatomi word "che-ca-gou," meaning "where the wild onion grows," from which Chicago gets its name. When Chicago was settled, the mouth of the Chicago River was filled with wild rice, and its banks were covered with wild onion plants.

The Wild Onion Brewing Company brewed beer as a microbrewery from 1997 until 2000. The Onion Pub and Brewery opened in 2003 and kept part of the name out of recognition for its microbrewery beginnings and ties to Chicago. But the owners and business associates also wanted a new beginning, so the "wild" was dropped to indicate a new direction for the company.

Actually, there is much more to this story than merely the name and beer. The Wild Onion Brewing Company was established by the Kainz family. The mother and father, Sue and Joe, along with their sons Michael, Patrick, and John, began a family brewery just down the street from where the Onion Pub and Brewery is located today. But their lives changed dramatically in May 2000, when Joe picked the winning numbers for a lottery jackpot worth $363 million. Needless to say, but still worth mentioning, the brewery got a big infusion of cash!

Mike and his father, Joe, are the main owners of Onion Pub and Brewery. The general manager (and the contractor for the construction of the brewpub), Mike Kowal, is a long-time friend of Mike Kainz. Kowal, Kainz, and the Onion's brewmaster, Steve Mazylewski, were coworkers at the now closed Weinkeller Brewpubs in Berwyn and Westmont. Mazylewski is no stranger to the local brewery business, having worked at the FireHouse Restaurant and Brewing Company in Morris, the now-closed O'Grady's Brewery and Pub of Arlington Heights, and downtown Chicago's former River West Brewing Company.

In case you're wondering just how much of the jackpot the Kainzes received, the overall jackpot was split with another winning ticket holder from Shelby Township, Michigan. Joe Kainz opted for the lump sum payment, so before taxes Joe and Sue received a check for approximately $90 million. The local convenience store that sold the winning ticket received $1.8 million.

DON'T MISS THIS

The large plot of land on which the Onion Pub and Brewery sits makes this brewpub unique—especially given its proximity to Chicago. Developing the grounds of a former quarry has been, and will continue to be, a tremendous project for the Kainzes and general contractor Mike Kowal. The land around the brewpub and the adjacent eight-acre lake were carefully researched so that native plants, including wildflowers, could be reintroduced. Much of Pepper Lake's shoreline, its wetlands, and its earthen berms are part of an extensive landscaping effort. The brewpub has recently constructed a waterfall that is visible from the patio and many viewpoints inside the building.

Most of those who visit the Onion Pub and Brewery will indeed miss the hidden features that are found within the soothing waters of Pepper Lake—that is, unless they're scuba divers. There was once a scuba instruction business near where the Onion Pub and Brewery is located, and deep in Pepper Lake there are submerged boats, an airplane, and even a helicopter. Local fire departments and rescue crews still use the lake for training.

ONION PUB BREWS

Golden Lager   🍺🍺🍺   *Your Ranking* _____
A Bavarian-style lager. Clean, no nose or finish. Clear golden color with a light, bubbly, white head. A mild malty start with a crisp, light hoppy background.

Paddy Pale Ale   🍺🍺🍺🍺   *Your Ranking* _____
An American pale ale with lots of hoppiness. Strong hoppy aroma. A light copper color with a slight haziness. A thick, soft, tan head. Medium bodied and soft. Strong bitterness throughout. A dry finish.

OTHER ONION PUB BREWS YOU MAY WANT TO TRY

Jack Stout   *Your Ranking* _____
A full-bodied, dark oatmeal stout. Malty flavor with lots of roasted coffee tones.

Pumpkin Ale   *Your Ranking* _____
A fall seasonal.

Summer Wit   *Your Ranking* _____
A Belgian-style white beer with hints of coriander and orange.

Winter Warmer   *Your Ranking* _____
A big beer for the colder season.

BREWERY RATING

	Your Rating	Shepard's Rating (1 to 4 Mugs)	General Description
Location		🍺🍺🍺	Commercial/industrial
Ease of Finding Location		🍺🍺🍺	Easy, but requires some planning
Brewery Atmosphere		🍺🍺🍺🍺	Family restaurant

	Your Rating	Shepard's Rating	General Description
Dining Experience		🍺🍺🍺	Family style/variety
The Pint		🍺🍺🍺	A good experience

MENU

Onion Pub and Brewery offers an English American pub style menu. Appetizer selections include nachos, buffalo wings, beer-battered onion rings and shrimp, onion quiche, crab cakes, and the ploughman's platter of smoked sausage and salmon. The Onion Pub also has a wood-fired stone oven for its own pizzas and calzones. Sandwich choices include basic hamburgers, Reubens, beer-braised bratwursts, and the B.L.A.S.T. wrap (bacon, lettuce, avocado, shrimp, and tomato). The entree portion of the pub's menu includes Maple Ale glazed pork chops, barbecue ribs, rack of lamb Dijonnaise, seared ahi tuna, bangers and mash, fish and chips, and stone-roasted meatloaf. There are also several vegetarian options, including a veggie burger, salads, and pastas. To finish your meal it's a tough decision between the carrot cake, cheesecake du jour, and traditional bread pudding.

OTHER THINGS TO SEE OR DO IN THE AREA

Just a few blocks away from the Onion Pub and Brewery is the Barrington Ice Arena (28205 West Commercial Drive, 1-847-381-4777). The arena is home to the Barrington Redwings hockey organization as well as Barrington's and Lake Zurich's high school hockey teams. Public skating is regularly held on Sunday afternoons.

The Barrington Ice House Mall (200 Applebee Street) was an actual ice-house built in 1904. Located in downtown Barrington, the Ice House has been transformed into a mall that includes many specialty shops and restaurants that link its historic architecture to the modern structure. Also in Barrington you can walk inside a giant heart, fill a cavity on a colossal tooth, or take a video ride in an ambulance during a visit to Health World (1301 South Grove Avenue).

The Barrington Area Arts Council Gallery (207 Park Avenue) in the heart of Barrington is home for art activities, jazz to classical music events, and theater performances. The council also organizes bimonthly shows and has developed a sculpture garden at the local public library.

Throughout Lake County there are more than 340 acres of preserved areas that are owned or cared for by the Citizens for Conservation (www.save-livingspace.org). Among the most beautiful and natural are the Flint Creek Savanna and Grigsby Prairie. The Citizens for Conservation headquarters (across from Good Shepherd Hospital on Route 22, between Kelsey Road and Highway 59) offers educational programs, information, and maps of the Flint Creek Watershed.

In Fox River Grove, just east of the Onion Pub and Brewery, the Norge Ski Club was founded in 1905 and hosts tournaments, including ski jumping events. The Bettendorf Castle, now a private residence, was built single-handedly by resident Ted Bettendorf and is a local landmark. You might also enjoy a view from above with a stop at Windy City Balloon Port (100 Ski Hill Road), the only hot air balloon port in the northwest suburbs of Chicago.

North of Onion Pub and Brewery on Route 12, the Wauconda International Professional Rodeo is held each July on the Golden Acres Ranch (Case Road and Route 12, Wauconda); events include bronco riding, barrel racing, and other events sanctioned by the Professional Rodeo Association. About ten miles north of Barrington, the Volo Auto Museum (27582 Volo Village Road) has four collector car showrooms and over 250 collector cars, including celebrity owned cars and vehicles that television made famous. You'll see the "General Lee" from *The Dukes of Hazzard*, the De Lorean time machine from the movie *Back to the Future*, and even the Batmobile.

Barrington also is known for a legendary gun battle that took place on November 27, 1934, at the entrance to North Side Park. The shootout left two federal agents dead and mortally wounded outlaw "Baby Face" Nelson, who escaped but later bled to death from seventeen bullet wounds. The agents who died in the confrontation, Samuel Cowley and Herman F. Hollis, had only four months earlier been part of the ambush that killed John Dillinger outside the Biograph Theater on Chicago's near west side (see also the listing for Goose Island–Clybourn Avenue).

DIRECTIONS

The Onion Pub and Brewery is located northwest of Barrington. Once in Barrington, travel about three miles northwest on Route 14 and turn right (north) on Pepper Road. The Onion Pub and Brewery is about two blocks north of Route 14 (West Northwest Highway).

Barrington (201 South Spring Street) and Fox River Grove (4015 North Northwest Highway) have Metra train links to Chicago. However, both of these stations would likely require a cab ride to and from the brewpub. The Onion Pub and Brewery is roughly halfway between Fox River Grove and Barrington.

Piece

Chicago

Visit Date	*Signed*

ABOUT THE BREWERY

Piece (as in "piece of pizza") is a brewpub with a great deal of individual character and uniqueness that serves Chicago's Bucktown and Wicker Park neighborhoods well. While you can expect great beer and pizza anytime, Piece has a number of amenities going for it that make it ideal for a beer after work, especially in the summer.

The two-story brick building would be almost unidentifiable as a brewpub if not for the plain-looking Piece logo above the door. In the summer, the large picture windows, nearly six by ten feet, are opened, making for a great place to have a beer or two and just people-watch. The brick exterior comes through inside and is accented with an arched ceiling and concrete floor that allow you to see how this building was once used as a warehouse. The building's renovations leave you with an interior that takes full advantage of the skylight in the center of the dining room. A wall separates the main room from a more secluded area of tables. This area is seen through open window frames that have a variety of photos situated between them.

The long, arching bar has a red-burgundy top, and it almost fills the west side of the dining room. The brewing equipment is mostly hidden from sight, leaving few clues that Piece is actually a brewery. But just look around, because most evenings you'll likely find brewer Jonathan Cutler talking with patrons.

Piece regularly has a half-dozen of its own beers on tap, plus you'll find about a dozen guest drafts and several bottled beers. On one fall visit I was pleasantly surprised to find Autumnal Fire from Wisconsin's Capital Brewery, Hoegaarden's Belgian White, and even a Framboise on tap. Piece also has an impressive wine list. While the Worryin' Ale and Prodigal Porter are among the mainstays of Piece, you won't go wrong with a Collars and Cuffs Blonde Ale that has a lot of character for a light beer.

HISTORY

Piece served its first beers in September 2001. The seven-barrel system is composed of some of the equipment from the former Box Office Brewery in De Kalb.

The restaurant and brewery is the creation of Matt Brynildson and Bill Jacobs. Brynildson is known for his brewing talents at Goose Island. Jacobs and his brothers started Jacobs Brothers Bagels, a business that grew into a twenty-four-store chain in the Chicago area. Matt and Bill met through playing ultimate frisbee and sealed their business plans at a homebrew and barbecue party.

Brewmaster Jonathan Cutler is a local boy who came back home to brew. After getting involved in homebrewing while at Southern Illinois University, Jonathan began thinking about the brewing industry. To ensure that his hobby didn't overtake his interest, Jonathan's father offered him a deal to finish college, after which he'd help with brewery training at Siebel Institute. While attending Siebel, Jonathan worked his way into several Chicagoland breweries, including Mickey Finn's and Goose Island, where he met Matt Brynildson. That working relationship eventually opened the door for Jonathan to become the brewer when Brynildson and Jacobs opened Piece.

DON'T MISS THIS

You'd better know the symbols for man and woman. If you don't, you might find the restrooms a little embarrassing!

PIECE BREWS

Collars and Cuffs Blonde Ale 🍺🍺🍺🍺 *Your Ranking* _____
An excellent summertime light beer. A light hoppy nose that complements a light bitter background. Deep yellow golden color with a thick, smooth, white head. Mild malty tones give it a light sweet tone, but the hops provide a nice accent. It has a clean finish.

Dolemite 🍺🍺🍺 *Your Ranking* _____
Just a fun beer to enjoy. Named after the campy 1975 cult film, starring Rudy Ray Moore, about a pimp trying to reclaim his nightclub. An American malt liquor that has a complex and competitive blend of flavors. Made with German hops and 25 percent Illinois corn. A malty nose. Clear, golden color and a thin, bubbly, off-white head. Full bodied and soft. A light sweetness with aggressive hoppiness in the background that lingers, even builds in the finish. At first I wasn't sure about the hoppiness because of the many malty qualities that impart both sweet and earthy tones. However, after a while the beer has a mild bitterness that grows on you. It is a seductive brew. A fun twist is that a glass of Dolemite is served wrapped inside a brown paper bag!

Dysfunctionale   🍺🍺🍺🍺   *Your Ranking* _____

A fresh, sharp hoppy ale. Starts with a floral nose. Bronze color and slightly hazy body. A thick, soft, tan head. Full bodied and sharp textures. Malty caramel flavors are found in the beginning with a dry, hoppy background. A strong fruity and hoppy finish. Firm, assertive bitterness like an IPA with a fruity background and finish.

Golden Arm   🍺🍺🍺🍺   *Your Ranking* _____

A Kolsch-style beer. No nose. Clear, straw color with a thin, soft, white head. Medium to light texture. Malty tones with a light fruity accent. Crisp and dry finish. Won a bronze medal at the 2002 Great American Beer Festival and a bronze medal in the 2002 World Beer Cup competition. An exceptional beer.

IPA   🍺🍺🍺🍺   *Your Ranking* _____

Described as generously hopped and it is! Strong resiny hoppy nose. Orange to copper color, mostly clear except for a faint haziness. A thick, long-lasting, soft, white head. Full bodied and soft texture. Strong hop flavor that stamps out a struggling malty background. The finish has a long-lasting bitterness. A great India Pale Ale.

J. Diddy's E.S.S.S.B.B.   🍺🍺🍺   *Your Ranking* _____

All the qualities of an extra special bitter, only hoppier! A strong flowery nose quickly lets you know you'll be drinking a bitter. A clear, dark gold color with a thin, bubbly, white head. Medium bodied and dry. Starts with a whiff of malt, but the aggressive hoppiness really dominates. The bitterness lingers long into the finish and beyond. This beer has many qualities you'd expect in a four-mug IPA, but it is labeled as an ESB-style; it's a little rough with the hoppiness, but still a great beer. "E.S.S.S.B.B." stands for "Extra Special Super Secret Best Bitter." It commemorates the life and times of the irrepressible and often misunderstood rapper J. Diddy, who died in 1997.

Oktoberfest   🍺🍺🍺   *Your Ranking* _____

A lager that has great malty character in aroma and finish. Clear, copper color. A thin, bubbly, off-white head. Medium bodied. Smooth mild caramel malty flavor. A clean, bubbly, light caramel malt finish.

Passive-Aggressive Porter   *Your Ranking* _____

A very strong roasted coffee nose. Gorgeous dark color with ruby tints. A thin, bubbly, tan head. Full bodied and very silky texture. Smooth chocolate malt flavors and a lightly roasted finish. All flavors work in perfect concert with each other for an incredible taste experience.

Prodigal Porter   🍺🍺🍺🍺   *Your Ranking* _____

The first beer brewed at Piece. A light roasted nose. Very dark color with a thick, bubbly, tan head. Full bodied and soft texture. A strong roasted malt flavor lingers from beginning to end. You can really taste the sweetness from the roasted chocolate malt. It is a smooth porter with great color and body.

Top Heavy Hefe-Weizen   *Your Ranking* _____

A traditional Bavarian Hefe-Weizen. Strong aroma of banana and cloves. A cloudy, light golden to copper color and a thick, bubbly, white head. Light bodied and very carbonated. Strong fruity esters dominate; the banana tones are very strong and assertive. It finishes with the same strong fruity flavors. Overall, it's light bodied and very bubbly with lots of banana notes. It's brewed with 66 percent wheat, Bavarian yeast, and imported German Pilsner malt and hops.

West Side Wheat   *Your Ranking* _____

An American-style wheat that begins with faint malty nose. Deep, clear yellow color with a thin, creamy, off-white head. A light bubbly texture. A smooth malty start that turns clean and crisp. A warm and sweet finish.

Wing Nut   *Your Ranking* _____

This strong malty beer is a great winter brew from brewmaster Jonathan Cutler. Assertive hoppy nose. Brownish bronze color with a light cloudiness. Full bodied. Very strong malty flavors with a bitterness way in the background. Warm and malty finish. A very complex beer because almost all of the flavors seem very pronounced. Served in a tulip glass.

Worryin' Ale   *Your Ranking* _____

An English-style ale. A light hoppy nose. Clear, deep golden color with a thick, soft, white head. Medium bodied and mildly hopped. The light malty body has some caramel tones in the background. There are some assertive hop qualities in the finish. It won a silver medal in the 2002 World Beer Cup competition.

OTHER PIECE BREWS YOU MAY WANT TO TRY

Gentrification Ale   *Your Ranking* _____

An extra pale ale. Introduced in summer 2002. Named in tribute to the gentrification of the Wicker Park and Bucktown neighborhoods.

BREWERY RATING

	Your Rating	Shepard's Rating (1 to 4 Mugs)	General Description
Location		🍺🍺🍺	Entertainment district
Ease of Finding Location		🍺🍺🍺	Easy, but requires some planning
Brewery Atmosphere		🍺🍺🍺🍺	Like an inside beer garden
Dining Experience		🍺🍺🍺🍺	Limited (pizza and sandwiches)
The Pint		🍺🍺🍺🍺	A perfect experience

MENU

As the name indicates, Piece is known for its pieces of pizza. You'll find several choices of salads and appetizers, and a limited sandwich menu is offered until 4 P.M., but Piece specializes in pizza. There are three sizes on the menu, and three styles make the basic pizza choice difficult between a plain (tomato sauce, parmesan, and garlic), the white (olive oil, garlic, and mozzarella cheese), and the red (tomato sauce, garlic, parmesan, and mozzarella cheeses). You have more than fifteen toppings to choose from. On a conservative evening you might go with the basic pepperoni or Italian sausage, but on a more adventuresome night out try the anchovies and hot peppers!

OTHER THINGS TO SEE OR DO IN THE AREA

Piece is located along West North Avenue, which serves as the boundary between Chicago's thriving neighborhoods of Bucktown to the north and Wicker Park to the south. Major streets such as North Avenue, North Damen, North Milwaukee, and West Armitage provide a great deal of activity.

On Thursday evenings in the summer you might be able to catch an outdoor movie in Churchill Park (1825 North Damen Avenue). For video and television buffs, in 2001 MTV's *Real World* came to Chicago and filmed its eleventh edition of the show (spring 2002) in an apartment loft just down North Avenue and across the street from Piece (1934 West North Avenue/the North-Damen-Milwaukee "six-way" intersection). Also west of Piece along North Avenue, just beyond the North Milwaukee Avenue intersection on the south side of the street, is a series of buildings located on the site of the former Luxor Baths (2039 West North Avenue). Here in the 1920s, the public bath was a vital institution for this neighborhood. About all that is left is portions of the terra cotta façade, which bears a nautical motif.

The historic "Flat Iron Building" (at the corner of North and Milwaukee Avenues) is home to many artists and their studios. The actual park of Wicker Park, located south of Piece along Damen Avenue, is a great place to take a walk and view the work of local artisans. The Wicker Park and Bucktown Chamber of Commerce is establishing a sculpture walk on the northwest side of the park.

About five blocks south on Damen Avenue, then a couple of blocks west on Potomac Avenue, is the former home of the Spies family (2132 West Potomac). Family patriarch August Spies, a German-born leader of Chicago's growing trade-union movement and editor of the newspaper *Arbeiter-Zeitung*, was executed along with several other labor leaders after taking part in the Haymarket Riot in May 1886.

Throughout history, the neighborhoods south of Piece have been home to several breweries that have long since closed, but a few buildings remain to give evidence of their location. In his book *The History of Beer and Brewing in Chicago 1833–1978*, Bob Skilnik identifies the West-Side Brewery Company as operating between 1890 and 1919 in the 900 block of North Paulina; the Pfeifer's Berlin Weiss Beer Company was in business from 1892 to 1909 at 718–742 North Leavitt Street; and the City Brewery Company operated under several names, including Francis J. Dewes, from 1882 to 1906 at 764 West Chicago Avenue.

Some other area bars that might be fun to visit include the Zakopane Lounge (1734 W. Division), which is known for polka music and hosts the "Extreme Polka Fest" in June; the Matchbox (770 North Milwaukee Avenue), which is Chicago's so-called smallest bar; and the Map Room (1949 North Hoyne, about nine blocks north and west of Piece) is well known for its beer selection, beer tastings, and beer events.

For entertainment, you may not have a reason to go much farther than Piece, because it has a stage for live music. Rick Nielsen, from the band Cheap Trick, is an investor in Piece. Maybe you'll see him perform sometime.

DIRECTIONS

Take exit 48b on the Kennedy Expressway (Interstates 90/94). Piece is located on North Avenue (Highway 64) a couple miles west of the expressway. Look for the brick building on the south side of the street, near the intersection with Winchester. The building doesn't have much identification except for the Piece emblem above the main door. Piece is also about a block from a CTA Blue Line station connecting O'Hare and the downtown.

Prairie Rock Brewing Company

Elgin

Visit Date	*Signed*

ABOUT THE BREWERY

The Prairie Rock Brewing Company has two locations: Elgin and Schaumburg. The Elgin location is Prairie Rock's original brewpub. Sitting at the corner of South Grove and Prairie Streets, it anchors the southern edge of downtown Elgin in a historic building that many locals remember as the neighborhood theater. Prairie Rock is only a block from the Fox River and just a few blocks north of the Grand Victoria Casino riverboat.

As you walk through the doors, the brewhaus is immediately to your left, while straight ahead two wooden-framed French-style doors open into the main dining room. The dining room is very open with a high arched ceiling, brick walls, stonework, and exposed wooden beams. This room was once the heart of Elgin's Grove Theater! The interior area makes use of its height with a loft. From above you look down on a two-story-high, floor-to-ceiling, four-sided fireplace that leaves you with a physical and emotional sense of warmth. Upstairs there is a private party room called the Rialto Room, a cigar bar, and a banquet area called the Loft.

The main bar for Prairie Rock is to the left of the entryway, just beyond the brewhaus. It's actually separated from the dining room. The bar is long and wooden with high stools. Again, brick walls and a ceiling of wooden joists accent the rustic old character and charm of the building. In the entryway to the bar, windows expose the brew kettle and fermentation tanks. Additional windows inside the main bar allow you to observe the inner workings of the brewhaus. Behind the bar are more serving tanks. The daily beer offerings are listed on wooden plaques that hang over the bar.

Each Prairie Rock brewpub brews its own beers, and while you will find a few similar brews, the seasonal specialties are likely to vary. Prairie Rock–Elgin regularly has six to eight of its own beers on tap. The Prairie Rock Ale is considered the flagship beer of the Elgin location, but brewmaster Rob Hunter does a great job with the Prairie Porter and Oatmeal Stout. In midsummer

Prairie Rock–Elgin hosts the annual Prairie Rock Brewfest. The event, with its beer, music, and food, often showcases more than a dozen other breweries from the Chicago area. Prairie Rock also offers quarterly brewmaster's dinners.

HISTORY

On my initial visit, I had trouble being impressed with the building housing Prairie Rock–Elgin. At first glance I almost wrote it off as an uninspiring former riverbank warehouse. But don't do that! Look close and make sure you explore the building. Prairie Rock is in a structure with a great deal of history. The building was originally constructed in 1920 as the Grove Theater. In its day it was the first silent movie house in Elgin and seated a thousand people. The first movie to show here was a film called *Trumpet Island*, starring Arthur Hoyt and directed by Tom Terriss. The Grove Theater sat unused for much of the Depression period, but it reopened in 1936 and showed "talkies" up until 1976, when it closed for good. In 1994 a local, family-owned real estate development company purchased the structure. Renovations on the building began in January 1995, and within only ten months the Prairie Rock Brewing Company was established and opened in October of that year.

The head brewmaster for the Prairie Rock Brewing Company, Rob Hunter, oversees both the Elgin and Schaumburg breweries. Rob's introduction to beer came while he was in the Air Force when he went to visit a friend's family in Brussels. As Rob remembers, "Once we got off the base, three friends and three Belgium beers later it was all over, and there was no looking back at bland beers!"

After his hitch in the Air Force, Rob attended the University of Arkansas in Fayetteville, where he earned a degree in psychology. He then relocated with his wife to Nashville, Tennessee, where he explored employment options. But in Nashville he found trouble finding work in his field of study. One afternoon while sitting at home and enjoying a beer with his landlord, his commiseration led to career advice Rob hasn't forgotten. The landlord told Rob, "You need to focus on what you like!" So Rob turned over the six-pack carton, called the brewery number, and asked for a job! You probably thought this kind of thing only happens in the movies such as the flicks shown at the old Grove Theater, but Rob's inquiry actually led to a job at Bohannon Brewing and Market Street Brewery and Public House in Nashville (134 N. 2nd Avenue, www.market-streetbrewery.com). There he eventually worked his way up to assistant brewmaster. When Prairie Rock in Elgin was built, Bohannon Brewing was a consultant for brewing operations, and that led Rob to Elgin. Nothing like the happy ending you find in the movies!

DON'T MISS THIS

The heritage of the building is proudly reflected by displaying the old projector that was once used in the building. Made in the early 1900s by the Century Projector Corporation of New York, it now rests in the upper seating area in the main dining room—just outside the Rialto Room. Old posters from movies once shown at the Grove Theater adorn the walls of the Rialto Room with the likes of Humphrey Bogart, James Dean, and Marilyn Monroe. Exploring the building, you'll find various beer photos, signs, and memorabilia. Inside the bar there's a framed 1903 certificate for the Union Saloon, marking membership in the Illinois Liquor Dealers Protective Association.

PRAIRIE ROCK–ELGIN BREWS

Doppelbock 🍺🍺🍺🍺   *Your Ranking* _____
A full-bodied and very smooth bock. Malty nose and finish. Very dark bronze color with a thin, soft, tan head. Strong maltiness, but smooth and consistent flavor will be appreciated by anyone. Just great color and flavor.

ESB (Extra Special Bitter) 🍺🍺🍺🍺   *Your Ranking* _____
An ESB that has solid, firm hoppy qualities and a smooth malty background that provides flavor but allows the hops to dominate. Begins with a crisp hoppy nose. Clear bronze color and a thick, soft, tan head. Medium bodied and smooth texture. Starts hoppy and finishes hoppy with a smooth caramel malt complement. Brewed with roasted malts and U.K. hops for a traditional British-style bitter. This is one of those beers that are rotated through the seasonal taps, so when it's on, better make the trip to Prairie Rock.

Honey Brown Ale 🍺🍺🍺   *Your Ranking* _____
A malty nose. Very dark color with bronze highlights. A thin, bubbly, tan head. Medium bodied and round. A malty flavor and somewhat dry. A lightly roasted finish with hints of honey helps to bring out the dryness.

IPA (India Pale Ale) 🍺🍺🍺   *Your Ranking* _____
A mild hoppy nose. Clear bronze color with a thin, bubbly, tan head. Light to medium bodied and rough texture. Begins with a light malty tone, after which the dry bitterness continues to build. It takes a while for this beer to get started with its hoppy tones, but after it gets going, the bitterness lasts a long time. I really liked this IPA, but it just seems to have too quiet of a start for the "hophead" in me!

Moana's Maple Ale 🍺🍺   *Your Ranking* _____
If you like maple syrup on your pancakes, this beer just might be the way to start your day. Strong maple aroma. Clear bronze color and a thin, soft, creamy, tan head. Medium bodied and somewhat sticky. Sweet syrupy qualities of caramel and sugar. Finishes with an aggressive maple flavor and aroma. If you like maple flavor, try this beer, but it was just a little too assertive for me.

Oatmeal Stout 🍺🍺🍺🍺   *Your Ranking* _____
A strong, assertive malty nose. Very dark color and a thin, soft, tan head. Full bodied and bubbly. A firm maltiness that eventually becomes heavy and long lasting. Finishes smooth and malty with caramel and chocolate tones. This beer has some complexity in its character as it balances its malty qualities and smooth texture. It is similar to the Prairie Porter, but with much more flavor.

Oktoberfest 🍺🍺🍺   *Your Ranking* _____

A mild malty nose. Clear, light copper color with a thin, soft, white head. Medium bodied and a crisp texture. A soft malty flavor with a quiet hoppy background. A light bitterness to the finish but the caramel flavors dominate. This Oktoberfest has a lighter color and milder flavor than most, but the Prairie Rock description clearly describes this beer, and for that it gets slightly higher marks. It is brewed with Vienna malt from Kulbach, Germany.

Pale Rider Ale 🍺🍺🍺🍺   *Your Ranking* _____

An inviting hoppy nose that lures you into this smooth pale ale. Clear, deep golden color and a thick, bubbly, white head. Medium bodied and soft texture. Strong bitter burst in the beginning with a smooth malty complement. A light but firm bitter finish. Described by Prairie Rock as a traditional English-style pale ale with an American twist. Brewed with Yakima Cascade hops and Wisconsin malt. A bronze medal winner at the 2002 North American Beer Awards.

Prairie Hefeweizen 🍺🍺   *Your Ranking* _____

No nose. Light golden color with a thin cloudiness. Thin, bubbly, white head. Light bodied and soft. A smooth sweetness of banana with mild fruity tones. Finishes with a light hint of cloves and fruity sourness. This unfiltered Hefe-Weizen seemed just a little mild for the hot summer day that encouraged me to try it. However, it's still worth a repeat order on a follow-up visit.

Prairie Light 🍺🍺🍺   *Your Ranking* _____

An American-style lager, the lightest of the Prairie Rock beers. A faint malty nose. Clear, light golden to straw color with a thin, soft, white head. Light bodied and very crisp. Mild fruity beginning with a light, crisp hoppy background. Finishes with a slight fruity sourness. Brewed with two-row malt and Liberty hops. This beer will indeed please those looking for a light beer with its solid flavor.

Prairie Porter 🍺🍺🍺🍺   *Your Ranking* _____

A light sweet nose. Very dark color with a thick, creamy, brown head. Medium to full bodied and silky. Great malt beginning, well balanced with a firm bitterness that lingers through the finish. The bitterness helps to gently accent some of this beer's delicate roasted coffee tones. This beer is distinctive for its balance and use of controlled hoppiness. It is considered an English-style porter.

Prairie Rock Ale 🍺🍺🍺   *Your Ranking* _____

A golden ale made with two-row malt and a hint of caramel malt for body. No nose. A light golden to copper body with a thin, off-white head. Light bodied and soft texture. A mild maltiness dominates. Cascade and Liberty hops provide the balance and clean crispness. The finish is sweet with a very light smokiness. This is Prairie Rock's flagship brew.

Raspberry Wheat 🍺🍺   *Your Ranking* _____

Strong fruity nose. Orange to copper color and hazy. A thin, bubbly, white head. Light bodied and soft. Sweet fruity qualities are very strong. A sweet raspberry finish will linger and linger. Raspberry beer fans might enjoy the overwhelming fruitiness. Each fifteen-barrel batch is brewed with 50 percent malted wheat and is infused with fifteen gallons of raspberries.

Rock'n Red   *Your Ranking* _____

An American-style amber ale. No nose. Dark bronze color with a thick, soft, white head. Medium bodied and round. A nice malty middle, especially hints of caramel malt. Finishes very clean. Light, dark caramel, and two-row pale malts with a touch of roasted barley give this amber ale a well-rounded malt body. Cascade and Willamette hops offer balance.

Stout   *Your Ranking* _____

Very similar to the Oatmeal Stout (I had a very difficult time distinguishing them). A strong malty nose. Dark color and a thin, soft, tan head. Full bodied and highly carbonated. A long-lasting malty flavor. The difference between this and the Oatmeal Stout seemed to be in a mild drier finish with a hint of sourness to this brew.

Vanilla Crème Ale   *Your Ranking* _____

Made with two-row pale and caramel malts and a touch of vanilla, which gives this unique beer the flavor and aroma of an old-fashioned crème soda. This will be a great beer for those looking for strong sweetness, but it just didn't work for me. A strong vanilla nose, flavor lasts from beginning to end. It has a deep golden color with a copper tint and a soft, white head. The texture is medium bodied and soft. All of this does help accent the vanilla notes. It is a fun beer for an after-meal dessert, and it won the 2000 World Expo of Beer "People's Choice" gold medal.

OTHER PRAIRIE ROCK–ELGIN BREWS YOU MAY WANT TO TRY

Classic Pilsner   *Your Ranking* _____

A European-style light lager with brilliant golden color. A soft, full malty body and a firm spicy hop flavor and finish.

Coffee Stout   *Your Ranking* _____

Very rich, dark and full of flavor. An inviting, strong roasted coffee aroma. Full bodied and silky. Strong chocolate malt flavor with a firm roasted background. Finishes with smooth texture and smoky tones.

Winter Warmer Wheat   *Your Ranking* _____

A winter seasonal at Prairie Rock—Elgin that doesn't last long.

BREWERY RATING

	Your Rating	Shepard's Rating (1 to 4 Mugs)	General Description
Location		🍺🍺🍺🍺	Central city/community Entertainment district
Ease of Finding Location		🍺🍺🍺	Easy, but requires some planning

	Your Rating	Shepard's Rating	General Description
Brewery Atmosphere		🍺🍺🍺	Historic Family restaurant
Dining Experience		🍺🍺🍺	Family style/variety
The Pint		🍺🍺🍺🍺	A perfect experience

MENU

Prairie Rock–Elgin has a diverse menu of appetizers, salads, burgers, pastas, seafood, steaks, chops, prime rib, and homemade desserts. The menu ranges from bar food to traditional American cuisine. Some of the house favorite appetizers are the chicken and mushroom quesadillas, beer-battered calamari made with Prairie Rock's Amber Lager, the spicy marinated chicken wings called "Rockin' Wings," and the crab cakes prepared with roasted red pepper sauce and tomato-caper salsa. On the lighter dinner or lunch sections of the menu you'll find about a half-dozen sandwiches that offer various combina- tions of grilled chicken, pork loin, and the standard half-pound Prairie burger topped with your choice of Swiss, smoked mozzarella, cheddar, or bleu cheese. You'll also find pizza options that include a margherita pizza, a grilled vegetable pizza, and a Hawaiian pizza with ham and pineapple. The main entree selections feature steaks, seafood and pastas, and choosing is difficult. But one of my favorites is the horseradish-crusted catfish. Daily specials feature choices such as crab, shrimp, and Friday night fish with Icelandic cod. There are also vegetarian items such as pasta primavera with fresh vegetables tossed with tricolor rotini and a tomato-Alfredo sauce. The vegetable radiatore is made with sautéed mushrooms, broccoli, zucchini, yellow squash, toma- toes, garlic, and shallots topped with white wine and olive oil. The handmade desserts at Prairie Rock–Elgin are as memorable as the beer. The Artic Sum- mer is made with raspberries, blackberries, and strawberries flambéed with rum and served over vanilla ice cream in a phyllo dough cup. The Arctic Sum- mer paired with Prairie Rock's Vanilla Crème Ale took first place in the 2003 Chicagoland Brewpub and Microbrewery Shootout's food and beer category. You'll also find raspberry crème brûlée and the over-the-top chocolate of the Volcano Cake!

OTHER THINGS TO SEE OR DO IN THE AREA

Elgin is well known for the Elgin National Watch Company, but that business closed in 1965. At one time it was the largest watch-manufacturing complex in the world. The original buildings (known as plant number 1) opened in 1866 and occupied a large portion of National Street (National Street is directly south of Prairie Rock and just a few blocks long between Route 20 and the Fox River). When the company was sold in the 1960s, plant 1 was razed. In 1910 the watchmaker constructed a company observatory in an attempt to convert stellar observations into more accurate timekeeping. Today the obser- vatory is known as the Elgin U-46 Planetarium (312 Watch Street). The com- pany donated the facility to the local school system in 1960. If you would like to know more about the Elgin Watch Company you'll find a number of exhibits at the Elgin Area Historical Society Museum (360 Park Street).

Other history is preserved in the Elgin Historic District, which has more than 660 structures on the National Register of Historic Places. You can see many of these by picking up a walking-tour map from the Elgin Visitors Bureau (1-847-695-7540). Other great walking tours include the Treasured Gardens Walk of ten private homes and the Trout Park Spring Wildflower Walk during the peak of the spring bloom in Elgin.

Elgin has also been a center for the dairy industry. Gail Borden, the inventor of condensed milk, established the Elgin Milk Condensing Company here in 1856. The Elgin Milk Condensing Company, also known as the Illinois Condensing Company, was located at Brook and Water Streets but was torn down in 1998. While Borden never lived in Elgin, his second wife and stepsons called the city home. In his honor, the Gail Borden Public Library has carried his name since 1892. The library was originally located at 50 North Spring Street, but a new Gail Borden Library facility opened in 2003 at 200 North Grove Avenue (north of Kimball Street on the Fox River).

Elgin Fire Barn No. 5 (533 St. Charles Street) is a museum of the 1904 structure that once housed horses and a horse-drawn fire wagon. Today it offers displays and antique fire engines. In mid-March, Fire Barn No. 5 holds its annual swap meet. The Elgin Public Museum (225 Grand Boulevard) was built in 1907 and remains the oldest building in Illinois built to house a museum. The exhibits provide insights to natural history and anthropology. The Lord's Park Pavilion (100 Oakwood) was the home of George P. Lord; built in 1894, it now houses a collection of mounted animals.

The State Street Market (701 North State) offers about three dozen shops and antique stores in a former 1920s millworks building. Each September Elgin hosts the Midwest Antique Clothing and Jewelry Show and Sale at the Hemmens Cultural Center (150 Dexter Court). The Hemmens Center is regularly home to the Elgin Symphony Orchestra. The Elgin Community Theatre (355 East Chicago Street) is an award-winning community theater offering musicals and plays. During the summer, the Wing Park band shell (west side of the Fox River along Tyler Creek) supports a concert series. Each July Elgin holds the National Road Race Car Show, which brings antique and custom cars in a reenactment of the "Elgin National" held in 1910. The Grand Victoria Casino (250 South Grove) is just south from Prairie Rock–Elgin along the Fox River. You will find not only slot machines and card games but also restaurants, banquet facilities, and three movie theaters.

The Fox River provides the backdrop to a number of community events. One of the largest is the Four Bridges of Elgin International Bike Race and Inline Skating Competition, held in July. Along the river's east banks in the downtown there are several sculptures by Elgin resident Trygve A. Rovelstad. Among the most impressive is the Pioneer Family Memorial near the Kimball Street Bridge. This sculpture was designed by Rovelstad, but he died before its completion. Rovelstad was the first Heraldic Artist and medalist of the U.S. War Department. He also designed the Combat Infantryman's Badge and the Bronze Star. A few blocks south of this point is the twelve-hundred-seat theater of the Hemmens Cultural Center (150 Dexter Court). Across from the Hemmens Center, in the Fox River, is a beautiful island with a footbridge, walking trails, and benches to enjoy the water and scenery.

The Fox River Trail is a hiking trail that follows the Fox River from Algonquin through Elgin, St. Charles, and Geneva on its way south to Aurora. Route 31 follows the western banks of the Fox River.

The trek from Elgin south to Aurora is winding and tree lined, making for a very beautiful drive between quaint small towns and two great brewpubs (Prairie Rock and America's Brewing Company). Another way to experience the scenic beauty is in a canoe on the Fox River. Canoe liveries can provide you with everything you might need for an excellent day or two on the water, whether you choose to paddle north to Algonquin or south to Aurora.

In South Elgin, the Fox River Trolley Museum offers a three-mile, thirty-minute ride along the Fox River. The museum (on Route 31 in South Elgin) also has vintage railway cars on display. For those interested in railroad history, northwest of Elgin the Illinois Railway Museum (7000 Olson Road, Union) contains America's largest collection of railroad equipment. About twelve miles south of Elgin in Geneva the Kane County Cougars, a Class A affiliate of the Florida Marlins, will entertain you with professional minor league baseball.

A great way to finish the day is with a stop at Al's Cafe and Creamery (43 DuPage Court) for a malt or ice cream cone.

DIRECTIONS

Prairie Rock–Elgin is located in downtown Elgin, only a few blocks from the Fox River. Perhaps the best-known landmark is the Grand Victoria Casino, which is directly south, down South Grove Street. With the municipal parking and casino parking, finding a place to leave your car isn't a problem. Elgin is also served by a Chicago Metra line. The Milwaukee District West Line has a station (109 West Chicago) on the west bank of the Fox River.

Elgin is accessible from several major highways. One of the easiest ways is from Interstate 90. If you're traveling west from Chicago, take Route 25/58 (exit mile 22) and drive south into central Elgin. If traveling east from northern Illinois, exit from I-90 onto Route 31 (exit mile 24) and drive south to either the Kimball or the Highland Avenue Bridge and then turn into the downtown.

Also, Business Route 20 will bring you into the downtown; watch for Prairie Street, then turn west toward the river.

Prairie Rock Brewing Company
Schaumburg

Visit Date	Signed

ABOUT THE BREWERY

The Prairie Rock Brewing Company has two locations: Schaumburg and Elgin. The Schaumburg location was opened in November 1999. Nearly twice the size of the Elgin brewpub, Prairie Rock–Schaumburg's building was constructed new for the purpose.

The Schaumburg location has some features similar to its sister location in Elgin: high ceiling, brick and stone work, wooden accents, and large windows. The main entryway brings you to the largest room, which opens two stories in height. The brewhaus is to the right in the corner of the room, with a concrete arching bar in front of the brewing equipment and fermentation vessels. This is actually the main bar. Further in, you see the open kitchen with its wood-fired oven. The main dining room is in the western half of the first floor, and large windows provide plenty of light, overlooking the busy Meacham Road and McConnor Parkway intersection. The private Chicago Room is separated from the main dining room and is more intimate, with its own fireplace.

The second floor has additional seating that meets the needs of restaurant overflow, banquet facilities, or parties. Upstairs there is also a wine bar, and the menu reflects an extensive selection. The lower floor—rather, the building's basement—is home to the nightclub DEEP Blue and Comedy Spot. Outside, Prairie Rock–Schaumburg has two patios, each with its own stone fireplace.

The Prairie Rock brewpubs brew their own beers with a few styles common to each as well as a number of unique brewmaster's specials, which makes for a different experience at each location. Prairie Rock–Schaumburg regularly has six to eight of its own beers on tap. The Prairie Light is the best seller, but brewmaster Rob Hunter brews an excellent Clocktower Amber Lager that is unique to the Schaumburg location. Other brewmaster's specials to watch for at the Schaumburg location include Belgian Saison and the Coffee Stout.

HISTORY

Prairie Rock–Schaumburg was established in 1999. It is the second brewpub in the Prairie Rock family. The first, located in Elgin, began in 1995. Both brewpubs are owned by the same Elgin-based real estate development company.

The head brewmaster for the Prairie Rock Brewing Company, Rob Hunter, oversees both the Elgin and Schaumburg breweries. Rob's introduction to beer came while he was in the Air Force when he went to visit a friend's family in Brussels. As Rob remembers, "Once we got off the base, three friends and three Belgium beers later it was all over, and there was no looking back at bland beers!"

After his hitch in the Air Force, Rob attended the University of Arkansas in Fayetteville, where he earned a degree in psychology. After relocating with his wife to Nashville, Tennessee, he explored employment options but found trouble finding work in his field of study. One afternoon while he was sitting at home and enjoying a beer with his apartment landlord, his commiseration led to career advice Rob hasn't forgotten. The landlord told Rob, "You need to focus on what you like!" So Rob turned over the six-pack carton, called the brewery number, and asked for a job! Rob's inquiry actually led to a job at Bohannon Brewing and Market Street Brewery and Public House in Nashville (134 N. 2nd Avenue, www.marketstreetbrewery.com). There he eventually worked his way up to assistant brewmaster. When Prairie Rock in Elgin was built, Bohannon Brewing was a consultant for brewing operations, and that led Rob to Elgin in 1995, and eventually to Schaumburg when the second location opened in 1999.

DON'T MISS THIS

Looking around the brewpub you might notice a replica street sign of State and Fulton Streets hanging from a lamppost. Outside in the beer garden, to the right of the door, you might notice a four-foot-tall wooden bear made by a chainsaw artist. Prairie Rock–Schaumburg is also very impressive at night with its backlit brewhaus, patio, lit fireplaces, and tall stone entryway.

PRAIRIE ROCK–SCHAUMBURG BREWS

Belgian Saison _Your Ranking_ _____

A light citrus nose. Very cloudy, bright copper color. Thick, bubbly, white head. Medium bodied, bubbly, and crisp. Some sweet, musty, malty qualities, but the citrus flavors really give this beer great flavor and unique character. Finishes with a light dry bitterness. A very impressive beer. The seasonal nature of this beer makes it even more special—worth the wait, though you really don't want to! This beer is brewed only at the Schaumburg location.

British Pub-Style Mild _Your Ranking_ _____

Very strong and malty aroma. The color is clear deep bronze, and the head is thick, bubbly, and off-white. Medium bodied and round texture. Smooth, clean malty flavor that offers a sweet caramel malt taste. Finishes clean and crisp. A brewmaster's special.

Chestnut Brown Ale 🍺🍺🍺🍺   *Your Ranking* _____

Great nutty flavor in the ale. A lightly roasted nose. Clear, deep bronze color and a thin, soft, tan head. Medium bodied, round, and bubbly texture. Strong caramel malty flavor and nearly perfectly sweet, complemented by a mild roasted, nutty finish. Great color, character, and flavors. An exceptional beer.

Clocktower Amber Lager 🍺🍺🍺🍺   *Your Ranking* _____

A very special, clean, crisp, amber lager. Clear bronze color with a thin, bubbly, off-white head. Medium bodied and crisp. A malty body with hints of caramel and a background that features fruity and spicy tones. Finishes clean and crisp with just a whiff of hoppiness. Made with imported German malt and considered to be an adaptation of the classic Vienna lager. This beer is brewed only at the Schaumburg location.

Coffee Stout 🍺🍺🍺🍺   *Your Ranking* _____

Very rich, dark, and full of flavor. A strong aroma of roasted coffee. Very dark color and bronze tints in the bottom of the glass. A thin, soft, brown head. Full bodied and silky. Strong chocolate malty flavor with a firm roasted background and finish. Although you can detect that the roasted flavors are coffee, the finish is well balanced and not overwhelming. Made with ten pounds of coffee in each fifteen-barrel batch. A brewmaster's special.

ESB (Extra Special Bitter) 🍺🍺🍺🍺   *Your Ranking* _____

An ESB that has solid, firm hoppy qualities and a smooth malty background that provides flavor but allows the hops to dominate. Begins with a crisp hoppy nose. Clear bronze color and a thick, soft, tan head. Medium bodied and smooth texture. Starts hoppy and finishes hoppy with a smooth caramel malt complement. Brewed with roasted malts and U.K. hops for a traditional British-style bitter. One of those beers that is rotated through the seasonal taps, so when it's on, better make the trip to Prairie Rock.

IPA (India Pale Ale) 🍺🍺🍺   *Your Ranking* _____

A mild hoppy nose. Clear bronze color with a thin, bubbly, tan head. Light to medium bodied and rough texture. Begins with a light malty tone, after which the dry bitterness continues to build. It takes a while for this beer to get started with its hoppy tones, but after its gets going, the bitterness lasts a long time. I really liked this IPA, but it just seems to have too quiet of a start for the "hophead" in me!

Oatmeal Stout 🍺🍺🍺🍺   *Your Ranking* _____

A strong, assertive malty nose. Very dark color and a thin, soft, tan head. Full bodied and bubbly. A firm maltiness that eventually becomes heavy and long lasting. Finishes smooth and malty with caramel and chocolate tones. This beer has some complexity in its malty qualities and smooth texture. Similar to Prairie Porter, but with much more flavor.

Oktoberfest 🍺🍺🍺   *Your Ranking* _____

A mild malty nose. Clear, light copper color with a thin, soft, white head. Medium bodied and a crisp texture. A soft malty flavor with a quiet hoppy background. A light bitterness to the finish but the caramel flavors dominate. This Oktoberfest has a lighter color and milder flavor than most, but the Prairie Rock description clearly describes this beer, and for that it gets slightly higher marks. It is brewed with Vienna malt from Kulbach, Germany.

Pale Rider Ale   🍺 🍺 🍺 🍺   *Your Ranking* _____

An inviting hoppy nose that lures you into this smooth pale ale. Clear, deep golden color and a thick, bubbly, white head. Medium bodied and soft texture. Strong bitter burst in the beginning with a smooth malty complement. A light, but firm bitter finish. Described by Prairie Rock as a traditional English-style pale ale with an American twist. Brewed with Yakima Cascade hops and Wisconsin malt. A bronze medal winner at the 2002 North American Beer Awards.

Prairie Hefeweizen   🍺 🍺   *Your Ranking* _____

No nose. Light golden color with a thin cloudiness. Thin, bubbly, white head. Light bodied and soft. A smooth sweetness of banana with mild fruity tones. Finishes with a light hint of cloves and fruity sourness. This unfiltered Hefe-Weizen seemed just a little mild for the hot summer day that encouraged me to try it. However, it's still worth a repeat order on a follow-up visit.

Prairie Light   🍺 🍺 🍺   *Your Ranking* _____

An American-style lager, the lightest of the Prairie Rock beers. A faint malty nose. Clear, light golden to straw color with a thin, soft, white head. Light bodied and very crisp. Mild fruity beginning with a light, crisp hoppy background. Finishes with a slight fruity sourness. Brewed with two-row malt and Liberty hops. This beer will indeed please those looking for a light beer with its solid flavor.

Prairie Porter   🍺 🍺 🍺 🍺   *Your Ranking* _____

A light sweet nose. Very dark color with a thick, creamy, brown head. Medium to full bodied and silky. Great malt beginning, well balanced with a firm bitterness that lingers through the finish. The bitterness helps to gently accent some of this beer's delicate roasted coffee tones. This beer is distinctive for its balance and use of controlled hoppiness. It is considered an English-style porter.

Prairie Rock Ale   🍺 🍺 🍺   *Your Ranking* _____

A golden ale made with two-row malt and a hint of caramel malt for body. No nose. A light golden to copper body with a thin, off-white head. Light bodied and soft texture. A mild maltiness dominates. Cascade and Liberty hops provide the balance and clean crispness. The finish is sweet with a very light smokiness. This is Prairie Rock's flagship brew.

Raspberry Wheat   🍺 🍺   *Your Ranking* _____

Strong fruity nose. Orange to copper color and hazy. A thin, bubbly, white head. Light bodied and soft. Sweet fruity qualities are very strong. A sweet raspberry finish will linger and linger. Raspberry beer fans might enjoy the overwhelming fruitiness. Each fifteen-barrel batch is brewed with 50 percent malted wheat and is infused with fifteen gallons of raspberries.

Rock'n Red 🍺🍺🍺🍺   *Your Ranking* _____

An American-style amber ale. No nose. Dark bronze color with a thick, soft, white head. Medium bodied and round. A nice malty middle, especially hints of caramel malt. Finishes very clean. Light, dark caramel, and two-row pale malts with a touch of roasted barley give this amber ale a well-rounded malt body. Cascade and Willamette hops offer balance.

Stout 🍺🍺🍺   *Your Ranking* _____

Very similar to the Oatmeal Stout (I had a very difficult time distinguishing them). A strong malty nose. Dark color and a thin, soft, tan head. Full bodied and highly carbonated. A long-lasting malty flavor. The difference between this and Oatmeal Stout seemed to be that this brew had a mild drier finish with a hint of sourness.

Vanilla Crème Ale 🍺   *Your Ranking* _____

Made with two-row pale and caramel malts and a touch of vanilla, which gives this unique beer the flavor and aroma of an old-fashioned crème soda. This will be a great beer for those looking for strong sweetness, but it just didn't work for me. A strong vanilla nose and flavor lasts from beginning to end. It has a deep golden color with a copper tint and a soft, white head. It is medium bodied with a soft texture. All of this does help accent the vanilla notes. It is a fun beer for an after meal dessert; it won the 2000 World Expo of Beer "People's Choice" gold medal.

OTHER PRAIRIE ROCK–SCHAUMBURG BREWS YOU MAY WANT TO TRY

Classic Pilsner   *Your Ranking* _____

A European-style light lager with brilliant golden color. A soft, full malty body and a firm spicy hop flavor and finish.

Coffee Stout   *Your Ranking* _____

Very rich, dark, and full of flavor. An inviting, strong roasted coffee aroma. Full bodied and silky. Strong chocolate malt flavor with a firm roasted background. Finishes with smooth texture and smoky tones.

German Bock   *Your Ranking* _____

Deep copper color and a clean malty flavor. A spring seasonal at Prairie Rock–Schaumburg.

BREWERY RATING

Rating	Your Rating	Shepard's Rating (1 to 4 Mugs)	General Description
Location		🍺🍺🍺	Entertainment district
Ease of Finding Location		🍺🍺	Difficult, out of the way, need a map (toll roads and exits are difficult)

	Your Rating	Shepard's Rating	General Description
Brewery Atmosphere		🍺🍺🍺🍺	Family restaurant
Dining Experience		🍺🍺🍺	Family style/variety Fine dining
The Pint		🍺🍺🍺	A good experience

MENU

Prairie Rock–Schaumburg's menu has choices ranging from sandwiches to upscale entrees. Appetizers include Southwest chicken quesadillas, beer-battered calamari made with Prairie Rock's Amber Lager, the spicy marinated chicken wings called "Rockin' Wings," and the crab cakes prepared on saffron cream sauce and fried spinach. On the lighter dinner or lunch sections of the menu you'll find about a half-dozen sandwiches that offer combinations of grilled chicken, prime rib, and the standard half-pound Prairie Burger topped with your choice of Swiss, smoked mozzarella, cheddar, or bleu cheese. The main entree selections feature steaks, seafood, and pastas. One of my favorites is the tenderloin fettuccini paired with a Clocktower Amber Lager. Prairie Rock–Schaumburg offers wood-fired pizza. Pizza selections include a margherita pizza with plum tomatoes, mozzarella cheese, and fresh basil; a BLT pizza, just like the sandwich with bacon, lettuce, and tomato topped with mozzarella cheese; and the house favorite, Prairie Rock pizza, a "build your own" with choices of pepperoni, sausage, mushrooms, peppers, red onions, and a variety of cheeses.

OTHER THINGS TO SEE OR DO IN THE AREA

There are numerous opportunities for shopping near Prairie Rock–Schaumburg. The brewpub is located near the Woodfield Village Green stores. IKEA home furnishings (1800 East McConnor Parkway) is directly east on McConnor Parkway. South of the brewpub, the large Woodfield Shopping Center (Golf Road and Route 53) has over 250 shops and forty restaurants. Inside Woodfield a favorite of video game fanatics is the NASCAR Silicon Motor Speedway with its race car simulators that give a real feel to driving a 700-horsepower racecar at speeds up to 200 miles per hour. For a similar experience, Game-Works (601 North Martingale Road) provides interactive games and entertainment. For more fantasy try the Medieval Times Dinner and Tournament (2001 North Roselle Road), where you can eat and be merry at an eleventh-century-style medieval banquet and witness jousts and sword fights in a castle.

Just west of Prairie Rock–Schaumburg, at the intersection of McConnor Parkway and Roosevelt Road, is Roosevelt University's Albert A. Robin campus. Considered the largest university in the northwest suburbs of Chicago, it serves about three thousand students. The campus offers computer-ready classrooms, laboratories, a library, student lounges, and a bookstore.

Despite what the neighborhood around Prairie Rock suggests with its concrete parking lots, major roadways, and shopping centers, Schaumburg is a city known for its commitment to community green space. The extensive Schaumburg Park District includes more than a thousand acres of parkland and hosts more than six hundred educational programs and one hundred special events throughout the year. In addition to urban green space, the district manages several recreational centers: the Community Recreation Center (505 North Springinsguth Road), Meineke Neighborhood Center (220 East Weathersfield Way), the Bock Neighborhood Center (1223 W. Sharon Lane), two golf courses, and the Ken Alley Safety Park (421 North Springinsguth Road), where kids can learn about sidewalk, bicycle, and fire safety.

The Spring Valley Nature Sanctuary (111 East Schaumburg Road) is a very special outdoor park with over 135 acres of forest, meadows, prairies, and wetlands. The Vera Meineke Nature Observatory, also at Spring Valley, houses a natural history library, meeting room, and classroom for educational programs. One of Spring Valley's hands-on exhibits is the 1880 Volkening Heritage Farm (south of Schaumburg Road on Plum Grove Road). Here you can help with farm chores, participate in family activities and games of the 1800s, or just see the livestock. Jumping ahead just a bit in history, electronic technology, from the basics of early radio to modern satellites, is uncovered at the Motorola Museum of Electronics (1297 East Algonquin Road).

The Chicago Athenaeum Museum (190 South Roselle Road; 1-847-895-3950) offers permanent exhibits and an International Sculpture Park on architecture and design. Founded in 1988, the museum is dedicated to the art of design in all areas of the discipline: architecture, graphics, urban planning, and industrial and product design. If going to the Athenaeum, it's best to call ahead for times and reservations. The park is located south of the municipal building. The Robert O. Atcher Municipal Center (101 Schaumburg Court) and the Prairie Center for the Arts (201 Schaumburg Court) feature plays, concerts, and exhibits. During August, the Atcher Municipal Center is also host to the Summer Breeze Outdoor Concert Series.

Schaumburg's major community events include the annual Septemberfest, which features an arts and crafts show, carnival, live entertainment, and a parade held over Labor Day weekend. Schaumburg also has a strong sense of historical preservation. The village's Great Hall and Old Village Hall were at one time a farmstead and a barn. Today they stand as community buildings, a youth and senior center. The Olde Schaumburg Centre District is the original center of the community and is the focus of a number of revitalization projects. The village also owns and maintains Olde Schaumburg Centre Park with its pond, native plants, wildflowers, brick sidewalk, and turn-of-the-(twentieth)-century park furnishings.

For those who like professional sports, just north of Prairie Rock on Mannheim Road the Allstate Arena (6920 Mannheim Road) is home to arena football's Chicago Rush. During the summer, the Schaumburg Flyers of the Independent Northern League play baseball at Alexian Field (1999 Springinsguth). North of Prairie Rock–Schaumburg in Arlington Heights is the Arlington Park Racecourse (Euclid Avenue and Wilke Road).

If you like amateur sports, you might try a round of golf at Ahlgrim's Funeral Home (201 Northwest Highway) in Palatine, north of Prairie Rock–Schaumburg. The nine-hole course, "Ahlgrim Acres," includes obstacles such as coffins and headstones, with a one-stroke penalty for bypassing the coffin on the second hole.

In midsummer, Prairie Rock hosts the annual Prairie Rock Brewfest in Elgin. This event, with its beer, music, and food, often showcases more than a dozen other breweries from Chicagoland. The Lynfred Winery (15 South Roselle Road) is a worthwhile stop for a weekend tour or the annual Oktoberfest celebration.

You may also want to check the brewery descriptions for Ram–Schaumburg, Brass, and Millrose of South Barrington for other things to see and do in the area.

DIRECTIONS

Prairie Rock–Schaumburg is just north of Woodfield Mall at the intersection of Meacham Road and McConnor Parkway. It's not far from the interchange of Interstates 90 and 290. When traveling on I-90, take I-290 south. While on I-290, exit immediately at the Woodfield Road exit. (West Frontage Road is the road onto which you turn off I-290, and it runs adjacent to the east side of Woodfield Mall.) On the southern edge of the mall, turn west on Woodfield Road and continue until you reach Meacham Road, then turn right (north) and continue on for about a mile to the intersection with McConnor Parkway. Prairie Rock is on the southeast corner of the intersection.

If you are approaching from the south on I-290, you can take the Route 72 exit, turn west and take Route 72 until it intersects with Meacham. Turn north on Meacham and travel about a mile north. Prairie Rock's driveway is on the right (east) side of Meacham, just before you reach the stoplight at the intersection of Meacham and McConnor. A major landmark in the area is the Schaumburg water tower near this intersection.

Ram Restaurant and Big Horn Brewery

Schaumburg

Visit Date	Signed

ABOUT THE BREWERY

Ram Restaurant and Big Horn Brewery in Schaumburg is located in the bustling area of Woodfield Mall. Ram–Schaumburg sits at the interchange of Interstates 90 and 290. You can see Ram at the southwest corner of this major interchange, but its frontage road location on McConnor Parkway helps insulate it from the actual traffic volume. While it's a very visible location, exiting from the major roadways and then winding your way through the Wood-field Mall area can be a little challenging. As you walk up to the building, you might pause a moment to notice the hop vines that are growing up the ladder of the brewery's grain bin.

Ram Restaurants all follow a comparable floor plan and sports theme. While they are not identical, their floor plans are similar or reversed from restaurant to restaurant. When this regularity is coupled with so many common decor elements, visitors should feel at home in any location—which, after all, is part of marketing a consistent image for a national restaurant chain of any kind.

Inside Ram–Schaumburg it's basically a large room where you'll find a high, arched ceiling and an open or "show" kitchen. There is a private room for parties or banquets, called the Woodfield Room. The main bar itself is multi-sided and angular, extending into the main lounge. Ram offers a family restaurant feeling in the main dining room with tables and high-backed booths. The main lounge has an upscale sports bar atmosphere, aggressively stated by the large television bank of eight screens that hang behind the bar. To the left and right of the television screens are Ram's serving vessels behind glass windows.

Ram Restaurant and Big Horn Brewery focuses on microbrewing, but you'll also find a wall of other spirits on display behind the bar. You'll understand what "wall" means when you see the ten-foot-high wall lined with different vodkas, tequilas, rums, and gins. Throughout the year, Ram Restaurant and Big

Horn Brewery has five or six standard beers and a few regular seasonal beer offerings, such as its Mai Bock and Oktoberfest. Beyond that, you'll find different specialty beers offered at each location depending upon the brewer's preferences or desires. While the standard beers carry similar descriptions at both Schaumburg and Wheeling, they are brewed separately at each location.

Of the Big Horn brews in Schaumburg, the Chicago Blonde and Ram Premium Pilsner are solid, lighter bodied beers that are always popular. The Big Red IPA has plenty of hops but is a little tame for IPA lovers. The Buttface Amber is a very good American amber ale, and if you appreciate a well-done unfiltered wheat beer, don't miss the Big Horn Hefeweizen. The specialty beers, Schaumburger Alt and Bubba's Brown Ale, are well worth a specific trip to Ram–Schaumburg.

HISTORY

Ram Restaurant and Big Horn Brewery of Schaumburg became the twentieth brewery in the Ram's chain in March 2000. Ram International got its start as a local restaurant in 1971 in the Tacoma, Washington, suburb of Lakewood. The "Ram Pub," as it was known, focused on a cook-your-own burgers, steaks, and sandwiches theme. The success of this formula for founders Cal Chandler and Jeff Iverson allowed them to expand their restaurants through many western states during the 1970s and 1980s. By the 1990s Ram International continued with a round of rapid expansion of more than twenty locations that included restaurants and breweries in Colorado, Texas, Washington, and Illinois.

In the fall of 2001, Chandler and Iverson decided to turn the day-to-day operations of Ram International over to their sons. Raised in the restaurant business, Jeff Iverson Jr., Dave Iverson, and Jeff Chandler are now leading the company that has more than thirty Ram International properties, including other familiar restaurant names: Shenanigan's (Washington), Murphy's Seafood and Steakhouse (Idaho), Texas Bar & Grill (Texas), Humperdinks (Texas), and C. B. & Potts (Colorado and Wyoming).

Ram–Schaumburg brewmaster Tom Nelson got his start with an intense interest in homebrewing. After first working at a homebrew supply store, he found himself working at a small brewpub in Dallas, Texas. From there, in 1997 he moved on to join a Ram Restaurant and Big Horn Brewery in Dallas. He came to Schaumburg as an assistant brewer, working with Lanny Fetzer, when it opened in 2000. When the Wheeling location began brewing in 2001, Fetzer became head brewer there, and Nelson took over in Schaumburg.

Ram–Schaumburg's sister brewpub in Wheeling opened in 2001. Ram opened its Rosemont location in 2003. Ram–Rosemont is a new concept for the company and is called the Ram Restaurant and Bar (9520 Higgins Road, north of O'Hare Airport). The Rosemont restaurant is not in Ram's distinctive stand-alone building, but it does offer similar decor, menu, and Big Horn beer. The exception is that it does not brew on the premises—rather it gets its beer from Ram–Wheeling.

DON'T MISS THIS

Midwesterners might know of Grain Belt beer. You'll find an old neon Grain Belt sign on the wall to the left of the bar. If you're from the area, you might discover the banner from the high school you attended hanging from Ram's rafters. The Rolling Meadows Mustangs, the Mt. Prospect Knights, and the Palatine Pirates are a few of the teams celebrated by the flags flying over the dining room. Also hanging from the ceiling is a former eight-person Harvard crew boat. Above the main entrance there is a large marlin fish, obviously something that wasn't caught in nearby Lake Michigan! It does, however, give you a clue to the intensive love of fishing and outdoor sports shared by Ram owners Jeff Iverson Jr., Dave Iverson, and Jeff Chandler.

BIG HORN BREWERY–SCHAUMBURG BREWS

Big Horn Hefeweizen 🍺🍺🍺🍺 *Your Ranking* _____

Don't let the season steer you away from this beer, any time is a good time for a Big Horn Hefeweizen. A strong fruity nose. Cloudy, solid golden color. A thick, bubbly, white head. Light bodied and very crisp. Firm, solid banana and clove flavors. The finish continues to allow the fruity banana esters to build as you enjoy a pint. Overall, a great pick from the Ram beer list. This unfiltered Bavarian-style Hefe-Weizen is well done and consistent among the Illinois Ram locations.

Big Horn Light 🍺🍺 *Your Ranking* _____

No nose. A very clear, pale straw color that makes this the lightest-looking of the Ram beers. Thick, soft, white head. Light bodied and soft. A mild sweetness dominates, almost an earthy maltiness. It finishes with a light smoky or roasted tone. It is made with 100 percent malted barley.

Big Red IPA 🍺🍺🍺 *Your Ranking* _____

This is a nice bitter, but it might be a little too controlled for those who like aggressively hopped India Pale Ales. It begins with just a faint hoppy nose. It has a clear copper color and a thin, soft, tan head. It is medium bodied with a soft and somewhat round texture. The bitterness is firm, but at the crispness and dryness of a good American pale ale. The finish is not very hoppy. This is a good bitter beer; it just doesn't quite live up to a what IPA lovers would like in hoppiness. Compared to this IPA, the Big Red at Ram–Wheeling is stronger with a rough bitterness and long-lasting hoppy finish.

Bubba's Bourbon Red 🍺🍺🍺 *Your Ranking* _____

A special beer, aged in Wild Turkey barrels for loads of bourbon flavor. A faint floral aroma that is mixed with the scent of bourbon. Clear copper color and a thin, bubbly, off-white head. Medium to full bodied and silky. A light hoppy start but the sweet bourbon flavors dominate. Finishes warm and smooth. The name honors Ram–Schaumburg brewer Tom "Bubba" Nelson.

Bubba's Brown Ale 🍺🍺🍺 *Your Ranking* _____

Brewed exclusively for the Ram–Schaumburg location. Begins with a malty nose. Clear, dark bronze color and a thin, soft, white head. Medium bodied. A sharp, sweet caramel malt dominance. The finish is light and fruity, with just a hint of bitterness.

Buttface Amber 🍺🍺🍺🍺 *Your Ranking* _____
A light malty nose. Clear, deep copper color and a thick, soft, tan head. Medium bodied and round. A mild malty smooth flavor. Dominated by a caramel maltiness. The finish has a mild bitterness. This smooth American-style amber ale is made with five malts and Willamette hops.

Chicago Blonde 🍺🍺 *Your Ranking* _____
This light lager has a faint malty nose. Clear, light straw color and a thick, soft, white head. Light bodied and thin texture. A dry bitterness dominates the flavor with a mild sour malty background. Not much finish, just a hint of light smokiness.

Ram Premium Pilsner 🍺🍺🍺 *Your Ranking* _____
A brewmaster's special in which Ram takes a lot of pride. This classic Pilsner is made with Noble Saaz hops. No nose. Clear, light gold color with a thick, soft, white head. Light bodied and crisp. There is a slight sweetness at the beginning, but then it quickly turns to a smooth, long-lasting bitterness. This is a clean and crisp beer.

Schaumburger Alt 🍺🍺🍺🍺 *Your Ranking* _____
A hoppy German-style Alt. A very light malty nose. Clear, deep copper color and a thick, soft, tan head. Medium bodied and crisp. Begins with a mild malty, caramel flavor with a crisp hoppy background. Finishes smooth and nicely balanced with an emphasis on a light crisp bitterness. A brewmaster's special at Ram–Schaumburg.

Total Disorder Porter 🍺🍺🍺 *Your Ranking* _____
A light, roasted nose. Very dark color and a thin, bubbly, off-white head. Medium to full bodied and highly carbonated. Strong malty flavors with sweetness, especially chocolate overtones. The finish is light and roasted. This porter has some great body and malt flavor. On a cold winter day this beer would get higher marks. It was a silver medal winner at the 1996 Great American Beer Festival.

OTHER BIG HORN–SCHAUMBURG BREWS YOU MAY WANT TO TRY

Chi Town Brown *Your Ranking* _____
A traditional English-style brown ale.

Knock Out Stout *Your Ranking* _____
Dark brown color, medium bodied. Light roasted qualities, with a balanced hoppiness.

Mai Bock *Your Ranking* _____
A late-spring into summer seasonal brew found at all Illinois Ram and Big Horn Breweries.

Oktoberfest *Your Ranking* _____
A fall seasonal brew found at all Illinois Ram and Big Horn Breweries.

Ole St. Mick's Stout   *Your Ranking* _____

A classic Irish-style dry stout. Distinctive rich caramel flavor and finishes with a dry roasted barley character. A seasonal beer brewed for St. Patrick's Day.

BREWERY RATING

Rating	Your Rating	Shepard's Rating (1 to 4 Mugs)	General Description
Location		🍺🍺🍺	Entertainment district
Ease of Finding Location		🍺🍺	Difficult, out of the way, need a map (toll roads and exits are difficult)
Brewery Atmosphere		🍺🍺🍺	Family restaurant
			Sports
Dining Experience		🍺🍺🍺	Family style/variety
			Fine dining
The Pint		🍺🍺🍺	A good experience

MENU

Ram–Schaumburg offers a diverse menu with steaks, poultry, seafood, pasta, burgers, pizza, and calzones. Appetizer choices outnumber all sections of the menu, with nearly fifteen different selections. You'll find chicken quesadillas, potato skins, fried mozzarella, calamari, and Zingers, which are actually boneless hot wings. There is also a Ram appetizer platter for two, which has a little of nearly everything, and a party platter for large groups. Ram features three or four soups, including a beer cheese. Salad options include a very basic house salad and several others with combinations of Thai chicken, turkey, a hot chicken Caesar, and north Atlantic shrimp. The barbecue chicken pizza is considered Ram's signature pizza, but you'll also find other versions, including an Italian pizza and the Rambo with its pepperoni, sausage, and mushrooms. Ram also has calzones with Canadian bacon, Italian sausage, pepperoni, and four cheeses. There are about a dozen burgers and sandwiches. Some of the most flavorful to consider are the Cajun burger with pepperjack cheese, the teriyaki chicken burger made with a teriyaki ginger glaze and pineapple, and the salmon baguette. If you are looking for a hearty entree, you might find that the Tuscan meatloaf may be more than a meal. Several entrees are made with Ram's house beers. The Bighorn fajitas are made with southwestern spices and the Buttface Amber Ale; if you have a taste for ribs, a one-pound rack is slow roasted in Big Red Ale then flame grilled; the lemon Hefeweizen chicken is pan seared in olive oil and finished with Big Horn Hefeweizen and fresh basil on garlic mashed potatoes; and the fish and chips platter includes cod fillets dipped in a Buttface Amber Ale batter. To end the meal, if the Ole St. Mick's Stout is on tap, you will want to try that. But also consider the Mile High Mud Pie with almond mocha and cookies and cream ice cream on an Oreo cookie crumb crust.

You'll find similar menus at Ram–Wheeling and Ram–Rosemont, but it's also a good idea to watch for different daily specials.

OTHER THINGS TO SEE OR DO IN THE AREA

There are two very visible landmarks to watch for that indicate that you're very close to Ram–Schaumburg. The Woodfield Shopping Center (Golf Road and Route 53) has over 250 shops and forty restaurants, and the large blue and yellow IKEA home furnishings building (1800 East McConnor Parkway) is visible from Interstate 90. IKEA is directly north of Ram, while Woodfield is directly south. Inside Woodfield you might quench your thirst for speed at the NASCAR Silicon Motor Speedway, with its race car simulators that provide the look and feel of driving at 200 miles per hour.

The village of Schaumburg maintains an impressive commitment to urban green spaces with more than a thousand acres of parkland. Olde Schaumburg Centre Park offers a pond, native plants, wildflowers, and brick sidewalks. The Spring Valley Nature Sanctuary (111 East Schaumburg Road) contains over 135 acres of forest, meadows, prairies, and wetlands. The 1880 Volkening Heritage Farm (south of Schaumburg Road on Plum Grove Road) offers a log cabin and exhibits.

The Chicago Athenaeum Museum (190 South Roselle Road; 1-847-895-3950) contains permanent exhibits and an International Sculpture Park on architecture and design. Founded in 1988, the museum is dedicated to the art of design in all areas of the discipline: architecture, graphics, urban planning, and industrial and product design. If going to the Athenaeum, it's best to call ahead for times and reservations. The park is located south of the municipal building. The Robert O. Atcher Municipal Center (101 Schaumburg Court) and the Prairie Center for the Arts (201 Schaumburg Court) feature plays, concerts, and exhibits. During August, the Atcher Municipal Center is also host to the Summer Breeze Outdoor Concert Series.

The Spring Brook Nature Center (130 Forest Avenue, Itasca) is open year-round and includes two miles of trails, offering the opportunity to walk through a tunnel of prairie grasses or stand four feet above a cattail marsh on the 700-foot-long boardwalk. In the fall Spring Brook holds its annual Anniversary Family Festival with historical recreations, displays, and exhibits.

Directly east of Ram–Schaumburg, the Busse Forest Nature Preserve is a 437-acre woodland within the 3700-acre Ned Brown Preserve. This area is also classified as a Registered National Landmark by the Department of the Interior. The area features a forest of oak, sugar maple, and basswood. There is an abundance of wildflowers and shrubs; exceptionally rich and colorful are the spring wildflowers, which include the large-flowered trillium. Busse Lake is a 590-acre impoundment lake on Salt Creek.

North of Ram–Schaumburg in Arlington Heights, the Arlington Park Racecourse (Euclid Avenue and Wilke Road) features the thunder of thoroughbreds. For those who like professional sports, the Schaumburg Flyers are members of the eighteen-team Independent Northern League and play baseball from May through September at Alexian Field (1999 Springinsguth). Arena football's Chicago Rush play at the Allstate Arena (6920 Mannheim Road, Des Plaines).

You may also want to check the brewery descriptions for Prairie Rock–Schaumburg, Brass, and Millrose of South Barrington for other things to see and do in the area.

DIRECTIONS

Ram Restaurant and Big Horn Brewery of Schaumburg is easy to see but it's a little tricky navigating the tollway exits. You'll have a great view of Ram as your turn south from Interstate 90 onto Interstate 290, but you need to continue driving south so that you can exit onto Woodfield Road. You'll actually be driving adjacent to the east side of the Woodfield Shopping Mall while on I-290. Woodfield Road runs east and west, and you'll want to turn west, drive until you see Meacham Road, and then turn right (north) on Meacham. About a mile north, turn back to the east on East McConnor Parkway. (At the corner of McConnor and Meacham you'll also see Prairie Rock Brewing Company.) Ram–Schaumburg is located only about three-fourths of a mile east of Prairie Rock on McConnor.

If you're approaching from the south on I-290, it's easy to watch for the Route 72 (Higgins Road) exit and turn west. Route 72 will intersect with Meacham; turn north there and continue in that direction until you reach the intersection of Meacham and McConnor Parkway, where you turn right (east) on McConnor.

Ram Restaurant and Big Horn Brewery

Wheeling

Visit Date	Signed

ABOUT THE BREWERY

Ram Restaurant and Big Horn Brewery of Wheeling is the second Ram to be built in the Chicago area. Located on Milwaukee Avenue (Route 45/21), it's only about a block south of Lake Cook Road, and it's within about twenty minutes of two other northern Chicago breweries: Flatlander's (Lincolnshire) and Mickey Finn's (Libertyville). Both are north of Ram–Wheeling on Milwaukee Avenue.

A similar floor plan and sports theme is found in most Ram Restaurants. While they are not identical, their floor plans are similar from restaurant to restaurant. When this regularity is coupled with so many common decor elements, visitors should feel at home in any location—which is, after all, part of marketing a consistent image for a national restaurant chain of any kind.

Outside Ram–Wheeling there is a changeable sign above the front door, somewhat like a marquee at a movie theater. The sign announces the specials of the day, current live entertainment, and parties at Ram.

Inside Ram–Wheeling it's basically a large room where you'll find high ceilings and an open or "show" kitchen. There is a private party or banquet room called the Tower Room, no doubt in acknowledgment of the Wheeling water tower, which stands just west of the Ram parking lot. It's so close that as you approach the brewpub from Milwaukee Avenue, the tower appears to be coming out of Ram's roof.

The main bar is multisided and extends into the main lounge. Similar to the sign above the front door is a large marquee above the bar that announces the beer specials. As in all Rams, the main lounge has an upscale sports bar atmosphere, aggressively stated by the large multiscreen television bank that hangs over and behind the bar.

Ram offers a family restaurant feeling in the main dining room with tables and high-backed booths. Ram–Wheeling's floor plan is nearly identical to those at Schaumburg and Rosemont, but it feels more open, perhaps because of the large northern windows and multiple mirrors along the west wall.

Ram and Big Horn Brewing of Wheeling stresses beer, but behind the bar you see the ten-foot-high wall lined with different vodkas, tequilas, rums, and gins. You can see the brewhaus and serving vessels through glass to the left and right of this main wall of liquor.

Throughout the year, Ram–Wheeling has five or six standard beers and a few regular seasonal beer offerings such as its Mai Bock and Oktoberfest. Beyond that, you'll find different specialty beers offered at each location depending upon the brewer's preferences or desires. While the standard beers carry similar descriptions at both Schaumburg and Wheeling, they are brewed separately at each location.

Of the Big Horn brews in Wheeling, the Chicago Blonde and the Ram Premium Pilsner are solid, lighter bodied beers that are always popular. The Buttface Amber is a very good American amber ale. The Big Horn Hefeweizen is a well-done unfiltered wheat beer and is the flagship for this brewery. The Big Red IPA has plenty of hops, and if you have the opportunity to compare, you might find it's stronger and more assertive. A very special beer from Ram–Wheeling is Lanny Fetzer's Russian Imperial Stout. Because it's a brewmaster's special, it is not always available, but that only makes it even more special when it's on tap!

HISTORY

Opening in April 2001, Ram Restaurant and Big Horn Brewery of Wheeling became Ram's twenty-eighth brewery. At the time of its opening the brewhaus capacity was the largest in the company. Ram International began as a local restaurant in 1971 in the Tacoma, Washington, suburb of Lakewood. The "Ram Pub," as it was known, focused on a cook-your-own burgers, steaks, and sandwiches theme. The success of this formula for founders Cal Chandler and Jeff Iverson allowed them to expand their restaurants through many western states during the 1970s and 1980s. By the 1990s Ram International continued with another round of rapid expansion of more than twenty locations that included restaurants and breweries in Colorado, Texas, Washington, and Illinois.

In the fall of 2001, Chandler and Iverson decided to turn the day-to-day operations of Ram International over to their sons. Raised in the restaurant business, Jeff Iverson Jr., Dave Iverson, and Jeff Chandler are now leading the company, which has more than thirty Ram International properties, including such familiar restaurant names as Shenanigan's (Washington), Murphy's Seafood and Steakhouse (Idaho), Texas Bar & Grill (Texas), Humperdinks (Texas), and C. B. & Potts (Colorado and Wyoming).

Ram–Wheeling's brewmaster Lanny Fetzer has been brewing for Ram since 1996. Fetzer began homebrewing while in college. After meeting Ram's corporate brewer at a brewfest in Lake Oswego, Oregon, he landed a job as an assistant brewer in Spokane, Washington. From there, Fetzer moved his way through the company with jobs in Seattle, then Schaumburg, and finally to Wheeling. Lanny remarks that he's very happy as a brewer: "It's great when you're able to turn your hobby into your career!"

Ram–Wheeling's sister brewpub in Schaumburg opened in 2000. Ram opened its Rosemont location in 2003. Ram–Rosemont is a new concept for the company and is called the Ram Restaurant and Bar (9520 Higgins Road, north of O'Hare Airport). The Rosemont restaurant is not in Ram's distinctive stand-alone building, but it does offer a similar decor, menu, and Big Horn beer. The exception is that it does not brew on the premises—rather it gets its beer from Ram–Wheeling.

DON'T MISS THIS

With the sports bar theme you expect to see television sets and sports team logos, but one unusual item in Ram–Wheeling's decor is a six seat, four-oar crew boat hanging upside down over the main dining room. The boat was formerly used by the crew at Harvard. Also throughout the restaurant, you find local high school banners hanging from Ram's rafters. Near the bar (its left side) you find a large jukebox. If you look closely at the dials on the jukebox, you'll see the locations of other Ram Restaurants and Big Horn Breweries.

BIG HORN BREWERY–WHEELING BREWS

Big Horn Hefeweizen   🍺 🍺 🍺 🍺   *Your Ranking* _____
Don't let the season steer you away from this beer, any time is a good time for a Big Horn Hefeweizen. A strong fruity nose. Cloudy, solid golden color. A thick, bubbly, white head. Light bodied and very crisp. Firm, solid banana and clove flavors. The finish continues to allow the fruity banana esters to build as you enjoy a pint. Overall, it is a great pick from the Ram beer list. This unfiltered Bavarian-style Hefe-Weizen is well done and consistent among the Illinois Ram locations.

Big Horn Light   🍺 🍺   *Your Ranking* _____
No nose. A very clear, pale straw color that makes this the lightest looking of the Ram beers. Thick, soft, white head. Light bodied and soft. A mild sweetness dominates, almost an earthy maltiness. It finishes with a light smoky or roasted tone. It is made with 100 percent malted barley.

Big Red IPA   🍺 🍺 🍺 🍺   *Your Ranking* _____
A firm hoppy nose. Clear, copper color and a thin, soft, tan head. Medium to full bodied. Firm, strong, assertive bitterness that continues through into the finish. This beer is best at the Wheeling Ram location. This beer just seemed more assertive in its flavors when compared to its sister brew in Schaumburg. The Wheeling bartender suggested that IPA might not move as quickly here as in Schaumburg, so it has time to age. If that's the case, don't tell anyone, because that way it would continue to improve here in Wheeling for IPA fans like me!

Buttface Amber   🍺 🍺 🍺 🍺   *Your Ranking* _____
A light malty nose. Clear, deep copper color and a thick, soft, tan head. Medium bodied and round. A mild malty smooth flavor. Dominated by a caramel maltiness. The finish has a mild bitterness. This smooth American-style amber ale is made with five malts and Willamette hops.

Chicago Blonde 🍺🍺   *Your Ranking* _____

A light lager that has a faint malty nose. Clear, light straw color and a thick, soft, white head. Light bodied and thin texture. A dry bitterness dominates the flavor with a mild sour malty background. There is not much finish; just a hint of light smokiness.

Magnificent Mile Ale 🍺🍺🍺🍺   *Your Ranking* _____

A brewmaster's special you'll find at the Ram–Wheeling location. No nose. Clear, light copper color and a thin, bubbly, off-white head. Light bodied. A mild hoppy start with malty balance. A light fruity finish. This brewmaster's special has great balance with some fruity finish.

Ram Premium Pilsner 🍺🍺🍺   *Your Ranking* _____

A brewmaster's special in which Ram takes a lot of pride. This classic Pilsner is made with Noble Saaz hops. No nose. Clear, light gold color with a thick, soft, white head. Light bodied and crisp. There is a slight sweetness at the beginning, but then it quickly turns to a smooth, long-lasting bitterness. This is a clean and crisp beer.

Total Disorder Porter 🍺🍺🍺   *Your Ranking* _____

A light, roasted nose. Very dark color and a thin, bubbly, off-white head. Medium to full bodied and highly carbonated. Strong malty flavors with sweetness, especially chocolate overtones. The finish is light and roasted. This porter has some great body and malt flavor. On a cold winter day this beer would get higher marks. It won a silver medal at the 1996 Great American Beer Festival.

OTHER BIG HORN–WHEELING BREWS YOU MAY WANT TO TRY

Bubba's Bourbon Red   *Your Ranking* _____

A special beer, brewed in Wild Turkey barrels at Ram–Schaumburg. Carries the name "Bubba," as in Ram–Schaumburg brewer Tom "Bubba" Nelson.

Ice Breaker Imperial Stout   *Your Ranking* _____

A strong, full bodied stout offered in February.

Knock Out Stout   *Your Ranking* _____

Dark brown color, medium bodied. Light roasted qualities with a balanced hoppiness.

Mai Bock   *Your Ranking* _____

A late spring into summer seasonal brew found at all Illinois Ram and Big Horn Breweries.

Oktoberfest   *Your Ranking* _____

A fall seasonal brew found at all Illinois Ram and Big Horn Breweries.

Ole St. Mick's Stout   *Your Ranking* _____

A classic Irish-style dry stout. Distinctive rich caramel flavor, finishing with a dry roasted barley character. A seasonal beer brewed for St. Patrick's Day.

Russian Imperial Stout   *Your Ranking* _____

A February seasonal beer brewed by Lanny Fetzer. A big beer with lots of chocolate and spice flavors.

BREWERY RATING

	Your Rating	Shepard's Rating (1 to 4 Mugs)	General Description
Location		🍺🍺🍺	Commercial/industrial
Ease of Finding Location		🍺🍺🍺	Easy, but requires some planning
Brewery Atmosphere		🍺🍺🍺	Family restaurant Sports
Dining Experience		🍺🍺🍺	Family style/variety Fine dining
The Pint		🍺🍺🍺	A good experience

MENU

Ram–Wheeling offers a diverse menu, with steaks, poultry, seafood, pasta, burgers, pizza, and calzones. Appetizer choices include chicken quesadillas, potato skins, fried mozzarella, calamari, and Zingers, which are actually boneless hot wings. There is also a Ram appetizer platter for two that has a little of nearly everything, and the party platter for large groups. Ram features three or four soups, including a beer cheese. Salad options include a very basic house salad and several others with combinations of Thai chicken, turkey, a hot chicken Caesar, and north Atlantic shrimp. The barbecue chicken pizza is considered Ram's signature pizza. Other pizza selections include an Italian and the Rambo with pepperoni, sausage, and mushrooms. Ram also makes calzones with Canadian bacon, Italian sausage, pepperoni, and four cheeses. Ram has about a dozen burgers and sandwiches. Some of the most flavorful to consider are the Cajun burger with pepperjack cheese, the teriyaki chicken burger made with a teriyaki ginger glaze and pineapple, and the salmon baguette. If you're looking for a hearty entree, you might find the Tuscan meatloaf may be more than a meal. Several entrees are made with Ram's house beers. The Bighorn fajitas are made with southwestern spices and the Buttface Amber Ale; a one-pound rack of ribs is slow roasted in Big Red Ale then flame grilled; the lemon Hefeweizen chicken is pan seared in olive oil and finished with Big Horn Hefeweizen and fresh basil on garlic mashed potatoes; and the fish and chips platter includes cod fillets dipped in a Buttface Amber Ale batter. To end the meal, if the Ole St. Mick's Stout is on tap, you will want to try that. But also consider the Mile High Mud Pie with almond mocha and rich cookies and cream ice cream on an Oreo cookie crumb crust.

You'll find similar menus at Ram–Schaumburg and Ram–Rosemont, but it's also a good idea to watch for different daily specials.

OTHER THINGS TO SEE OR DO IN THE AREA

Wheeling is known for one of the largest concentrations of antiques dealers in the Chicago area. The Antique Center of Illinois (1920 South Wolf Road) is home to over fifty sellers, featuring crystal, china, pottery, lamps, jewelry, clocks, and the unusual. The Sale Barn Square (971 North Milwaukee [Route 21]) is another antique center, located on the 1835 Redlinger Farm.

The Wheeling Historical Society Museum (251 North Wolf Road, in Chamber Park) was once used as the original Village Hall from its construction in 1894. Wheeling marked its centennial in 1994 with a year-long celebration and dedication of the Centennial Plaza Fountain. Wheeling's first church was built by German Presbyterians in the fall of 1865; they erected their church on a site located on the north side of Dundee Road and west of Milwaukee Avenue. The last worship services were held there on December 16, 1962. The church has since been moved to the Chamber of Commerce Park on Wolf Road, pending movement to a permanent location.

On Wheeling's eastern boundary, the Cook County Forest Preserve lies along the Des Plaines River. The forest preserve provides jogging and equestrian trails, canoeing, fishing, and cycling opportunities as it stretches through Cook, Lake, and Du Page Counties. South of Wheeling on Route 21, the River Trail Nature Center (3120 Milwaukee Avenue) provides insights into the forests, the prairie along the riverbanks, and the area's glacial geology. Wheeling itself supports nine parks throughout the village.

When driving through Wheeling, take a close look at some of the homes near the intersection of Dundee and Elmhurst, an area known as the Dunhurst Heights neighborhood. The land was once a cornfield owned by Techny, a Catholic community. In the 1950s an explosion of residential construction occurred with many homes built by the Harnischfeger Corporation of Port Washington, Wisconsin, and put together by the Herzog Construction Company. The homes were built assembly-line fashion in only two bungalow styles, with modern amenities for their time that included electric kitchen appliances, built-in ranges and ovens, washers, dryers, and gas heat. Five hundred and fifty of these three-bedroom, 900-square-foot homes were built by the Harnischfeger Corporation.

Long Grove is a charming small town about five miles northwest of Ram–Wheeling. Long Grove's historic business district offers galleries, cafés, restaurants, specialty shops, and antique dealers. The village also hosts a number of events including a May Chocolate Festival, the June Strawberry Festival, the Cobblestone Sidewalk Sale in August, and the Apple Festival in October, and Countryside Christmas lasts from Thanksgiving until Christmas. A kid's favorite in Long Grove is Dave Herzog's Marionettes (Old McHenry Road and Route 83). For adults, the Valentino Vineyards and Winery (5175 Aptakisic Road) grows twelve different varieties of grapes and makes more than twenty different wines.

The Ravinia Festival (Highland Park) is known for its outdoor live music. Ravinia's open-air, covered pavilion seats 3,200 and is used for symphony concerts, dance, and pop concerts. The companion Martin Theatre, an indoor venue, seats 850 and is used for chamber music performances and recitals. A third venue, Bennett Gordon Hall, seats 450, primarily for the Steans Institute concerts.

In nearby Deerfield, the historical society (Deerfield and Kipling Roads) supports the Deerfield Historic Village, which includes tours of the Caspar Ott Log House, George Luther House, and the Little Red Schoolhouse. The Ott house is considered the oldest standing building in Lake County. Deerfield also hosts a fall festival in September as the society's annual fundraiser offering food, musical entertainment, reenactment groups, crafts, and pioneer demonstrations.

Wheeling is close to a number of professional sports venues. The Arlington Park Racecourse (Euclid Avenue and Wilke Road, Arlington Heights) features thoroughbred events. The Chicago Rush, of the Arena Football League, play at the Allstate Arena (6920 Mannheim Road, Des Plaines).

You may also want to check the brewery descriptions for Flatlander's (Lincolnshire) and Mickey Finn's (Libertyville) for other things to see and do in the area.

DIRECTIONS

Ram Restaurant and Big Horn Brewery in Wheeling is one of the easiest brewpubs to find. When traveling north on either Interstate 94 or 294, watch for the Lake Cook Road exit as those major interstates come together. Turn west on Lake Cook Road and stay in the right-hand lane for about two miles, then exit at Route 45/21. Just south of this exit is Ram–Wheeling (Lake Cook Road goes over the top of Route 45/21). Ram is approximately one stoplight south of Lake Cook Road.

If you are traveling north on Route 45/21 (Milwaukee Avenue) from Chicago, you'll want to turn west at the stoplight marking North Wolf Road. North Wolf Road is the intersection that is immediately south of Ram, and because of the way the turn lanes are marked, you'll have difficulty turning left if you pass the North Wolf Road stoplight.

Rhodell Brewery and Bar
Peoria

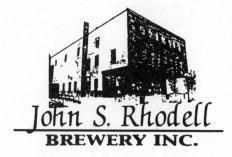

Visit Date	Signed

ABOUT THE BREWERY

If you want to share your enthusiasm with others looking for good beer, all you have to do is visit Rhodell Brewery and Bar on one of the nights when the brew-your-own crowd arrives. The bar comes alive with the excitement of children opening Christmas presents, as local folks either brew or bottle in the brew-your-own section of Rhodell. As I sat at the bar one evening and just watched, I could feel the exhilaration of these small-batch brewers exchanging tips about recipes, bragging in anticipation of their handcrafted brews, and sharing stories of their own perfect pints. If you're looking for the holy grail of beer aficionados, then put Rhodell on the list of breweries to visit.

Rhodell is situated along the Illinois River in Peoria's entertainment and recreation district. Rhodell is typically open in the evenings, but the hours can be somewhat irregular, so if you are not from the local area, it's a good idea to call ahead.

The three-story brick building really adds to the unique character of Rhodell. Inside, the history as an old warehouse is felt through the wooden floors and high open ceilings. The front half of the brewery includes a small bar with only about ten stools. There are a few tables and chairs, a pool table, and a large picture window looking out on the front sidewalk. The back half of Rhodell is where the brew-your-own operations take place. Overall, the inside atmosphere is really like a warehouse because of the way the bar is arranged and the large area that's been set aside for mass homebrewing. The building also contains a comedy club on the third floor, a common area between buildings serves as a beer garden, and next door is Kelleher's Irish Pub and Eatery.

Throughout the course of a year you'll likely find more different house beers being served at Rhodell Brewery and Bar than at any other place in Illi-

207

nois. That's partly because brewmaster and owner Mark Johnstone uses the same four-barrel equipment his brew-your-own customers use. Given the small quantities, Johnstone is able to keep eight to twelve of his beers on tap, and they always change, so every trip to Rhodell's offers something different. Johnstone's brewing philosophy is that he wants to make beers that will get people to sit and appreciate them for awhile. Among the standard beers that remain on tap are the Brave Heart Ale, Scottish Ale, a wheat, and the Dark Star Porter. The special beers worth asking about include the MoJo and the strong Scotch ale called Tartan Terror.

HISTORY

Rhodell Brewing was established in 1998. The name is actually a combination of initials and syllables from the names of the brewery's owners and friends. Rhodell is run by Mark Johnstone, who is the brewmaster, the president of the company, the bar manager, and the self-described "cleaner of many things and surfaces" at the brewery-bar-and-brew-your-own business. Mark is from Edinburgh, Scotland. His wife and partner, Suzanne, is originally from Peoria, but the two met while attending Scotland's University of Stirling. Both enjoy beer and started homebrewing prior to being married in 1991. The "odell" in Rhodell comes from O'Dell, Suzanne's maiden name. Mark and Suzanne remained in Scotland until 1998, when they relocated to Peoria. Mark was looking for work opportunities in the area, and, after they researched the brew-your-own business and found the riverfront location, Rhodell Brewing came to be.

The area south from Rhodell Brewery and Bar, along the river, was once home to Peoria's Distillery Row. In the book *Peoria Spirits*, Bryan Ogg documents the city's boom years, the 1860s and 1870s. During that time there were as many as fourteen distilleries and six breweries in Peoria. The earliest brewer was Andrew Eitle, who built his brewery in 1837 (located south of the Robert Michel Bridge). Among the most famous brewers to call Peoria home were Joseph Huber and Sons, who operated the Old City Brewery, and John Gipps, who owned Gipps and Eagle Breweries. Huber's brewery was purchased by Edward and Albert Leisy, who operated the Leisy Brothers Brewery until Prohibition. Gipps's brewery also operated until Prohibition, but it reopened in 1933 and continued brewing for another twenty years until 1953. It was well known for its "Give me a Gipps!" slogan. There was even a major Pabst brewery in Peoria (Peoria Heights) until 1982. But Peoria was perhaps better known for its distilleries. By 1900 it was called the "Whiskey Capital of the World." Among the whiskey barons who called Peoria home were Samuel Woolner, J. B. Greenhut, and Hiram Walker and Sons. In 1881 Joseph Greenhut, Nelson Morris, and John Francis built the Great Western Distillery, which was known as the largest distillery in the world. Hiram Walker purchased Great Western in 1933 and ran the facility until 1982.

The building containing Rhodell Brewing was constructed in the 1890s as a wholesale liquor warehouse to serve the thriving distilleries of Peoria. In the early 1900s it was transformed into a storage building for a farm equipment factory; then it eventually became the O'Neill Brothers Trucking and Storage Company. During the 1930s, local historians say, it was not just a trucking company but was allegedly used by Al Capone to store gambling tables. Trucks would transport the tables to Joliet, where two uniformed policemen would take possession of the tables and deliver them wherever Capone wanted them in Chicago.

DON'T MISS THIS

The building containing Rhodell Brewing has a lot of character and ties to local history. In the area where the homebrewing is done, on the north wall there is a black-and-white photo of the building when it was home to O'Neill Brothers Trucking. Owner and brewmaster Mark Johnstone has hung a number of national flags from the ceiling. The banners of Great Britain, Scotland, Wales, and the United States are prominently displayed.

RHODELL BREWS

Brave Heart Ale *Your Ranking* _____

This medium-bodied Scottish ale has an aggressive malty nose. Deep copper color and a thick, bubbly, white head. There is a firm caramel malty flavor with a nice balance of hops. The maltiness comes on strong in the finish.

Dark Star Porter 🍺🍺🍺 *Your Ranking* _____

One of brewmaster Mark Johnstone's favorite combinations of malt. A porter that begins with a light roasted nose. Very dark with a thick, soft, brown head. Full bodied and round. Strong malty flavors with a smooth roasted background and finish. There is a lot of flavor in this beer.

English Ale 🍺🍺🍺🍺 *Your Ranking* _____

A special treat when you are visiting Rhodell. A crisp malty nose. Deep, rich copper color and a thick, bubbly, white head. Full bodied. The hops begin the taste but there is smooth malty background; the taste lingers and builds throughout the finish. This ale has great character and strong flavor.

Golden Ale 🍺🍺 *Your Ranking* _____

A malty nose. Hazy golden color with a thin, soft, white head. Light bodied. A weak malty flavor. Finishes with a sweet, sugarlike aftertaste.

Light Lager 🍺🍺 *Your Ranking* _____

A light malty nose. Clear golden color and a thick, soft, white head. Malty, earthy flavor and a sour finish.

Scottish Ale 🍺🍺🍺🍺 *Your Ranking* _____

A malty nose. Clear, deep copper color. The head is thin, soft, and white. Medium bodied and round. A malty, caramel dominance. A light hoppy finish. This is a smooth, bold malty beer. If you're looking for some assertive flavors, yet controlled and smooth, this beer will be the one you spend your time with.

Wheat 🍺🍺🍺 *Your Ranking* _____

A German-style wheat that has a strong fruity nose. Cloudy golden color and a thick, soft, white head. Light bodied and soft. Strong yeasty qualities with great banana flavor. A sweet finish. This beer provides a base beer for a number of fruit adjuncts that you might find on any visit to Rhodell.

OTHER RHODELL BREWS YOU MAY WANT TO TRY

Black Angus Stout   *Your Ranking* _____
A complex blend of roasted malts. Similar to a Scottish-style stout. Made with dark crystal and British malts.

Cream Ale   *Your Ranking* _____
A smooth-bodied, light golden ale.

Honey Lager   *Your Ranking* _____
A light golden lager with a hint of honey sweetness.

Honey Wheat   *Your Ranking* _____
Fruit beginning with a sweet finish. This wheat is light and crisp.

Midwest Red Ale   *Your Ranking* _____
A reddish amber ale. Full bodied and well balanced.

MoJo   *Your Ranking* _____
A strong ale with an amber color. Dry hopped with Cascade hops. The name comes from the movie *Austin Powers* in reference to Dr. Evil's description of Austin's life force. After all, beer is life for many of us.

Natural Blonde   *Your Ranking* _____
A light pale ale. Dry hopped with Cascade hops. One of Rhodell's most popular beers.

Pale Ale   *Your Ranking* _____
A firm hoppy aroma and flavor. Dry hopped with Australian and Cascade hops.

Pumpkin Pilsner   *Your Ranking* _____
A special seasonal for the fall. There is a heavy emphasis on the spices. You'll detect nutmeg and cinnamon, to name a few.

Tartan Terror   *Your Ranking* _____
A strong Scotch ale. The emphasis of this beer is almost entirely on the malt; the hops are hard to find. A beer Robert the Bruce would be happy to consume.

BREWERY RATING

Rating	Your Rating	Shepard's Rating (1 to 4 Mugs)	General Description
Location		🍺🍺🍺🍺	Entertainment district
Ease of Finding Location		🍺🍺🍺	Close to major roads and intersections

Rating	Your Rating	Shepard's Rating	General Description
Brewery Atmosphere		🍺🍺	Rustic
Dining Experience		n/a	Limited
The Pint		🍺🍺🍺	A good experience

MENU

Rhodell Brewing doesn't try to compete with nearby restaurants. The focus is clearly on the beer! You can get premade pizza and a few light bar appetizers such as chicken strips, beer-battered cheese strips, and mushrooms.

OTHER THINGS TO SEE OR DO IN THE AREA

A great way to begin your visit is with a stop at the Apollo Fine Arts and Entertainment Center to view the film *Discover Peoria* and gain insights into the area's history and culture. Another option for learning and actually seeing Peoria is by signing up for one of the guided historical tours or historical trolley rides offered by the Peoria Historical Society (942 Northeast Glen Oak Avenue, 1-309-674-1921). The Pettengill-Morron House Museum (1212 West Moss Avenue) is part of the historic Moss Avenue neighborhood. The Pettengill-Morron House is an 1868 Victorian mansion containing decorative arts, antique furniture, and a silver collection. The John C. Flanagan House Museum (942 Northeast Glen Oak Avenue) is located in a red brick Georgian and early Federal-style home overlooking the scenic bluffs of the Illinois River. The Flanagan House Museum has collections that date from early local settlement. The African American Museum and Hall of Fame (309 Dusable Street) offers numerous collections and exhibits of African American life and culture. The Illinois American Historical Water Museum (123 Southwest Washington) has gargoyles, winding staircases, and a museum dedicated to equipment that has been used throughout history to treat drinking water.

Peoria's Grandview Drive winds through majestic homes in Peoria Heights. It was once called "the world's most beautiful drive" by President Teddy Roosevelt. Also in Peoria Heights, Tower Park (1222 East Kingman) offers a panoramic view of the Illinois River from a 175-foot observation tower. There are three viewing decks and a glass elevator for appreciating the local vista.

A great way to experience the Illinois River and see the Peoria skyline is with a cruise on the *Spirit of Peoria* (225 Northeast Adams Street). The paddle wheeler offers short excursions, dinner cruises, private charters, and even overnight trips on the riverboat. If a paddle wheeler isn't for you, perhaps you'll enjoy the Wheels O' Time Museum (11923 North Knoxville Avenue [Route 40]). The museum contains displays of autos, farm equipment, trains, bicycles, toys, clothing, and fire equipment. For those who enjoy baseball, about two blocks southwest of Rhodell Brewing is O'Brien Field (730 Southwest Jefferson), the home of the Peoria Chiefs of the Midwest Baseball League.

The Glen Oak Zoo (2218 North Prospect Road) is home to more than 175 animals from around the world. The Peoria Park District maintains the Luthy Botanical Garden (2218 North Prospect Road) along the west banks of the Illinois River. The George L. Luthy Memorial Botanical Garden has been part of Peoria since the 1950s, but the City of Peoria first opened the conservancy with the Victorian-style Palm House in 1896. The Palm House was located on the grounds that eventually became the Glen Oak Zoo. The Lakeview Museum of Arts and Sciences (1125 West Lake Avenue) contains a planetarium, Illinois folk art, and a children's discovery center. Another way to see the area is by taking the Rock Island State Trail, which stretches some twenty miles from Peoria to Toulon. The trail is an excellent path for bikers and hikers.

East of Peoria in Eureka, on the campus of President Ronald Reagan's alma mater, Eureka College, the Donald B. Cerf Center houses the Reagan Exhibit with over two thousand items from Reagan's college days, movie career, governorship of California, and two terms as president. Also east of Peoria, the Wildlife Prairie State Park (3826 North Taylor Road [Route 2]) is a two-thousand-acre park with wolves, bison, waterfowl, black bear, elk, and otters. It's a restored prairie that offers a glimpse of what Illinois was like in the early 1800s. The Dickson Mounds Museum (10956 North Dickson Mounds Road, Lewistown) is a fascinating way to learn about the Native American cultures that once lived in the Illinois River valley.

Back in Peoria, along Water Street and just a few blocks north of Rhodell Brewing, the Illinois Antique Center (311 Water Street) has more than two hundred antique dealers in a renovated warehouse. The Riverfront (200 Northeast Water Street) is a revitalized area for Peoria that serves as a community gathering place for festivals, events, or just walks along the Illinois River. The Riverfront Visitors Center is located in the 1852 Schwab-Powell Building at the north end of Water Street.

DIRECTIONS

When arriving in Peoria on Interstate 74, exit south into the downtown. From the east, I-74 crosses the Illinois River via the Murray M. Baker Bridge. From the north, scenic Route 29 winds along the west bank of the Illinois River and becomes one road with Route 24 just north of the downtown. Jefferson Street is a one-way thoroughfare and will bring you south into the city. As you near the Civic Center, turn left (east) onto State Street, which will bring you directly into the riverfront area and Water Street. There's ample parking to be found along Water Street.

Rock Bottom Restaurant and Brewery

Chicago

Visit Date	*Signed*

ABOUT THE BREWERY

The Rock Bottom Restaurant and Brewery in downtown Chicago is in the heart of the River North area, only a couple of blocks from the famous Magnificent Mile. What makes Rock Bottom–Chicago distinctive in the national chain of thirty-plus Rock Bottoms is that it's one of only a few that are located in old buildings. Located at the corner of State and Grand, Rock Bottom's home is three stories tall. The first floor holds the main dining room and bar, the second floor holds the banquet facilities, and the third floor is actually a rooftop patio.

Inside Rock Bottom, the main bar room, dining room, and pool hall take advantage of the building's charm and character with a wooden bar, beams, parquet flooring, and brick walls. While the dining room has some great views of Grand and State Streets, the best view is from the rooftop patio. It's a great place to watch the activity of Chicago while enjoying a Walleye Wheat or Roof Top Pilsner.

Rock Bottom regularly has six to eight of its own beers on tap plus a few guest beers. The Chicago Gold is one of the brewery's best sellers, but brewmaster Pete Crowley also has a few specials on tap that are always worth a try. Watch for the special seasonal tapping of the Fire Chief Ale. Rock Bottom Restaurants and Breweries throughout the country offer a portion of every pint sold as a donation to the local firefighters' charity of choice. Even though all Rock Bottoms participate in the event, each brewery's version of Fire Chief Ale reflects the local brewmaster's unique recipe. Rock Bottom–Chicago also holds a chili cookoff, where the chili is made by local firefighters and the winner's concoction is served at the restaurant during the Oktoberfest season.

HISTORY

Rock Bottom arrived in downtown Chicago in October 1995. It was the sixth in the national chain of Rock Bottom brewpubs. The building that is home to Rock Bottom–Chicago is actually remodeled from two buildings that date back to the Chicago construction boom following the Great Chicago Fire of 1871. Remodeling was very extensive; the fermentation tanks had to be lowered into the building by a helicopter. Prior to becoming Rock Bottom, the building housed a cafe and record store, and upstairs were several apartments.

The Rock Bottom Restaurant chain is based in Louisville, Colorado. Building on his successful brewpub formula at the Walnut Street Brewery in Boulder, owner Frank Day came up with the name Rock Bottom as he began the business venture in downtown Denver. The first Rock Bottom opened in 1991 in Denver's Prudential Insurance Company building (1001 Sixteenth Street). Playing on Prudential's slogan, "Own a Piece of the Rock," Day figured "Rock Bottom" was appropriate, given the brewpub's location on the ground floor of a multibuilding high-rise in the Mile High City.

Rock Bottom has two breweries in Illinois, as well as breweries in other Midwestern states including Indiana, Iowa, Minnesota, Ohio, and Wisconsin. While you'll likely see some common themes in beer and food as you visit other Rock Bottoms, each one has its own chef and brewmaster who take local interests and flavors seriously, so you will find some common things but many unique approaches too. Rock Bottom is part of the family of national restaurant chains that include Old Chicago, ChopHouse & Brewery, Walnut Brewery, and Sing Sing restaurants and bars.

DON'T MISS THIS

Rock Bottom has a number of older black-and-white, historic photographs on the walls. Some feature the Chicago skyline before and after the Great Chicago Fire of 1871. In the pool hall there's an interesting portrait of three priests playing pool. In the summer, try a Chicago Gold on the rooftop patio; if the weather's cold, ask for the Liquid Sun Malt Liquor.

ROCK BOTTOM–CHICAGO BREWS

American Dream Pale Ale 🍺🍺🍺🍺 *Your Ranking* _____
An American pale ale that has no nose. Clear, copper color and a thin, bubbly, off-white head. Medium bodied and round. A malty start quickly gives way to a bitterness that lingers and builds beyond the finish. There is some great hoppy flavor in this beer.

Belgian Wit 🍺🍺🍺 *Your Ranking* _____
A smooth, soft Wit. Begins with a fruity nose that offers hints of orange. A hazy yellow color and a thin, soft, white head. Light to medium bodied with soft textures. Fruity flavor includes orange and coriander. A light hoppy finish.

Bourbon Stout 🍺🍺🍺 *Your Ranking* _____
A stout aged three months in whiskey barrels. A roasted, sweet nose. Very dark color with a very, very thin, bubbly, off-white head. Full bodied and very round. Begins with the flavor of whiskey. The maltiness does come out, but it's overwhelmed by the liquor tones and warmth. Served in a brandy snifter.

Brown Bear Brown 🍺🍺🍺🍺 *Your Ranking* _____
A subtle roasted nose. Deep brown color with a slight haziness. Thick, soft, tan head. Full bodied and round. A smooth, creamy maltiness dominates. The

finish has just a light bitterness. Some nice smooth maltiness makes this a memorable beer.

California Mike's IPA

Your Ranking _____

This is a great crisp, assertive American-style IPA. A strong floral and resiny nose. Cloudy, golden to copper color and a thick, bubbly, off-white head. Sharp hoppy bitterness dominates throughout. A dry bitter finish. Those who like IPAs will appreciate the floral nose and aggressive hop body. "California Mike" refers to assistant brewer Mike Barher.

Chicago Gold

Your Ranking _____

The flagship beer of Rock Bottom–Chicago, poured from a tap whose handle bears the image of Chicago's famous Water Tower. A very clean-tasting ale with no nose or finish. Clear, golden color and a thin, soft, off-white head. Light bodied and soft texture. A light hoppy dryness complements a mild malty flavor. Brewed with three different varieties of Pacific Northwest hops.

Erik the Red Ale

Your Ranking _____

A light fruity nose. Clear amber to copper color and a thick, soft, tan head. Medium bodied with a light roundness to the texture. A mild but firm malty taste. Just a hint of bitterness in the finish. Made with Cascade hops. Very similar to the Ragtop Red Ale served by Rock Bottom–Warrenville.

IPA

Your Ranking _____

A light flowery nose. Dark yellow color and a thin, bubbly white head. Medium bodied and soft. A malty start that doesn't allow the hop qualities to bloom completely. A mild yet firm bitter finish. A mild IPA, really more of the hoppy qualities found in an American pale ale, so it's considered a little light for those who really enjoy India Pale Ales. A brewmaster's special.

Line Drive Light Lager

Your Ranking _____

A light malty nose. Clear straw color and a thin, soft, white head. Light bodied and bubbly. There is a light malty dominance with a slight sour background. This German-style lager is brewed with a blend of six-row barley, rice, and Hallertauer hops. A summertime seasonal at Rock Bottom–Chicago.

Liquid Sun Malt Liquor

Your Ranking _____

A malt liquor with some smooth, assertive malty flavor and a malty nose that helps define this beer from the start. A hazy, golden color and a thin, bubbly, white head. Fully bodied. Sweet flavor that borders at times on syrupy. The finish is malty and sweet with a smoky tone. I'm not ordinarily a malt liquor fan, but are some great strong flavors that make this a fun beer—just watch how much you drink, because it'll sneak up on you.

Mike's Schwarz Bier

Your Ranking _____

A very clean dark lager. No nose. Dark bronze color with a thick, very soft, brown head. Medium bodied with some silkiness. A nice crisp caramel flavor with a dry background. Mildly bitter finish. This beer was brewed to mark Rock Bottom–Chicago's seventh anniversary.

Naughty Scot Scotch Ale 🍺🍺🍺   *Your Ranking* _____

This strong Scotch ale is brewed with seven different specialty malts that offer a variety of flavors that include malty, resiny, coffee, sherry, and wood. A light, grainy nose. Cloudy, bronze color and a thin, soft, brown head. Full bodied and soft texture. Malty flavors dominate with a caramel, light roasted, woody finish.

Oktoberfest 🍺🍺   *Your Ranking* _____

This fall seasonal was somewhat timid. No nose. A clear light copper color and thick, tan head. Medium bodied and very soft. A mild malty and worty taste. Finishes with a roastedness that builds.

Roggendampf Rye Lager 🍺🍺🍺🍺   *Your Ranking* _____

A California common style, a special treat from brewmaster Pete Crowley. A flowery nose. Light copper color with a light cloudiness. A thin, soft, off-white head. Medium to full bodied and creamy. A complex balance of maltiness and hoppiness that seem to be in competition for dominance, which provides some great flavor and distinctive character. The finish features a firm dryness.

Roof Top Pilsner 🍺   *Your Ranking* _____

A Czech-style Pilsner. A faint, hoppy nose. Clear golden color and a thick, soft, white head. Light bodied with a soft texture. A light malty flavor with a thin bitter background. The finish is fruity and sour. Brewed especially for enjoyment on Rock Bottom's rooftop patio, this beer is guaranteed to taste good on a sunny summer day, three stories above the corner of State and Grand.

Terminal Stout 🍺🍺🍺🍺   *Your Ranking* _____

A faint malty nose. Very thick appearance, dark color. Thick, soft, brown head. Full bodied and soft texture accentuated by the nitrogen line. Malty flavor with some light crisp bitterness in the background. The roasted qualities are found in the finish. This stout is creamy and has enough chocolate qualities to make a great dessert beer.

Walleye Wheat 🍺🍺🍺   *Your Ranking* _____

An unfiltered wheat that has a light citrus nose. Cloudy golden color and a thin, soft, white head. Light bodied and soft. A smooth banana and fruity flavor. Light and smoky finish. This wheat is overall creamy and smooth with a lingering sweetness. It is made with a special Canadian malt called "honey malt" to give it a unique smooth sweetness.

Wild Berry Wheat 🍺🍺🍺   *Your Ranking* _____

This beer is made with real blueberries, cherries, and raspberries. All combine for a strong fruity nose. Cloudy, copper to orange color with a thick, soft, tan head. Medium bodied and crisp texture. A strong berry flavor dominates the taste and finish.

OTHER ROCK BOTTOM–CHICAGO BREWS YOU MAY WANT TO TRY

Belgian Cheery Ale   *Your Ranking* _____
This brewmaster's special is aged in oak casks.

Hefeweizen   *Your Ranking* _____
A seasonal beer available in summer.

BREWERY RATING

	Your Rating	Shepard's Rating (1 to 4 Mugs)	General Description
Location		🍺🍺🍺🍺	Central city/community Entertainment district
Ease of Finding Location		🍺🍺	Difficult; traffic or roads are problematic Parking can be challenging
Brewery Atmosphere		🍺🍺🍺🍺	Family restaurant
Dining Experience		🍺🍺🍺	Family style/variety
The Pint		🍺🍺🍺	A good experience

MENU

The Rock Bottom menu has an American flair with a southwestern twist. You'll find Santa Fe lasagna and smoked chicken enchiladas on the pub favorite section of the menu. But the Brown Ale chicken and the Brewery's Best meatloaf are always favorites. Rock Bottom has a number of choices including burgers, steaks, seafood, pastas, and salads. The main entree choices include a Texas Fire steak that is made with jalapeño brewery butter. The tenderloin with roasted garlic features a hickory-smoked filet that is stuffed with roasted garlic and dressed in a rich creamy Jack Daniel's and gorgonzola sauce. Pasta selections include chicken Genovese, fettuccine with shrimp and artichokes, and the Bangkok chicken bowl. There are about a half-dozen salad choices including a Brewer's Cobb, the Georgia spinach salad, Mrs. Chow's sizzling shrimp salad, and the basic plate of greens and vegetables called the "Rock the House Salad." There are also ten or twelve appetizer choices including an Asiago cheese dip, Thai coconut shrimp, brewery nachos, and the Titan Toothpicks made from rolled tortillas stuffed with smoked chicken, jack cheese, and southwestern seasonings.

OTHER THINGS TO SEE OR DO IN THE AREA

Downtown Chicago has many, many things to see and do, so it's difficult to give them all attention. But from the perspective of someone who enjoys a good meal and great beer, it's important to focus one's attentions.

The best place to start is with a local guidebook or a search of the few tourism-oriented Web sites: Chicago Convention and Tourism Bureau (www.choosechicago.com) and the City of Chicago Visitor Information Centers (www.cityofchicago.org). Another excellent option is to stop by one of the downtown visitors' centers at either Chicago Water Works (163 East Pearson at Michigan Avenue) or the Chicago Cultural Center (77 East Randolph at Michigan Avenue). Located just south of the river, the Chicago Cultural Center might be a better start, because a number of tours begin there, tickets can be purchased for the Loop Tour Train, and it's a landmark itself. The building's main entrance on Washington Street brings visitors to a grand staircase made of white Carrara marble. Upstairs is the Preston Bradley Hall, known for the world's largest Tiffany stained-glass dome.

While in this part of the Chicago Loop, the Loop Tour Train runs from May through September on Saturdays. The forty-minute tour is on a CTA "El" train and is narrated by Chicago Architecture Foundation docents.

There are many Loop-area attractions, but a few that top the list for consideration include the 220-acre Grant Park (along Michigan Avenue); the Chicago Art Institute (111 South Michigan Avenue); the Illinois Art Gallery (100 West Randolph Street); and the Museum of Broadcast Communications (78 East Washington Street). The Field Museum (1400 South Lake Shore Drive) is home to six acres of exhibits, including mummies, dinosaurs, and many hands-on displays for all ages. The John G. Shedd Aquarium (1200 South Lake Shore Drive) is the world's largest indoor aquarium. You can see sharks, otters, and many other sea animals.

Some general ways to enjoy the "big" Windy City are to check out a few guidebooks that help you identify the skyscrapers. The Sears Tower (233 South Wacker Drive), at 110 stories, was once the world's tallest building before it was surpassed by the Petronas Towers in Kuala Lumpur, Malaysia. To get to the skydeck of the Sears Tower you'll take a seventy-second elevator ride. Other buildings that deserve a mention include the Monadnock Building (53 West Jackson Boulevard) at sixteen stories, the tallest building ever constructed with weight-bearing walls, which at their base are six feet thick, and the Chicago Board of Trade, topped by a statue of Ceres, the Roman goddess of agriculture.

Buildings in the River North area include the William Wrigley Jr. Building (400 North Michigan Avenue), constructed by the chewing gum family between 1919 and 1924, with its gallery that includes original prints from naturalist John James Audubon; the thirty-six-story Tribune Tower (435 North Michigan Avenue), with bits of historical ruins (the Parthenon, the Pyramids, Westminster Abbey, and the Alamo) embedded in the structure's exterior; and the ninety-fourth-floor observation deck of the John Hancock Center (875 North Michigan Ave.), or "Big John," which at its time of construction in 1969 was briefly the tallest building in the world.

Another fun way to enjoy the loop is to make a game of looking for sculptures. Try to find a few that include: a Pablo Picasso, Flamingo, Centennial Fountain, Buckingham Fountain, the Universe, Gem of the Lakes, and the Fountain of the Great Lakes.

While in the Loop a common standard among beer drinkers is the Berghoff Restaurant (17 West Adams). This hearty German American restaurant serves some great wienerschnitzel and sauerbraten and its own beer! Berghoff beer is actually brewed by the Huber Brewery in Monroe, Wisconsin. Berghoff beer was originally made in Fort Wayne, Indiana, by the Herman Berghoff Brewing Company. But after a fire in 1899, founder Herman Berghoff moved to Chicago and opened the Berghoff Restaurant and beer garden. The Berghoff Brewery continued operating under the direction of several family members and was eventually sold to Falstaff in 1954. Huber Brewing began producing Berghoff beer in 1960 under contract with the Chicago restaurant, and today it is considered one of Huber's flagship beers.

If the Rock Bottom is your principal destination, the neighborhood surrounding it is River North. Given there's so much to see and do in the downtown, this area will likely capture your attention due to simple logistics. The Magnificent Mile, only three blocks east, is almost beyond description with its glitz, upscale shopping, fine restaurants, and luxury hotels. The main shopping part of the avenue stretches from the Chicago River northward to Oak Street Beach. Chicago actually began in this area, along the banks of the river. Fort Dearborn was built at what is now the south end of the Michigan Avenue Bridge. Like many of the downtown bridges, this bridge is a drawbridge that is very functional and often used—you might even get to see it in operation. The Michigan Avenue Bridge may merit a little extra attention for its ornate sculptures on the pylons.

Navy Pier is a major attraction in downtown Chicago. The 150-foot Ferris wheel is modeled after the very first Ferris wheel, which was built for the World's Columbian Exposition. You can be one of 240 people who take an eight-minute ride. Also at Navy Pier is the historical Musical Carousel with its hand-painted scenes and animals, and the one-acre indoor botanical park, Crystal Gardens. There are also restaurants and many shops. You can also catch an old-fashioned trolley to Navy Pier from just outside of Rock Bottom.

The Water Tower (163 East Pearson Street) is a major landmark for River North and the Magnificent Mile. It was one of the few buildings to survive the Great Chicago Fire of 1871. It also contains a visitors' center. About a block away is the Museum of Contemporary Art (220 East Chicago Avenue).

For a fun diversion, DisneyQuest (55 East Ohio Street) is located in a five-story building. It offers plenty of room to enjoy the amazing number of high-tech video and interactive games and displays.

Some other great ways to explore downtown Chicago include taking a sightseeing boat tour on the Chicago River and Lake Michigan. Many offer narration that explains the sights of the city's skyline and its architecture. Another way to enjoy the Magnificent Mile is in a horse-drawn carriage. Several tours depart from locations along Michigan Avenue including Pearson, Huron, and Chestnut Streets.

A little further north, near Lincoln Park, is the International Museum of Surgical Science and the Hall of Immortals (1524 North Lake Shore Drive). You'll find a seven-thousand-piece exhibit that includes a copy of Napoleon's death mask, Florence Nightingale's nurse's cap, a working iron lung from the 1920s, one of the world's first stethoscopes, and Xavier Cugat's painting of an operating room where a surgeon reads Playboy and a dog waits for scraps. Also in this area is the Peggy Notebaert Nature Museum (2430 North Cannon Drive), which offers permanent exhibits on the relationship between people and nature and the impact humans have on their environment.

Chicago has an endless number of festivals and events. During National Beer Month (July) the Rock Bottom has activities that have included beer specials, a brewfest and special tastings, and you might even put your name in the drawing to become "brewer for the day." A few other downtown events that might go well with a beer tour include the Taste of Chicago in Grant Park (late June to early July); the Magnificent Mile Art Festival (July); Grant Park Music Festival (June to August); Chicago's Folk and Roots Festival in Welles Park (July); the Chicago Yacht Club Race to Mackinac (July); the Chicago Outdoor Film Festival at Butler Field (Tuesday nights, July to August); the Chicago Jazz Festival (late August to early September); and the annual St. Patrick's Day celebration, where the Chicago River is turned a bright fluorescent green! For another type of event you could consider being part of a talk show. Chicago is known for three major talk show hosts—Jenny Jones, Jerry Springer, and Oprah. Tickets require reservations in advance.

There are a couple of old brewery sites near Rock Bottom. Near Sedgwick and West Huron Streets was the Bartholomae and Leicht Brewing Company, which closed in 1911. Al Capone's Sieben Brewery (1464–1478 Larrabee) was one of the largest breweries in Chicago during Prohibition. Federal agents raided it on August 29, 1923, and arrested Johnny Torrio, Louis Alterie, and Hymie Weiss.

The River North area has some other interesting ties with Chicago's organized crime icons. In 1924 near 738 North State Street, now a parking lot but once the Schofield flower shop, was the site where gangster Dion O'Bannion was killed, allegedly by members of the Capone mob. Two years later, while heading to his office in the same building, Hymie Weiss was gunned down in a spray of bullets—some of which struck the nearby Holy Name Cathedral (the bullet marks are now hidden behind a stairway near the church's front door). In the 1930s, John Dillinger is said to have had a favorite restaurant in the 600 block of North Clark. In this area today, you'll find the Clark Street Ale House (742 North Clark), which is a favorite beer bar for many locals. Clark Street doesn't brew on premises, but it does offer a great selection on tap, including a few house beers that are brewed with the help of Two Brothers Brewing Company of Warrenville.

A little further north, near the Lincoln Park Zoo, Bugs Moran lived at the Parkway Hotel at 2100 north Lincoln Park West. About a block away on North Clark, Moran's S-M Garage was the site of the 1929 St. Valentine's Day Massacre (the building at 2122 North Clark was torn down in the late 1960s), where six people were machine-gunned to death. The Untouchable Tour (1-773-881-1195) leaves from the northwest corner of North Clark and West Ohio Streets.

The Museum of Holography (1134 West Washington Boulevard) may leave you wondering what's real and what's not. You'll find images of Michael Jordan, a very large *Tyrannosaurus rex*, and even the late Chicago newspaper columnist and beer lover Mike Royko. Royko deserves a special note for his occasional mention of beer in his column, but mostly for his 1976 commentary that American beer tasted as though it had been "filtered through a horse." When some brewers complained, Royko apologized—to the horse!

DIRECTIONS

Rock Bottom isn't difficult to find, but if you are driving, you'll need to plan just a little and consider parking. When traveling into downtown from Interstate 90, take the Ohio Street exit and drive east toward the lake. Turn right onto State

Street and watch for the intersection with Grand. There are several indoor and surface parking lots in the immediate area with prices generally from about eight to about seventeen dollars.

Rock Bottom is very convenient for using the train system. There is a Red Line stop at the corner of Grand and State.

Rock Bottom Restaurant and Brewery

Warrenville

Visit Date	Signed

ABOUT THE BREWERY

It's probably more than just a coincidence that a business named Rock Bottom was built on a former quarry. Rock Bottom–Warrenville was constructed as part of a massive redevelopment area for this western Chicago suburb and is actually on the site of the former Cantera Rock Quarry—accented by a boulder to the left of the front door.

Rock Bottom has a multilevel floor plan that features an open, almost barnlike atmosphere. With brick walls, wood floor, vaulted ceiling, and lots of natural light, you get a very "lofty" feel, even before you have a beer. The building has some southwestern and prairie style features that include soft earth-tone colors and stucco interior walls. There are a couple of private party rooms, but the best view in the house is from Paavey's Loft, which overlooks the main dining room and bar. This second-floor bar makes a great private party room. It offers a pool table for a game or two. While in Paavey's Loft, look around; you'll find a large mounted collection of beer bottle openers, a collection that would make most antique dealers envious.

Rock Bottom is also a venue for live entertainment. There is a small area that provides a stage, and it comes in handy on open mic night (a.k.a. Karaoke Tuesday). If you're looking for music or karaoke, it's best to call ahead to check the evening schedule. Rock Bottom in Warrenville is also known for its brewmaster dinners and extra-special treatment of mug club members, with advance information on various activities occurring at the brewery. In the warmer months there is an outdoor beer garden along the east side of the building. This patio has an awning, pull-down walls, and heaters that will allow you to enjoy it much later in the fall than most outdoor dining areas.

Rock Bottom–Warrenville regularly offers four to six of its beers on tap. Among the beers to give attention to are the Warrenwiezen and the cask-conditioned Peashooter Pale Ale. Barnaby Struve became brewmaster in Warrenville in 2002 after previous stints at Rock Bottoms in downtown Chicago and Arlington, Virginia. He follows the Rock Bottom tradition and offers a couple of dozen different styles of beer during the course of a year.

HISTORY

Rock Bottom Restaurant and Brewery in Warrenville opened in November 1998. Rock Bottom Restaurants are based in Louisville, Colorado. Building on his successful brewpub formula at the Walnut Street Brewery in Boulder, owner Frank Day came up with the name Rock Bottom as he began the business venture in downtown Denver. The first Rock Bottom opened in 1991 in Denver's Prudential Insurance Company building (1001 Sixteenth Street). Playing on Prudential's slogan, "Own a Piece of the Rock," Day figured "Rock Bottom" was appropriate, given the brewpub's location on the ground floor of a multibuilding high-rise in the Mile High City.

Rock Bottom has two breweries in Illinois, as well as other Midwestern states including Indiana, Iowa, Minnesota, Ohio, and Wisconsin. While you'll likely see a number of common themes in beer and food as you visit other Rock Bottoms, each one has its own chef and brewmaster who take local interests and flavors seriously, so you find common things but many unique approaches too. Rock Bottom is part of the family of national restaurant chains that include Old Chicago, ChopHouse & Brewery, Walnut Brewery, and Sing Sing restaurants and bars.

DON'T MISS THIS

Paavey's Loft offers a second, somewhat secluded upper bar that looks down over the main bar. When Rock Bottom was being constructed in Warrenville, a fly became stuck in the varnish of the bar in the upper loft. The fly was named "Paavey," and so the upper bar became "Paavey's Loft." It's obviously not a big tourism draw for the restaurant, but it does put a name and a face to the term "bar fly."

ROCK BOTTOM–WARRENVILLE BREWS

American Honey Wheat   🍺🍺🍺🍺   *Your Ranking* _____
A light hoppy aroma. Cloudy, light gold color and a thick, soft, tan head. A full bodied wheat that really has great flavor qualities! Creamy, wheat malty flavor with a light bitter background. The finish has a light graininess and strong fruity tones.

Frostbite Trippel Ale   🍺🍺🍺🍺   *Your Ranking* _____
A beautiful beer from all aspects of taste, color, and finish. It's the beer to watch for at Rock Bottom–Warrenville. The strong, sweet aromatic qualities are very inviting. Its solid golden color makes you appreciate how some describe the Belgian Tripel style as nectar! Full bodied with soft textures that bring out the earthy sweetness and warm finish. This is a special beer.

Lumpy Dog Brown   🍺🍺🍺🍺   *Your Ranking* _____
A malty nose. Dark bronze color. A thick, soft, brown head. Full bodied and creamy. Strong, assertive caramel and chocolate malt flavors. A smooth,

sweet, lightly roasted finish. Strong flavors and nice overall balance. Similar to Rock Bottom–Chicago's Brown Bear Brown, but more flavor is found in the Warrenville brown ale.

Mud in Your Eyes Light   🍺🍺🍺   *Your Ranking* _____

I'm a sucker for any beer with a pig on the label! This beer is very clean and light with no nose, a clear, straw color, and a thick, soft, white head. A very mild malty start with a fruity, slightly sour background and finish. There are also hints of crispness and light bitterness to the ending.

Peashooter Pale Ale   🍺🍺🍺🍺   *Your Ranking* _____

An American-style pale ale with a firm hoppy nose. Clear copper body and a thin, soft, tan head. Medium bodied and soft texture. Strong bitter qualities with a pleasant dryness. The bitter finish is long lasting.

Peashooter Pale Ale on Cask   🍺🍺🍺🍺   *Your Ranking* _____

This is the best way to enjoy the Peashooter. While it has many of the same qualities of the "on-tap" Peashooter, the hoppy nose, bitter body, and long-lasting finish all are accentuated, while the cask fermentation helps soften this beer's overall texture. When you visit Rock Bottom, your search for the perfect pint is over for the day when this beer appears!

Ragtop Red Ale   🍺🍺🍺   *Your Ranking* _____

Not much nose, only a light whiff of maltiness. Clear amber to copper color and a thick, soft, tan head. Medium bodied with a light roundness to the texture. A mild but firm malty taste. Just a hint of bitterness in the finish. Very similar to its cousin, the Erik the Red Ale served at Rock Bottom in downtown Chicago.

Saison Belgian Ale   🍺🍺🍺   *Your Ranking* _____

The nose offers sweet tones of cloves and banana. Clear copper color and a thin, soft, tan head. Medium bodied and very soft. A light fruity sweetness that complements a solid malty flavor. Finishes with a sweet fruitiness. Offered as a summertime Belgian by Rock Bottom–Warrenville.

Terminal Stout   🍺🍺🍺   *Your Ranking* _____

A faint malty nose. Very thick appearance, dark color. Thick, soft, brown head. Full bodied with soft texture accentuated by the nitrogen line. Malty flavor with some light crisp bitterness in the background. A mild, dry, coffee-type roastedness is found in the finish.

Warrenwiezen   🍺🍺🍺🍺   *Your Ranking* _____

A German-style wheat beer. Strong banana and clove aroma. Cloudy, deep yellow color with a thick, soft, white head. Light bodied and soft. The taste is dominated by a soft graininess and strong banana esters. The cloves and overall sweetness build throughout the finish and continue to linger long after the pint is finished. This beer has some excellent, assertive wheat qualities, and Hefe-Weizen drinkers will appreciate it.

OTHER ROCK BOTTOM–WARRENVILLE BREWS YOU MAY WANT TO TRY

IPA   *Your Ranking* _____

A medium-bodied India Pale Ale full of hop flavor. Not always on tap at Rock Bottom–Warrenville, but very much worth watching for.

Oktoberfest   *Your Ranking* _____

A medium-bodied, clear copper fall seasonal.

BREWERY RATING

	Your Rating	Shepard's Rating (1 to 4 Mugs)	General Description
Location		ᗡᗡᗡ	Commercial/industrial
Ease of Finding Location		ᗡᗡᗡᗡ	Close to major roads and intersections
Brewery Atmosphere		ᗡᗡᗡ	Family restaurant
Dining Experience		ᗡᗡᗡ	Family style/variety
The Pint		ᗡᗡᗡ	A good experience

MENU

The Rock Bottom menu features a full complement of salads, brick oven pizzas, pub favorites, burgers, sandwiches, and pastas. Many selections have a spicy southwestern twist. The chicken Genovese pasta is a great example of this, with its seasoned chicken breast on a walnut pesto cream sauce, sun-dried tomatoes, and Asiago cheese on tossed penne pasta. It had my eyes watering from the spicy heat, and it paired well with a Peashooter Pale Ale. Other entrees that you'll have a tough time deciding on include the alder-smoked fish and chips, the Santa Fe lasagna, and the southwestern shrimp and chicken pasta. Rock Bottom–Warrenville makes a great stop for dinner before or after a movie, so you'll find about twenty choices of burgers and sandwiches combined. One of the differences between the downtown Chicago Rock Bottom and the Warrenville location is that you'll find brick oven pizzas at Warrenville. These pizzas feature a special hand-stretched honey and Brown Ale crust. Elsewhere in the menu there are about a half-dozen salad choices including a Brewer's Cobb, the Georgia spinach salad, Mrs. Chow's sizzling shrimp salad, and the basic plate of greens and vegetables called the "Rock the House Salad." There are about ten or twelve appetizer choices, including an Asiago cheese dip, Thai coconut shrimp, brewery nachos, and the Titan Toothpicks made from rolled tortillas stuffed with smoked chicken, jack cheese, and southwestern seasonings. Another fun starter is the Ball Park pretzels, which are brushed with Brown Ale and seasoned with garlic and parsley.

OTHER THINGS TO SEE OR DO IN THE AREA

Warrenville is a western Chicago suburb, about forty-five minutes from downtown. Known mainly as a quiet, secluded residential area, it is surrounded on three sides by DuPage County Forest Preserves. Downtown Warrenville is north of Rock Bottom, and it offers connections to both the Illinois Prairie Path and the DuPage River. The Prairie Path can be accessed about a mile northwest of Rock Bottom, just off of Route 59. The western branch of the DuPage River is only about a half-mile west of Rock Bottom; and the Great Western Trail is on the DuPage County section of the former Great Western right of way from Villa Avenue in Villa Park to the Elgin branch of the Illinois Prairie Path west of Prince Crossing Road.

The Fermi National Accelerator Laboratory is only about a few miles northwest of Rock Bottom–Warrenville. Scientists at Fermilab carry out research in high-energy physics to answer the questions of what the universe is made of and how it works. Fermi provides both organized and self-guided tours, scheduled lectures, an art gallery, and "Ask a Scientist" on every Saturday afternoon.

In nearby Naperville, located southwest of Rock Bottom, the Naper Settlement (523 South Webster Street) is a replica of a nineteenth-century village on a thirteen-acre site. Downtown Naperville has numerous opportunities for shopping, browsing antique stores, and strolling along the riverwalk that lines the DuPage River and links park land, covered bridges, and fountains by a red brick pathway.

About six miles northeast of Warrenville is Wheaton, home of the DuPage County Historical Museum (102 East Wesley Street). One of Wheaton's most famous sons is football legend Red Grange, and you can learn more about this three-time All-American and Chicago Bear running back, known as the Galloping Ghost, at the Red Grange Museum and Heritage Gallery (421 County Farm Road).

One of the most well-known landmarks is the AMC Cantera Theatres (28250 Diehl Road), with its thirty-seven screens. The theater complex is very

Rock Bottom Restaurant and Brewery–Warrenville   227

close; it actually shares parking with Rock Bottom. Another option for entertainment is the annual Warrenville car show and street dance every August. You'll also want to watch for the schedule of summer events, such as a Brewfest at Rock Bottom. A couple miles north and west of Rock Bottom–Warrenville is Two Brothers Brewing Company (30 West 114 Butterfield).

DIRECTIONS

When traveling from downtown Chicago, you'll want to consider Interstate 88. Take the Winfield Road exit from I-88 and travel south to the first major set of stoplights (intersection of Winfield and Diehl Road). Turn west on Diehl Road and Rock Bottom will be on the north side of the road.

There is a Metra station in nearby Naperville. A Pace bus route through Warrenville picks up passengers and connects them to locations in Warrenville and Naperville.

Taylor Brewing Company
Lombard

Visit Date	Signed

ABOUT THE BREWERY

Taylor Brewing Company is a combination of pub, sports bar, burger place, and family tavern. As you walk through the doors, you're greeted on your left by the brewhaus with its six stainless steel tanks and brew kettle. But the most eye-catching element of this brewpub lies straight ahead as you walk through the front doors. That's where you see a square bar that is recessed about three feet in the center of the brewpub. In the middle of the bar there is a partial, open kitchen for bar-ordered food preparation. As you sip a beer from the green and black bar top, you can actually watch your burger being grilled! Taylor is probably best known for its burger selection, having been recognized by the *Chicago Tribune*'s "Best of" competition in the late 1990s.

Taylor Brewing is located in Lombard, near the massive Yorktown Mall along Butterfield Road. It's a new building that is nestled among several hotels and directly across the street from Northern Baptist Theological Seminary. From the outside you'll catch a glimpse of the brewery through large windows. The inside ambiance is loud and bustling with numerous televisions, a wide-open interior, and cinder block walls. Several of Taylor's beer labels are found on painted murals throughout the brewpub. There are two outer areas of the main dining room that are separated by partial dividers, and they offer some seclusion from the bar activity. Taylor Brewing has modest seating capacity and supports a menu that includes pub food as well as family tavern-type dishes.

Taylor Brewing is a great bar for those looking for a variety of beers. There are regularly up to a half-dozen of Taylor's own, brewed-on-premises beers, with at least that many other house beers that are contract brewed by Capital Brewing of Middleton, Wisconsin, and Two Brothers Brewing of Warrenville. There are another thirty tap handles with local, regional, national, and imported beers. The menu offers an honest insight into which beers are made on-site and which are contractually brewed for Taylor—just look under the menu's beer descriptions. Among Taylor's handcrafted favorites, watch for the Banter Blonde Ale, Poseidon Pale Ale, IPA, and Sunset Red Ale. One of Taylor's best-selling beers is the Rusty Dog Amber, a medium-bodied malty brew from Capital Brewing. For a great summertime treat try the Weisen, which is made by Two Brothers.

HISTORY

Taylor Brewing actually started in the basement of Glen Taylor's home. His sons Gary and Steve gave him a homebrewing kit as a Father's Day gift in the early 1980s. All three liked to brew together in five-gallon batches. When Steve went away to college, homebrewing went with him, and when it was Gary's turn to go to college, he too benefited from the fruits of their combined labor. Upon completing college, Gary and his father decided to venture into the brewing business and graduated from the Taylor family basement to the restored turn-of-the-century furniture factory building called the Fifth Avenue Station in Naperville. It was at the Naperville location in 1994 that Taylor Brewing was established, and at the time it was one of only four microbreweries in Illinois.

After five years their lease ended, so Glen and Gary decided to look for a place to relocate and eventually built their brewpub from the ground up. The Lombard location, with its close proximity to Yorktown Mall and easy access to Interstates 88 and 355, fit their plans. They moved to the present location on Butterfield Road in 1999. Taylor Brewing is very much a family business. Gary's wife, Jean, handles much of the staff relations; his mother, Amy, takes care of the business paperwork; and Gary and his father, Glen, continue to brew together.

DON'T MISS THIS

Taylor Brewing has a number of large, framed, black-and-white beer-related photos. On the south wall you see an old photo of the Carling National Brewing Company bottling operation. You can actually see the bottles of Carling's Black Label Beer on the bottling line.

TAYLOR BREWS

Banter Blonde Ale　🍺🍺🍺　　　　　　*Your Ranking* _____
A faint hoppy nose. Clear, golden color and a thin, bubbly, off-white head. Light bodied and soft. A light maltiness with strong sour background and finish.

Cream Ale　🍺🍺🍺　　　　　　*Your Ranking* _____
A very smooth golden ale. Starts with a very light malty nose. Golden color and hazy. Thin, soft, white head. Medium bodied and a soft, creamy texture. The maltiness begins, but a mild hoppiness comes through the background and finish.

Golden Diamond    *Your Ranking* _____

A strong, fruity, sour nose. Clear golden color and a thick, soft, white head. Medium bodied. Strong fruity sourness and earthy maltiness. The sweetness and slight musty qualities did not work for me; perhaps you'll find this a better beer on your visit. It is one of Taylor's lighter beers.

IPA   *Your Ranking* _____

The hoppiness in the nose is strong and very pushy. Clear, light copper color. A very thin, bubbly, white head. Medium bodied and soft. The taste really lives up to the strong hoppy nose with great bitter flavor. There are some hints of maltiness in the background, but the hops continue to dominate and last a long time throughout the finish.

Maibock   *Your Ranking* _____

A malty nose. Dark golden to copper color with a thick, soft, tan head. Medium bodied. Strong sweetness, especially caramel malt flavors. A malty finish. While the maltiness dominates, this beer seemed to have a confusing fruitiness that builds in the finish. This is a seasonal beer brewed in the spring.

Papa's Porter   *Your Ranking* _____

A very dark porter that begins with a strong roasted, chocolate malt aroma. Dark black with reddish tints. A thin, soft, tan head. Medium bodied and a soft texture. A caramel malt dominance. Finishes with a roasted, light coffee flavor. A similar Taylor porter in the past was called Palpitations Porter.

Poseidon Pale Ale   *Your Ranking* _____

A light hoppy aroma. Clear, deep golden color and a thin, bubbly, off-white head. Medium bodied and bubbly. Mainly a firm, solid bitterness from beginning to end. Finishes hoppy with a light dryness that builds.

Pure Pilsner   *Your Ranking* _____

No nose. Clear, golden color with a thin, bubbly, white head. Light bodied and soft. A smooth, mild, but firm creamy malty flavor. Finishes clean. Made with four malted grains and two varieties of hops.

Raspberry Wheat   *Your Ranking* _____

Strong, aggressive raspberry aroma. Golden cloudy color. Thick, soft, and white head. Medium to full bodied and soft. Strong fruity sweetness with very prominent raspberry flavors.

Rusty Dog Amber   *Your Ranking* _____

A clean nose with just a light hint of malt. Clear, copper color and a thin, soft, tan head. Medium bodied and round. Well balanced with a slight dominance by a smooth malty flavor and a mild caramel finish.

Weisen   *Your Ranking* _____

A strong banana aroma. Very cloudy golden color with a thick, soft, white head. Light to medium bodied and soft texture. A strong fruity sweetness flavored with assertive banana and clove tones. Finishes with banana and yeasty flavors. Described as true Bavarian-style Weizen.

OTHER TAYLOR BREWS YOU MAY WANT TO TRY

American Wheat   *Your Ranking* _____

A lightly hopped golden copper ale. Smooth texture and malty tones with a subtle wheat character.

Dark Satin   *Your Ranking* _____

A reddish-brown German Dunkel. Soft texture with solid, complex malty palate accentuated by great malt-to-hop balance. A hint of toffee flavor.

G.W. Cherry Wheat   *Your Ranking* _____

A smooth ale. Light in body with a pleasing aroma and taste of fresh cherries.

Northern Light Ale   *Your Ranking* _____

A clean pale to golden light ale. Well balanced with a pleasing malt character and a light floral hop aroma.

Nut Brown Ale   *Your Ranking* _____

A traditional British brown ale. Deep chestnut color. A roasty, malty flavor.

Sunset Red Ale   *Your Ranking* _____

A malty beer with low hop bitterness and aroma highlighted by a sunset orange hue. Made with imported grains and German Hallertau hops. In the past this beer was also called Munich Helles.

Taylor ESB   *Your Ranking* _____

A traditional English-style extra special bitter. A higher level of maltiness and increased hop bitterness offer lots of flavor.

Velina Pale Ale   *Your Ranking* _____

A crisp classic pale ale with a slight citrus-like aroma. Named for one of Taylor's hardworking employees.

Voodoo Raspberry   *Your Ranking* _____

A mixture of Taylor's Raspberry Wheat and a dark ale creates chocolate flavor with a hint of raspberry.

Winterfest   *Your Ranking* _____

A dark orange color. Creamy with low carbonation.

BREWERY RATING

	Your Rating	Shepard's Rating (1 to 4 Mugs)	General Description
Location		🍺🍺🍺	Commercial/industrial Entertainment district

	Your Rating	Shepard's Rating	General Description
Ease of Finding Location		◐◐◐	Easy, but requires some planning
Brewery Atmosphere		◐◐◐	Sports
Dining Experience		◐◐◐◐	Family style/variety Pub fare
The Pint		◐◐◐	A good experience

MENU

Taylor Brewing Company offers an extensive American menu, specializing in burgers. In 1998 it was recognized by the *Chicago Tribune* as the Best in Burgers. The standard bar burger is based on a ten-ounce hamburger with a variety of seasonings and toppings. The most basic is the brew pub burger, which is topped with bacon and sautéed onions and a choice of Swiss, cheddar, or mozzarella cheese. Other burger selections include bacon, parmesan, Skinny Minnie, char burger, cheeseburger, hamburger, and blue cheeseburger. Beyond the burgers, Taylor makes over a dozen sandwiches. Taylor Brewing also offers a number of other entrées. Among the favorites are the barbecue ribs, which received first place in the 1996 Arlington Park Rib Fest. The Cajun catfish is a boneless catfish fillet with mild Cajun spices, and the salmon pesto pasta is served over fettuccini and topped with parmesan cheese and served with garlic bread. Appetizers include common pub starters such as stuffed potato skins, buffalo wings, jalapeño poppers, mozzarella triangles, and a couple varieties of nachos. You'll also find chili and French onion and daily soup specials, complemented with several salad options. The dessert considerations feature cheesecake, carrot cake, apple pie, and the chocolate lover's Kentucky Derby Pie.

OTHER THINGS TO SEE OR DO IN THE AREA

One of Lombard's top tourism attractions is the eight-and-a-half-acre Lilacia Park on the village's historic Maple Street. Lilacia Park was designed by famed landscape architect Jens Jensen. It contains over 200 varieties of lilacs and 75,000 tulips. The best time to visit for flowers is in early May. Across the street from the park is the Lombard Historical Museum (23 West Maple Street), which resides in the former home of William R. Plum, an early local politician, who gave the community the land for the park. It was his collection of lilacs that became the nucleus of Lilacia Park. Today, the Plum home and museum offer a glimpse of what life was like in the nineteenth century. This area of Maple Street, between Main and Elizabeth Streets, offers many historical homes and provides a pleasant walking tour. The oldest home in Lombard is the Sheldon Peck house (Parkside and Grace Streets), which was constructed between 1837 and 1839. It was originally home to the Peck family and later was the first school for the area.

Lombard also was once home to Harold Gray (119 North Main Street), creator of Little Orphan Annie. The finicky feline and cat actor "Morris" was discovered in 1968 at the nearby Humane Society of Hinsdale, and Bob Martwick, Morris's discoverer, trainer, handler, housemate, and owner (as if anyone ever owns a cat), lived in Lombard. The original Morris (from Hinsdale/Lombard) died in 1978 at the age of nineteen and was buried with great pomp in Martwick's back yard. (Sorry, but try as I might, I couldn't find an address for Morris's gravesite—anyway, it's probably best not to trample the flowers and catnip of the home's current owners.)

Moran Water Park in the Lombard Commons (East Maple Street is the southern border, while St. Charles Road borders the north, between Grace and Edgewood) has two 210-foot water slides, a swimming pool, diving well, and sand play areas. Lombard Commons also offers basketball, soccer, baseball, and softball fields. Lombard's largest park, Madison Meadow (Madison and Ahrens), is the location for the annual Taste of Lombard over the July 4 holiday. Its festivities also include a fireworks display.

The 216-acre Brookfield Zoo (First Avenue and 31st Street) has everything from aardvarks to zebras. It has great landscaping, entertainment, and special events such as the Living Coast, with its re-creation of the western coasts of Chile and Peru; the Swamp, which features a southern cypress swamp; and an Illinois River with underwater views. Another outdoor experience is found at the Morton Arboretum (4100 Route 53), consisting of 1,700 acres of trees, gardens, and natural landscapes. The Old Graue Mill (York and Spring Roads, Oak Brook) is the only operating waterwheel mill in the state. You can purchase stone-ground cornmeal at the country store. The mill was also a stop on the Underground Railroad. The mill is located at the edge of the Fullersburg Woods and Nature Center, which includes a 200-acre preserve and hands-on nature discovery room.

Directly across Butterfield Road from Taylor Brewing is the Northern Baptist Theological Seminary (660 East Butterfield Road). The seminary's Lindner Conference Center hosts inspirational lectures and special programs.

For shopping there are a number of options. The Yorktown Mall (203 Yorktown, Highland and Butterfield Roads) is across the street from Taylor Brewing Company. Other local strip malls are located along St. Charles Road in downtown Lombard and along South Main Street and Roosevelt Road; they include High Point Centre, Lombard Pines, Northgate, and Eastgate. Fountain Square is directly east of Taylor Brewing (Meyers and Butterfield Roads). If you're looking for a good movie, try the Yorktown Cinemas (97 Yorktown Shopping Court). In nearby Oak Brook, the Oakbrook Center (Route 83 and 22nd Street) offers more than 160 shops and small boutiques.

For seasonal fun, you might try the Lombard Jaycees Haunted House (800 East Roosevelt Road), one of the oldest and longest-running haunted houses in Illinois. West of Lombard in Berwyn there is some unusual artwork at the Cermak Plaza (7043 Cermak Road, about twelve miles east of Taylor Brewing) that features "The Spindle," which consists of eight cars that have been skewered on a giant spike in the middle of the mall's parking lot. The plaza also has about twenty other such sculptures, including a "Pinto Pelt," which is the shell of a Ford Pinto.

Taylor Brewing is actually part of a western Chicago "triangle" of great brewpubs. Within about fifteen minutes of each other, Lunar, Glen Ellyn, and Taylor Brewing all provide unique choices for good food and beer. You might also check those brewpub listings for other things to see or do in the area.

DIRECTIONS

When in Lombard, just locate the Yorktown Mall, and Taylor Brewing Company is located near the southeastern corner of the mall, but across Butterfield Road to the south. When you are approaching Taylor Brewing from the north or south, Interstate 355 will be a possible route. I-355 is west of Taylor Brewing about one mile. Connecting from I-355 on Butterfield Road (Route 56) will take you directly to Taylor.

When traveling east and west, consider Interstate 88. The Highland Avenue Parkway exit will take you to Butterfield Road, which parallels I-88 on the north. Once on Butterfield (also known as Route 56), you will find Taylor Brewing about three-quarters of a mile east of the Highland Avenue and Butterfield Road intersection.

Three Floyds Brewing Company
Munster, Indiana

Visit Date	Signed

ABOUT THE BREWERY

Okay, so Munster is technically in Indiana. But you can throw a rock into Illinois from Three Floyds' parking lot, and, furthermore, anyone who drinks beer in the Chicagoland area knows about Alpha King. Three Floyds is located in an industrial park in Munster, about three miles south of Interstate 80. The brewery actually got its start just a few miles north, in Hammond, Indiana, but moved to its current headquarters when it outgrew the mere three thousand square feet of its original space. That first location wasn't much more than a garage; all the bottle washing was done by hand, and the brew kettle was heated by an open flame. The location in Munster is five times that size. Three Floyds plans to expand further in 2003–2004 with an attached brewpub and beer garden, which will likely enrich the brewery's attractiveness to those searching for the perfect pint.

The area around Three Floyds is very sparse, mostly warehouses and industry. The building itself is somewhat plain looking, and without the large yellow sign in front of the parking lot you might not realize there is a working brewery behind the loading dock and the large bay doors.

Inside the brewery there is basically one large room, where the twenty-barrel system and series of thirty- and sixty-barrel fermenters, keg filler, and empty kegs line the warehouse walls. Three Floyds has a tasting area rather than a tasting room. Tours offer a chance to sample most of the Three Floyds brews, which are dispensed from a small, eight-by-ten-foot, boothlike kitchen. It is after all a working brewery; so don't expect a lot of superfluities. On my tour, I just sat at the folding table and chairs, enjoying a Robert the Bruce Scottish Ale, while the weekend tour guide just pointed to select brewery equipment while he talked from his place behind the serving booth. It was one of the most "no frills" tours I've ever been on. However, it must be pointed out that once you have a Three Floyds beer in your hand, you really don't want to stray far from the taps anyway.

Three Floyds Brewing Company makes more than a dozen beers. Anyone who really enjoys bitter beers knows these two words: "Alpha King." This beer is actually much more bitter than most American pale ales, but its complex hop and malt flavors really make it unique. Alpha King is considered the signature beer for Three Floyds. The brewery really lives up to its "Not Normal" motto with all of its beers. The Dreadnaught Imperial IPA is an in-your-face hop monster. The Robert the Bruce Scottish Ale has a rich, robust, thick, maltiness that will raise the kilt of any Scot.

HISTORY

The name Three Floyds refers to brothers Nick and Simon and father Michael Floyd. Nick is the principal owner and brewmaster of the company, while Simon is a chef in the restaurant industry and Mike is a local doctor. The Floyds are actually from Homewood, Illinois (near Flossmoor)—yet another reason for putting Three Floyds in with Illinois breweries.

Nick Floyd began as a homebrewer in the late 1980s. By the time he was twenty-one years old, he had enrolled in the Siebel Institute of Technology. He got his start as a professional brewer at the Florida Brewing Company in Auburndale, Florida, where he worked from 1993 to 1994. In 1994 he moved back to the Chicago area as a brewer for Weinkeller brewpubs in Berwyn and Westmont. When Weinkeller closed, he became the brewmaster at the Golden Prairie Brewing Company from 1995 to 1996. Golden Prairie, which closed in 2001, was located in the historic former home of the Brand Brewing Company that operated from 1899 to 1935. When he left Golden Prairie, Nick determined it was time to be part of his own fate and company, so he opened Three Floyds with his brother and father in October 1996.

When Three Floyds began, it was basically serving draft-only accounts, supplying bars and restaurants in Chicagoland and northwest Indiana from a small warehouse in Hammond. But the "Not Normal" beers of Three Floyds gained a following, and expansion was inevitable. From 1997 to 2002, Nick Floyd partnered with LeRoy Howard to produce a line of beers under the Burnham Brewing Company name. In 1999, Three Floyds shifted some of its bottling to August Schell Brewing of New Ulm, Minnesota. That year, Three Floyds was reaching all Big Ten states and a handful of others. In 2000, Three Floyds badly needed space, so it moved from Hammond to Munster.

During 2002 Three Floyds actually reduced distribution from more than fifteen states to focus primarily on Illinois, Indiana, Wisconsin, Kentucky, Pennsylvania, and New York. In 2003 the brewery installed a twenty-two-ounce bottling machine in the Munster facility. The company plans to expand again into the brewpub business by 2004, with enhancements to the Munster brewery to serve food and host a beer garden.

DON'T MISS THIS

The tasting area of Three Floyds has a number of interesting newspaper and media clippings about the brewery. You might also give some extra attention to the artwork and illustrations that Three Floyds uses in its promotional materials, packaging, and bottle labels. The eye-catching graphics were drawn by a friend of Nick Floyd's who also designs album covers in New York.

THREE FLOYDS BREWS

Alpha King Pale Ale 🍺🍺🍺🍺 *Your Ranking* _____
A floral hoppy aroma. Hazy, deep orange color and a thick, tan head. Full bodied and dry throughout. The strong malty character actually competes with an aggressive hoppiness. The finish is somewhat dry and bitter. This beer has an abundance of flavor from the malty start to the aggressive hoppiness in the body of flavor and the finish. The bitterness is strong, at more than sixty IBUs (International Bitterness Units), almost overwhelming. This beer is unique among unique beers—that's why it's the flagship of Three Floyds' "Not Normal" beers. It won a silver medal in the 1998 World Beer Championships.

Behemoth Blonde Barleywine 🍺🍺🍺 *Your Ranking* _____
A strong and assertive caramel malty nose. Dark copper color with ruby highlights. Full bodied and round, even chewy. Huge sweet flavors, and a complex caramel maltiness with generous hoppiness. Brewed as a fall seasonal. A gold medal winner at the 1998 World Beer Championships.

Calumet Queen Kolsch-Style Ale 🍺🍺🍺 *Your Ranking* _____
An earthy nose. Light golden color and a very thick, white head. Light to medium bodied and grainy. Great malty flavor with a fruity background that is more sweet than sour. Finishes with a light fruitiness. A summer seasonal.

Dreadnaught Imperial IPA 🍺🍺🍺 *Your Ranking* _____
If you think Alpha King has a distinctive flavor, prepare your taste buds for an over-the-top hoppy beer! It has a very strong hoppy nose and a deep copper color with a slight cloudiness. The head is thick, soft, and white. This ale is full bodied and smooth with strong, aggressive hoppy flavor from beginning to end. Though a wonderfully distinctive beer, it's so hoppy that it literally "stains" the taste buds, making it difficult to enjoy other beers during the same sitting. Don't take this observation as negative—I liked the beer; it's just that this IPA will challenge the serious hophead!

Rabbid Rabbit Saison 🍺🍺🍺🍺 *Your Ranking* _____
A Belgian-style Saison ale that begins with a spicy nose, with hints of coriander and yeast. A light copper color and slightly hazy. A very thick, soft, white head. Light to medium bodied and very soft. Smooth and creamy flavors of orange and coriander dominate a light malty background. Finishes with a sweet fruitiness. This late-spring-to-summertime seasonal has distinctive flavor and great spicy tones that are well balanced and complement the yeasty qualities.

Robert the Bruce Scottish Ale   🍺🍺🍺🍺   *Your Ranking* _____

Lots of malty flavor in this beer. Dark brown and slightly hazy with a thick, creamy, tan head. A lightly sweet, malty nose. Full bodied and creamy texture. Strong malty flavor. There is some balance in the beer, but it's at the end, after lots of chocolate and caramel flavor. Full bodied and full flavored, it is a great beer any time, but especially nice on a cool fall day!

X-tra Pale Ale   🍺🍺🍺   *Your Ranking* _____

A clean malty nose. Clear, golden color and a soft, small-bubbled, white head. Medium bodied and sharp. Moderate malty start with a strong, firm hoppy body. A dry bitter finish. While the firm bitterness dominates, there is a smooth, caramel malty background that continues to build through a pint of this pale ale.

OTHER THREE FLOYDS BREWS YOU MAY WANT TO TRY

Alpha Klaus Xmas Porter   *Your Ranking* _____

Rich and chocolatey. Made with English chocolate malt and Mexican sugar.

Black Sun Stout   *Your Ranking* _____

Available only on draft. Roasted nose. Deep dark coffee color. Dry and surprisingly light bodied. Malty sweetness and caramel flavors turn to a distinctive dry-roasted background.

Brian Boru   *Your Ranking* _____

An old-style Irish red.

Dark Lord   *Your Ranking* _____

A full-bodied and full-flavored Russian imperial stout.

Drunk Monk   *Your Ranking* _____

Three Floyds' weissbier.

Harvest Ale   *Your Ranking* _____

A fall seasonal introduced in 2003.

Oktoberfest   *Your Ranking* _____

This fall lager has deep copper color and smooth malty flavor.

Pride & Joy Mild Ale   *Your Ranking* _____

A light hoppy nose. Deep amber color. Medium bodied. A mild sweetness and hoppiness. Brewed with Cascade hops, which offer some fruity aroma and flavor. A bronze medal winner at the 1998 World Beer Championships.

Quadrupel   *Your Ranking* _____

If Three Floyds makes it, you just have to know this Belgian-style beer will have lots of maltiness and fruity flavor. This is a big beer. Introduced in 2003.

BREWERY RATING

	Your Rating	Shepard's Rating (1 to 4 Mugs)	General Description
Location		🍺🍺🍺	Commercial/industrial
Ease of Finding Location		🍺🍺🍺	Easy, but requires some planning
Brewery Atmosphere		🍺🍺🍺🍺	Brewery and business park
Dining Experience		n/a	No food (may add brewpub fixtures in future)
The Pint		🍺🍺🍺🍺	A perfect experience

MENU

Three Floyds Brewing Company is a working brewery and does not serve food. However, plans for expanding Three Floyds into a brewpub may be fulfilled in 2003–2004. When the brewpub begins, owner and brewmaster Nick Floyd promises "Not Normal" food, in the way of bratwurst corndogs, dishes made with curry, and a healthy complement of Cajun selections including jambalaya.

OTHER THINGS TO SEE OR DO IN THE AREA

Munster is well known for its performing arts and theater. It has a multimillion-dollar Center for the Visual and Performing Arts, which is home to Northwest Indiana Symphony and the Northern Indiana Arts Association (1040 Ridge Road). The Munster Theatre Company (8808 Columbia Avenue) produces productions at Munster High School and supports an extensive year-round schedule.

The Carmelite Shrines (1628 Ridge Road) are grottos built of crystals and colorful rocks that have been collected from around the world. The shrines are part of the monastery gardens of the Polish Carmelite Friars, who established themselves in the area in 1949.

Nearby, Indiana's Lake County Welcome Center (7770 Corrinne Drive, Hammond) will provide you with information about the area. The Welcome Center also has an art center, a gift shop, and the John Dillinger Museum, which traces his life from childhood through Prohibition to his death outside Chicago's Biograph Theatre. Also in Hammond, the Gibson Woods Nature Preserve (6201 Parrish Avenue) is 130 acres of woods, wildlife, and trails.

The Indiana Dunes National Lakeshore offers fifteen thousand acres on the southern shore of Lake Michigan. The largest of the dunes, 123-foot Mount Baldy, actually moves four to five feet inland from the lake each year. You can also visit swamps, bogs, and ponds. The superintendent's quarters (1100 North Mineral Springs Road, Porter) has information and even guided tours.

Just across the Illinois border, the Sand Ridge Nature Center (15891 Paxton Avenue) teaches visitors about the unique natural history of the Calumet region. The Lan-Oak Park District includes twenty-two parks throughout Lansing, Illinois. The Hollywood Park Family Entertainment Center (2635 Bernice Road, Lansing, Illinois) offers over a hundred games and two eighteen-hole miniature golf courses.

There are several casinos nearby. The Horseshoe Casino (825 Empress Drive) is located in Hammond. The Majestic Star Casino (Cline Avenue off Interstate 90 Skyway) and Trump Hotel Casino (One Buffington Harbor Drive) are both in Gary, Indiana. Balmoral Park Race Track (26435 South Dixie Highway) in Crete, Illinois, offers live and intertrack racing year round. In Crown Point, Indiana, the Crown Point Speedway offers Saturday night races that feature different-sized cars including Super Street and Mini Stock. Crown Point is also home to the Lake County Fair each August.

The Griffith Art Fair (Central Park) is held the third weekend in July. Griffith is about five miles east of Three Floyds. Further east, in Hobart, the Skystone N'Silver (1350 South Lake Park Avenue) offers Native American art.

East of Munster, the Old Jail Museum (153 South Franklin Street) in Valparaiso has been restored to its original 1871 condition and, together with the Porter County Sheriff's home, is on the National Register of Historic Places. While in Valparaiso, you might want to tour the Hoosier Bat Company (4511 E. Evans Avenue), which produces over fifty thousand baseball bats a year, many of which are specially ordered by major league players such as Rafael Palmeiro, Ray Durham, and Roberto Alomar. Sammy Sosa used a Hoosier bat to hit homers 64, 65, and 66 in 1998.

Northern Indiana supports two other breweries and two wineries. Breweries within about a half-hour drive include the Back Road Brewery (308 Perry Street) in La Porte and the Aberdeen Brewing Company (210 Aberdeen Drive) in Valparaiso. Anderson's Orchard and Winery (420 East U.S. Highway 6) in Valparaiso offers wine and has a country market. Dune Ridge Winery (1240 Beam Street) in Porter is only five minutes from the Lake Michigan shore.

DIRECTIONS

Three Floyds is located in a business park about three miles south of Interstate 80. From I-80 take Calumet Avenue south (exit 1) to Superior Avenue and turn right (west). Continue on Superior for two blocks and turn left (south) on Indiana Parkway. Watch for the red-and-white-striped water tower, which is directly behind Three Floyds.

Two Brothers Brewing Company

Warrenville

Visit Date	*Signed*

ABOUT THE BREWERY

Two Brothers Brewing Company is unique in the Illinois brewing business. First, it's family owned and operated by two brothers, Jim and Jason Ebel. Second, it is distinctive because it is an Illinois microbrewery only, without an attached brewpub or bar business. When you ask other brewers who they look to for good beer, Two Brothers is always at the top of everyone's list.

The brewery is located in Chicago's western suburbs, in a business park that is somewhat poorly marked. If you blink at the wrong time, you just might miss the building. But keep looking; it's well worth the trouble you might have finding it. Two Brothers is located in the northern part of a long building that houses several other businesses. Two Brothers has its own space, which is both a brewery and a homebrewing supply store, called the Brewers' Coop. If you're a homebrewer, there's got to be something very reassuring about purchasing your supplies from a brewery—sort of like getting your vegetables directly from a farmer. On one visit, I watched as Jim walked out of his office to personally help a new homebrewer develop a recipe and select the ingredients, and then he took extra care to make sure the person got a few tips that would ensure success. Without sounding like some "beer geek, know-it-all," Jim offered a level of professional courtesy and personal service to an inexperienced homebrewer that seemed special, even rare. While this just sounds like good business, I could tell that the motivation for Jim came from the individual contact and exchange of ideas.

Two Brothers offers about nine different beers throughout the year. About half of the Two Brothers brews are available in bottles. Draft beer distribution is mainly in the Chicago area, whereas the bottles turn up in Illinois, Indiana, Minnesota, Missouri, Ohio, and Wisconsin. The Ebel's Weiss, a traditional German Hefe-Weizen, is what started it all for Jim and Jason, and it is considered the company's mainstay—perhaps why it carries their name! The Prairie Path Golden Ale, Brown Fox Session Ale, and the Bitter End Pale Ale are the core Two Brothers brews. Among the seasonal favorites to watch for are the Dog Days and the Monarch Wit Beer. As a special treat, Two Brothers produces a Bare Tree Weiss Wine, which appears in late fall in champagne bottles.

Two Brothers also helps produce house beers for the Clark Street Ale House (742 North Clark) and Sheffields (3258 North Sheffield, near Wrigley Field) in Chicago.

HISTORY

Two Brothers Brewing Company was established in 1996 by Jim and Jason Ebel. Jason began his professional brewing career in the early 1990s in Colorado at Tabernash Brewing Company. During the same time, Jim, who was working in the commercial architecture field, opened a part-time business with a homebrew supply store called the Brewers' Coop. The Brewers' Coop was originally in Jim's house before it moved to a storefront in Naperville. When Jason decided to return to Illinois, he found work at Mickey Finn's brewpub in Libertyville and offered part-time assistance to his brother at the Brewers' Coop. In the fall of 1996, Jason attended the Siebel Institute in Chicago, and a few months later the two Ebel brothers officially opened Two Brothers Brewing in 10,000 square feet of space in a business park on Butterfield Road in Warrenville. The front of their brewery continues to house the Brewers' Coop, with the actual brewery in the back.

Both brothers shared in designing the brewery and homebrew store. While most of the current brewing equipment was built specifically for brewing, the early days of the company weren't so mainstream. The Ebels' first fermenters were used milk tanks, which they got from their grandfather's farm in Creighton, Nebraska. They also purchased used equipment from the former Golden Prairie Brewery of Chicago.

DON'T MISS THIS

Related, because beer is tied to good food, and interesting, to-say-the-least, is the collection of hot sauces that you'll find in the Brewers' Coop.

TWO BROTHERS BREWS

Brown Fox Session Ale 🍺🍺🍺   *Your Ranking* _____
A mild English-style brown ale. A light malty nose. Very dark, clear, bronze color. Thick, bubbly, tan head. Medium bodied and silky texture. A strong nutty and caramel flavor. The roasted chocolate malts come out in the finish and linger lightly without overwhelming the great flavors. This ale is made with eight different malts.

Dog Days 🍺🍺🍺🍺   *Your Ranking* _____
A clear, golden Dortmunder-style lager that has a delicate caramel nose and flavor. Medium bodied and crisp texture. Finishes with a light bitterness that is well balanced against the malty start. Crisp and clean. Available June through August.

Ebel's Weiss 🍺🍺🍺🍺   *Your Ranking* _____

A traditional German Hefe-Weizen. A faint fruity aroma. Deep golden and unfiltered color. A thick, soft, white head. Great sweetness with hints of clove, vanilla, and banana in the taste and aroma. Finishes with a smooth yeast flavor. A silver medal winner in 1998 and a bronze medal winner in 1997 at the World Beer Championship.

Heavy Handed IPA 🍺🍺🍺🍺   *Your Ranking* _____

A special brew in which freshly picked "wet hops" are used. Lots of hoppy aroma. Clear, golden color and a thin, soft, off-white head. Full bodied. Strong bitterness, a resiny flavor. A dry, bitter finish. This is a solid and well-bittered beer. Available in September and October. An exceptional beer.

Monarch Wit Beer 🍺🍺🍺   **Your Ranking** _____

Two Brothers' anniversary ale. Brewed only once a year, in small batches. Made with unmalted wheat and a touch of oats for a light body and crisp finish. It is spiced with coriander and orange peel, giving this Belgian-style white beer its traditional citrus aroma and flavor. Available in April.

The Bitter End Pale Ale 🍺🍺🍺🍺   *Your Ranking* _____

A classic American pale ale. A medium hoppy nose. Clear, copper color and thick, soft, tan head. Medium bodied and crisp bubbly texture. A firm, hoppy flavor with some maltiness and fruity tones in the background. Finishes with bitterness and dry texture. Don't just write this beer off as a light version of the Heavy Handed IPA. It's a different beer in color and texture and the fruit tones add to its sharpness. It is made with three American hop varieties to add citrus and floral hop complexity.

OTHER TWO BROTHERS BREWS YOU MAY WANT TO TRY

Bare Tree Weiss Wine   *Your Ranking* _____

A barley wine style weiss wine that is offered in limited quantities during the holidays. Made with the first runnings from a batch of Ebel's Weiss. Fermented with the yeast used to make Ebel's Weiss, then finished with a Scottish ale yeast and aged in oak. Limited release, and you might watch for it in a champagne bottle.

Bock   *Your Ranking* _____

The first lager brewed by Two Brothers. Brown color with great malty smoothness.

Domaine DuPage—French Country Ale   *Your Ranking* _____

A northern France amber colored ale. Brewed with specialty malts and imported hops. Deep copper color, malty and soft texture. The finish has a gentle floral and spicy hop balance. Available February through May.

Northwind Imperial Stout   *Your Ranking* _____

Deep, dark, and robust. This velvety stout starts with a nice caramel sweetness and is loaded with chocolate and firm roasty maltiness. It is available November through February.

Prairie Path Golden Ale   *Your Ranking* _____

Brewed with Belgian malts that lend a golden hue and toasty malt character, it is balanced with Saaz and Goldings hops for a slight hop flavor and finish. A clean, crisp, beer that is light in color but not in flavor.

BREWERY RATING

	Your Rating	Shepard's Rating (1 to 4 Mugs)	General Description
Location		🍺🍺🍺	Commercial/industrial
Ease of Finding Location		🍺🍺🍺	Easy, but requires some planning
Brewery Atmosphere		🍺🍺🍺🍺	Brewery and business park
Dining Experience		n/a	No food
The Pint		🍺🍺🍺🍺	A perfect experience

MENU

Two brothers is a combination of home brewing supply store and working brewery. The business does not sell food.

OTHER THINGS TO SEE OR DO IN THE AREA

Warrenville is a western Chicago suburb, about forty-five minutes from the Loop. Known mainly as a quiet, secluded residential area, it is surrounded on three sides by DuPage County Forest Preserves. Downtown Warrenville offers connections to both the Illinois Prairie Path and the DuPage River. The Prairie Path can be accessed about a half-mile south of Two Brothers off of Route 59. The Western Branch of the DuPage River winds its way just about a half-mile north and east of Two Brothers. The Great Western Trail is on the DuPage County section of the former Great Western right-of-way from Villa Avenue in Villa Park to the Elgin Branch of the Illinois Prairie Path west of Prince Crossing Road.

The Fermi National Accelerator Laboratory is only about a mile west from Two Brothers. Scientists at Fermilab carry out research in high-energy physics to answer the questions "What is the universe made of?" and "How does it work?" Fermi provides both organized and self-guided tours, scheduled lectures, an art gallery, and "Ask a Scientist" on every Saturday afternoon.

Warrenville hosts an annual car show and street dance every August. If you want to catch a movie, the AMC Cantera Theatres (28250 Diehl Road) offer thirty-seven screens. In the same area as the theatre, roughly two miles south and east of Two Brothers, the Rock Bottom Brewpub of Warrenville is located on Diehl Road.

The Warrenville Cenacle Retreat House (29 W 012 Batavia Road) offers 42 acres of wooded grounds along the DuPage River. The Cenacle offers a variety of retreats and spiritual programs. The Warrenville Historical Museum is located in the Albright Building (3 S 530 Second Street) in Warrenville.

DIRECTIONS

Two Brothers is located on Butterfield Road (Route 56). If you are traveling from downtown Chicago, Butterfield Road will take you there, but you may want to consider Interstate 88. Take exit 123 from I-88 and travel north on Route 59. Turn west on Butterfield (Route 56) and watch for the first opportunity to turn north (the place to turn is onto a frontage road on the north side of Route 56), into a modestly marked set of buildings that are part of a business park. Two Brothers is located in the far north end of the easternmost set of buildings.

An alternative travel mode is to take the train to the Metra station in nearby Naperville. A Pace bus route through Warrenville picks up passengers and connects them to Naperville.

Just Over the Border
Searching the Region for the Perfect Pint

Many great beers can be found just beyond the Illinois state line. Therefore the following section captures some of those breweries and brewpubs that are within about a half-hour drive beyond the Illinois border. These brewpubs and breweries are listed in an abbreviated form. While the focus of the book remains on Illinois, some of these breweries offer a potential to expand the search for that perfect pint or two that you might have otherwise missed.

Some of my favorite Just Over the Border breweries are in towns like Valparaiso and La Porte, Indiana. For those in the northern part of Illinois, Wisconsin's lower third has many opportunities to find great beer. New Glarus is one of the hardest working breweries in the state, producing more than twenty beer styles a year. Brewmasters–Friarswood in Kenosha was Wisconsin's first brewpub and has a unique design that makes use of a hundred-year-old barn. The cities of Madison and Milwaukee are not documented in this book in detail, but both offer numerous opportunities for good beer and food. For those in Madison, the brewpubs include Angelic, J. T. Whitney's, and the Great Dane in Madison and Fitchburg. The Capital Brewery in the Madison suburb of Middleton is a very special brewery because of the attention it gives to German-style lagers. The Märzen-style Capital Oktoberfest is as good as, if not better than, what one might find in the fall celebrations in Munich. Just to the east of Madison in the town of Lake Mills, Tyranena Brewing Company has a small, charming bar, a tasting room, and beer garden. Milwaukee is more difficult to describe because it offers not only the large Miller Brewing Company, but it also has a number of smaller brewpubs in the downtown. If you find yourself with a couple of days, pay a visit to Water Street and the Milwaukee Riverfront for the concentration of brewpubs. And don't overlook some of the city's small working breweries such as Lakefront and Sprecher.

Illinois's western border features three small breweries in Iowa that offer a great way to explore old river towns lining the Mississippi. One of the most scenic trips would take you into northwest Illinois to Galena, where you could shop for antiques or tour the home of Ulysses S. Grant, then drive a short twenty minutes to the picturesque community of Dubuque, Iowa, and a stop at the Bricktown Brewery in the center of town. Leaving Dubuque, traveling south on Routes 52 and 67, you'll end up in Clinton and the Upper Mississippi Brewing Company, which is located in a century-old papermaking warehouse. Further south, on Route 67 into Davenport, you'll find the Front Street Brewery. From there, it's merely a short crossing of the Mississippi River via the Centennial Bridge and you'll be just a few blocks from the Blue Cat Brew Pub and the Bent River Brewing Company. In the summer months you might take the *Channel Cat Water Taxi* to see the Quad Cities.

St. Louis, Missouri, makes up for a lack of breweries in southwestern Illinois. Anheuser-Busch Brewing is impressive for its size and historical significance to the industry. The world's largest brewer has made a significant commitment to preserving many of the brewery's original buildings. A tour of Anheuser-Busch will show you the big business side of the industry, while giving tribute to the historical past. But no brew tour of the "Gateway to the West" is complete without a stop at Schlafly Tap Room, where you'll find some of the best beer and food of any brewpub. Schlafly certainly has figured out what the pursuit of the perfect pint is about.

Illinois has many great beer makers, but so do the other states in the Great Lakes region. This section will introduce you to some of the best that lie near the borders with Illinois. Remember, when traveling, it's always best to call ahead for hours of operation and directions. Traveling also brings with it a responsibility to remember that finding the perfect pint is not about quantity; rather it's about finding quality beer and food and enjoying the scenic landscape and interesting people you meet along the way.

Aberdeen Brewing Company
Valparaiso, Indiana

Visit Date	Signed

ABOUT THE BREWERY

The Aberdeen Brewing Company has the feel of a Scottish pub, complete with a number of wonderful historic accents. Inside, the maple plank floor, wainscot on the walls, and marble windowsills create a traditional pub atmosphere. If you look closely at the pub's message board, you'll find it is hand-carved oak and was once used in a service club in Glasgow, Scotland, where it honored local World War I veterans. The bar in the lounge was found at the Great Gatsby Auction House in Atlanta, but it was traced back to northwest Indiana. When it was restored, it was found to have originated in a basement saloon of a boarding house in nearby Hammond. The bar is made from solid mahogany and dates to the late nineteenth century. The Aberdeen Brewing Company was originally founded by the Emig family. Greg Emig began home-brewing in the late 1980s and eventually became the brewmaster for the Broad Ripple Brewing Company in Indianapolis. By 1992, Greg, his wife, Nancy, and his brother Joe opened the Lafayette Brewing Company. Eight years later, in 2000, the Emigs opened Aberdeen Brewing Company. In 2002 it was purchased by John and Cora Bosak. The Emigs still own and operate Lafayette Brewing Company.

BEERS

You'll find about a half-dozen beers at Aberdeen Brewing. Given the Scottish accents of the brewpub, the Aberdeen Scottish Ale (🍺🍺🍺🍺) is a good one to start with. This 80 Schilling Ale has a dark ruby color and aggressive malty character. A beer well worth taking home in a growler is the Skadi Pale Ale

($\mho\mho\mho\mho$). This classic pale ale has a clear copper color, bubbly tan head, and an assertive floral, hoppy aroma and finish. Skadi is the name of the goddess of winter, for whom Scandinavia was named. The Country Porter ($\mho\mho\mho\mho$) is smooth and well balanced with creamy chocolate tones and a subtle, dry, bitter finish. But the Braveheart Barleywine ($\mho\mho\mho$) is a great way to finish lunch on a cold Saturday in February. Its deep, inviting malty nose, bronze color, and full body is a wonderful way to warm up on a snowy day. Other beers to try include the Kolsch-style Aberdeen Golden Ale ($\mho\mho\mho$), Queen Mum India Pale Ale ($\mho\mho\mho$), Beyond the Pale Stout ($\mho\mho\mho$), Aberdeen Brown ($\mho\mho\mho$), and Aberdeen Raspberry Ale ($\mho\mho$).

MENU

The appetizers include stuffed mushrooms, baked crab dip, margherita pizza, ale-battered onion rings, and something all European pubs must have— Scotch eggs. Entree choices feature beef tenderloin medallions, steak Delmonico, cottage pie, roast rack of lamb, blackened yellow fin tuna, and ale-battered fish and chips. There are a few vegetarian options such as veggie pasta, stuffed spinach, and artichoke ravioli.

Anheuser-Busch
St. Louis, Missouri

Visit Date	Signed

ABOUT THE BREWERY

When it comes to the big breweries, Anheuser-Busch is a must stop for the beer tourist. There is a major part of American brewing history that is revealed by a tour of the Anheuser-Busch grounds. If there's one big brewery to visit, the St. Louis facility offers a remarkable look into a family business that became the world's largest beer maker. The tours will take you through the modern, computer-controlled operations center, buildings that are listed on the National Registry of Historic Sites, and into the round barn that is home to the famous Budweiser Clydesdales. The stables have stained glass windows and house the massive eight-horse hitch and beer wagon. Anheuser-Busch began in St. Louis in 1860, when Eberhard Anheuser invested in the Bavarian Brewery, a small St. Louis beer company that had begun in 1852. Adolphus Busch was the son-in-law of Anheuser, and he entered into partnership with Anheuser in 1869. The Anheuser-Busch Brewery isn't far from downtown St. Louis, only about three miles south of the Gateway Arch.

BEERS

Anheuser-Busch is the world's largest brewer. The company makes about thirty beers in its U.S. breweries. Among the most common are Budweiser, Bud Light, Busch, Busch Light, Michelob, Michelob Amber Bock, Michelob HefeWeizen, Michelob Honey Lager, Michelob Black & Tan, Natural Light, Red Wolf, Killarney's Red Lager, and the nonalcoholic O'Doul's. In recent years, Anheuser-Busch entered into distribution agreements with West Coast micro-breweries Redhook and Widmer Brothers.

MENU

None. This is a brewery.

Back Road Brewery
La Porte, Indiana

Visit Date	Signed

ABOUT THE BREWERY

There's a lot about this brewery that might seem understated, especially given its warehouse location in La Porte, limited if not nonexistent advertising, and simple packaging. But the beers are assertive and full of flavor. Their tours really give you a feel for how special small breweries are. Back Road's three-story brick building is huge. It was originally constructed in the 1870s by the Rumley Company, which made threshing machines and coal oil tractors. Back Road occupies just a small rectangular room in the southwest corner of the first floor. The building is adjacent to Norfolk Southern rail lines and when trains pass through town you can actually feel the building tremble. With just a seven-barrel brew kettle, double batches are required to fill the fermenters. There's a great amount of handcrafting, not only in the beer but also in the brewery. Its conditioning tanks were modified from former dairy equipment. During a tour you'll likely meet owner Chuck Kreilek and part-time brewer Matt Peterson who serve as the primary guides. The Back Road Brewery name really seems to capture the essence of this brewery, because unless you live in La Porte, it seems a little out of the way—yet very worth the trip. The brewery's name was controversial. In 1996, Kreilek established his brewery with the name "Brick Road Brewing." However, that caused a conflict over names and trademarks registered in the United States by Ontario's Brick Brewing Company, so Kreilek decided on the similar yet different name of "Back Road." It has also inspired the catchy marketing theme of "Take the Back Road Home."

BEERS

The Back Road Amber (🍺🍺🍺) is the company's flagship beer. This amber colored English ale is crisp with some nice hop to malt balance and a light, dry finish. The Belle Gunness Stout (🍺🍺🍺🍺) is a dry Irish-style stout; it has a deep dark color, soft brown head, and a roasted body that helps bring out a firm bitterness. Back Road also makes a Bavarian lager called the Millennium Lager

(🍺🍺🍺), which offers a complex malt-dominated flavor with a mild smooth bitterness to the finish. The Midwest IPA (🍺🍺🍺) is full of hoppy flavor and aroma. Other Back Road brews to watch for include a Bock, the "Aviator" Doppelbock, Hefe-Weizen, Oktoberfest, Belgium Wit, a Barley wine, and Maple City Gold (La Porte is known as "The Maple City" because of its impressive fall foliage). Seasonals include Autumn and Christmas Ales that will change in specific styles from year to year.

MENU

None. This is a brewery.

Brewery Creek Restaurant, Bed & Breakfast, and Microbrewery

Mineral Point, Wisconsin

Visit Date	Signed

ABOUT THE BREWERY

Brewery Creek is one of the most inviting pubs in Wisconsin. It offers a restaurant, bed and breakfast, and microbrewery. The bar and restaurant occupy the first floor of this beautifully restored limestone building; guest rooms are on the upper two floors. Original oak posts and beams and salvaged antique wainscoting all impart a historic feeling. Many of the furnishings were either made by local craftsmen or imported from England. As you sip your pint you can't help but ask about the back bar, which owner Jeff and Deborah Donaghue rescued from an old clothing store in Edina, Minnesota. The five guest rooms upstairs have whirlpool tubs and private baths, all in the same decor of hand-hewn timbers and exposed stone walls. Four of the five rooms have their own fireplace. The Phillips Brewery, one of the earliest breweries in Wisconsin, was located just a few hundred yards north on Commercial Street. The building housing Brewery Creek was constructed in 1854 and originally served as a railroad warehouse. Later it housed an agricultural implements business and then a veterinary surgery ward. Horses were stabled near the area that is now used for dining. Until 1995, the building had a dirt floor and no plumbing, heating, or electricity. Brewery Creek is the name of the small stream behind the building. The town of Mineral Point makes a wonderful weekend destination with its antique shops, stone buildings, historical structures, and the Brewery Pottery Studio, which was home to the Mineral Springs Brewery from 1852 to 1961.

BEERS

Oatmeal Stout–Victoria's Secret (🍺🍺🍺🍺) is a sweet, full-bodied stout that matches well with the barbecue ribs! New-Old Ale (🍺🍺🍺) has a light malty nose, clear copper color, a thin, bubbly, tan head, and a full body with silky texture. This beer has a beautiful appearance and pleasant warm finish. It's based on a recipe that Jeff Donaghue adapted from the Truman Brewery in England from the mid-1800s. Mahogany Ale (🍺🍺🍺) begins with a little earthiness in the nose and flavor but turns smooth with a bold malty middle. The All American Wheat (🍺🍺🍺) is a slightly cloudy and golden wheat with medium body and a fruity sweetness that dominates the taste. Other Brewery Creek beers to try include the Bière Blonde; the Chewy Oatmeal Stout, which is based on a 1909 recipe that includes twenty percent oats; an IPA; and a Schwarzbier.

MENU

The Brewery Creek menu features pub style items with daily specials. The main sandwich menu consists of about ten choices, ranging from the brewery burger, a quarter pound of black Angus beef seasoned with roasted garlic and spices, to the classic salmon burger with Hook's cheddar cheese. Hook's cheeses are made locally, just two blocks away. Other sandwiches to consider are the Brewery Creek MLT, a crisp portobello mushroom with red onions and aïoli on whole wheat sesame seed sourdough, and the Brewery Creek walnut burger, which has portobello slices, cheddar cheese, and caramelized onions. Nightly dinner specials vary. Hours also vary, especially closing time and all hours during winter. It's a good idea to call ahead to check the schedule.

Brewmasters Pub–Friarswood

Kenosha, Wisconsin

Visit Date	Signed

ABOUT THE BREWERY

Opening in 1987, Brewmasters Pub–Friarswood was the first brewpub in Wisconsin and the sixteenth in the nation since Prohibition. Located on Kenosha's south side, about twenty minutes north of the Illinois-Wisconsin border, you will find Brewmasters Pub in a century-old three-story barn. Its brick walls, three-foot-thick stone foundation, and arching roof accent the rural farmstead appearance of a building that was once part of a massive monastery. The Allen family of New York constructed it in the late 1890s as a tannery and place to spend summers. In 1945 the barn and property were sold to the Brothers of May Town. The barnlike building served as a meeting hall and dormitory until the early 1980s, when it was sold to developers. Present owner Jerry Renzy gained his enthusiasm for microbrewing on a trip to Germany in 1982. When he came home, somewhat by coincidence, he saw an ad for a homebrewing kit on the back of a magazine. After a little research at the local library, Renzy started homebrewing, and in 1985 his light lager won a first-place medal at the Wisconsin State Fair. From that inspiration he decided to enter the brewing business and make his beer for all of us to enjoy.

Inside Brewmasters the atmosphere is warm, with brick accents, wooden beams, and low ceilings. The bar is a small square with a seating area to the left as you enter. Most of the restaurant seating, along with banquet facilities for private parties, is to the right of the bar. If you look closely on the north wall of the bar area, you will see a newspaper clipping dated May 23, 1987, with a photo and story describing beer guru Michael Jackson's visit to Brewmasters.

BEERS

Brewmasters Pub commonly has about ten regular beers and two or three seasonal specials on tap. Among the beers to ask about is the Gobbler Brau (🍺🍺🍺🍺)

with its light flowery nose and lots of fresh hoppy aroma; it is medium bodied with a clear copper color, a thick tan head, and a bitterness that is firm throughout. The Kensoha Gold (🍺🍺🍺🍺) is a Czech-style Pilsner made with German Spalt and Tettnang hops that offers a strong aroma; it consists of an assertive collection of flavors, yet overall it remains well balanced. The Kenosha Gold is considered the flagship beer for Brewmasters. The Southport Amber (🍺🍺🍺) has vivid orange color, a thin white head, and medium body with a light hoppiness in the beginning that gives way to a smooth malty dominance. Southport was Kenosha's original name. Of the seasonals to watch for, the Winter Warmer (🍺🍺🍺) is a bronze beer with a strong caramel malt flavor. A few other beers to make note of at Brewmasters include Abbott Ale, East Coast Porter, Gran Cru, Icemaster, Indian Pale Ale, Johnson's Honey Lager, Illuminator Dopplebock, Irish Mocha Stout, Saint Brendan's Oatmeal Stout, and Nort's Cream Ale.

MENU

The menu features English pub and German specialties. Potato skins, chicken wings, and nachos round out a range of appetizers. Signature dishes include ribs, beer-battered shrimp, and fish and chips. On the hearty German side of the menu, the Wiener Schnitzel is a veal cutlet sautéed in caper butter, and the Bavarian Trio features a pork chop, barbecued ribs, and bratwurst served with sauerkraut. The English pub offerings are highlighted by the shepherd's pie. The smothered steak is charbroiled and topped with melted cheddar cheese, sautéed mushrooms, onions, and green peppers. The lighter portion of the menu includes more than a dozen sandwiches and burgers. There are also daily specials such as barbecued pork ribs, steak, shrimp, prime rib, roasted chicken, and pasta. It's also a good idea to look for several entrées that are made with house beer.

Bricktown Brewery & Blackwater Grill

Dubuque, Iowa

Visit Date	Signed

ABOUT THE BREWERY

As the name suggests, the brick and stonework are striking as you arrive at Dubuque's Bricktown Brewery and Blackwater Grill. This four-story building has a strong historical tie to the community. The building, the former home of Augustine A. Cooper Wagon Works Factory, was constructed in the mid-nineteenth century. The wagon maker reached its peak around 1900, producing over five thousand wagons a year on grounds that covered nearly twenty-seven acres of Dubuque. Cooper Wagon Works closed as the automobile caught on in the early 1900s. During the first half of the twentieth century the factory suffered from decay and even a major fire. Since the 1950s it was used as apartments. Renovations for the Bricktown Brewery began in 1999. The brewery and its companion businesses, the Blackwater Grill, Stonewall Lounge, and Underground Night Club, opened in 2002. Bricktown offers two floors of banquet facilities. The Stonewall Lounge and the Underground are in the lower level of the building. The Blackwater Grill and Bricktown Brewery are located on the first floor. The brew kettle and fermentation vessels sit in the middle of the main dining area, behind brick and glass walls. The high ceilings of the first floor work well with heavy wooden tables, spacious booths, and large windows that overlook the corner of Third and Main. The Bricktown Brewery, with its great beer, food, and historic charm, will a make great weekend visit to the picturesque river city of Dubuque.

BEERS

The Black Eye Stout (ᗡᗡᗡ) has a roasted nose, a deep black color and a thick soft tan head, strong chocolate malt flavor, and a clean, somewhat dry finish; this stout has some very roasted flavors. Almost opposite is the traditional American light called Laughing Ass Light, which is the lightest of the Bricktown beers. The Laughing Ass (ᗡᗡᗡ) has a straw color, thin body, and mild malty tones with a dry finish. A winter seasonal favorite is a strong English ale called Rudolf's Red Nose Ale (ᗡᗡᗡᗡ), which has a floral nose, a clear, deep reddish bronze color, and is full bodied and bubbly, with a malty flavor and a sharp hoppy background and finish. The Blitzen (🍺🍺🍺🍺) is a strong winter ale with an assertive malty nose, a deep cloudy bronze color, and a very thick, bubbly brown head; the Blitzen has a very caramely flavor and warm finish. The Bricktown Nut Brown (🍺🍺🍺) offers a malty nose, light caramel flavor, and a dry roasted finish, combined with medium body and a somewhat slick texture. The English-style pale ale called Get Fuggled (🍺🍺🍺) offers a light hoppy nose, clear deep copper color, and strong dry bitter flavor. Other Bricktown beers include the Bully Porter, the Wheat, the Stone Cutters Ale, the Munich Dunkel, the Mexican, the Gorilla Vanilla, a Scottish ale called the Grounds Keeper Willie Ale, and the seasonals Bull Dog Double Bock and Oktoberfest.

MENU

The Blackwater Grill is the restaurant that is attached to the Bricktown Brewery. It offers a range of salads, soups, pastas, pizzas, burgers, and meaty entrees, some of which are prepared on an open-flame hickory-fired grill. The lighter selections worth a close look include the smoked pork farfalle pasta, the Bricktown patty melt, and the Blackwater club. If you are looking for a larger meal, try the meatloaf with its garlic, peppers, and onions served with roasted brown ale catsup. There is also a pub-style sirloin, a twelve-ounce Pittsburgh prime rib basted with Cajun Creole sauce, and brewery-smoked ribs.

Front Street Brewery and Beer Garden

Davenport, Iowa

Visit Date	Signed

ABOUT THE BREWERY

The Front Street Brewery opened in 1992 in a narrow brick warehouse that is sandwiched between a couple of taller brick buildings along Davenport's riverfront. Inside Front Street the brick walls and wooden booths and tables offer a neighborhood tavern feel. The bar is L-shaped with a beautiful oak back bar. Because there isn't much room in the building, the brewing equipment is stuck in the front part of the bar area. A small outside beer garden is located to the rear of the building, but, although you can enjoy a blue Iowa sky and fresh air, the view is rather constricted because the patio is behind all the buildings in something of an alley. Front Street is worth the trip, and an added benefit is its proximity to the other brewpubs in the Quad Cities (Blue Cat in Rock Island and Bent River in Moline). A great way to get around the Quad Cities in the warm months is via the *Channel Cat Water Taxi* on the Mississippi River.

BEERS

If you are passing through town on an Iowa summer's day, the Hefe-Weizen (🍺🍺🍺🍺) has some great German wheat qualities in its cloudy yellow color, citrus nose, and smooth, light banana tones. The Raging River Ale (🍺🍺🍺), the flagship beer for Front Street, gets its name from the 1993 floods; the Raging River has a light flowery nose, a cloudy copper color, a soft tan head, light sharp texture, and a mild caramel malt flavor that finishes with a light dryness. The Bucktown Stout (🍺🍺) takes its name from the notorious red light district of a century ago in the Front Street area; it is a light-bodied stout with great color but is a bit shy in character. Other Front Street beers include the light-bodied Old Davenport, a Cherry Ale, Scotch Ale, and brewmaster specials such as a Spring Fest.

MENU

There is a nice range of food to choose from at Front Street, with an emphasis on sandwiches and burgers, of which more than a dozen are on the menu. Sandwich selections include a slow-roasted Italian beef, ahi tuna, grilled chicken, grilled portabello mushroom, and one of my favorites, a turkey Reuben. Entrees include steaks, chicken, and seafood. The bangers and cakes feature a choice of bratwurst or Polish sausage with sauerkraut and sautéed onions on potato pancakes. There is baked salmon, fish and chips, and the hearty spinach- and mushroom-stuffed pork loin.

Gray's Brewing Company
Janesville, Wisconsin

Visit Date	Signed

ABOUT THE BREWERY

Gray's Brewing Company is believed to be the nation's oldest beverage company owned and operated continuously by the same family. Now in its fifth generation, it has been in Janesville since 1856. Irish immigrant Joshua Converse Gray started Gray's Brewing and Beverage Company in this southern Wisconsin town in a wood frame building near the intersection of Locust and McKinley Streets. The company brewed beer until 1912, and then it switched to soft drinks. In 1959 it moved to its present location on the west side of the town. In 1965 the original building was razed. In 1992 the business survived a devastating fire, and when the company rebuilt in 1994, it returned to brewing. Tours at Gray's feature the uniqueness of a small-town brewery with actual family members taking part in the tour.

BEERS

Gray's continues to make both beer and soda. The company makes about a dozen different beers; about half are seasonals. Among those that are considered the company's mainstays are Gray's Classic American Pale Ale (🍺🍺🍺) with its mildly hoppy nose, deep golden color, and thin, soft, white head; with medium body and a caramel beginning, the hoppiness remains firm throughout the finish. The Honey Ale (🍺🍺🍺) has a light malty nose with subtle fruity tones, and a golden body that is highly carbonated with a thick frothy head and creamy texture; it's made with 100 percent pure Wisconsin honey and three types of two-row malted barley. The Honey Ale is a 1994 gold medal winner at the Great American Beer Festival and a bronze medal winner at the 1996 World Beer Championships. A seasonal favorite is the Winter Porter (🍺🍺🍺🍺), with a dark color; smooth, silky texture; distinct malty aroma; and warm finish. Other Gray's brews to try include the Autumn Ale, Black & Tan, Cream Ale, Irish Ale, Oatmeal Stout, and Wisconsin Weissbier.

MENU

None. This is a brewery.

Joseph Huber Brewing Company

Monroe, Wisconsin

Visit Date	*Signed*

ABOUT THE BREWERY

Joseph Huber Brewing is the second oldest operating brewery in the United States and the oldest in the Midwest. This brewery and several local cheese plants are the heart and soul of this southern Wisconsin community. Huber Brewing is located in a large white brick building, less than a block from the town square. Through many renovations, equipment upgrades, and even a fire, the brewery has stood at this location since 1845. Huber Premium and Huber Bock are the mainstays of the brewery, but it also brews the popular Berghoff line of beers. The Berghoff beer, first brewed by Huber in 1960, was originally made in Fort Wayne, Indiana, by the Herman Berghoff Brewing Company, but after a fire in 1888, founder Herman Berghoff moved to Chicago and opened the Berghoff Restaurant. Today, Berghoff is one of Huber's most popular beers. Huber officially purchased the Berghoff label in 1995.

BEERS

Huber not only brews its own main labels of Huber Bock (🍺🍺🍺) and Huber Premium (🍺🍺), but it also makes a number of long-standing Wisconsin beers such as Wisconsin Club (🍺🍺), Rhinelander (🍺🍺) and Rhinelander Bock (🍺🍺🍺), Bavarian Club, Braumeister, Regal Brau, and Dempsey's Pale Ale and Extra

Stout. The Berghoff line includes Berghoff Bock (🍺🍺🍺), Genuine Dark (🍺🍺🍺🍺), Hazelnut Winterfest (🍺🍺🍺), Hefe-Weizen, Honey Maibock, Oktoberfest, Original Lager, Raspberry Wheat, and Red Ale.

MENU

None. This is a brewery.

Lafayette Brewing Company
Lafayette, Indiana

622 Main St., Lafayette, IN. 765/742-2591

Visit Date	Signed

ABOUT THE BREWERY

Lafayette Brewing is located in the turn-of-the-century Kaplin Furniture build-ing along Main Street. The four-story brick building with its vivid green awning has somewhat of a rustic inside with heavy wood accents, beams, ceiling posts, and thick wooden tables. The brewery is always on view, enclosed in a glass room behind the bar. There is also a collection of memorabilia from the city's former breweries. The last of those local breweries, the Lafayette Brew-ery (also known as Theime and Wager), closed in 1953. The modern Lafayette Brewing Company brewpub opened in September 1993.

BEERS

My pick is the Eastside Bitter (🍺🍺🍺🍺), with a clear, deep copper color, a tan head, medium body, great bitterness, and a strong competitive malty flavor. The Eighty-Five (🍺🍺🍺) is another great bitter beer that is a little lighter than the Eastside; it has a light floral nose, clear golden color, smooth texture, and long lasting, firm bitterness. The Black Angus Oatmeal Stout (🍺🍺🍺🍺) has a malty nose, a thick dark color, and a tan soft head; it is medium bodied with a strong roasted flavor and finish. Other Lafayette brews include Whitetail Wheat, Prophet's Rock Pale Ale, Piper's Pride Scottish Ale, the Smokehouse Porter, Heritage Trail Amber Ale, Digby's Irish Stout, Weeping Hog IPA, and cask-conditioned ales including an IPA. Followers of Lafayette also watch closely for Big Boris Barleywine, which is brewed in summer and served in the winter.

MENU

Lafayette Brewing's menu emphasizes hearty pub dishes such as Tippecanoe BBQ, which consists of house pork shoulder and cornbread. You'll also find a bison sirloin, house steak, and prime rib. There are four different salads and a few different soups.

Morgan Street Brewery
St. Louis, Missouri

Visit Date	Signed

ABOUT THE BREWERY

Morgan Street Brewery is located in Laclede's Landing, one the oldest parts of St. Louis. It's within a five-minute walk of the Gateway Arch. Also nearby is the St. Louis Convention Center, the Trans World Dome, and Busch Stadium. The building housing Morgan Street is one of the oldest buildings on the landing. The present building was constructed in the 1890s as the Schoelhorn-Albrecht Machine Company, which made capstans for the Mississippi River barges. As you walk up the actual Morgan Street in Laclede's Landing, toward Third Street, you might notice that the sidewalks are uneven. That's because they conceal a room underneath Morgan Street that was once used to hide runaway slaves. Morgan Street Brewery began its brewing heritage in September 1995. The first floor of the building is the main dining room and brewery, while the second floor has its own bar and private party rooms. Brewmaster Marc Gottfried actually started brewing at the age of thirteen in the basement of his mother's house, under her watchful eye. She's a well-respected biology professor who noted his interest as the pursuit of scientific inquiry. After working for a local homebrew supply store, Marc became Morgan Street's assistant brewmaster at the age of twenty. By the time he was twenty-two, he was brewmaster and at that time was considered the youngest brewmasters in North America by the National Association of Brewers.

BEERS

Morgan Street has an ambitious beer list. The Altbier (🍺🍺🍺🍺) has a strong malty nose and clear bronze body with a thin, bubbly, tan head; it is medium bodied with crisp, nice, smooth balance and a dry finish. The Cobblestone Steam Lager (☙☙☙) has a light, fruity nose, clean deep golden color, and a thin white head; it is medium bodied with a crisp hoppiness. The Dark Wheat (☙☙☙) begins with a malty nose and has a clear, deep bronze body, soft texture, strong sweet malty flavor, and fruity finish. The Red Lager (☙☙☙☙) is similar to the Vienna style, with a very light malty nose and a clear, reddish-bronze color; it is medium bodied and has a great malt-to-hops balance that finishes very clean. Other Morgan Street beers include the Bohemian-style Golden Pilsner, a dry Irish Stout, and the very popular Honey Wheat. Seasonal specialties to watch for include the Doppelbock, Krystäl, Maibock, Oktoberfest, and Winter Lager.

MENU

Morgan Street offers a diverse menu selection. Starters include baked beer pretzels served with Steam Lager mustard. You'll also find pastas, pizzas, and sandwiches that come with house *coniques* (mashed potato balls). The Brewery Favorites, the main entree section of the menu, offers some great choices, with Applewood smoked bacon-wrapped buffalo meatloaf, herb crusted Atlantic salmon, baby back ribs, blue crab cakes, and lobster ravioli.

New Glarus Brewing Company
New Glarus, Wisconsin

Visit Date	Signed

ABOUT THE BREWERY

Probably one of the most ambitious brewers in Wisconsin, New Glarus always seems to be expanding its brewery or introducing a new beer. In 1998 the Beverage Testing Institute named it one of the eleven best breweries in the country. It was established by the husband-and-wife team of Dan and Deb Carey. The couple chose New Glarus because Deb was originally from Milwaukee and, together, they wanted to raise their children in a small town. The proximity to Madison offered a beneficial market niche, with which they've continued to do well. Both had considerable brewery experience before moving to southern Wisconsin. Dan had served as a brewer's apprentice in the Ayinger Brewery near Munich, Germany. They both worked for Anheuser-Busch in Colorado before relocating and creating the New Glarus Brewing Company in 1993.

New Glarus Brewing is located in the Sugar River valley on the eastern edge of the town of New Glarus. It's about a half-hour drive from Madison or fifteen minutes from the Illinois border. Rolling hills, dairy farms with their red barns, and fields dotted with the black and white spotted Holsteins make for a relaxing journey. New Glarus is often called Little Switzerland for its scenic countryside and the cultural heritage of many of its residents.

Inside the New Glarus brewery you'll find green corian tile floors and high ceilings that direct attention to the copper brew kettles. Much of the Careys' equipment—including the brew kettles, lauter tun, mill, and the brewery's control panel—was salvaged from a German brewery.

BEERS

New Glarus Brewing produces about sixteen different styles of beer a year. Spotted Cow (🍺🍺🍺) is one of the company's most recognized brews, with its mild malty nose, clear straw to golden color, and light body; it has a soft maltiness with a soft fruity background. New Glarus's Uff-Da Bock (🍺🍺🍺🍺) has an assertive malty nose with generous chocolate, caramel, and coffee flavors and a dark color that looks heavy but is really crisp and medium bodied; Uff-Da won a silver medal at the 1996 Great American Beer Festival. In 2003 New Glarus introduced its Native Ale (🍺🍺🍺🍺) with a deep hazy bronze color, medium body, and soft smooth caramel flavors. Of the seasonals, Cabin Fever (🍺🍺🍺🍺) is a light Belgian Tripel with a strong flower nose, cloudy orange body, strong malty flavor, and warm, sweet finish. A few other New Glarus beers include Celtic Stout, Copper Kettle Weisse, Edel-Pils, Extra Pale Totally Naked, Hop Hearty Ale, Norski Honey Bock, Snowshoe Ale, Solstice Wheat, and Staghorn Oktoberfest. New Glarus also makes the popular Wisconsin Belgian Red (🍺🍺🍺), which has won a number of national and international awards. Known for its strong, fruity, cherry flavors, it is purchased in a 750-milliliter bottle that is sealed with distinctive red wax.

MENU

None. This is a brewery.

Route 66 Brewery & Restaurant

St. Louis, Missouri

Visit Date	Signed

ABOUT THE BREWERY

The famous Route 66 passed through St. Louis, Missouri, and brought many a traveler to the "Gateway to the West" as they followed the winding road from Chicago to Los Angeles. Route 66 Brewery and Restaurant isn't actually on the old Route 66 in St. Louis; in 2000 it moved from a previous location, which was on the route (Watson Road), in southwest St. Louis. It is now located in a very memorable location, calling St. Louis's old Union Station its home. The brewery is at the main entrance of this grand, ornate building, which was once one of the busiest rail terminals in the United States. The brewery's fermenters actually stand inside the cathedral-like center of Union Station and greet beer lovers as they enter the brewpub. Black-and-white paintings, photos, postcards, memorabilia, and even a map adorn the pub's walls to tell the story of Route 66. Focal points of the brewpub are its green tiled ceiling and the gray-and-white-checkered tile floor in the main bar. Route 66 Brewery and Restaurant was started in 1998 by Rao Palamand, a twenty-three-year veteran of Anheuser-Busch and student of the Institute of Brewing in London.

BEERS

The Munich Lager (🍺🍺🍺🍺) has a clean aroma and taste, medium body, assertive malty tones, and warm finish. The River City Red Ale (🍺🍺🍺) has no aroma, an amber to brown color, a thick, bubbly, tan head, a creamy soft texture, bold malty flavor, and a sweet finish. The Mile Marker Amber Lager (🍺🍺🍺) offers a light malty nose, amber color, malty dominance, and a fruity background and finish. One of Route 66's best sellers is the Lakeshore Light

(🍺🍺🍺), which is brewed with two-row barley and wheat malts and bittered with Perle and Tettnag hops. The seasonal Maple Stout (🍺🍺🍺🍺) is dark and full bodied, with solid caramel malty flavor and a warm maple finish. Other Route 66 beers include the American ESB and Scottish Ale. Seasonals include the Imperial Pale Ale, Rambling Raspberry Ale, Streamline Oatmeal Stout, Continental Wheat Ale, and the Classic Blonde Ale.

MENU

Route 66 offers more than mere pub food. You can expect hearty dishes with entrees like bison meatloaf, sirloin strip steak, grilled chicken pasta, and jambalaya. There are also some trendy selections with names such as martini chicken and tequila lime chicken.

Schlafly Tap Room
St. Louis, Missouri

Visit Date	Signed

ABOUT THE BREWERY

Okay, this is my favorite Missouri brewpub. It's worth the trip to St. Louis all by itself—even if you're driving from Wisconsin! Schlafly has all the things that make a perfect pint in my book: a renovated building with local history, a diverse but Midwestern menu, and an overall focus on, if not celebration of, beer. Established in 1991, Schlafly (also known as the Schlafly and St. Louis Tap Room and the St. Louis Brewery), is located in the historic Swift Printing Building, which was constructed in 1902. The building and the neighborhood were nearly destroyed by a devastating 1976 fire that engulfed all four corners of Locust and 21st Streets. Much of the area sat vacant though the late 1970s and 1980s. In its dilapidated state it made a brief appearance in John Carpenter's 1981 action film, *Escape from New York,* with Kurt Russell. When Schlafly opened in December 1991, it was Missouri's first brewpub. Opening in the backyard of Anheuser-Busch was no simple matter. Schlafly was the state's test case for revised legislation that lifted restrictions on production and off-premises sales, enabling the brewery to bottle and distribute. But what makes Schlafly great is the commitment to beer, with more than thirty styles throughout a year. Schlafly does bottle about six of its beers. Bottling was done at the August Schell Brewery in New Ulm, Minnesota, but in 2003 Schlafly opened a local production facility in Maplewood. Schlafly also ventured into the D concourse at Lambert International Airport in 2002. And, even though I don't make it to St. Louis as often as I would like to enjoy Schlafly beer, every time I walk into the bar, it just feels like a neighborhood tavern. Schlafly is always the first place I mention when friends ask me for recommendations about St. Louis beer and food.

BEERS

You will find ten or more beers on tap for any visit to Schlafly. The Pale Ale (🍺🍺🍺🍺) has a crisp hoppy flavor, with a golden to copper color, thin tan head, and medium body. The unfiltered Hefeweizen (🍺🍺🍺🍺) has a cloudy light yellow color, fruity nose, light texture, and strong banana and clove tones. The Pilsner (🍺🍺🍺🍺) has a lot of individual character; it has a crisp resiny nose, a deep clear golden body, and thick, soft, white head, with an assertive malty beginning and crisp dry hoppy background. The Oatmeal Stout (🍺🍺🍺🍺) offers a malty nose and very dark thick appearance; it is full-bodied with a dry malty body and a lightly bitter and dry finish. While most brewpubs refer to their brewmasters' specials as seasonals, Schlafly offers enough to be considered monthly specials. Each month may have three to five new beers, in addition to regular taps. Yes, you'll also find the normal calendar seasonals, such as Oktoberfest and Maibock. Some of those monthly beers include Smoked Porter, Dopplebock, Belgian Dubbel, Welsch Ale, Irish Stout, Munich Dunkel, Weissbier, Dortmunder, Witbier, IPA, Nut Brown Ale, and Imperial Stout. For me, Schlafly's most special beer is the December-released Belgian Trippel (🍺🍺🍺🍺), with its deep golden color, thin white head, and rich sweet fruity character— this exceptional beer meets the definition of the perfect pint!

MENU

For starters you have choices that include house-made pretzel sticks, peel-and-eat shrimp, Tap Room pâté, goat cheese rarebit, pickled herring, and the English ploughman's plate, which makes a great dish for friends to share. The beer cheese soup is made with the pub's Pale Ale. There are both hot and cold sandwiches. The main entrees offer tough choices such as Tap Room meat pie, Pilsner lamb sausage pasta, chicken andouille pasta, and Wiener schnitzel. The garlic mashed potatoes make a great complement to a steak or burger. Finishing the meal is a perfect opportunity to try the sticky toffee pudding matched with Schlafly's Oatmeal Stout.

Trailhead Brewing Company
St. Charles, Missouri

Visit Date	Signed

ABOUT THE BREWERY

"Trailhead" in this brewery's name refers to the three western trails that originated in St. Charles, Missouri: the route of Lewis and Clark's expedition; the Boone's Lick Trail, which connected to the Oregon and Santa Fe trails; and the Katy Trail, which connected Missouri with Kansas and Texas. Trailhead Brewing is located in a renovated gristmill in historic Old St. Charles. It's just a short walk to the banks of the Missouri River. The brewpub has a multilevel design that offers four levels of seating. Inside the decor features exposed brickwork, wood, and stainless steel. Over the bar hangs a cedar strip canoe, and above the bar seating is a seven-seat bicycle. There is also an outside patio. Trailhead Brewing was established in 1995. The nearby Lewis and Clark's American Restaurant and Public House is also part of the same ownership. There is also a Trailhead Brewing tavern in the B concourse at Lambert International Airport in St. Louis.

BEERS

The Missouri Brown Dark Ale (🍺🍺🍺) is a full-bodied beer with lots of flavor; it has a malty sweet nose, deep reddish-brown color, and memorable caramel flavor, with a lightly roasted finish. The Old Courthouse Porter (🍺🍺🍺🍺) makes a nice pairing with the smoked baby back ribs, offers a clean nose, deep dark color and tan bubbly head, a medium round body, and smooth chocolate malt dominance. The Pale Ale (🍺🍺🍺) has a light to medium body, a crisp hoppy bite that overall has a very clean taste without much finish. The seasonal Winter Ale (🍺🍺🍺🍺) is a special treat with its vivid copper color, smooth malty flavor, and warm finish. Other Trailhead beers include the Old Courthouse Stout, Riverboat Raspberry, Trailblazer Blond Ale, and Trailhead Rainbow Red Amber Ale.

MENU

The Trailhead Brewing menu is very much American cuisine. You'll find sandwiches, burgers, soups, salads, pizzas, and a variety of house specialties that
are prepared with a wood-fired smoker. Among the entrées are ale-battered
fish and chips, smoked baby back ribs, prime rib, a hot beef or portabello
sandwich, and a sausage platter with slow-smoked bratwurst, knockwurst,
and weisswurst.

Upper Mississippi Brewing Company

Clinton, Iowa

Visit Date	Signed

ABOUT THE BREWERY

Located in the old Clinton Paper Company building, Upper Mississippi Brewing makes a great stop along a scenic Mississippi River drive. The brewery opened in May 2000 in a building that was constructed in 1909 on the eastern edge of downtown Clinton, not much more than a block from the river. Inside, the east and west walls are brick, which helps maintain the old working industrial feel. The bar, main dining room, and brewhaus are all separated by interior glass walls. Local history is kept alive with a great collection of old black-and-white photos that provide a glimpse of the Clinton riverfront, as seen in the old paddle wheelers, the *W. W. Washer* and *High Bridge*. Look closely because among those photos on the far west wall, you'll find images of the Western Brewery and the Clinton Brewing Company.

BEERS

The Hefeweizen (🍺🍺🍺🍺) offers an inviting banana nose, a cloudy deep yellow color, medium soft body, and lots of banana and bubble gum tones with a subtle but very evident light smoky finish. The Bartels & Lager (🍺🍺🍺🍺) has no aroma but a clean sharp crisp hoppy tone makes for a firm, hoppy light-bodied lager. The Mullin Brown (🍺🍺🍺) is a very memorable beer with its roasted nose, reddish brown body, tan bubbly head, light texture, and strong caramel malty flavor with a crisp dry background and finish. But my favorite is the Cherek

Cream Stout (🍺🍺🍺🍺), which was perfect after a cold, cloudy winter day of driving the Mississippi River valley. This stout offers a strong aggressive malty nose, clear but very dark color, medium bodied and soft texture, and loads of chocolate malt. It finishes with a smooth roasted aftertaste. Other Upper Mississippi brews include the Pale Pale Boss Ale, Mudcat Stout, and the Hannan Blue, with its smooth blueberry sweetness.

MENU

The Upper Mississippi Brewing Company has a full range of salads, pastas, sandwiches, and steaks. The menu offers a lot of diversity that makes choosing difficult. Appetizers feature some basic pub style starters such as poppers, nachos, wings, and white cheddar cheese nuggets. Sandwiches include a tenderloin, Reuben, eight-ounce pub burger, and the sliced prime rib called the Bridge Sandwich. You'll also find chicken and mushroom pasta, shrimp imperial, and the Rajun Cajun, which is a sautéed chicken breast. The entrees offer pork loin chops, ribeyes, and New York strips.

BEER TASTINGS AND FESTIVALS

BOOKS ABOUT BEER, BREWERIES, AND BREWPUBS

WEB SITES ABOUT BEER, BREWERIES, AND BREWPUBS

DIRECTORY OF ILLINOIS BREWERIES AND BREWPUBS

DIRECTORY OF JUST OVER THE BORDER BREWERIES AND BREWPUBS

BEER STYLES

INDEX

Beer Tastings and Festivals

Attending a beer festival or a beer tasting is an excellent way to discover some of Illinois's best beers. Such events occur all around the state, and many occur annually. Before leaving, it's always a good idea to check a few Web sites or even call the local chamber of commerce to confirm date, time, location, driving directions, cost, and phone numbers for more information. Dates, sponsors, and other details can change.

While the list that follows is by no means all-inclusive, it offers some ideas on which events to watch for. Also included are a few regional and national events that could be of interest depending upon where you live and how much you like to travel. Many Illinois breweries and brewpubs will hold their own special events that feature tastings and brewmaster dinners, so it's best to call the brewery directly and ask about upcoming events. Because phone numbers and specific event addresses can change from year to year, try using the Internet by typing in the event name and city for exact dates, locations, and contact information.

ALTAMONT
Schuetzenfest — September

BELLEVILLE
Breweriana Blowout — April

CHICAGO AREA
Berghoff Annual Oktoberfest — September
Blues and Brews Cruise — August
Chicago Beer Society's Annual Spring Beer Tasting and Dinner — May
Chicago Beer Society's Annual Fall Beer Tasting and Dinner — November
Chicagoland Brewpub-Microbrewery Shootout — January
Goose Island's Annual Czech Beer Festival — October
May Fest Chicago German Celebration — May
Planet Buzz Mead and Cider Festival — November
Real Ale Festival — March
Southside Whiskey Barrel Brew-in and St. Patrick's Day Parade — March
Summer Beer Festival by Illinois Craft Brewers Guild — July
Urban Knaves of Grain Annual Train Crawl — February
WhiskeyFest-Chicago — March

DAVENPORT, IOWA
Brew-Ha-Ha — September

DES MOINES, IOWA
Brewfest   August

DOWNERS GROVE
Annual Spring Brewer's Festival   May

ELGIN
Prairie Rock's Annual Beer Festival   June

ELK GROVE VILLAGE
Breweriana Show   March

INDIANAPOLIS, INDIANA
Indiana Microbrewers Festival   August

IOWA CITY, IOWA
Brew Fest   September

LIBERTYVILLE
Brewers on the Bluff Febfest   February

MADISON, WISCONSIN
Great Taste of the Midwest   August
Quivey's Grove Beer Festival   October

MILWAUKEE, WISCONSIN
Food and Froth   February
Blessing of the Bock   March
Prosit and Paddle Canoe Race   June
Germanfest   July
Oktoberfest   September
Louie's Last Regatta, Milwaukee Ale House   October

MONROE, WISCONSIN
Monroe Oktoberfest   October

NEW GLARUS, WISCONSIN
New Glarus Beer Fest   February
New Glarus Oktoberfest   October

PALATINE
Annual Northwest Suburban Beer Festival   April

PEORIA
International Beer Festival   March

ST. LOUIS, MISSOURI
HOP in the City Beer Festival   September

URBANA
Annual International Beer Tasting and Chili Cook-off   October

VICTORIA, BRITISH COLUMBIA
The Great Canadian Beer Festival   November

WARRENVILLE
Rock Bottom Brewfest   June

YPSILANTI, MICHIGAN
Michigan Brewers Guild Annual Summer Beer Festival   July

Books about Beer, Breweries, and Brewpubs

Apps, Jerry. *Breweries of Wisconsin.* Madison: University of Wisconsin Press, 1992.

Asbury, Herbert. *Gem of the Prairie: An Informal History of the Chicago Underworld.* Garden City, New York: Garden City Publishing Company, 1942. Republished by Northern Illinois University Press, 1986.

Association of Brewers, comp. *Evaluating Beer.* Boulder, Colorado: Brewers Publications, 1993.

Beaumont, Stephen. *The Great Canadian Beer Guide.* Toronto, Ontario, Canada: McArthur and Company, 2002.

Beaumont, Stephen. *A Taste for Beer.* Pownal, Vermont: Storey Publishing, 1995.

Beaumont, Stephen. *Premium Beer Drinker's Guide: The World's Strongest, Boldest and Most Unusual Beers.* Buffalo, New York: Firefly Books, 2000.

Bice, John. *Tap into the Great Lakes.* Holt, Michigan: Thunder Bay Press. 1999.

Dikty, Alan S., ed. *The Beverage Testing Institute's Buying Guide to Spirits.* New York: Sterling Publishing, 1999.

Dornan, Marc, ed. *The Beverage Testing Institute's Buying Guide to Beer.* New York: Sterling Publishing, 1999.

Eckhardt, Fred. *Essentials of Beer Style: A Catalog of Classic Beer Styles for Brewers and Beer Enthusiasts.* Portland, Oregon: Fred Eckhardt Communications, 1989.

Glover, Brian. *The Complete Guide to Beer.* (Original Title: *The World Encyclopedia of Beer.*) New York: Anness Publishing, 2000.

Hieronymus, Stan, Michael Jackson, and Daria Labinsky. *The Beer Lover's Guide to the USA: Brewpubs, Taverns, and Good Beer Bars.* New York: St. Martin's, Griffin, 2000.

Jackson, Michael. *The Simon & Schuster Pocket Guide to Beer.* New York: Simon & Schuster, Fireside, 1996.

Jackson, Michael. *Michael Jackson's Beer Companion: The World's Great Beer Styles, Gastronomy, and Traditions.* 2d ed. Philadelphia: Courage Books/Running Press Publishers, 2000.

Jackson, Michael. *Michael Jackson's Pocket Beer Book.* United Kingdom: Mitchell Beazley, 2000.

Jackson, Michael. *The New World Guide to Beer.* Philadelphia: Running Press, 1997.

Jackson, Michael. *Ultimate Beer.* New York: DK Publishing, 1998.

Lamoureux, Debbie. *A History of Brewing in Thornton, Illinois.* Thornton, Illinois: Village of Thornton Historical Society, 2001.

Lindberg, Richard. *To Serve and Collect: Chicago Politics and Police Corruption from the Lager Beer Riot to the Summerdale Scandal, 1855–1960.* Carbondale: Southern Illinois University Press, 1998.

Mercer, Todd Bryant. *Bike & Brew American: Midwest Region.* Boulder, Colorado: Brewers Publications, 2001.

Nachel, Marty. *Beer across America: A Regional Guide to Brewpubs and Microbreweries.* Pownal, Vermont: Storey Publishing, 1995.

Nachel, Marty, and Steve Ettlinger. *Beer for Dummies.* New York: IDG Books, 1996.

Ogg, Bryan J. *Peoria Spirits.* Peoria, Illinois: Peoria Historical Society, 1996.

Papazian, Charlie. *The New Complete Joy of Home Brewing.* New York: Avon Books, 1991.

Protz, Roger. *The Taste of Beer.* New York: Sterling Publishing Company Inc., 2000.

Protz, Roger. *The Ultimate Encyclopedia of Beer.* London: Carlton Books, 1998.

Protz, Roger. *The World Beer Guide.* London: Carlton Books, 2000.

Rabin, Dan, comp., and Carl Forget, ed. *Dictionary of Beer and Brewing.* Boulder, Colorado: Brewers Publications, 1998.

Rhodes, Christine P., ed. *The Encyclopedia of Beer.* New York: Henry Holt, 1997.

Robertson, James D. *The Beer-Taster's Log: A World Guide to More Than 6000 Beers.* Pownal, Vermont: Storey Publishing, 1996.

Skilnik, Bob. *The History of Beer and Brewing in Chicago, 1833–1978.* St. Paul, Minnesota: Pogo Press, 1999.

Skilnik, Bob. *The History of Beer and Brewing in Chicago, volume 2.* Haverford, Pennsylvania: Infinity Publishing, 2001.

Shepard, Robin. *Wisconsin's Best Breweries and Brewpubs.* Madison: University of Wisconsin Press, 2001.

Smith, Gregg. *The Beer Enthusiast's Guide: Tasting and Judging Brews from around the World.* Pownal, Vermont: Storey Publishing, 1994.

Smith, Gregg. *Beer in America: The Early Years, 1587–1840.* Boulder, Colorado: Siris Books, 1998.

Sneath, Allen Winn. *Brewed in Canada: The Untold Story of Canada's 350-Year-Old Brewing Industry.* Toronto, Ontario, Canada: Dundurn Group, 2001.

Wood, Heather, comp. *The Beer Directory: An International Guide.* Pownal, Vermont: Storey Publishing, 1995.

Web Sites about Beer, Breweries, and Brewpubs

BEER RATING AND GENERAL BEER INFORMATION

American Brewery History Page: www.beerhistory.com
American Homebrewers Association:
    www.beertown.org/homebrewing/about.html
Associated Beer Distributors of Illinois: www.abdi.org
B Is for Beer: www.BisforBeer.com
BeerAdvocate: www.beeradvocate.com
Beer Books: www.beerbooks.com
Beer Expedition: www.beerexpedition.com
The Beer Info Source, Virtual Library of Beer and Brewing: www.beerinfo.com
Beer Judge Certification Program: www.mv.com/ipusers/slack/bjcp
Beer Lovers World: www.beer-lover.com
Beerme (database of beers and breweries): www.beerme.com
Beertown, Home of the Association of Brewers: www.beertown.org
Beer Travelers: www.beertravelers.com
Beverage Testing Institute (BTI): www.tastings.com
The Brewery, Total Homebrewing Information: www.brewery.org
BrewPubZone: www.brewpubzone.com
BrewsTraveler Guides: www.brewstraveler.com
Chicago Beer History: www.chicagolandbeerhistory.com
Chicago Beer Society: www.chibeer.org
Indiana State Fair's Brewer's Cup Competition: www.hbd.org/indiana
Iowa Brewpub and Brewery Information: www.beerstuff.com/ibg
Marcobrau Beer Pages (Chicago & Illinois): www.marcobrau.com
Michael Jackson's The Beer Hunter, World Guide to Beer:
    www.beerhunter.com
Michigan Beer Guide: www.michiganbeerguide.com/beerguide.asp
Minnesota Home Brewers Association: www.mnbrewers.com
Museum of Beer & Brewing: www.brewingmuseum.org
Pubcrawler: www.pubcrawler.com
RateBeer: www.ratebeer.com
The Real Beer Page: www.realbeer.com
The Real Beer Page Events Calendar: www.realbeer.com/search/eventscalendar
Siebel Institute of Technology: www.siebelinstitute.com
Stephen Beaumont's World of Beer: www.worldofbeer.com

BREWERS' GUILDS

American Brewers Guild: www.abgbrew.com
Brewers of Central Kentucky (B.O.C.K.): www.hbd.org/bock/
Indiana Brewers Guild: www.theoysterbar.com/guild.htm
Iowa Brewers Guild: www.beerstuff.com/ibg/
Michigan Brewers Guild: www.michiganbrewersguild.org
Minnesota Craft Brewer's Guild: www.mncraftbrew.org

BEER NEWSPAPERS AND MAGAZINES

Ale Street News: www.alestreetnews.com
All About Beer: www.allaboutbeer.com
American Brewer: www.ambrew.com
Beer Notes: www.beernotes.com
Brewing News: www.brewingnews.com
BrewingTechniques: www.brewingtechniques.com
Brew Your Own: www.byo.com
The Celebrator Beer News: www.celebrator.com
Cream City Suds: www.creamcitysuds.com

ILLINOIS HOMEBREW CLUB WEB SITES

ABNORMAL [Association of Bloomington/Normal Brewers]:
    www.hbd.org/abnormal/
B.a.b.b.l.e! [Brewers Association of Beer and Beverage Libations Extraordinare]
    (Grayslake): www.babble.freeservers.com
B.O.B. [Brewers on the Bluff] (Lake Bluff): www.clubbob.org
B.O.S.S. [Brewers Of South Suburbia] (Crete):
    http://members.core.com/~bethke/boss/
Brew Rats (Oak Park): www.brewrats.org
B.U.Z.Z. [Boneyard Union of Zymurgical Zealots] (Urbana):
    www.uiuc.edu/ro/BUZZ/
Chicago Beer Society (La Grange Park): www.chibeer.org
Club Wort (Palatine): www.clubwort.org
Forest City Brewers (Rockton): www.drink.to/fcb
Headhunters Brewing Club (Sugar Grove):
    www.bigscary.com/headhunter.php3
Quincy Braumeisters HomeBrew Club (Quincy): www.letsbrew.com
Urban Knaves of Grain (Warrenville): http://hbd.org/ukg

TOURISM

Chicago Convention and Tourism Bureau: www.choosechicago.com
Eastern Iowa Tourism Association: www.easterniowatourism.org
Illinois Department of Commerce and Community Affairs:
    www.enjoyillinois.com
Indiana Tourism Division, Department of Commerce: www.in.gov/enjoyindiana
Iowa Tourism Office: www.traveliowa.com
Kentucky Department of Travel: www.kytourism.com

Missouri Tourism Commission: www.missouritourism.org
Northwest Indiana Guide: www.northwestindiana.com
St. Louis, City of: www.stlouis.missouri.org/tourism
Travel Michigan, Economic Development Corporation:
    http://travel.michigan.org
West Michigan Tourist Association: www.wmta.org
Wisconsin Department of Tourism: www.tourism.state.wi.us
Wisconsin Festivals and Events Association: www.wfea.com
Wisconsin's Directory of Attractions: www.wistravel.com
    (brewery directory at www.wistravel.com/breweries.htm)

Directory of Illinois Breweries and Brewpubs

AURORA

America's Brewing Company and Walter Payton's Roundhouse

205 North Broadway
Aurora, IL 60505
GPS Coordinates: N 41°45'37.36"
 W 088°18'32.14"
Web site:
 www.auroraroundhouse.com or
 www.paytonsroundhouse.com
E-mail:
 miker@auroraroundhouse.com
Telephone: 1-630-264-BREW
 (2739) or 1-630-892-0034
Established Brewing Operations:
 1994
Gift Shop: yes
Mug Club: none
Homebrew Club: no official
 connection
Growlers: yes
Tours: yes
Tasting: yes
Bottling/Distribution: yes, but limited
Bar Toys: assorted in other
 roundhouse bars
Bar Stools: 20
Beer Garden/Outside Seating: yes
Tourism: Aurora Convention and
 Visitors Bureau, 1-800-477-
 4369 (www.enjoyaurora.com,
 www.ci.aurora.il.us, and
 www.aurorachamber.com)

BLOOMINGTON

Illinois Brewing Company

102 North Center Street
Bloomington, IL 61701
GPS Coordinates: N 40°28'42.74"
 W 088°59'42.75"
Web site: www.illinoisbrewing.com
E-mail: not available
Telephone: 1-309-829-2805
Established Brewing Operations:
 2000
Gift Shop: yes
Mug Club: none
Homebrew Club: no official club
 connection, but it is also a
 homebrew supply store
Growlers: yes
Tours: yes
Tasting: yes
Bottling/Distribution: none
Bar Toys: pool table, dart boards,
 video games
Bar Stools: 28
Beer Garden/Outside Seating: none
Tourism: Bloomington-Normal Area
 Convention and Visitors
 Bureau, 1-800-433-8226 or
 1-309-829-1641
 (www.visitbloomingtonnormal.
 org)

CARBONDALE

Copper Dragon Brewing Company and Pinch Penny Pub

700 East Grand Avenue
Carbondale, IL 62901
GPS Coordinates: N 37°43'05.70"
 W 089°12'25.02"
Web site: not available
E-mail: jimmygk9@aol.com

Telephone: 1-618-549-3348
Established Brewing Operations:
  1996
Gift Shop: yes
Mug Club: none
Homebrew Club: no official
  connection
Growlers: yes
Tours: yes
Tasting: yes
Bottling/Distribution: yes, southern
  Illinois
Bar Toys: video games
Bar Stools: 28 in the Pinch Penny
  Pub
Beer Garden/Outside Seating: yes
Tourism: Carbondale Convention
  and Tourism Bureau, 1-800-
  526-1500 (www.cctb.org); City
  of Carbondale, 1-618-549-
  5302 (www.ci.carbondale.il.us)

CHICAGO
Goose Island Beer
Company–Clybourn Avenue
1800 North Clybourn Avenue
Chicago, IL 60614
GPS Coordinates: N 41°54'48.52"
  W 087°39'15.33"
Web site: www.gooseisland.com
E-mail: info@gooseisland.com
Telephone: 1-312-915-0071
Established Brewing Operations:
  1988
Gift Shop: yes
Mug Club: none
Homebrew Club: Chicago Beer
  Society
Growlers: yes
Tours: yes
Tasting: yes
Bottling/Distribution: yes, regionally
  in the Midwest
Bar Toys: pool tables and video
  games
Bar Stools: 24

Beer Garden/Outside Seating: yes
Tourism: The Lincoln Park Chamber
  of Commerce, 1-773-880-5200
  (www.lincolnparkchamber.com);
  Chicago Convention and
  Tourism Bureau, 1-877-
  CHICAGO or 1-312-567-8500
  (www.choosechicago.com);
  City of Chicago,
  1-877-CHICAGO or
  1-312-742-1084 (www.city-
  ofchicago.org/tourism)

Goose Island Beer
Company–Wrigleyville
3535 North Clark Street
Chicago, IL 60657
GPS Coordinates: N 41°56'47.61"
  W 087°39'21.09"
Web site: www.gooseisland.com
E-mail: info@gooseisland.com
Telephone: 1-773-832-9040
Established Brewing Operations:
  1999
Gift Shop: yes
Mug Club: no
Homebrew Club: no official
  connection
Growlers: yes
Tours: yes
Tasting: yes
Bottling/Distribution: yes, regionally
  in the Midwest
Bar Toys: video games
Bar Stools: 18
Beer Garden/Outside Seating: yes
Tourism: Lakeview Chamber of
  Commerce, 1-773-472-7171
  (www.LakeviewChamber.com);
  the Northcenter Chamber of
  Commerce, 1-773-525-3609
  (www.northcenterchamber.com);
  Chicago Convention and
  Tourism Bureau, 1-877-
  CHICAGO or 1-312-567-8500
  (www.choosechicago.com);

City of Chicago, 1-877-
CHICAGO or 1-312-742-1084
(www.cityofchicago.org/tourism)

Piece
1927 West North Avenue
Chicago, IL 60622
GPS Coordinates: N 41°54'37.69"
W 087°40'34.21"
Web site: not available
E-mail: not available
Telephone: 1-773-772-4422
Established Brewing Operations:
2001
Gift Shop: yes
Mug Club: none
Homebrew Club: no official
connection
Growlers: yes
Tours: yes
Tasting: yes
Bottling/Distribution: no
Bar Toys: none
Bar Stools: 15
Beer Garden/Outside Seating: no
Tourism: Wicker Park and Bucktown
Chamber of Commerce, 1-773-
384-2672 or 1-773-384-2699
(www.wickerparkbucktown.com)

**Rock Bottom Restaurant and
Brewery**
One West Grand Avenue
Chicago, IL 60610
GPS Coordinates: N 41°53'29.58"
W 087°37'41.95"
Web site: www.rockbottom.com
E-mail:
operations@rockbottom.com
Telephone: 1-312-755-9339
Established Brewing Operations:
1995
Gift Shop: yes
Mug Club: yes
Homebrew Club: no official
connection
Growlers: yes
Tours: yes

Tasting: yes
Bottling/Distribution: none
Bar Toys: pool tables and about 20
televisions throughout the
brewpub
Bar Stools: 18
Beer Garden/Outside Seating: yes,
rooftop beer garden
Tourism: Chicago Convention and
Tourism Bureau, 1-877-
CHICAGO or 1-312-567-8500
(www.choosechicago.com);
City of Chicago, 1-877-
CHICAGO or 1-312-742-1084
(www.cityofchicago.org/tourism)

DOWNERS GROVE
**Founders Hill Restaurant and
Brewery**
5200 Main Street
Downers Grove, Illinois 60515
GPS Coordinates: N 41°47'58.74"
W 087°58'13.98"
Web site: not available
E-mail: not available
Telephone:
1-630-963-BREW (2739)
Established Brewing Operations:
1996
Gift Shop: yes
Mug Club: yes
Homebrew Club: no official
connection
Growlers: yes
Tours: yes
Tasting: yes
Bottling/Distribution: no
Bar Toys: upstairs billiards lounge,
dart board
Bar Stools: 15
Beer Garden/Outside Seating: yes
Tourism: Downers Grove Area
Chamber of Commerce and
Industry, 1-630-968-4050
(www.downersgrove.org);
Village of Downers Grove,

1-800-934-0615
(www.vil.downers-grove.il.us)

ELGIN
Prairie Rock Brewing Company
127 South Grove Avenue
Elgin, IL 60120
GPS Coordinates: N 42°02'04.52"
W 088°16'54.84"
Web site: www.prairierock
brewingcompany.com
E-mail: Triclamp@msn.com
Telephone: 1-847-622-8888
Established Brewing Operations:
1995
Gift Shop: yes
Mug Club: yes
Homebrew Club: no official
connection
Growlers: yes
Tours: yes
Tasting: yes
Bottling/Distribution: no
Bar Toys: dart boards, a video golf
game
Bar Stools: 20
Beer Garden/Outside Seating: yes
Tourism: Elgin Area Convention and
Visitors Bureau, 1-800-217-
5362 (www.enjoyelgin.com);
City of Elgin 1-847-931-5615
(www.cityofelgin.org)

ELMWOOD
**Elmwood Brewing Company and
Parkview Restaurant**
118 East Main Street
Elmwood, IL 62529-0057
GPS Coordinates: N 40°46'41.23"
W 089°57'55.36"
Web site: not available
E-mail: potts@elmnet.net
Telephone: 1-309-742-4200
Established Brewing Operations:
2001
Gift Shop: yes

Mug Club: no
Homebrew Club: Peoria and
Galesburg Clubs
Growlers: yes
Tours: yes
Tasting: yes
Bottling/Distribution: yes, Galesburg,
Peoria, and Bloomington area
Bar Toys: none
Bar Stools: 8
Beer Garden/Outside Seating: no
Tourism: Elmwood Association of
Commerce, 1-309-742-8878
or 1-309-742-8643

FLOSSMOOR
**Flossmoor Station Restaurant and
Brewery**
1035 Sterling Avenue
Flossmoor, IL 60422
GPS Coordinates: N 41°32'36.13"
W 087°40'43.53"
Web site:
www.flossmoorstation.com
E-mail: info@flossmoorstation.com
Telephone:
1-708-957-BREW (2739)
Established Brewing Operations:
1996
Gift Shop: yes
Mug Club: no
Homebrew Club Connections:
Chicago Beer Society and the
Brewers of South Surburbia
(B.O.S.S.)
Growlers: yes
Tours: yes
Tasting: yes
Bottling/Distribution: no
Bar Toys: video trivia game
Bar Stools: 15
Beer Garden/Outside Seating: yes
Tourism: Village of Flossmoor,
1-708-798-2300
(www.flossmoor.org) or
(www.lincolnnet.net/users/

lmflssmr); Chicago Southland
Convention and Visitors Bureau,
1-888-895-8233
(www.cscvb.com/calendar.cfm)

GLEN ELLYN
Glen Ellyn Sports Brew
433 North Main Street
Glen Ellyn, IL 60137
GPS Coordinates: N 41°52'31.29"
W 088°03'59.72"
Web site: not available
E-mail:
ryan@glenellynbrewingco.com
Telephone: 1-630-942-1140
Established Brewing Operations:
1996
Gift Shop: yes
Mug Club: yes
Homebrew Club: no official
connection
Growlers: yes
Tours: yes
Tasting: yes
Bottling/Distribution: yes, keg distri-
bution in limited area
Bar Toys: none
Bar Stools: 10
Beer Garden/Outside Seating: no
Tourism: Glen Ellyn Chamber of
Commerce 1-630-469-0907
(www.glenellynchamber.com);
Glen Ellyn Community Profile
(www.glen-ellyn.com)

LAKE BARRINGTON
Onion Pub and Brewery
22221 Pepper Road
Lake Barrington, IL 60010
GPS Coordinates: N 42°11'10.89"
W 088°11'04.34"
Web site: www.onionpub.com
E-mail: not available
Telephone: 1-847-381-7308
Established Brewing Operations:

2003 as the Onion Pub and
Brewery; 1997 as the Wild
Onion Brewing Company
Gift Shop: yes
Mug Club: none
Homebrew Club: no official
connection
Growlers: yes
Tours: yes
Tasting: yes
Bottling/Distribution: no
Bar Toys: none
Bar Stools: 20
Beer Garden/Outside Seating: yes
Tourism: Barrington Area Chamber
of Commerce, 1-847-381-2525
or 1-847-381-2540
(www.barringtonchamber.com);
Lake County, Illinois,
Convention and Visitors
Bureau, 1-800-LAKE-NOW or
1-847-662-2700
(www.lakecounty.org)

LAKE IN THE HILLS
Govnor's Public House Restaurant
and Brewery
220 North Randall Road
Lake in the Hills, IL 60156
GPS Coordinates: N 42°10'39.82"
W 088°20'11.86"
Web site: www.govnors.com
E-mail: ron@govnors.com or
jim@govnors.com
Telephone: 1-847-658-4700
Established Brewing Operations:
2001
Gift Shop: yes
Mug Club: no
Homebrew Club: Midnight Carboys
of the McHenry and Crystal
Lake Areas
Growlers: yes
Tours: yes
Tasting: yes
Bottling/Distribution: no

Bar Toys: video golf , NTN Trivia
Bar Stools: 37
Beer Garden/Outside Seating: yes
Tourism: Village of the Lake in the
Hills, 1-847-658-4213
(www.lith.org); Lake County,
Illinois, Convention and Visitors
Bureau, 1-800-LAKE-NOW
(www.lakecounty.org)

LIBERTYVILLE
Mickey Finn's Brewery
412 North Milwaukee Avenue
Libertyville, IL 60048
GPS Coordinates: N 42°17'14.10"
W 087°57'14.76"
Web site:
www.mickeyfinnsbrewery.com
E-mail:
mickeyfinnsinfo@ameritech.net
Telephone: 1-847-362-6688
Established Brewing Operations:
1994
Gift Shop: yes
Mug Club: yes
Homebrew Club: Brewers on the
Bluff (BOB)
Growlers: yes
Tours: yes
Tasting: yes
Bottling/Distribution: no, ended
bottling in 2002
Bar Toys: video golf
Bar Stools: 20 seats at the main bar
Beer Garden/Outside Seating: yes
Tourism: Lake County, Illinois,
Convention and Visitors Bureau,
1-800-LAKE-NOW or 1-847-
662-2700 (www.lakecounty.org);
IMAGES Magazine, 1-847-680-
0750 (www.glmvmag.com);
Village of Libertyville, 1-847-
362-2430; Libertyville Township,
1-847-816-6800
(township.libertyville.il.us);
Libertyville village profile

(www.villageprofile.com/
illinois/libertyville/index.html)

LINCOLNSHIRE
Flatlander's Restaurant and Brewery
200 Village Green
Lincolnshire, IL 60069
GPS Coordinates: N 42°12'9.61"
W 087°55'51.96"
Web site: www.flatlanders.com
E-mail:
brewmaster@flatlanders.com
Telephone: 1-847-821-1234
Established Brewing Operations:
1996
Gift Shop: yes
Mug Club: no
Homebrew Club: Brewers on the
Bluff (BOB)
Growlers: yes
Tours: yes
Tasting: yes
Bottling/Distribution: yes, on-
premises sales only
Bar Toys: pool table, video games
Bar Stools: 18
Beer Garden/Outside Seating: yes
Tourism: Lake County, Illinois
Convention and Visitors Bureau,
1-800-LAKE-NOW or 1-847-
662-2700 (www.lakecounty.org)

LOMBARD
Taylor Brewing Company
717 East Butterfield Road
Lombard, IL 60148
GPS Coordinates: N 41°50'22.12"
W 087°59'53.88"
Web site: www.taylorbrewing.com
E-mail: not available
Telephone: 1-630-990-8700
Established Brewing Operations:
1994
Gift Shop: yes
Mug Club: no

Homebrew Club: no official
    connection
Growlers: yes
Tours: yes
Tasting: yes
Bottling/Distribution: no
Bar Toys: NTN Trivia
Bar Stools: 35
Beer Garden/Outside Seating:
    none
Tourism: Village of Lombard,
    1-630-620-5700
    (www.villageoflombard.org);
    Lombard village profile
    (www.villageprofile.com/
    illinois/lombard/index.html)

MOLINE
Bent River Brewing Company
1413 5th Avenue
Moline, IL 61265
GPS Coordinates: N 41°30'22.03"
    W 090°31'00.66"
Web site: findusat309.com/
    venues/bentriver.html
E-mail: bentriver@qconline.com or
    TimBo@qconline.com
Telephone: 1-309-797-2722
Established Brewing Operations:
    1997
Gift Shop: yes
Mug Club: yes
Homebrew Club: M.U.G.Z.
    (Mississippi Unquenchable
    Grail Zymurgists)
Growlers: yes
Tours: yes
Tasting: yes
Bottling/Distribution: yes, but limited
Bar Toys: shuffle board, pool table,
    dart board, video games
Bar Stools: 22
Beer Garden/Outside Seating: yes
Tourism: Quad Cities Convention
    and Visitors Bureau, 1-800-
    747-7800 or 1-309-788-7800

(www.visitquadcities.com) or
    (www.moline.il.us)

MORRIS
FireHouse Restaurant and
Brewing Company
124 West Illinois Avenue
Morris, IL 60450
GPS Coordinates: N 41°21'24.22"
    W 088°25'29.10"
Web site:
    www.firehousebrewery.com
E-mail: jroberts@nmu.net
Telephone: 1-815-941-4700
Established Brewing Operations:
    2000
Gift Shop: yes
Mug Club: no
Homebrew Club: no official
    connection
Growlers: yes
Tours: yes
Tasting: yes
Bottling/Distribution: no
Bar Toys: FireHouse Interactive
    Game Center is next door
Bar Stools: 15
Beer Garden/Outside Seating: yes
Tourism: Morris Visitors Center,
    1-815-942-0245 (www.morris
    illinois.com); Grundy County
    Chamber of Commerce and
    Industry, 1-815-942-0113
    (www.grundychamber.com);
    Grundy County Tourism Office,
    1-815-942-6172

MUNSTER, INDIANA
Three Floyds Brewing Company
9750 Indiana Parkway
Munster, IN 46321
GPS Coordinates: N 41°32'7.08"
    W 087°30'58.78"
Web site: www.threefloyds.com
E-mail: alphaking1@msn.com
Telephone: 1-888-266-0294

Established Brewing Operations:
1996
Gift Shop: yes
Mug Club: no
Homebrew Club: no official
connection
Growlers: no
Tours: yes
Tasting: yes
Bottling/Distribution: yes, regionally
in the Midwest
Bar Toys: no
Bar Stools: no bar, just a tasting area
Beer Garden/Outside Seating: no
Tourism: Munster Chamber of
Commerce, 1-219-836-5549;
Munster village profile (www.
villageprofile.com/indiana/
munster/index.html); Lake
County Indiana Convention and
Visitors Bureau, 1-219-989-
7770 or 1-800-ALL-LAKE
(www.alllake.org); Online Guide
for Northwest Indiana
(www.northwestindiana.com/
cities/munster/munster.html)

ORLAND PARK
Harrison's Restaurant and
Brewery
15845 LaGrange Road
Orland Park, IL 60462
GPS Coordinates: N 41°36'11.59"
W 087°51'07.70"
Web site:
www.harrisonsbrewpub.com
E-mail:
info@harrisonsbrewpub.com
Telephone: 1-708-226-0100
Established Brewing Operations:
1997
Gift Shop: yes
Mug Club: no
Homebrew Club: no official
connection
Growlers: yes

Tours: yes
Tasting: yes
Bottling/Distribution: no
Bar Toys: video games
Bar Stools: 20
Beer Garden/Outside Seating: yes
Tourism: Village of Orland Park,
1-708-403-6140 (www.orland
park.il.us); Chicago Southland
Convention and Visitors
Bureau, 1-888-895-8233
(www.cscvb.com/calendar.cfm)

PEORIA
Rhodell Brewery and Bar
619 Water Street
Peoria, IL 61602
GPS Coordinates: N 40°41'07.36"
W 089°35'40.05"
Web site: not available
E-mail: not available
Telephone: 1-309-674-7267
Established Brewing Operations:
1998
Gift Shop: yes
Mug Club: no
Homebrew Club: Homebrewers of
Peoria (HOPS), and it is also a
homebrew supply store
Growlers: yes
Tours: yes
Tasting: yes
Bottling/Distribution: no
Bar Toys: pool table
Bar Stools: 10
Beer Garden/Outside Seating: yes
Tourism: Peoria Area Convention
and Visitors Bureau, 1-800-
747-0302 or 1-309-672-2860
(www.peoria.org)

QUINCY
O'Griff's Irish Pub and Brew
House
415 Hampshire Street
Quincy, IL 62301

GPS Coordinates: N 39°55'59.26"
W 091°24'33.58"
Web site: www.ogriffs.com
E-mail: griffin@adams.net
Telephone: 1-217-224-2002
Established Brewing Operations:
2001
Gift Shop: yes
Mug Club: no
Homebrew Club: River City
Brewmasters of Quincy
Growlers: yes
Tours: yes
Tasting: yes
Bottling/Distribution: no
Bar Toys: pool tables, video
games, dart board
Bar Stools: 12
Beer Garden/Outside Seating: no
Tourism: Quincy Convention and
Visitors Bureau, 1-800-97-VISIT
(1-800-978-4748) (www.quincy-
cvb.org)

RICHMOND
J.W. Platek's Restaurant and Brewery
8609 Highway 12 (Intersection of
Routes 12 and 31)
Richmond, IL 60071
GPS Coordinates: N 42°27'4.93"
W 088°18'21.74"
Web site: www.plateks.com
E-mail: jamesplatek@rsg.org
Telephone: 1-815-678-4078
Established Brewing Operations:
1997
Gift Shop: no
Mug Club: no
Homebrew Club: no official
connection
Growlers: yes
Tours: no
Tasting: yes
Bottling/Distribution: no
Bar Toys: none

Bar Stools: 10
Beer Garden/Outside Seating: no
Tourism: Village of Richmond, 1-815-
678-4040 (www.richmond-
il.com); Richmond/Spring Grove
Chamber of Commerce, 1-815-
678-7742; McHenry County
(www.mchenryonline.com)

ROCKFORD
Carlyle Brewing Company
215 East State Street
Rockford, IL 61104
GPS Coordinates: N42°16'8.65"
W 089°5'25.65"
Web site: not available
E-mail:
carlylebrewing@hotmail.com
Telephone: 1-815-963-2739
Established Brewing Operations:
2002
Gift Shop: yes
Mug Club: none
Homebrew Club: no official
connection
Growlers: yes
Tours: yes
Tasting: yes
Bottling/Distribution: yes, but limited
to Rockford area
Bar Toys: none
Bar Stools: 15
Beer Garden/Outside Seating: no
Tourism: Rockford Area Chamber of
Commerce, 1-800-521-0849 or
1-815-963-8111
(www.rockford.il.us)

ROCK ISLAND
Blue Cat Brew Pub
113 18th Street
Rock Island, IL 61201
GPS Coordinates: N 41°30'41.94"
W 090°34'27.87"
Web site:
www.bluecatbrewpub.com

E-mail: bluecatbrew@
    bluecatbrewpub.com
Telephone: 1-309-788-8247
Established Brewing Operations:
    1994
Gift Shop: yes
Mug Club: no
Homebrew Club: no official
    connection
Growlers: yes
Tours: yes
Tasting: yes
Bottling/Distribution: yes, but limited
Bar Toys: pool tables, dart boards,
    video games
Bar Stools: 12 downstairs, 15 up-
    stairs
Beer Garden/Outside Seating:
    planned
Tourism: Quad Cities Convention
    and Visitors Bureau, 1-800-747-
    7800 or 1-309-788-7800
    (www.visitquadcities.com) or
    (www.rigov.org)

SCHAUMBURG
Prairie Rock Brewing Company
1385 North Meacham
Schaumburg, IL 60173
GPS Coordinates: N 42°03'21.24"
    W 088°02'39.98"
Web site: www.prairierock
    brewingcompany.com
E-mail: Triclamp@msn.com
Telephone: 1-847-605-9900
Established Brewing Operations:
    1999
Gift Shop: yes
Mug Club: yes
Homebrew Club: no official
    connection
Growlers: yes
Tours: yes
Tasting: yes
Bottling/Distribution: no
Bar Toys: none

Bar Stools: 10 in main bar
Beer Garden/Outside Seating: yes
Tourism: Village of Schaumburg,
    1-847-895-4500
    (www.villageofschaumburg.org);
    Schaumburg village profile
    (www.villageprofile.com/illinois/
    schaumburg/index.html);
    Northwest Regional Chamber of
    Commerce, 1-847-517-7110
    (www.nsaci.org); Greater
    Woodfield Convention and
    Visitors Bureau, 1-800-VISIT-GW
    (www.chicagonorthwest.com)

Ram Restaurant and Big Horn
Brewery
1901 McConnor Parkway
Schaumburg, IL 60173
GPS Coordinates: N 42°03'14.22"
    W 088°01'50.05"
Web site: www.theram.com and
    www.theram.com/pages/
    restaurants/the_ram/illinois/
    schaumburg.asp
E-mail: feedback@theram.com
Telephone: 1-847-517-8791
Established Brewing Operations:
    2000
Gift Shop: yes
Mug Club: yes
Homebrew Club: no official
    connection
Growlers: yes
Tours: yes
Tasting: yes
Bottling/Distribution: no
Bar Toys: none
Bar Stools: 25
Beer Garden/Outside Seating: yes
Tourism: Village of Schaumburg,
    1-847-895-4500
    (www.villageofschaumburg.org);
    Schaumburg village profile
    (www.villageprofile.com/illinois/
    schaumburg/index.html);

Northwest Regional Chamber of
Commerce, 1-847-517-7110
(www.nsaci.org); Greater
Woodfield Convention and
Visitors Bureau, 1-800-VISIT-GW
(www.chicagonorthwest.com)

SOUTH BARRINGTON
Brass Restaurant and Brewery
105 Hollywood Boulevard
South Barrington, IL 60010
GPS Coordinates: N 42°04'16.93"
    W 088°08'38.86"
Web site: not available
E-mail: not available
Telephone: 1-847-765-1200
Established Brewing Operations: 2003
Gift Shop: yes
Mug Club: yes
Homebrew Club: no official
    connection
Growlers: yes
Tours: yes
Tasting: yes
Bottling/Distribution: none
Bar Toys: none
Bar Stools: 25
Beer Garden/Outside Seating: yes
Tourism: Barrington Area Chamber
    of Commerce, 1-847-381-2525
    (www.barringtonchamber.com);
    Greater Woodfield Convention
    and Visitors Bureau, 1-800-
    VISIT-GW
    (www.chicagonorthwest.com)

Millrose Restaurant and Brewing Company
45 South Barrington Road
South Barrington, IL 60010
GPS Coordinates: N 42°04'14.44"
    W 088°08'31.88"
Web site:
    www.millroserestaurant.com
E-mail: manager@
    millroserestaurant.com

Telephone: 1-847-382-7673
Established Brewing Operations:
    1992
Gift Shop: yes
Mug Club: no
Homebrew Club: no official
    connection
Growlers: none
Tours: no
Tasting: yes
Bottling/Distribution: yes, but limited
    and sold through the Millrose
    Country Store
Bar Toys: none
Bar Stools: 25
Beer Garden/Outside Seating: yes
Tourism: Barrington Area Chamber
    of Commerce, 1-847-381-2525
    (www.barringtonchamber.com);
    Greater Woodfield Convention
    and Visitors Bureau, 1-800-
    VISIT-GW
    (www.chicagonorthwest.com)

VILLA PARK
Lunar Brewing Company
54 East St. Charles Road
Villa Park, IL 60181
GPS Coordinates: N 41°53'23.78"
    W 087°58'35.40"
Web site: not available
E-mail: not available
Telephone: 1-630-530-2077
Established Brewing Operations:
    1996
Gift Shop: yes
Mug Club: no
Homebrew Club: no official
    connection
Growlers: yes
Tours: yes
Tasting: yes
Bottling/Distribution: no
Bar Toys: dart board,
    video games
Bar Stools: 15

Beer Garden/Outside Seating: no
Tourism: Village of Villa Park, 1-630-
834-8500 (www.invillapark.com);
Villa Park Chamber of
Commerce, 1-630-941-9133
(www.villaparkchamber.org)

WARRENVILLE
Rock Bottom Restaurant and Brewery
28256 Diehl Road
Warrenville, IL 60555
GPS Coordinates: N 41°48'11.77"
W 088°10'17.76"
Web site: www.rockbottom.com
E-mail:
operations@rockbottom.com
Telephone: 1-630-836-1380
Established Brewing Operations:
1998
Gift Shop: yes
Mug Club: yes
Homebrew Club: no official
connection
Growlers: yes
Tours: yes
Tasting: yes
Bottling/Distribution: no
Bar Toys: pool tables
Bar Stools: 12
Beer Garden/Outside Seating: yes
Tourism: City of Warrenville, 1-630-
393-9427 (www.warrenville.il.us);
Warrenville Chamber of
Commerce, 1-630-393-9080
(www.warrenvillechamber.com);
Warrenville village profile
(www.villageprofile.com/illinois/
warrenville/index.html); West
Chicago Illinois Directory
(www.seekon.com/L/US/IL/West
_Chicago)

Two Brothers Brewing Company
30 West 114 Butterfield
Warrenville, IL 60555

GPS Coordinates: N 41°49'20.13"
W 088°12'30.63"
Web site: www.twobrosbrew.com
E-mail: info@twobrosbrew.com
Telephone: 1-630-393-4800
Established Brewing Operations:
1996
Gift Shop: yes
Mug Club: no
Homebrew Club: no official con-
nection, but it is also a home-
brew supply store
Growlers: yes
Tours: yes
Tasting: yes
Bottling/Distribution: yes, Illinois,
Indiana, Minnesota, Missouri,
Ohio, and Wisconsin
Bar Toys: none
Bar Stools: none
Beer Garden/Outside Seating: no
Tourism: City of Warrenville, 1-630-
393-9427 (www.warrenville.il.us);
Warrenville Chamber of
Commerce, 1-630-393-9080
(www.warrenvillechamber.com);
Warrenville village profile
(www.villageprofile.com/illinois/
warrenville/index.html); West
Chicago Illinois Directory
(www.seekon.com/L/US/IL/West
_Chicago)

WEST DUNDEE
Emmett's Tavern and Brewing Company
128 West Main Street
West Dundee, IL 60118
GPS Coordinates: N 42°05'52.83"
W 088°16'43.35"
Web site: not available
E-mail: not available
Telephone: 1-847-428-4500
Established Brewing Operations:
2000
Gift Shop: yes

Mug Club: yes
Homebrew Club: no official
    connection
Growlers: yes
Tours: yes
Tasting: yes
Bottling/Distribution: no
Bar Toys: none
Bar Stools: 10
Beer Garden/Outside Seating:
    yes
Tourism: Village of West Dundee,
    1-847-551-3800 (www.west-
    dundee.il.us); Mainstreet
    Dundee, 1-847-836-9212
    (www.mainstreetdundee.com)

WHEELING
Ram Restaurant and Big Horn
    Brewery
700 Milwaukee Avenue
Wheeling, IL 60090
GPS Coordinates: N 42°09'04.14"
    W 087°54'51.87"
Web site: www.theram.com and
    www.theram.com/pages/
restaurants/the_ram/illinois/
    wheeling.asp
E-mail: feedback@theram.com
Telephone: 1-847-520-1222
Established Brewing Operations:
    2001
Gift Shop: yes
Mug Club: yes
Homebrew Club: no official
    connection
Growlers: yes
Tours: yes
Tasting: yes
Bottling/Distribution: no
Bar Toys: none
Bar Stools: 22
Beer Garden/Outside Seating: yes
Tourism: Wheeling/Prospect Heights
    Area Chamber of Commerce
    and Industry, 1-847-541-0170
    (www.wphchamber.com);
    Village of Wheeling, 1-847-459-
    2600 (www.vi.wheeling.il.us);
    Wheeling Township Community
    Events, 1-847-259-7730
    (www.wheelingtownship.com)

Directory of Just Over the Border Breweries and Brewpubs

CLINTON, IOWA
Upper Mississippi Brewing Company
132 South Sixth Avenue
Clinton, IA 52732
Telephone: 1-563-241-1275
GPS Coordinates: N 41°50'24.57"
    W 090°11'14.78"
Web site: not available

DAVENPORT, IOWA
Front Street Brewery and Beer Garden
208 East River Drive
Davenport, IA 52801
Telephone: 1-563-322-1569
GPS Coordinates: N 41°31'14.73"
    W 090°34'20.53"
Web site: not available

DUBUQUE, IOWA
Bricktown Brewery & Blackwater Grill
299 Main Street
Dubuque, IA 52001
Telephone: 1-563-582-0608
GPS Coordinates: N 42°29'48.19"
    W 090°39'54.14"
Web site: www.
    bricktowndubuque.com

JANESVILLE, WISCONSIN
Gray's Brewing Company
2424 West Court Street
Janesville, WI 53545
Telephone: 1-608-752-3552
GPS Coordinates: N 42°40'46.34"
    W 089°03'02.34"
Web site:
    www.graybrewing.com/full.html

KENOSHA, WISCONSIN
Brewmasters Pub–Friarswood
4017 80th Street
Kenosha, WI 53142
Telephone: 1-262-694-9050
GPS Coordinates: N 42°33'28.15"
    W 087°51'24.51"
Web site: www.brewmasterspub.com
    or www.foodspot.com/brew
    masterspubsouth/index.html

LAFAYETTE, INDIANA
Lafayette Brewing Company
622 Main Street
Lafayette, IN 47901
Telephone: 1-765-742-2591
GPS Coordinates: N 40°25'8.68"
    W 086°53'23.74"
Web site:
    www.lafayettebrewingco.com

LA PORTE, INDIANA
Back Road Brewery
308 Perry Street
La Porte, IN 46350
Telephone: 1-219-362-7623
GPS Coordinates: N 41°36'41.54"
    W 086°43'39.64"
Web site:
    www.backroadbrewery.com

MINERAL POINT, WISCONSIN
Brewery Creek Restaurant, Bed & Breakfast, and Microbrewery
23 Commerce Street
Mineral Point, WI 53565
Telephone: 1-608-987-3298
GPS Coordinates: N 42°51'27.82"
W 90°10'37.12"
Web site: www.brewerycreek.com

MONROE, WISCONSIN
Joseph Huber Brewing Company
1208 Fourteenth Avenue
Monroe, WI 53566
Telephone: 1-608-325-3191
GPS Coordinates: N 42°35'58.66"
W 089°38'29.79"
Web site: www.huberbrewery.com
or www.berghoffbeer.com

NEW GLARUS, WISCONSIN
New Glarus Brewing Company
119 County Trunk West
New Glarus, WI 53574
Telephone: 1-608-527-5850
GPS Coordinates: N 42°49'02.67"
W 089°37'48.68"
Web site:
www.newglarusbrewing.com

ST. CHARLES, MISSOURI
Trailhead Brewing Company
921 South Riverside Drive
St. Charles, MO 63302
Telephone: 1-636-946-2739
GPS Coordinates: N 38°46'27.04"
W 090°29'04.99"
Web site:
www.trailheadbrewing.com

ST. LOUIS, MISSOURI
Anheuser-Busch
S. 12th and Lynch Streets
St. Louis, MO 63118
Telephone:
1-314-577-2626
GPS Coordinates: N 38°35'58.84"
W 090°12'51.30"
Web site: www.anheuser-busch.com

Morgan Street Brewery
721 North Second Street
St. Louis, MO 63102
Telephone:
1-314-231-9970
GPS Coordinates: N 38°37'50.37"
W 090°11'03.98"
Web site: www.morganstreet
brewery.com

Route 66 Brewery & Restaurant
1820 Market Street
St. Louis, MO 63103
Telephone:
1-314-231-4677
GPS Coordinates: N 38°37'46.70"
W 090°12'29.92"
Web site:
www.route66brewery.com

Schlafly Tap Room
2100 Locust Street
St. Louis, MO 63103
Telephone:
1-314-241-2337
GPS Coordinates: N 38°37'58.83"
W 090°12'36.28"
Web site: www.schlafly.com

VALPARAISO, INDIANA
Aberdeen Brewing Company
210 Aberdeen Drive
Valparaiso, IN 46385
Telephone:
1-219-548-3300
GPS Coordinates: N 41°26'19.46"
W 087°06'25.16"
Web site: www.
aberdeenbrewingco.com

Beer Styles

Beer styles fit rather loosely into two general classifications, known as ales and lagers. These two distinctions correspond to the type of yeast used. Ales are made at relatively warm temperatures, roughly 60 to 70 degrees Fahrenheit, and require less time to ferment. They are made with strains of yeast that are active in the warmer upper portions of the fermentation vessel. Ales tend to have fruity flavors, more assertive tastes and aromas, and especially bitter tones. Ales are considered the older, more traditional beers. Lagers are made with strains of yeast that live in colder temperatures, usually at the bottom of the fermentation vessel. The colder fermentation and aging temperatures slow down the activity of the yeast and in turn can reduce the production of fruity esters, in some cases leading to a mellower or cleaner tasting beer. Lagers became more popular once mechanical refrigeration became possible. Keep in mind that ales and lagers share many characteristics, so, unless the brewer specifies which beers are which, it can be difficult if not impossible for even the best beer connoisseur to tell the difference.

Within the general classifications of ales and lagers there are subgroups referred to as styles. The brewing industry recognizes fifty or sixty different styles of beer, and some of the styles have substyles. For example, a stout is an ale and can include such substyles as American stout, dry (Irish) stout, oatmeal stout, or even Russian Imperial stout.

For the most part, the beer styles recognized today evolved over centuries through trial and error in brewing processes. Brewers were either making beer in less than ideal situations, trying different grains, varying the amount of hops or spices, or looking for less costly ingredients. While some styles may initially have been created by accident, many years of consistent brewing helped establish particular beers as accepted styles.

The following list of styles is not meant to be all-inclusive. There are a number of good books and Web sites that offer more complete listings and more exact definitions of styles. See, for example, Michael Jackson's *New World Guide to Beer* and his Web site, www.beerhunter.com; the *Beverage Testing Institute's Buying Guide to Beer* and its Web site, www.tastings.com/beer/index.beer.lasso; the American Homebrewers Association and World Beer Cup Competition Styles Web site, www.beertown.org; the Beer Judge Certification Program Web site, www.mv.com/ipusers/slack/bjcp/; and Fred Eckhardt's book *Essentials of Beer Style*.

Finally, remember that the beer styles described in this book are merely guidelines for the average beer drinker and beer enthusiast. Brewers, especially those at microbreweries and brewpubs, often do not want to be held to strict style definitions. Because they brew smaller batches, they like to experiment. That may mean they begin with a general style and expand its characteristics, combining their creativity and their insights into what local beer drinkers want. Try to keep in mind, it doesn't make the beer wrong or bad, and it would not be fair to give the beer a bad mark for a style it really did not intend to be.

I have provided style definitions because many brewers often reference a particular style in their descriptions. As brewers experiment and try modified or new recipes, the results may go beyond formal definitions and offer a remarkable and rewarding beer drinking experience.

I have also provided examples of these styles; many of them are beers described in this book. The name of the beer is followed by the Illinois brew-pub or brewery that produces it; if my example is not from Illinois, its brewer and the brewer's location follow in parentheses.

ALES

Ales are characterized by fermentation at warmer temperatures. They are made with what is commonly referred to as a top-fermenting yeast, that is, a yeast that is active in the upper portions of the fermentation vessel. Ales generally require shorter aging processes. Compared with lagers, they are often distinguished by a greater variety of colors and more robust flavors, including fruity tones.

Some ales may be bottle or cask conditioned. Cask-conditioned ale is served the traditional British way, on draft from a hand pump from the cask or keg under its own carbonation rather than through lines that are pressurized by tanks of carbon dioxide (or some other gas). This hand pumping often provides a full head and smoother texture to the beer. Cask-conditioned ales are usually served at cellar temperatures of 50 to 55 degrees Fahrenheit, which is considerably warmer than what most Americans are used to. Cask-conditioned ales are sometimes referred to as "live" beers. This is because they are naturally self-carbonated during a secondary fermentation process that occurs in the keg or cask.

Alt

Alt (the German word for "old") usually has a malty nose, a color that is orange or copper to brown, a medium body, and assertive bitterness with a light fruity background. Some Alts will have a dry finish because of the large amounts of hops. While considered traditional German ales, some well-known northern German Alts are closer to a lager because they are fermented (with ale yeast) at lower lager-style temperatures.

Examples: Little Angel German Alt, Glen Ellyn Sports Brew; Nelson Algren Alt Beer, Goose Island Beer Company; Schaumburger Alt, Ram Restaurant and Big Horn Brewery–Schaumburg; Sam Adams Boston Ale (Boston Beer Company, Jamaica Plain, Massachusetts).

American
Amber or Red

Amber or red ale can have either a mild to strong hop aroma or some malty caramel nose. The light copper to light brown color and tan head most commonly distinguish them. Reds are very similar, often with a more vivid red hue (hence the name) and clearer color. The body is medium to full; carbonation is moderate. They are usually well balanced between maltiness and hoppiness, with emphasis on the malty-caramel flavor. The amber differs from the pale ale in its color and stronger caramel malt flavors.

Examples: Amber Ale, Elmwood Brewing Company; Hidden River Red Ale, Founders Hill; Panama Red Ale, Flossmoor Station; Frontier American Amber Ale (Alaskan Brewing, Juneau, Alaska).

Pale

An adaptation of the original British style, American pale ale is generally considered crisper and more hoppy than the English pale ale. Despite their name, most are a clear, rich golden to amber color. They often have moderate to high hop flavor, light to medium body, and high carbonation. Often brewers use all American hops. This style is a very common beer in many brewpubs.

Examples: Abe's Honest Ale, Flatlander's; Alpha King, Three Floyds Brewing Company; Pale Ale, Bent River Brewing Company; Pale Ale (Sierra Nevada Brewing, Chico, California); Pale Ale (Summit Brewing, St. Paul, Minnesota).

Barley Wine
American-style

Often made with American hops, the American-style barley wine is hoppier in both nose and taste than the English style. Barley wine has the strongest, most robust and assertive character of all the ales. The nose is often fruity. The color is dark, sometimes with a bronze hue. It has full-bodied and viscous texture and intense malt body with fruity overtones. High alcohol content and thick texture provide a very smooth taste experience. Finish can be very warm. To truly appreciate a barley wine, drink it from a snifter or tulip glass.

Examples: Behemoth Blonde Barleywine, Three Floyds Brewing Company; Kosmic Charlie's Y2K Catastrophe Ale (Central Waters Brewing, Junction City, Wisconsin); Old Scratch Barley Wine (Great Dane Pub & Brewing Company, Madison, Wisconsin); Old Foghorn (Anchor Brewing, San Francisco, California).

English-style

The English-style barley wine features British hops and gives more attention to the malty character. Barley wine has the strongest, most robust and assertive character of all the ales. The nose is often fruity. The color is dark, sometimes with a bronze hue. It has full-bodied and viscous texture, and intense malt body with fruity overtones. There is some hoppiness, but the balance is more to the malty flavors. It has high alcohol content. A thick texture provides a very smooth taste experience. Finish can be very warm. To truly appreciate a barley wine, drink it from a snifter or tulip glass.

Examples: Old Conundrum Barley Wine, Flossmoor Station; Old Nick (Young & Company, England).

Belgian
Dubbel

Dubbel originated at monasteries in the Middle Ages. It has a rich malty nose; sometimes cloves or spiciness are evident. Color is dark golden to dark amber with a thick, long-lasting head. Body is medium to full and often warm. Flavor has rich maltiness with a fruity background. The finish is usually warm from the alcohol content.

Examples: Abbey Dubbel, Flossmoor Station; Dingle Dubbel, Govnor's Public House; La Trappe Dubbel (Trappistenbierbrauwerij "De Schapskooi," Koning-shoeven, Holland, imported by All Saint's Brands, Minneapolis, Minnesota); Ommegang (Brewery Ommegang, Cooperstown, New York).

Red

Also considered "soured," this beer has strong fruity qualities; whole cherries are often used to produce a cherry flavor. The style is commonly associated with the Rodenbach brewery in northern Belgium. Many qualities are similar to those of the Trappist, but a sharp fruitiness really dominates. Hops can play a minor part in the taste associated with this beer.

Example: Wisconsin Belgian Red, New Glarus Brewing Company.

Saison

Saison originated in the French-speaking part of Belgium. Often a seasonal beer (summer), it was traditionally brewed at the end of winter. Characteristics include fruity nose with some light hoppiness, a pale orange body with a thick head, light to medium body, and bitter hoppiness with a strong fruity background.

Examples: Belgian Saison, Prairie Rock Brewing Company–Schaumburg; Saison Belgian Ale, Rock Bottom–Warrenville; Serenity Now Saison, Glen Ellyn Sports Brew; Hennepin (Brewery Ommegang, Cooperstown, New York); Monette-Saison (Brasserie Dupont, Belgium, imported by Vanberg & DeWulf, Cooperstown, New York).

Singel

Many abbeys are unique in hoppiness and malty-musty qualities, but nearly all feature fruity or spicy traits or both. Abbey ales are not always brewed in an abbey, but they may be licensed by one.

Examples: GPH Abbey Ale, Govnor's Public House; Abbaye de Leffe (Leffe Blonde, Belgium, imported by Wetten Importers).

Strong, Belgian-style

Belgian ales are sometimes distinguished by color into further categories as either pale or dark. Belgian strong ales are commonly brewed with Belgian candy sugar and are well attenuated. Most have low bitterness and are big on the fruity sweetness and intense maltiness. Herbs and spices are sometimes used to offer some light flavors. The high alcoholic characteristics can be deceiving, but are often very evident.

Examples: Govnor's Gaelic Golden, Govnor's Public House; Neil Armstrong Ale, Lunar Brewing Company; Santa's Magic, Mickey Finn's Brewery.

Trappist

By Belgian law an ale must be brewed at a Trappist monastery to be called a Trappist ale, and according to European law it can only come from six abbeys of the Trappist order that still brew. The term "Abbey" or "Trappist-style" is applied to beers that closely follow this style but do not originate from a Trappist monastery. Golden to deep amber color. They are often fruity and bittersweet. Characteristically these Belgians are brewed with candy sugar in the kettle and are bottle conditioned (secondary fermentation occurs once in the bottle).

Examples: Blue, an interpretation of a Grand Resérve Belgian ale, Goose Island Beer Company–Clybourn Avenue; Red (Chimay, Belgium, imported by Belukus Marketing).

Tripel
Tripel is complex from beginning to end. The nose shows a competition between malty and fruity aromas. The color is pale golden to deep gold with a light, bubbly, white head. It is medium bodied, crisp, and often very effervescent. A malty sweetness is balanced with both hops and fruity overtones. The finish is dry. Overall, the flavor shows strong fruity bursts yet is warm and smooth.

Examples: Anvers Cent Tripel, Govnor's Public House; Todd's Tupelo Tripel, Flossmoor Station; Trippel Play, Goose Island Beer Company–Wrigleyville; Cabin Fever, New Glarus Brewing Company; Tripel, Schlafly Tap Room; Tripel (New Belgium, Fort Collins, Colorado).

Witbier, or White Beer
Witbier has a sweet, citrus nose, often with hints of orange, herbs, or spice. The color is pale yellow or straw color and generally cloudy, with a light, soft, white head. This beer has light to medium body. While the malt may dominate, it may have hints of musty qualities, all accented with coriander, citrus, and spice.

Examples: Le Chien Blanc Witbier, Flossmoor Station; Solstice Wit, Govnor's Public House; Wit-Engeltje, Mickey Finn's Brewery; Celis White (Celis Brewing, San Antonio, Texas).

Bière de Garde
This French beer has a malty to fruity nose. The color is clear and sparkling gold, copper, or even reddish. The beer has a light to medium body, with moderate to high carbonation and a medium to full malty flavor. Light hints of caramel and toffee are common. Traditionally served in a corked bottle, it is meant to be aged in a cellar as wines are. Its name means "beer for keeping."

Examples: Chateau de Lune, Lunar Brewing Company; Domaine DuPage, Two Brothers Brewing Company; Bière de Garde (Brasserie Castelain, Bénifontaine, France, imported by Vanberg & DeWulf).

Brown
American
This brown was adapted by American brewers who wanted stronger hop flavors. The nose has a hoppy aroma. The color is dark amber to dark brown with a thick, tan head. It is medium bodied and sometimes dry. The hop bitterness dominates, despite assertive maltiness. There are often some toasty qualities in the background. With its high hop qualities, the finish is usually dry.

Examples: Brown Ale, Elmwood Brewing Company; Pullman Nut Brown Ale, Flossmoor Station; Brooklyn Brown Ale (Brooklyn Brewery, Brooklyn, New York).

Mild
It has a slight, mild, malty nose. The color can be medium dark brown, deep copper, or mahogany. Light to medium body; low carbonation; low or no hop flavor and finish. It is malty but usually well balanced.

Example: British Pub-Style Mild, Prairie Rock Brewing Company–Schaumburg; Dark Honey Brown, O'Griff's Irish Pub and Brew House.

Northern English
Also called nut brown ale, it is known for its drier, nuttier maltiness. With little or no hop aroma, it is more likely to have a malty or even roasted nose. The color is dark golden to light brown. Light to medium bodied, it has a soft sweetness with strong nutty character that dominates a caramel malt body. The finish is dry.

Examples: Hex Nut Brown Ale, Goose Island Beer Company; Nut Brown Ale (South Shore Brewery, Ashland, Wisconsin); Newcastle Brown Ale (Scottish & Newcastle Breweries, Newcastle-upon-Tyne, England); Nut Brown Ale (Samuel Smith's Old Brewery, Yorkshire, England).

Southern English
Nose is malty, sometimes with a light fruitiness. Color is dark brown and almost opaque. Medium bodied, it has a gentle sweetness with a malty dominance. There should be some hoppiness in the background, but nutty roasted tones are not appropriate.

Examples: Brown Eye Brown Ale, Govnor's Public House; Brown Ale (Capital Brewery, Middleton, Wisconsin); Pete's Wicked Ale (Pete's Brewing, San Antonio, Texas).

India Pale Ale (IPA)
American
An adaptation of the British IPA, it is lighter in color than most British versions, and the hoppy aroma may be more assertive. Somewhat bolder and cleaner, it is made with American malt and hops to create a crisper profile. Most often it has a strong aromatic hoppy nose, deep golden color, medium body, and assertive hoppiness. The finish is often dry and long lasting.

Examples: Donegal IPA, Govnor's Public House; River Black Jack IPA, Blue Cat Brew Pub; R. K's IPA, Mickey Finn's Brewery; India Pale Ale, Brewmasters Pub; Full Sail India Pale Ale (Full Sail Brewing, Hood River, Oregon).

British
Well known for its heavy hopping, British IPA was an attempt to make a beer that would survive long sea voyages from England to the colonies in India. It has a strong floral hoppy nose and a color that ranges from gold to a deep copper. Some versions may appear hazy or slightly cloudy. It is smooth and medium bodied and has a very strong hop flavor with assertive bitter taste. A warm, strong, bitter finish is also common.

Examples: Dreadnaught Imperial IPA, Three Floyds Brewing Company; IPA, Piece; Moondance IPA, Lunar Brewing Company; Todd and Bill's Excellent IPA, Flossmoor Station; Celebration Ale (Sierra Nevada Brewing, Chico, California); Sam Smith's India Ale (Samuel Smith's Old Brewery, Yorkshire, England).

Irish

Similar to Scottish ale, Irish ale has a malty nose, dark color, and often reddish hues. It is medium to full bodied. Malty sweet flavors dominate, with low hoppiness.

Examples: Brian Boru Old Irish Red, Three Floyds Brewing; Glen Ellyn Red, Glen Ellyn Sports Brew; Irish Ale, Gray's Brewing.

Kölsch (also Koelsch)

The Kölsch name can be applied only to beers from Köln (Cologne), Germany, brewed to strict legal standards, including 10 to 20 percent wheat. Kölsch is considered a blond Alt beer. It has a light hoppy nose and a clear pale to light golden color. It is light to medium bodied and soft and has a light fruity body and a crisp hoppy background. Some Kölsch beers have a dry finish.

Examples: Calumet Queen, Three Floyds Brewing Company; Golden Arm, Piece; Kosmic Kölsch, Lunar Brewing Company; Kölsch, Schlafly Tap Room; Sam Adams Spring Ale (Boston Beer Company, Jamaica Plain, Massachusetts).

Lambic

Traditionally the lambic style is open fermented with naturally occurring yeast.

Framboise

A lambic made with raspberry, framboise often has a cloudy reddish color. It has a strong fruity body and may be sour. It is light to medium bodied and highly carbonated. Typically it has very light or no hop flavor. The fruit will dominate.

Examples: Framboise de Flossmoor, Flossmoor Station; Raspberry Tart, New Glarus Brewing Company; Belle-Vue Framboise (Brewery Belle-Vue, which is owned by Interbrew, Belgium, imported by Labatt's).

Gueuze

Gueuze is traditionally made by blending young and old lambic, producing a smoother beer. Most often it has a fruity nose, but it can be sour, earthy, or even woody. Color is gold to amber and slightly cloudy. It can be intensely sour and acetic, but it is better balanced than the unblended lambic.

Example: Gueuze Cuvée René (Brouwerij Lindemans, Belgium).

Kriek

Kriek is a lambic made with cherries. Traditionally the cherries are not crushed; rather, the skins are lightly broken and added to the beer in the cellar. Some young lambic is also added. It has a fruity nose and pink color. It is light to medium bodied and highly carbonated. Kriek can be intensely sour and acetic, but it is better balanced than the unblended lambic.

Examples: Devils Kriek, Glen Ellyn Brewing Company; Kriek (Brouwerij Lindemans, Belgium).

Unblended
The straight lambic-style ale most often has a fruity nose, but it can be sour, earthy, or even woody. Color is yellow to golden and cloudy. Light to medium bodied, it has strong, sour, acidic flavor.

Examples: Very few straight lambics are bottled.

Light
Blonde or Golden
A soft, light malty flavor and a fruity or light hoppy nose. The blonde color is clear pale straw to deep golden. Most often blonde is light and thin, but it can range to medium bodied and soft. The fruitiness or hoppiness is in the background and usually well balanced with the maltiness.

Examples: Blonde Ale, Goose Island Beer Company; Canadian Golden Ale, O'Griff's Irish Pub and Brew House; Collars and Cuffs Blonde Ale, Piece; Harvest Gold, Emmett's Tavern and Brewing Company; Zephyr Golden Ale, Flossmoor Station.

Cream
Cream ale is a hybrid of an American pale lager fermented as an ale. Corn or rice may be used as adjuncts. It has a light hoppy aroma and a pale straw to light golden color. It is light bodied with a smooth texture and is well carbonated. A sweet graininess dominates the light malt character and even light hoppy background. This sweetness leaves almost a floury, or grainy, impression.

Examples: Cream Ale, Rhodell Brewery and Bar; Cream Ale, Taylor Brewing Company; Jumping Cow Cream Ale, Lunar Brewing Company; Cream Ale (Hales Ales Brewery, Seattle, Washington).

Porter
American
American versions of porter are often drier and hoppier than the British. Also classified as a robust porter style, it has a roasted malt or coffee nose and a dark brown to black color. It is medium to full bodied. The malty flavor has strong coffee tones and roasted dryness. Hoppiness is evident or even dominant.

Examples: Night Watch Dark, FireHouse Restaurant and Brewing Company; Badger Porter (Wisconsin Brewing, Black River Falls, Wisconsin); Black Diamond Porter (J. T. Whitney's, Madison, Wisconsin); Anchor Porter (Anchor Brewing, San Francisco, California).

British
This style of porter originated in England as a blend of beers and was a precursor to stout. It has a malty nose with a mild roastedness. Hoppiness should be low to moderate. The color is brown to dark brown. It is medium bodied. The flavor is maltier with some roasted tones, but generally it is sweeter, even with hints of chocolate malt, than the American porter style.

Examples: Porter from Hell, Illinois Brewing Company; XXX Porter, Goose Island Beer Company; Flag Porter (Darwin, England); Sam Smith's Taddy Porter (Samuel Smith's Old Brewery, Yorkshire, England); Yuengling Porter (D.G. Yuengling, Pottsville, Pennsylvania).

Scotch Ale and Wee Heavy

The maltiness can be overwhelming in these beers. They begin with a strong, aromatic malty nose. There is some roastedness that may even be in competition with the malt aroma. A peaty or smoky character is common. The color is dark amber to brown. It is full bodied and thick, almost chewy. There is intense maltiness and even some hints of caramelization. The Wee Heavy is dark brown, full bodied, and very malty with assertive flavors. "Wee Heavy" is the name more commonly used in Scotland.

Examples: Kilt Kicker Wee Heavy, Flossmoor Station; Tartan Terror Scotch Ale, Rhodell Brewery and Bar; Wee Heavy, Mickey Finn's Brewery; McEwan's Scotch Ale (McEwan and Younger, Fountain Brewery, Scotland, imported by Scottish & Newcastle).

Scottish

The common varieties of Scottish ales are light, heavy, and export. Almost all are malty, sweet, and full bodied. They often range from dark amber to brown or even bronze color with thick creamy heads. A strong malty nose is common. The taste is dominated by maltiness. Some may have a faint smokiness. Heavier versions may even have a warmth, especially in the finish.

Examples: Brave Heart Ale, Rhodell Brewery and Bar; 80 Shilling Ale, Flatlander's; Old Dundee, Emmett's Tavern and Brewing Company; Caber Tossing Scottish Ale (Fox River Brewing, Appleton and Oshkosh, Wisconsin); Kilt Lifter Ale (Pike Brewing, Seattle, Washington); Scottish Ale (Boundary Bay Brewing, Bellingham, Washington).

Specialty
Fruit-flavored

An important characteristic of quality fruit beer is balance. The fruit should complement the style and not overwhelm other characteristics. Color and texture of the fruit beer will vary depending upon style. Nose, taste, and finish should provide a distinctive opportunity for the fruit but not a venue to overpower the beer.

Examples: Old Orchard Ale, Flatlander's; Apple Ale, New Glarus Brewing Company; Pyramid Apricot Ale (Pyramid Ales, Seattle, Washington).

Rauchbier

Rauchbier is smoke flavored, and its smoky aroma ranges from faint to very assertive. Usually a clear dark beer, the color can be black, brown, or dark copper. It has medium body and smooth texture. While the smoke flavor may vary among brewers, it should remain in balance with the smooth maltiness of the body.

Examples: Rooftop Smoked Porter, Glen Ellyn Sports Brew; Rich's Rauchbier (J. T. Whitney's, Madison, Wisconsin); Rauchbier (Rogue Ales, Newport, Oregon).

Stout

American

Inspired by Irish and English styles, the American stout features more hoppy aromas and bitter flavors. It has a light, mildly hoppy or even roasted nose. The color is dark to black. Medium bodied, American stout has some malty flavors but a dry bitter dominance, and less fruity esters than an English or Irish stout.

Examples: Stout, J. W. Platek's Restaurant and Brewery; Sinner's Stout (Angelic Brewing Company, Madison, Wisconsin); Stout (Sierra Nevada Brewing, Chico, California).

Dry (Irish)

Irish stout is deep black in color, and it looks thick. The head is off-white to tan, very thick, and long lasting. It has a coffee or roasted nose, medium body, and creamy texture. A sharpness or sourness comes through in the beginning, but the strong hoppy body provides a dry or even tart finish. Overall, the Irish stout is smooth and creamy with a dry bitterness.

Examples: Black Star Stout, Lunar Brewing Company; Guinness (St. James Gate Brewery, Dublin, Ireland).

Oatmeal

Oatmeal stout has a mild roasted nose. It is black with a thick creamy head. The oats enhance its full body and smooth, sometimes oily, resinlike, or velvety texture. There is medium malty sweetness and mild hoppiness with a slight malty dominance. A nutty finish is not uncommon. The oatmeal stout gained popularity among the British in the early 1900s as an alternative to the Irish stouts.

Examples: Five Springs Oatmeal Stout, Mickey Finn's Brewery; Oatmeal Stout, Copper Dragon Brewing Company; Oatmeal Stout, Emmett's Tavern and Brewing Company; Sam Smith's Oatmeal Stout (Samuel Smith's Old Brewery, Yorkshire, England).

Russian Imperial

This style of stout was brewed to stand up to sea voyages from Britain to the Baltic and is said to have been popular with the Russian Imperial Court. It actually belongs in a category of strong ales. It has an intense roasted nose with fruity esters in the background. It is very full bodied and creamy. Usually low carbonation will add to a thick texture. The taste is a complex blend of heavy roasted maltiness and fruity tones. The high alcohol levels provide a rich, smooth, yet lingering dryness. Imperial stouts are usually found in winter months.

Examples: Imperial Delusion, Mickey Finn's Brewery; Imperial Eclipse Stout, Flossmoor Station; Russian Imperial Stout, Gray's Brewing Company; Sam Smith's Imperial Stout (Samuel Smith's Old Brewery, Yorkshire, England).

Sweet (English)

This stout, also known as a milk stout, has a mild roasted nose. Some may have fruity or even light hoppy aromas. The color is very dark amber to black. A full body and creaminess may accentuate the malty dominance in the flavor.

While this stout still isn't truly sweet, the malts dominate, and the roastedness may stand out above any mild hoppy flavor.

Examples: Sam Adams Cream Stout (Boston Beer Company, Jamaica Plain, Massachusetts); Wildcatter's Refined Stout (Yellow Rose Brewing, San Antonio, Texas).

Strong

Often referred to as old ales, strong ales most commonly have deep amber colors but can be deep bronze to black. They are full bodied and assertive with sweet malty flavors, sometimes with a light fruity background or accent.

Example: Christmas Ale, Goose Island Beer Company; Santa's Little Helper, Founder's Hill.

Traditional English

Bitter

"Bitter" is considered an English term for the standard house ale or "session" beer. Bitter usually has a high hop aroma. The color is medium gold to copper with a light head. It is light to medium bodied. Medium to high bitterness will dominate the taste, but they do not completely stop some maltiness in the background. Commonly served on draft by gravity or hand pump at cellar temperatures.

Examples: Bella Luna Best Bitter, Lunar Brewing Company; Best Bitter, Copper Dragon Brewing Company; Special Bitter, Emmett's Tavern and Brewing Company; Bitter (Young & Company, London, England).

English Pale

Sometimes called a Burton (because it originated in the English town of Burton-upon-Trent), English pale is sometimes confused with the English bitter, but generally it has a fuller body and more assertive hoppiness. There is strong hop aroma and strong hop flavor with fruitiness. Color is copper with a light, bubbly head. It is medium to full bodied. There should be some evidence of malt, but clearly bitter dominance.

Examples: Public House Pale Ale, Govnor's Public House; Worryin' Ale, Piece; Bass Pale Ale (Bass Brewers, Burton-upon-Trent, England, imported by Guinness Import Company); Bishop's Finger (Shepherd Neame Brewery, Faversham, England, imported by Westwood).

Extra Special Bitter (ESB)

Extra special bitter is derived from the English bitter, but it has a richer maltiness. It has high hop nose, gold to copper color, and often a light or thin head due to low carbonation. Light to medium bodied, it has medium to high bitterness in the flavor. It should have some maltiness in the background, but the emphasis is clearly on the bitterness.

Examples: ESB, Prairie Rock Brewing Company; J. Diddy's E.S.S.S.B.B., Piece; Honkers Ale, Goose Island Beer Company; ESB (Red Hook Brewery, Seattle, Washington).

Old English

Traditionally these beers often undergo a long aging process. This prolonged fermentation is commonly done in the bottle. This type of ale has a light hoppy nose and dark amber to brown color with medium to full body. Fruity tones can be found in the nose and taste, but overall strong caramel sweetness dominates.

Examples: Big Bad Dog, Blue Cat Brew Pub.

Weisse (Wheat Beer)

American Wheat and Honey Wheat

The American wheat style is known for its hoppy aroma. The color is straw to golden, and clarity depends upon whether it has been filtered. The head is typically white and bubbly and long lasting. Light to medium bodied, the taste has a light graininess. Fruitiness and hoppiness dominate.

Examples: Heritage Wheat, Founder's Hill; Mickey Finn's Wheat Ale, Mickey Finn's Brewery; Wee Willy's Wheat Ale, Illinois Brewing Company; Honey Weisse (Leinenkugel Brewing Company, Chippewa Falls, Wisconsin); Unfiltered Wheat (Boulevard Brewing, Kansas City, Missouri).

Bavarian Dunkelweizen

This dark version of the Bavarian Weizen has low hoppiness, so the spicy aromas are evident in its nose. Color ranges from amber to light brown. It is light to medium bodied but is usually highly carbonated, so it's often considered a very refreshing beer. The Dunkel style is known for its complex malt and fruity tones. Wheat content is 25 percent or less.

Examples: Dunkelweizen, Flossmoor Station; Gudendark Dunkel Weizen, Mickey Finn's Brewery; Paulaner Hefe-Weizen Dunkel (Brauerei Paulaner, Germany).

Bavarian Krystal Weizen

This traditional wheat beer originated in southern Germany. As with the Bavarian Weizen, its qualities are spicy and have a strong clove nose and flavor. Krystal refers to the filtering of the Bavarian Weizen.

Examples: Club-Weissbier (Spaten-Franziskaner Brau, Germany); Pyramid Kristall Weizen (Pyramid Ales, Seattle, Washington); Weissbier Kristallklar (Hofbrau Kaltenhausen Edelweiss, Austria).

Bavarian Weizen

Unlike the American style, Bavarian Weizen is marked by a strong vanilla and clovelike, even banana nose. The color is pale straw to dark reddish golden. It is light to medium bodied and creamy. A soft grainy flavor consists of spicy clove and fruity esters. A strong banana taste is common. The finish is crisp and bubbly.

Examples: Warrenweizen, Rock Bottom–Warrenville; Kloster Weizen (Capital Brewery, Middleton, Wisconsin); Paulaner Hefe-Weizen (Brauerei Paulaner, Germany).

Berliner Weisse/Weissbier

This northern Germany style of weissbier is Berlin's classic white beer. Wheat malt content is typically under 50 percent. A fruity nose may appear sour. The color is pale straw to light golden. Light bodied and highly carbonated, it has sour fruitiness that dominates.

Examples: Weisse (Berliner Kindl Brauerei, Germany).

Hefe-Weizen

"Hefe" is the German word for yeast. Expect a Hefe-Weizen to be cloudy with a light golden color. The nose will offer hints of spices, cloves, or even bubblegum. The body of taste may feature a light citrus quality. It is brewed with at least 50 percent wheat (Weizen).

Examples: Ebel's Weiss, Two Brothers Brewing Company; Gudenteit Hefe Weizen, Mickey Finn's Brewery; Hefeweizen, Glen Ellyn Sports Brew; O'Kelly's Hefeweizen, Govnor's Public House; Pyramid Hefeweizen (Pyramid Ales, Seattle, Wash.).

Weizenbier

Weizenbier is the style found in southern Germany, mainly Bavaria, Munich, and Baden-Württemberg. It is made with 50 percent wheat, with a pale straw to golden color. Weizenbier usually has fuller flavor and is less acidic than Berliner Weisse. The flavors tend to be spicy, fruity, and tart.

Examples: Weisen, Taylor Brewing Company; Whitewater Weizen (Central Waters Brewing Company, Junction City, Wisconsin).

Weizenbock

Weizenbock has a strong fruity nose. The color is light amber to dark brown and cloudy. Medium to full bodied, it has strong earthy flavors, marked by fruitiness and maltiness, but the fruitiness dominates. Some clove spiciness is common. There may be smoky overtones.

Example: Pyramid Weizenbock (Pyramid Ales, Seattle, Washington).

LAGERS

Lagers are characterized by fermentation at colder temperatures. They are made with what is commonly referred to as bottom-fermenting yeast, meaning that the yeast is active in the lower portions of the fermentation vessel. Their color is lighter than most ales, most often a shade of golden or bronze, except for the bock and schwarzbier styles, which are much darker. Lagers are a younger style of beers, most having been refined since the mid-nineteenth century and especially in the twentieth, when mechanical refrigeration came to the brewing industry.

American
California Common Beer

Attributed to America's West Coast, this beer evolved in the absence of ice or refrigeration. It is sometimes considered a hybrid between an ale and a lager, because fermentation temperatures are between those of the two styles.

Anchor Steam Brewing in San Francisco often gets credit for setting the standard for this style. (Steam Beer is a trademark of Anchor Steam Brewing.) The nose is a complex combination of hoppy, fruity, and citric aromas. It has medium body and medium to high carbonation. Substantial bitterness stands out, with a dry finish.

Examples: Anchor Steam (Anchor Brewing, San Francisco, California).

Dark

Dark lager has no aroma or a very faint light roasted nose. The color is a clear and deep copper to dark brown with a long-lasting bubbly head. Light to medium bodied and smooth, it is crisp with subtle sweetness and roasted tones. The darker caramel malts may provide some dominance to a crisp hoppy background. Finish, if at all, can be lightly sweet.

Examples: Dark Star Lager, Millrose Restaurant and Brewing Company; Dixie Blackened Voodoo Lager (Dixie Brewing, New Orleans, Louisiana); Henry Weinhard's Private Reserve Dark (Blitz-Weinhard Brewing, Portland, Oregon).

Light

American light lager has a very light or no nose. If an aroma is present, it may be a faint fruity or very light flowery hoppiness. The color is pale straw to pale gold. It has light body and thin texture. The flavor is generally clean and crisp. There may be some sweetness, but more often a dryness is evident from the high carbonation. "Light" requires that it have fewer calories than the same style without the light label. In America, Miller Lite has become synonymous with the American light lager style. Miller Lite is known for its "Tastes great, less filling" slogan and its emphasis on fewer calories. In Canada and Australia, the term "light" usually indicates lower amounts of alcohol.

Example: Flatlander's Light, Flatlander's; Lager Light, Harrison's Brewing Company; Miller Lite (Miller Brewing Company, Milwaukee, Wisconsin).

Pilsner, American style

American Pilsner has a light hoppy nose, a clear light gold color, and a long-lasting, soft head on a light to medium creamy body. The flavor will be dominated by hoppiness, but not an assertive hop flavor. The taste is smooth or even slightly grainy.

Examples: Mickey's Pils, Lunar Brewing Company; Payton Pilsner, America's Brewing Company.

Premium Pilsner, American style

American premium Pilsner has a very light or no nose. If an aroma is present, it may be a faint fruity or very light flowery hoppiness. The color is pale straw to pale gold. It is light bodied and thin textured. The flavor is generally clean and crisp. It may have some sweetness, but more often a dryness is evident from the high carbonation.

Examples: Ram Premium Pilsner, Ram Restaurant and Big Horn Brewery; Miller High Life (Miller Brewing Company, Milwaukee, Wisconsin).

Red

Similar to the American light and premium lagers, the red lager uses darker malts for reddish color and strong malt flavor. American reds are not heavy beers by any means. They have little or no nose. The color is copper to reddish. Light bodied, they have a crisp taste, usually balanced between a light sweetness and a crisp hoppy background.

Examples: Devils Lake Red Lager (Great Dane Pub & Brewery, Madison, Wisconsin); Red (Leinenkugel Brewing Company, Chippewa Falls, Wisconsin).

Bock

American

American bock is a dark lager, though usually lighter than the traditional German style. The American style tends to be stronger in hoppiness and drier in taste.

Examples: FireHouse Bock, FireHouse Restaurant and Brewing Company; Berghoff Bock, Joseph Huber Brewing Company.

Doppelbock

A very strong malty nose and virtually no hoppiness. The color is deep clear gold to dark brown. Full bodied, it has rich maltiness and a strong roasted complement without a burnt flavor. It is smooth and warm to the finish.

Examples: Blackburn Doppelbock, Founder's Hill; Blonde Doppelbock (Capital Brewery, Middleton, Wisconsin); Spaten Optimator (Spaten-Franziskaner Brau, Germany).

Eisbock

A specialty from Kulmbach, Germany, Eisbock is made by freezing a bock or doppelbock and removing the ice to concentrate the flavor and alcohol content. It has a malty nose and golden to dark brown color. Full bodied, it has strong malty dominance and no hop flavor. A warming sensation comes from the high alcohol content.

Examples: Eisbock, New Glarus Brewing Company; Bayrisch G'frorns Eisbock (Kulmbacher Reichelbrau, Germany).

Helles Bock/Maibock

Helles Bock has a moderate to strong malty nose. As the German word "Helles" (bright, clear) indicates, this bock is light or pale in color—clear deep golden to amber, with a thick, soft, long-lasting white head. Medium bodied, it has a rich malty flavor that provides an assertive and sweet perception without being syrupy.

Examples: Maibock, Glen Ellyn Sports Brew; Maibock, Taylor Brewing Company; Maibock (Capital Brewery, Middleton, Wisconsin); Ayinger Maibock (Privatbrauerei Aying, Germany).

Traditional

The traditional-style bock has a strong malty nose. The color is clear deep amber to bronze. It is medium to full bodied with a rich, complex maltiness and strong caramel flavors. Some roastedness is in the background, but it is kept quiet and only as an accent. The hoppiness is almost nonexistent. Finish can be raisiny.

Examples: Bock, Two Brothers Brewing Company; Huber Bock, Joseph Huber Brewing Company; Hacker-Pschorr Dunkeler Bock (Hacker-Pschorr Brauerei, Germany).

European
Bohemian Pilsner
The Bohemian Pilsner, and especially Pilsner Urquell, are often considered the standard by which all Pilsners are measured. The nose is rich and malty; some hoppiness is evident. Color is a clear, vivid golden with a thick, creamy, white head. Medium to full bodied, it has a smooth, soft hoppiness that stands out above the rich malty balance. A lingering hoppy finish.

Examples: Bohemian Pilsner, Bent River Brewing Company; Czech Pilsner, Flatlander's; Pilsner Urquell (Pilsner Urquell, Czech Republic, imported by Guinness Import Company).

Dortmunder Export
The color is clear and light golden with a bubbly white head. With light to medium body and hoppiness, there should be good balance between the hops and malt. The strongest trait is in its balance. It is clean tasting and not fruity. Dortmunder Export is not as malty as a Munich Helles nor as hoppy as a Bohemian Pilsner. This style originates from the German city of Dortmund.

Example: Dog Days, Two Brothers Brewing Company; Dortmunder Pils, Goose Island Beer Company; Dortmunder Union Original (Dortmunder Union Brauerei, Germany).

Munich Helles
The nose is malty, with just a hint of hoppiness. Color is clear and golden with a soft, white head. Medium to full bodied, it has a clean malt dominance, but a strong hop complement gives a balanced impression. This is a Bavarian version of light lager, distinctively malty.

Examples: Bavarian Lager (Capital Brewery, Middleton, Wisconsin); Spaten Premium Lager (Spaten-Franziskaner Brau, Germany).

Northern German Pilsner
Northern German Pilsner is considered to be very similar to the Bohemian Pilsner style, but it is drier in bitterness and finish. It has a flowery nose and a straw to gold color with a soft, white head. Light to medium bodied, it has crisp and dry hoppiness, clean taste, no fruitiness, and long-lasting dry finish.

Examples: Bitburger Premium Pilsner (Privatbrauerei Th. Simon, Germany).

German
Munich Dunkel
A malty nose with hints of chocolate and toffee. The color is amber to dark brown with a reddish hue. Medium to full bodied and firm. The rich Munich malt dominates this beer. Both roasted tones and hoppiness are restrained,

and only lightly in the background. It usually has a crisp, light hoppy finish. When compared with an American dark lager, the Munich Dunkel tends to be fuller bodied with sweet tones from the Bavarian malts.

Examples: Dunkel Munich Lager, Goose Island Beer Company; Ayinger Altbairisch Dunkel (Brauerei Aying, Germany); Denargo Dark (Tabernash Brewing, Denver, Colorado).

Oktoberfest/Märzen
Oktoberfest has a malty nose with light roastedness in the background. Color is dark gold to bronze. Medium bodied and creamy, it has a complex maltiness that may have light roasted tones. Its malty character is smooth and rich. There is a clean, crisp hoppiness in the background. Finish is clear, clean, and lightly bitter. Traditionally brewed in the spring, Oktoberfest was stored in caves or cellars during the summer until the autumn celebrations.

Examples: Oktoberfest, Emmett's Tavern and Brewing Company; Oktoberfest, Glen Ellyn Sports Brew; Oktoberfest (Capital Brewery, Middleton, Wisconsn); Spaten Oktoberfest (Spaten-Franziskaner Brau, Germany).

Schwarzbier
This German black beer has a malty nose with hints of roasted character. It is very dark, with a reddish or bronze hue. Light to medium bodied, it has a complex malt and hop balance that allows the chocolate malts to come out somewhat dry. The finish is lightly bitter.

Examples: Schwarz Lager, Goose Island Beer Company; Rocky's Revenge (Tyranena Brewing Company, Lake Mills, Wisconsin).

Vienna
The nose is malty, the color is reddish amber to light brown. Light to medium bodied, Vienna has a soft and malty body with a light hoppiness in the finish. It is made with Vienna malt, and roasted malt characteristics impart a light nutty or toasty aroma and taste.

Examples: Wisconsin Amber (Capital Brewery, Middleton, Wisconsin); Negra Modelo Dark Lager (Cerveceria Modelo, Mexico).

Malt Liquor
Neither malt nor liquor dominates. Sometimes it is made with cheaper sugars. Usually it is a high-alcohol version of an American lager. The Bureau of Alcohol, Tobacco, and Firearms (ATF) established the term to identify lager greater than 5 percent alcohol by volume.

Example: Dolemite, Piece; Liquid Sun Malt Liquor, Rock Bottom–Chicago; Mickey's Malt Liquor (Miller Brewing Company, Milwaukee, Wisconsin).

Specialty
Ice Beer
Ice beers have been frozen during fermentation. Water freezes before alcohol, so when the ice crystals are separated from the beer, the alcohol concentration can thereby increase. The freezing can rob the beer of some characteristics and

increase others. Ice beer is considered an American adaptation of the Eisbock style, but specific federal regulations apply to its production and marketing.

Examples: Mickey's Ice (Miller Brewing Company, Milwaukee, Wisconsin).

MEADS

Meads are made with honey, water, and yeast. They can offer many characteristics of beer, such as sweetness, dryness, and effervescence. Often recognized for long fermentation times and sweet, honey-like flavors.

Braggot or Bracket
Braggot meads are made with both honey and malt. The amount of honey must be greater than half of the fermentables, otherwise it is more likely a honey-enhanced beer.

Traditional Mead
The honey is evident in both the nose and the taste. The color ranges from gold to amber and is usually clear, and most have only light bubbly heads or no head at all. Meads are full bodied and smooth, almost wine-like in their texture. They will finish smooth and warm.

Melomel
Melomel is made with fruit. Both nose and color are enhanced by the type of fruit used. More specifically, a Cyser is a mead made with apples, and a Pyment is a mead made with grapes.

Metheglin
A mead made with herbs and spices. While the honey aromas are evident, their assertiveness depends upon what spices are used.

Index

Morris, 53–59, 234, 299. *See also* Fire-House Restaurant and Brewing Company

Morris Theater Guild, 58

Morton Arboretum, 88, 139, 234

Motorola Museum of Electronics, 190

Mount Baldy, 240

Mount Carmel Cemetery, 139

Mr. C's Nitro Pale Ale, 146

Mr. C's Pale Ale, 143, 146

MTV's *Real World,* 173

Mudcat Stout, 281

Mud in Your Eyes Light, 225

mugs, xii

M.U.G.Z. (Mississippi Unquenchable Grail Zymurgists), 11

Mullin Brown, 280

Mundelein, 65

Munich Dunkel, 261, 277

Munich Helles, 71, 232

Munich Lager, 274

Munster (Indiana), 236–42, 299. *See also* Three Floyds Brewing Company

Munster Theatre Company, 240

Murphysboro, 37

Murphy's Seafood and Steakhouse (Idaho), 193, 201

Murray, Bill, 97

museums: African American Museum and Hall of Fame, 211; American Movie Palace Museum, 139; Antique Auto Museum, 162; Arlington Heights Historical Museum, 26, 156; Aurora Regional Fire Museum, 8; Auto Museum, 150; Chester, 37; in Chicago, 98, 219, 220, 221; Chicago Athenaeum Museum, 190, 197; Cuneo Museum and Gardens, 65, 149; Dixon Mounds Museum, 213; Downers Grove, 79; Dundee, 50; DuPage County Historical Museum, 227; Elgin Area Historical Society Museum, 181; Elgin Fire Barn No. 5, 181; Elgin Public Museum, 181; Elmhurst Art Museum, 139; Elmhurst Historical Museum, 139; Elmwood, 43; Ernest Hemingway Museum and Birthplace, 139; Field Museum, 219; Flanagan House Museum, 211; Fox River Trolley Museum, 182; Galesburg, 44; Glen Ellyn, 88; Graue Mill and Museum, 80; Great Lakes Museum, 149; Illinois American Historical Water Museum, 211; Illinois and Michigan Canal Museum, 57, 119; Illinois Railway Museum, 182; International Museum of Surgical Science and the Hall of Immortals, 220; John Dillinger Museum, 240; John G. Shedd Aquarium, 219; Lakeview Museum of Arts and Sciences, 212; Lakewood Forest Preserve's Lake County Discovery Museum, 150; near Lewistown, 213; Lizzardo Museum of Lapidary Art, 139; Lombard Historical Museum, 233; Lorado Taft Museum, 43; McHenry County Historical Society Museum, 113; Midwest Carver's Museum, 73; Moline, 14; Morton Arboretum, 88, 139; Motorola Museum of Electronics, 190; Murphysboro, 37; Museum of Broadcast Communications, 219; Museum of Contemporary Art, 220; Museum of Holography, 221; Normal, 126; Old Jail Museum, 241; Peggy Notebaert Nature Museum, 98, 220; Pettengill-Morron House Museum, 211; Popeye, 37; pottery, 52; Prairie Aviation Museum, 126; Quincy Museum, 161, 162; Railway Museum, 113; Red Grange Museum and Heritage Gallery, 227; Rockford, 30–31; Rock Island, 21; Romeoville's Isle a la Cache Museum, 120; Southern Illinois University, 37; Thornton, 73; Vernon Hills, 65; Villa Park Historical Society Museum, 138; Volvo Auto Museum, 168; Warrenville Historical Museum, 246; Wheeling Historical Society Museum, 205; Wheels O' Time Museum, 211